WINDSOR TO SLOUGH
A Royal Branch Line
by
C.R. Potts

THE OAKWOOD PRESS

© C.R. Potts and Oakwood Press 1993

ISBN 0 85361 442 3

Typeset by Gem Publishing Company, Brightwell, Wallingford, Oxfordshire.

Printed by Alpha Print (Oxon) Ltd, Crawley, Witney, Oxfordshire.

Before the railway came, the Reading and London coach passing Windsor and Eton, c.1820.   *Author's Collection*

Other Oakwood Press books by the same author:
  The Brixham Branch (temporarily out of print)
  The Newton Abbot to Kingswear Railway, 1844–1988

Published by
The OAKWOOD PRESS
P.O.Box 122, Headington, Oxford.

Acknowledgements

Mrs Judith Hunter for access to material in the Madame Tussaud's Collection and the Royal Borough Collection.

Mrs Elizabeth Brown for the loan of station master Maun's diary.

Mrs Daphne Fido for three marvellous drawings and husband John for acting as intermediary; unfortunately only one drawing could be included.

Gerald Jacobs for providing a photocopy of volume 2 of Hubert Simmons' memoirs.

Professor Jack Simmons for permission to quote from his introduction to *Memoirs of a Stationmaster*.

Mrs Sheila Goldsmith for permission to quote from her articles re Eton College.

John Gillham for numerous journeys to obtain full size copies of various large plans for me and for drawing an excellent map.

David Castle for loan of several 'Windsor' items from his collection.

Laurence Waters for photographing, specially, items at the GWS Museum, Didcot.

John Morris for loan of photographs and for checking the section on signalling.

Ivor Smart for loan of photographs.

Ken Williams for loan of photographs and other material.

Material from the Royal Archives has been used by gracious permission of Her Majesty the Queen.

The Public Record Office; The House of Lords Record Office; Eton College Library; Slough Library; The Signalling Record Society; Colindale Newspaper Library; Ian Coulson; Chris Turner; Barry Cook; Colin Judge; Ken Smith.

Photographs are individually acknowledged following each caption.

Thanks to Modern Postcards Wholesale (081-570-7458) for permission to reproduce the 'Eton v. Harrow Cricket Match' card.

Finally many thanks to my wife Sue for fitting in the heavy task of typing, and retyping, the manuscript with her already onerous workload.

Author's Note

Although *Windsor to Slough: A Royal Branch Line* has been four years in the making, and is as comprehensive as space and price will permit, I know from past experience that as soon as the printing presses start to roll, fresh material will turn up that I wish I had included! However any such material will be kept and used should a Second Edition be requested at some future date.

It is inevitable in a work of this size and complexity that some errors will have slipped through, despite my best endeavours to prevent them. If you are aware of an error of fact, a note to my publisher with details of the source of your information would be helpful, as would any additional information for use in a subsequent Edition.

Christopher Potts
Didcot, Oxfordshire
January 1993

A specially posed picture of the Royal Train about 1890. Headed by 'Queen' class 2–2–2 locomotive No. 55, Queen, the train comprises a passenger brake van No. 473, 1st saloon No. 316, a saloon with guard's compartment, fourth is the 1874 Queen's saloon, next is the 1850 Queen's saloon (converted to narrow gauge in 1889), then followed an 8-wheel 1st saloon, two 6-wheel saloons and another

British Rail

Contents

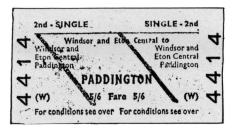

In this scene, dated between 1884 and 1892, a down narrow gauge train passes Slough West signal box on its way west. The narrow gauge-only relief lines (opened 1884) can be seen to the left. A goods train stands at the home signal on the West Curve, waiting 'the road'

J.P. Morris Collection

Chapter One
Eton *v.* The Rest: 1833–1840

The Great Western Railway was formed of two committees, one in London and one in Bristol, in 1833. From the very beginning, once a route from London to Bristol via Ealing, Slough, Reading, Swindon and Bath had been decided upon, the GWR had determined to have a branch to Windsor. This provoked strong feelings in the town: on the one hand the town and its council complained that Windsor should be on the main line; on the other hand the Provost and Fellows of Eton College opposed its coming implacably, fearing it would lead to a deterioration of discipline at the school. The Provost, Dr Goodall, had said publicly that 'the College would endeavour to prevent it to the utmost of their abilities and the extent of their purse'.

By the time the Great Western's Bill had reached its committee stage in the House of Commons, the Windsor branch had been dropped from its plans because of Eton's opposition (it must be remembered that many old Etonians were to be found in both Houses of Parliament). After a lengthy examination in Committee (57 days) the Bill received its second reading and passed to the House of Lords. Here it was speedily rejected by 47 votes to 30 (June 1834). Meanwhile Windsor itself had been supporting a London and Windsor Railway Company in preference to a line passing them by, but this proposal was withdrawn by its promoters, once the GWR Bill passed through the Commons.

The GWR London and Bristol Committees determined to submit a further Bill in the next Parliamentary session and in the meantime set about raising further subscriptions to fulfil the requirement set by Parliament's standing orders, namely that half the proposed capital should have been subscribed. Public meetings were arranged, not just in towns on the line of route but even in places like Gloucester and Exeter. After much hard work the necessary capital was raised by February 1835 and the Bill submitted to the Commons the following month. By now its main opponents were the London & Southampton Railway, promoting a rival line from Basingstoke to Bath and Bristol, and the Eton College masters. When the Bill reached the Commons' Committee stage, Brunel was able to show the superiority of his line to that of his southern rivals and the Bill received its third reading on 26th May, 1835 passing to the Lords the next day.

By now the Lords were seeing the Bill in a more favourable light and it passed its second reading on 10th June, being turned over to a Committee chaired by Lord Wharncliffe. Here it was to remain for a further 40 days.

Eton College remained resolutely opposed to the railway passing them at some two miles distance and in an attempt to remove this obstacle, Benjamin Shaw, the Chairman of the GWR London Committee wrote on 18th June to Dr Goodall, the Provost of Eton, *volunteering* to implement many restrictive clauses which would protect the College. In view of the impact this letter had some three years later, when the company was locked in a courtroom battle with the College, it is worth quoting in some detail:

> With reference to this point, it appears, from the opinion of Counsel, which I take the liberty of forwarding to you that there is no difficulty in providing a special prohibition under the provisions of the same clause in the Act against any such branch being made to connect with the Great Western Railway within a fixed

distance, either by this Company or by any other persons whomsoever.

The same prohibition may be made to apply also to the formation of a Depot.

Under a firm belief that such concessions must effectually remove the chief grounds of oppositions alleged, and so strongly advocated by the individuals presiding over the College, against the Bill, I am requested by the Directors to ask the favour of you submitting to them the following proposal as calculated to give permanent and substantial security against any injury or possible disadvantage to the institution from this measure.

A proviso to be introduced as an amendment to the clause in page 76 of the Bill specially preventing the making and connecting any Branch whatever with the Great Western Railway, by any Company or Persons, within the distance of three miles, in a direct line from Eton College without the consent in writing of the Provost or Fellows.

That no depot shall be made at Slough, nor within two miles thereof in either direction on the Great Western Railway.

That a close fence or wall shall be constructed on both sides of the line within the same distance.

That a sufficient and satisfactory Police shall be maintained at all times, within the same distance, by the Company to be appointed by, and subjected, to the control of the Provost and Fellows, for the purpose of preventing, restricting, under their orders, all access to the Railway for the Scholars of the College.

In the event of these terms being satisfactory to the Provost and Fellows of Eton College, the Directors cannot doubt they will signify their acquiescence in the arrangement by a declaration, through their Counsel or Agent in the Committee of the House of Lords, when the promoters of the Bill will proceed to carry it into immediate effect.

In communicating to the authorities of the College this proposition, I am requested to inform you that the Directors are, and ever have been, actuated by the strongest desire to remove every objections, which has been urged against the measure. And, as a further pledge of that disposition I beg to say that, if any point has been omitted which can be reasonably suggested, for the protection of the College, they will gladly accede to it, as far as may be consistent with the prosecution of the Undertaking. In the mode of carrying this proposition into effect, if sanctioned by the College, the Promoters of the Bill will readily acquiesce in a reference to Lord Canterbury, or any other Peer, who, being interested in the welfare of Eton College may be kind enough to undertake it.

I have the honor to be

Sir

Your most obed. Servant.

B. Shaw,

Chairman

However this appeal was not even considered by the Eton authorities, and Dr Goodall replied to Charles Saunders, the GWR Secretary, the next day as follows:

My Dear Sir,

I am compelled, after mature reflection, to come to this conclusion: that the unanimous decision of every one of the Fellows of Eton College on the proposal, which I was authorised to make to them from the Directors of the Great Western Railroad Company and I must add the conviction of their persevering inflexibly in the opinion, which, as Head of the College, I communicated to Mr Burke at their request, do not leave me at liberty to call them together a second time, for it would be an illiberal abuse of my authority to summon them, some of them from a considerable distance, into College, to pronounce upon a question which though it had undergone important modifications still remains essentially the same. I have moreover undoubted reason to know, that not only those individuals who were present when the question was proposed but also the three who where absent, coincided so fully in its rejection, that every vote would be given for uncompromised opposition. Your own observations must have convinced you, when we last met, that the only shade of opinion was the degree of energy, and, perseverance of application for aid in the opposition. It is I trust needless for me to say that my grateful sense of the liberality which I acknowledge that the Directors have uniformly shewn continues to have its due weight with me though I should feel that I deserved the excoration of every Etonian were I to attempt to exert an undue influence over those who, by the undeserved avowal of their motives I cannot but be sensible act under the impulse of pure and conscientious feelings.

I have passed an almost sleepness night and am at the moment afflicted by a severe headache the natural consequences of mental agitation and the regret which I feel because I am absolutely excluded from submitting the handsome proposals of the Directors, of which I most readily acknowledge the very favourable character, to ulterior discussion. Never were any one's hands more effectively tied than mine are; at the same time I must be permitted to recall to your recollection that the burthen of my song has been invariably the absolute obligation of my opposition, nor have I for a moment concealed from myself the inevitable danger to our institution, should the railroad be established. In as far as I could, I encouraged the hope that I might safely acquiesce in the protecting clauses which seemed to diminish the worst mischiefs which were to be apprehended from it.

It is not only a satisfaction and a pleasure, but also a duty to embrace this opportunity of declaring that throughout the entire course of this harassing business the College of Eton has experienced the considerable kindness and the fair, often candid treatment of every individual with whom I have come in contact engaged in the promotion of the Bill, and that I consider myself bound in honor and conscience to avow these sentiments on every allowable occasion.

Believe me to be with the truest esteem and respect,

My dear Sir,

Your obliged and faithful humble servant

(signed) J. Goodall

Lodge, Eton College, June 19, 1835

The Eton evidence to the Select Committee was heard on 11th August, 1835. The College case was put by Revd Thomas Carter, Fellow and Bursar (and vicar of Burnham) and Revd William Gifford Cookesley who had been a master for six years, following his own time at the school as a pupil. Both men laid great stress on the differences between Eton and other great schools such as Harrow, Winchester and Charterhouse that managed to exist close to a railway or other distractions.

As Cookesley said:

> . . . the tone and habit and more especially the wealth and rank of the boys at Eton must be taken into account.

and later,

> We have not been able to pass sumptuary laws to prevent boys having more money than does them good, and we must alter the system and discipline of the school if this railway passes.

Revd Carter intimated that any line 'within a distance where the boys could get to it' would be objected to, and when asked to be more specific indicated that four to five miles away was quite close enough. When asked whether a commitment by the company that no passengers should be *taken up* within a certain distance would satisfy him, said, tellingly,

> Not any distance if the railway was to go to Slough, we should think it a great evil without any Depot.

Revd Cookesley pooh-poohed the idea of police preventing access to the line saying that 'an Eton boy does not carry a badge upon his back', and, as for the wall '(it) might have been built as long as the Walls of China, I do not know the length of it, but I am satisfied they did not contemplate building a wall that would have been efficient'.

Asked why Eton would not accept the restrictions on a depot within a certain distance which the GWR had offered to impose upon itself, Rev. Cookesley said,

> Because it was considered insufficient and the College would not in the first place waive their objection to the line but in the next place it was considered an insufficient motive if any thing could induce them to withdraw their objection.

In other words, despite the very restrictive conditions which the GWR was prepared to accept (having already abandoned the idea of a branch to Windsor), Eton saw it as a point of principle that there should be no local railway whatsoever ('if the railway was to go to Slough we should think it a great evil *without any depot*') and did not concern itself with the feelings of the people of Windsor and Slough who would thereby be condemned to a life without fast transport (enjoyed by lesser places like Hanwell). Their own proposal was that between Reading and London the line should be diverted into the valley of the Blackwater River to Farnborough where it would join the London & Southampton Railway. This would have added about 7 miles to the distance but would have had the advantage of missing Eton by about 15 miles!

One might think, reading this, that the boys of Eton College were extremely susceptible to evil outside influences from which they had to be protected at all costs. But Sheila Goldsmith in her four-part article dealing with opposition in Windsor and Slough to the GWR at this period (News Bulletin of the Middle Thames Archaeological & Historical Society, 1966/7) has uncovered telling evidence of the true state of affairs at this time:

> In 1834 Eton College was the largest public school but even so it was not altogether successful. In common with the other schools, numbers were dropping rapidly. Westminster fell from 324 to 1818 to 100 in 1835, Rugby from 381 to 123 and Eton from 627 to 486 in 1834. The public school was declining in popularity and in danger of extinction for several reasons but all connected with the transition from eighteenth century to Victorian England.
>
> At this time the public schools still clung to an eighteenth century way of life but in several respects it was decadent or extremely inadequate. The curriculum had been designed for educating leisured gentlemen in the 'age of reason' so that, as a result, Sydney Smith is quoted as saying: 'A young gentleman goes to school at six or seven years old, and he remains in a course of education till twenty-three or

twenty-four years of age. In all that time his sole and exclusive occupation is learning Latin and Greek: he has scarcely a notion that there is any other kind of excellence: and the great system of facts with which he is the most perfectly acquainted are the intrigues of the heathen Gods; with whom Pan slept? – with whom Jupiter? – whom Apollo ravished?'

Other subjects were taught only as extras and at Eton, mathematics was included on the bill in the same list as 'extra washing' and 'journey money'. The mathematics master was not included in the staff and was not allowed to wear academic dress.

Organisation was also faulty in the school, accommodation being so primitive that some boys had to pay an extra fee to have a bed to themselves and food being so unappetizing and inadequate that most pocket money was devoted to supplementing it.

The number of assistant masters was extremely small. At Eton in the early 1830s when the number of boys was 570, there were only eight and at times the headmaster might be teaching two hundred boys at one time.

Because of the shortage of masters, a monitorial system was in operation in most schools with older boys teaching the younger as well as learning themselves. This led to a 'boy-rule' which was abused considerably. Because there was no organisation of leisure time, fighting and the type of bullying portrayed in 'Tom Brown's Schooldays' was rife.

When a boy graduated from slavery to the tyranny of upper school, he frequently indulged in dissipation. A schoolmaster said of schools in 1806: 'The youth at Eton are dissipated gentlemen: those at Westminster dissipated with a little of the blackguard: and those at St Paul's the most depraved of all'.

The only weapons which the masters could use were expulsion and flogging and the latter they did to excess. As a result rebellions were not uncommon. There was one at Harrow in 1808 because the headmaster had tried to reduce the power of the upper school. Another one occurred at Charterhouse in the same year for the same reason. At Winchester a rebellion occurred because the headmaster tried to make a Saint's day out of a school day without first asking the prefects. In 1818 the boys rebelled again at Winchester and were only quelled by the militia with fixed bayonets. At Shrewsbury in the same year the headmaster had his windows broken.

Eton was the most notorious school in this respect especially during the rule of Dr Keate (1809–1834) who began the campaign against the railway. This famous headmaster who was only five feet tall and an outstanding character at Eton faced three rebellions. The first was immediately after his appointment, the second he repressed while standing in the ruins of his shattered desk and the worst occurred in 1832, the year before the opposition to the railway began. He tried to flog a popular boy who resisted strongly. The boy's father was requested to remove him so that at the next rollcall the boys rebelled in protest. Biding his time, Keate waited until the boys were in bed and then sent for them in small batches to be flogged. He worked throughout the night until the early hours of the morning and eighty boys were punished.

The ordinary day to day activity of the school was far from humdrum. Boys burst into song during the lessons and expressed their feelings by booing and hissing. On Sunday afternoon when Keate read extracts from sermons he would be the target for atlases and dictionaries or even rotten eggs. His discipline was drastic. He would allow this behaviour to continue for several weeks and then pounce. Forty or fifty floggings and half a dozen expulsions would usually restore order.

In the light of this knowledge it is amusing to read such an understatement as that of the master who said 'Eton is founded on liberty'. This was the Eton of

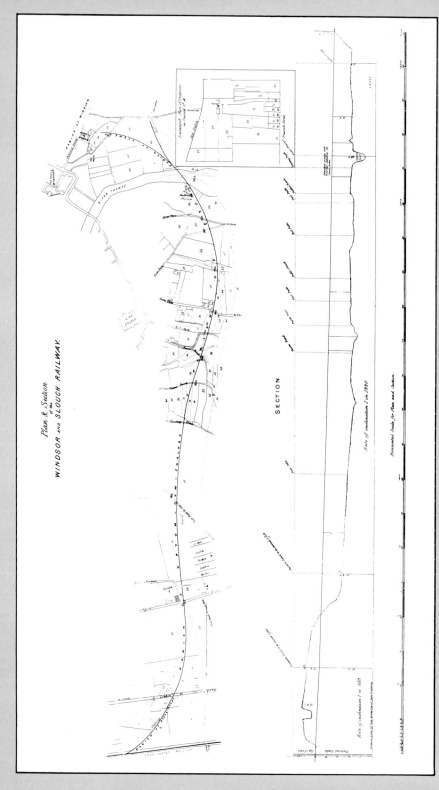

The Slough to Windsor Railway proposal of 1836 (Messrs Bedborough and Chadwick). Note how the line went straight through the Brocas Clumps, left of the River Thames crossing which was quite unacceptable to Eton College. Note also the separate location intended for the goods depot.

1833–5. The school which objected to the railway on the grounds that it would allow easy access to London and vice. In summing up Cookesley said: 'If the Parent of a boy at Eton was to come and say "You did not take decent precautions to prevent my boy coming upon the railway and getting into Vice" we should feel we had neglected that boy'.

At first sight it appears completely incongruous and very hard to believe until it is remembered that the school was declining. The reasons for its decline were undoubtedly the Hogarthian way of life and restricted curriculum.

If a line were built at Slough the college would have to change its whole system or risk an even greater decline in numbers. If the boys were given easy access to London it was very likely that they would become even more dissolute so giving the school a worse name. This would not encourage parents to send their children to the school. In order to prevent the boys going to London the only solution would be 'to alter the whole system because the combination of wealthy boys and shortness of distance would be disastrous. We must alter the whole system and discipline of the school if this railway passes'.

Despite Eton's resolute refusal to consider the GWR proposals, at the Lords' Committee the following clauses were added, the substance of which had first been put to Eton in Benjamin Shaw's letter (and turned down by them).

Clause 99:   Company not to make any branch to or through Eton.
Clause 100:   No person or Company to make a branch to or through Eton.
Clause 101:   No depot etc. to be within three miles of Eton College.
Clause 102:   Company to maintain a fence on each side of the line for four miles through certain parishes near Eton.
Clause 103:   Company to appoint an additional number of persons to prevent the Eton Scholars from using the Railway.

To obtain its line to Bristol, the GWR had had to sacrifice any hope of a branch to Windsor or a station at Slough and the Lords' Committee accepted that Eton's objections were insufficient to prevent the building of the line, despite an Eton petition to all peers recommending the adoption of the alternative proposal to join the Southampton line and the 'rejection of the Great Western Railroad Bill'. The Bill received the Royal Assent on 31st August, 1835.

In spite of the restrictive clauses included in the GWR Act, an attempt was made in 1836 to obtain permission to build a branch to Windsor. Captain Bulkeley, a resident of Windsor, and later to play a large part in the bringing of rail transport to the town, together with Messrs Bedborough and Chadwick (the latter, Engineer to the line) proposed a branch along a route later adopted by the unsuccessful Windsor Railway in 1846 (of which Bulkeley was Chairman). The GWR gave its support to the scheme but it will not surprise the reader to learn that the proposal was abandoned on account of 'a variety of objectionable restrictions' put forward by Eton College. Later Messrs Bedborough and Chadwick changed their allegiance and in 1846 were opponents to the Windsor Railway, being Directors of an alternative line, the Windsor, Staines and South Western Railway.

By the early part of 1838 the first section of the main line between Paddington and Maidenhead (a station near today's Taplow) was nearing completion and the GWR was receiving petitions as to the possibility of a

the old one there are gates, at which Policemen and Officers in the service of the Company are stationed, to prevent the ingress of all persons, except those going by the Railway.—There are also Policemen constantly attending outside of the booking Office.— Passengers are taken up and set down at this part of the Railway several times a day.:— Omnibuses from Windsor and Eton take passengers to and from the Booking Office, so that there is in reality a Station of this part of of. the Railway:—

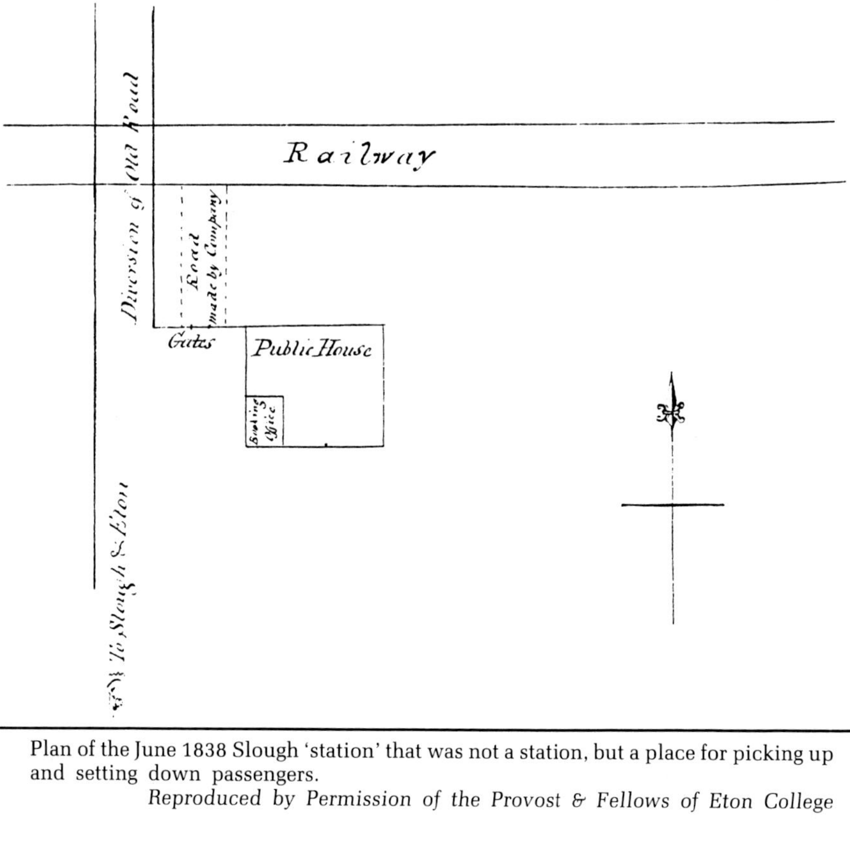

Diversion of old Road

Railway

Road made by Company

Gates

Public House

Booking Office

To Slough & Eton

Plan of the June 1838 Slough 'station' that was not a station, but a place for picking up and setting down passengers.
Reproduced by Permission of the Provost & Fellows of Eton College

station at Slough, of course banned by the 1835 Act. In response to an approach from William Bonsey, a solicitor and chief spokesman for Slough, the GWR replied that they would stop certain trains as they passed through Slough to allow passengers to alight or entrain. 'Slough' was also advertised as a calling point in the GWR's first timetable, to come into operation on 4th June, 1838.

Just two days before this, the Attorney-General (represented by the Solicitor General) spoke on behalf of Eton College in the Court of Chancery, presided over by the Vice Chancellor. Eton had presented an injunction to restrain the GWR from stopping their trains at Slough, quoting the restrictive clauses, particularly clause 101 on the school's behalf. The GWR's counsel made much of the fact that with no less a legal opponent than the Attorney-General as Plaintiff.

> ... it is to be supposed therefore that there is some very great general public mischief that will ensue if on Monday next, or on Tuesday next, a certain number of passengers shall go down to Slough by steam conveyance instead of going by road conveyance.

The GWR's case was that no depot (etc.) had been constructed. One or two rails had been removed in the boundary fence to enable passengers to gain access to the railway. Some 20 or 30 yards away 'a temporary house has been erected by an individual totally unconnected with the railway as a private speculation for the purpose of affording (waiting) accommodation'.

After hearing a laboriously argued case from the Solicitor General (the Hearing and Judgment runs to 58 handwritten pages) the Vice Chancellor ruled that stopping a train at the roadside was not the same as constructing a station, and that if the former action was intended to have been prevented by the Act, it should have said so clearly. When asked for costs by the GWR the Vice Chancellor, himself an old Etonian, injected a little humour into the proceedings with his remark, 'they will collect money enough at the Montem* to pay the costs'. So, on the following Monday the GWR opened for business, *and* stopped at Slough.

The Eton solicitors wrote rather bitterly of this defeat:

> ... the Lord Chancellor [sic] although an old Etonian, took the matter up strongly against our view ... nothing our counsel could allege ... had any affect on the Lord Chancellor ... who not only rejected the motion but as I think in an ungracious and uncalled for manner visited us with the costs to be paid to the other party.

However Mr Tooke, the solicitor, did admit that he agreed with the Lord Chancellor that the relevant clauses in the Act had been poorly constructed, for want of a little more care, and advised against an Appeal.

His advice was not heeded however. Ironically, even with an Appeal to the Lord Chancellor pending, Eton ordered a special train from Slough to take the boys to the Coronation on 28th June! On the strength of this, on 30th June George Gibbs (a GWR Director) wrote in his diary, 'It appears likely that

---

*A ceremony every third year in which the boys wore fancy dress and processed to a nearby hill, 'Montem', where they exhorted passers-by for money. This was to raise cash for the captain of the School who was leaving for University. However the ceremony was accompanied by much lawlessness and extravagance. The building of the GWR brought in huge numbers of spectators to the 'Montem' for the first time. An attempt was made to keep the next ceremony private, but without success, and so the event was abolished.

even Eton will allow us to have a station at Slough, and, strange to say, a train was provided on Thursday at the request of the Masters to convey the Eton boys up to town'. However a request by the GWR on 9th July to construct a station, with two persons (selected by Eton) appointed to prevent boys using the station, was rejected by the College. For the moment, Slough had to manage without a proper station (a tent was ordered for a shelter in May 1839!)

The following January (1839) the opponents were back in the Court of Chancery, arguing the same facts before the Lord Chancellor. The Reverends Carter and Cookesley, once again in combination, complained that up to 2,000 persons a day were passing through Eton in omnibuses to and from the Railway; these were driven at a furious rate, up to 10 buses together and put the scholars at great personal risk! (The GWR soon demolished this part of the argument by pointing out that the originally proposed branch line to Windsor would have obviated this nuisance!)

Apart from all the previously rehearsed arguments about 'booking office', 'station' etc., Eton this time drew into its case evidence that, in 1835, the terms of the Benjamin Shaw letter had effectively been written into the Act of Parliament with the GWR's agreement. However the GWR submitted evidence to show that this was not so; Mr Shaw's letter was written on the basis that the GWR would restrict itself if Eton would withdraw its opposition to the railway through Slough, and Eton refused to do so. Accordingly when on 27th August, 1835 the restrictive Clauses had been proposed by Eton for insertion by the Lords' Committee in the Bill then being discussed, the GWR said it had objected on the basis that Eton had never withdrawn its opposition to the railway. However, the GWR continued, all Counsel and the interested parties were ordered to withdraw from the Committee so it was not possible to state exactly what had gone on in closed session, but eventually the Bill was amended to include these clauses, but two important changes were made. In the clause prohibiting a depot, station etc. at Slough, the words 'no building whatsoever' (at this spot) were deleted, and so was the need for a brick wall 10 ft high on each side of the railway through the parishes stretching from Langley to Burnham.

Once again the lawyers sat back and listened (expensively) as the Lord Chancellor again went over all the old arguments about 'road', 'station', 'waiting place'. Finally, having revealed his own feelings ('I would be very glad undoubtedly if I could find in the Act anything that could enable me to say they are not authorised to do that' [stop trains]), the Chancellor concluded that the Act did not prevent the stopping of trains and refused the application, with costs granted to the GWR. Sheila Goldsmith wrote of the effect on Eton:

> In fact, although the line was built, the whole system of the school was not changed, partly because the Provost was so conservative but mainly because the magic name of Eton would always attract the aristocracy regardless of its reputation. Reforms were necessary, however, and occurred under Keate's successor, Dr Hawtrey (headmaster 1834–1852) who improved the teaching and the living conditions and at the same time tightened up on discipline. It was he who abolished the Montem ceremony, an ancient and famous custom but one which had become symbolic of the dissipation within the school.

On 14th November, 1839, Prince Albert made his first journey by train, from Slough to Paddington and, like everyone else, climbed up from ground level to join the train at the non-station called Slough at which trains halted. This may have helped the college to change its attitude to the matter and when the GWR wrote to the Provost giving notice of an Application to repeal and amend the 1835 Act 'to provide for a station at Slough', they at last relented. Thomas Batcheldor replied to the effect that the College could not affix its seal to the required consent, but would not take any steps in opposition. The Board recorded (Feb. 1840) that Eton had 'handsomely acquiesced in the request'. The Slough station finally opened on 4th June, 1840; it had been built in about 3 months. It consisted of separate up and down stations, both on the south side of the line, the up station being at the east, or London end. This of course meant that up trains calling had to cross the path of those in the opposite direction, and was a highly undesirable arrangement. But at least Slough and Windsor now had a proper station and for the next nine years, whilst various bodies sought to build a branch line to Windsor, it formed Windsor's 'gateway' to the slowly expanding railway system. The Queen, together with Prince Albert, made her first Royal journey from Slough to Paddington on 13th June, 1842, after which she used the train regularly. To quote from the Queen's own journal:

At half past eleven we left Windsor . . . we drove to Slough station . . . the saloon we travelled in on the train was very large and beautifully fitted up. It took exactly 30 minutes going to Paddington, and the motion was very slight and much easier than a carriage. Also no dust or great heat, in fact it was delightful and quick.

Slough station 1841/42 with a train in the down station. *British Rail*

SPECIAL Instructions to be observed at each Terminus of the Railway, and also at Slough and Reading Stations.

The signals are the same in every respect as those described in the General Instructions. The cross bar is always to be kept full on by day, and the red light always to be shown after dusk and at night; to close the entrance to those stations until a train or locomotive engine shall come distinctly in sight, and until a bell shall have been rung by the policeman, to give notice thereof at the station.

If the line, and the station, and all the crossings into it shall be perfectly clear, the disc is then to be put full on to the railway, (the cross-bar being reversed so as not to be seen on the line,) and the green light is to be shown to admit the train at a slow speed.

When one disc is shown full at one side or entrance to the Reading or Slough station, the other disc is on no account whatever to be put on full, in the same manner; but the cross-bar and red light must be kept shown, to prevent any engine or train approaching the station in the opposite direction.

As soon as the train has entered the station, and is quite clear of the crossing, and not sooner, the round disc is to be reversed, and the green lamp changed for the red light; the cross-bar being again shown full on to the line.

Particular attention must be paid by the signal men, after ringing the bell, to see that the other signals in the Reading or Slough stations, or at the other end of either station, are so given as to close admittance to it, before the round disc or green lamp is put on to the line, to permit any train or engine to approach.

The up-train must never be allowed to move from the platform of the Reading or Slough station, when the disc or green light is full on to the railway, to admit the down-train; nor must the disc or green light be put full on to the railway, after the whistle of the engine has given notice that the up-train is about to start; nor until it shall have completely cleared the crossing into the north line.

At each terminus the signal man must refuse to admit any engine or train into the station, until he knows that the line in the station is quite clear from the preceding engine, or train of carriages, trucks, or waggons, which it his duty to ascertain as soon as possible.

By order of the Directors,

CHARLES A. SAUNDERS,
February, 1841.   General Superintendent of the Line.

I, the undersigned, being appointed in the service of the Great Western Railway Company, do hereby bind myself to observe and obey the foregoing regulations.

Date_____

Appointment_____

Witness to Signature.   Signature.

INSTRUCTIONS to Policemen, and Others, for the Management and Method of giving Signals.

EVERY policeman, on the railway, will be furnished with a lamp having three different glasses; viz. red for *Danger*, green for *Caution*, and white for *All right* signals.

The use of each colour is more clearly described in the printed list of signals, and it is of the utmost importance that attention be at all times given to the accurate display of the proper signal according to circumstances, for which purpose each policeman must take care that his lamp is well trimmed and kept clean, and the glasses quite clear and unbroken. In the event of the lamp or glass requiring repair, he is to procure another from the station, to be used until his own be restored to him.

The signals, both by day and night, are to be kept steadily shown by every policeman on the line, until every carriage or truck in the train shall have passed him. In all cases the policeman signalling, is to stand on the opposite side of the railway, that he may be quite conspicuous to the driver and fireman, as well as to the conductor and guards, taking great care not to be in the way of any engine or train approaching in the opposite direction.

At and after dusk, each policeman will show the red light to any train or engine which may be following another train, or carriage, or engine, upon the same line, within three minutes of each other, in order to stop the latter.

Instructions dated February 1841 for working the signals at Slough.
Courtesy House of Lords Records Office

Chapter Two
No Branch for Windsor

Between 1844 and 1846 several attempts were made to connect the town of Windsor with the railways running nearby, (or at least as close as the 'Eton clauses' had permitted). The first of these was the Windsor Junction Railway, formed at a meeting in Windsor on 17th October, 1844. A committee was set up including James Bedborough, a Windsor councillor, under the chairmanship of Capt. John Forbes RN, Deputy Lieutenant of Berkshire. This line was planned as an atmospheric railway, which found much favour locally, and its Engineer, Thomas Page, was also a Consultant Engineer to the Crown Commissioners (of Woods and Forests). The route proposed was from a station at Windsor Bridge via Dachet to Staines, where it would have joined the intended Staines and Richmond Junction Railway, another line from Richmond taking it to Hungerford Bridge in London.

Despite Page's influence and the early placing of the plans before the Queen, no definite answer could be obtained from the Crown and matters were frozen in November as it was obvious that nothing would be achieved in the ensuing session of Parliament. Attempts were made to reinvigorate the matter of a railway the following June (1845) and a new Committee was formed, again with Capt. Forbes in the chair. At a public meeting in Windsor on 2nd July those attending made it clear that what the inhabitants of Windsor sought was an independent direct line to the heart of London, not a connection with the GWR which ended at Paddington on the outer fringe of the metropolis.*

Following the meeting a letter was put to the Crown Commissioners of Woods and Forests asking that they receive a deputation. Within days, however, a reply was received that the Commissioners had decided that the proposed line would injure Crown property and that such a deputation would be pointless. Despite further correspondence from the Committee which suggested a private branch and terminus for the Queen's use, a final rejection was given by the Commissioners on 13th August and this scheme was dead.

Within a matter of weeks, however, a new proposal surfaced. Some of those involved in the formation of a Windsor, Slough and Staines Atmospheric Railway had been prominent in the Windsor Junction Railway, including James Bedborough and Thomas Clarke, Mayor of Windsor. Charles Vignoles who had constructed the Kingstown to Dalkey atmospheric line in Ireland was appointed its Engineer.

It proposed to commence at Thames Street to cross the Barge Canal to Romney Island and to continue thereon to the eastern extremity thereof, that island being in the middle of the Thames and lying between Windsor Home Park and the playing fields of Eton College and thence over the Thames between Eton College playing fields and the Black Potts Fishery by a continuous viaduct, after crossing the Thames one line proceeded to a junction with the Great Western Railway at Slough and the other line diverged to Staines where it was proposed to form a junction with the projected Staines and Richmond Railway ... The scheme was a strictly independent undertaking ...

*Under consideration at this meeting was a London & Windsor Railway, commencing on the south side of Victoria Street, Windsor 'about 250 yds west of the Lower Lodge ... situate at the entrance of the Little Park and immediately at the end of the Long Walk.' It would have tunnelled under the Long Walk, and passed through Crown property for nearly a mile and a half. It was 21 miles 45 chains long and terminated opposite Knightsbridge Barracks in London.

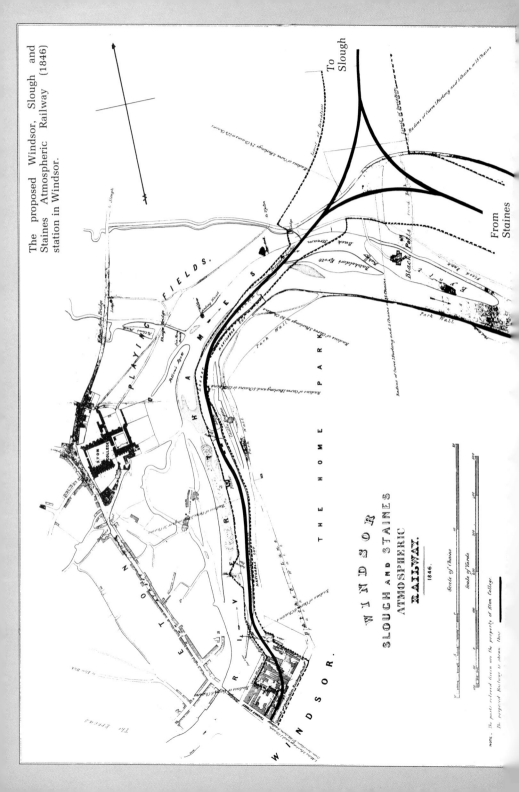

The proposed Windsor, Slough and Staines Atmospheric Railway (1846) station in Windsor.

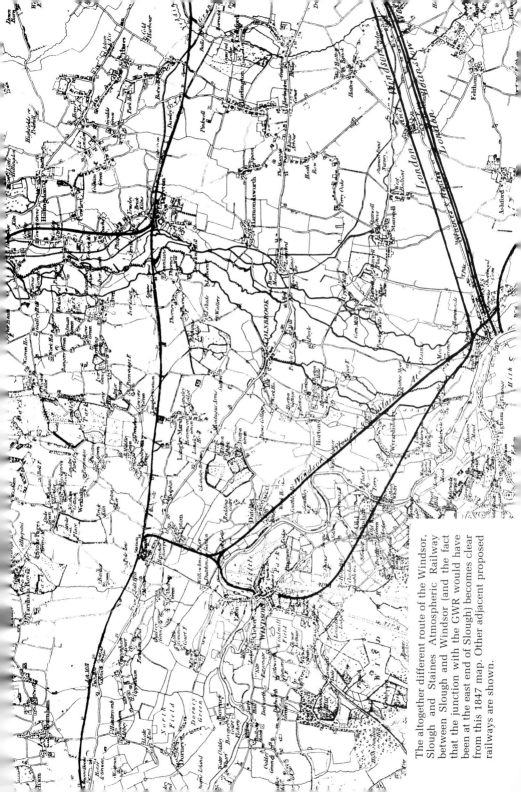

The altogether different route of the Windsor, Slough and Staines Atmospheric Railway between Slough and Windsor (and the fact that the junction with the GWR would have been at the east end of Slough) becomes clear from this 1847 map. Other adjacent proposed railways are shown.

The cost of the enterprise was estimated at £150,000, later amended to £158,000.

The question of gauge naturally interested the GWR since the line would be connecting with a broad gauge line at one end and a narrow gauge line at the other! Furthermore as the GWR's Brief to counsel opposing the eventual Bill pointed out, the atmospheric company had no power to lay their pipes nearer to Slough station than the point 200 yds east of the station where their line would end, and the GWR wondered how the carriages would be moved from Slough station to the commencement of the atmospheric line.

A Subscription Contract published early in 1846 shows that 6,100 £20 shares had been subscribed for, of which about 10 per cent, or somewhat over £12,000, were paid up. So there is no doubt of the support for the line. Of the 161 subscribers, 60 were 'local' with 'trades' varying from Plumber and Carpenter to Surgeon and Gentleman.

A Traffic Survey carried out for the Atmospheric Railway between 1st and 14th October, 1845 produced information of an estimated 649,411 passengers travelling between Windsor and Slough annually, 353,998 of whom were on foot. To this figure another 35,000 needed to be added for Ascot Race week, plus 3,600 Eton Collegians, giving a grand total of 688,011 passengers annually available to a railway company.

Public opponents to the scheme were the GWR, Eton College, the inhabitants of Eton, and several large and influential landowners (Windsor of course favoured it). The GWR's main objection was that they had been prevented by the clauses inserted in their 1835 Act from building a branch to Windsor, which they had always wanted, and that if a branch was to be built, they should build it. Furthermore, it contended, traffic could be much more efficiently carried on by the company possessing the main line than by one working the branch independently.

Eton College circulated a printed statement of the chief points on which the Provost and Fellows based their opposition. Summarised as briefly as possible:

1. The approach of the railway within a few yards of the playing field would inflict permanent and irremediable evil on the school . . . by affecting the privacy of its position and the security of the scholars.
2. The railway by its peculiar construction of a bridge or viaduct up, rather than *across* the Thames would injure the property of the College . . . beyond the reach of any compensation.
3. The consequence of the proposed Works would dam or pen up the waters . . . so as to subject the College to extensive inundations.
4. A better link between Windsor and Slough would be answered by a railway entirely on the west side of Eton, crossing the River some distance above Windsor Bridge.
5. The cost of the line would exceed the estimates; should the Flood water rise above the rails, a very probable occurrence, it would cause much obstruction to an atmospheric railway.
6. The GWR Act 1835 prevented construction of a line within three miles of Eton College without the latter's consent, which had not been sought.

The chief reason for the routeing of the line via Romney Island had been to avoid the crossing of Crown land. By the time the Atmospheric Railway Bill reached its Select Committee stage, Eton College had bought Romney Island and this would almost certainly have killed the scheme, even if it had got through Parliament.

However there was further *private* opposition to the proposal which counted even more than Eton College. The Crown was not represented at the Select Committee hearing but, time after time, evidence was produced as to the effect the line would have on their lives – Prince Albert's privacy; the fact that the Engine House would be visible from the Castle; disturbance to the fisheries, and so on.

With all these powerful forces ranged against the Bill, it was inevitable that it would fail and on the ninth day of the Committee Hearing, 19th May, 1846, the Committee decided they would not recommend Parliament to sanction the line.

Despite this apparent opposition, in fact early in 1846 the Crown's objection to railways had begun to melt. After the expensive refurbishment of Windsor Castle which had taken place between 1824 and 1836 and cost over a million pounds, the need was felt to tidy up the slums surrounding the Castle (and, as a secondary feature, make Home Park private by diverting the roads that crossed it). Because the cost of the Castle's improvement had caused public criticism, money had to be obtained elsewhere. It was realised that the companies who were keen to bring railways to the town could be made to pay for the privilege. Furthermore the support for railways in Windsor was very strong.

After a summer of meetings with the Great Western and South Western Companies and much discontent, the majority of the disappointed locally-interested shareholders and Directors of the Atmospheric Company eventually proposed an amalgamation with the GWR. A minority joined with the Staines & Richmond and South Western companies in a new Windsor, Staines and South Western Railway. The latter company lost no time in approaching Lord Morpeth, HM Chief Commissioner of Woods & Forests with a view to agreeing a route for the railway into Windsor. The very next day, 4th October, the GWR had a similar meeting.

Both companies now began the process of drawing up plans to lay before Parliament for yet more attempts to build a railway or railways into Windsor, although the Crown was not prepared to allow the South Western line beyond Black Potts, between Dachet and Windsor. A public meeting was arranged for 7th December, 1846 to discuss the merits of the two proposals, to be chaired by the Mayor, now James Bedborough.

In an attempt to win the day, the GWR played some really dirty tricks! An up overnight express was stopped specially at Slough (a thing quite unheard of) and a special train run down from London in order to convey 'vast numbers of persons, perfect strangers to Windsor' to the meeting. The GWR had organised an array of 'clerks, check-takers, constables and even navigators' in a stream of coaches from Slough station to 'pack' the meeting! As a result a good proportion of the local residents were unable to enter the hall to express their views.

The meeting began at 1 pm and was extremely noisy and disorderly. At one stage Captain Bulkeley, on behalf of the Windsor Railway, promoted by

WINDSOR RAILWAY.

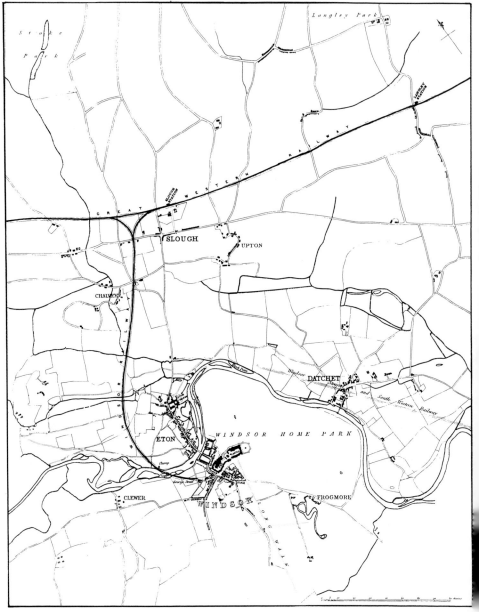

The Windsor Railway (promoted by the GWR) 1846, and its rival, the Windsor, Staines and South Western Railway which was forced to end in the middle of nowhere.

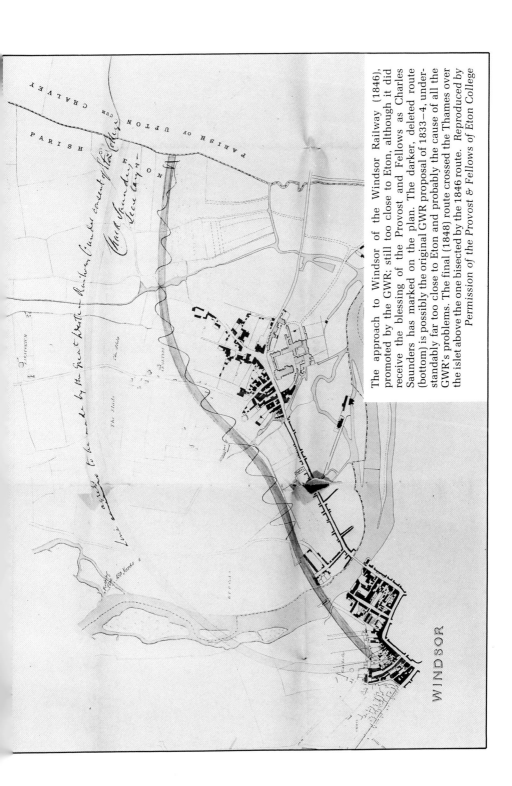

The approach to Windsor of the Windsor Railway (1846), promoted by the GWR; still too close to Eton, although it did receive the blessing of the Provost and Fellows as Charles Saunders has marked on the plan. The darker, deleted route (bottom) is possibly the original GWR proposal of 1833–4, understandably far too close to Eton and probably the cause of all the GWR's problems. The final (1848) route crossed the Thames over the islet above the one bisected by the 1846 route. *Reproduced by Permission of the Provost & Fellows of Eton College*

the GWR, asserted that a bribe had been given by the South Western Company to her Majesty's Government for the purpose of obtaining the assent of the Crown! Eventually a point was reached where a vote was required on an amendment proposed by Captain Bulkeley that 'as this railway . . . has obtained the consent of the Crown, HM Government, and the Provost and College of Eton, this meeting cordially approves the same in preference to the line proposed to terminate near Dachet, and that a petition to both Houses of Parliament be adopted, and signed by the Mayor . . . in favour of the Windsor bill'.

The Mayor asked that only those who resided locally should vote, by a show of hands. The amendment was then put to the vote and as the *Windsor Express* records:

> . . . a scene took place such as the Windsor folks have rarely if ever witnessed. Several hundred strangers to Windsor, but many of them known as clerks, porters, policemen, navigators, engineers, cabmen, etc., belonging to the Great Western Railway Company, including their directors and secretary, holding up both hands in favour of the amendment. A show of hands was taken against, when the Mayor declared the majority to be in favour of the amendment. Great cheering and turmult followed this announcement.

Captain Bulkeley then announced that he had had such confidence in the result of the meeting that he had a petition ready prepared (cries of 'You relied on your packed meeting'!).

> Captain Bulkeley here pressed the Mayor to sign the petition, which he, in the rudest manner, placed before him, and in like manner thrust a pen into his hand, which the Mayor threw on the table below him amidst great laughter and cheers.

The Mayor would not allow himself to be bullied by the GWR and its supporters and decided that the meeting was not representative of the inhabitants and that he would place the petition into the Town Hall for the next five days, for signatures to be obtained.

> The most disorderly and disgraceful noise was for a full hour kept up to induce the Mayor to put the adoption of the petition to the meeting and to sign it. The Mayor, however, coolly but fairly, refused; and darkness having arrived, the meeting separated . . .
>
> The meeting broke up in confusion, after a sitting of five hours, one hour of which was spent in darkness, and two hours in the most disorderly and disgraceful uproar. The Town Hall emptied by degrees; but the public houses became simultaneously full. There were 'treats' and 'spreads' provided with tolerable profusion, as we learn by Great Western generosity . . . (and) the curtain dropped on one of those scenes observed at rotten boroughs at elections . . .

The result of the written ballot, which only those who had attended the meeting and were residents of Slough, Chalvey, Eton Wick, Upton, Datchet, Wraysbury Horton or Old Windsor were permitted to sign was:

> For the adoption of the Great Western petition 14
> Against it 238

After this excitement the winter months were quiet but, as spring approached, the Town Council despatched two petitions to Parliament in support of the Town Improvements promoted by the Crown and the other supporting the South Western Railway proposals. The Crown also supported the South Western Bill, but so they did the Great Western Bill, as did the Provost and Fellows of Eton (but not, definitely not, the masters!).

In May 1847 the House of Commons looked at both Railways' Bills and threw out the Great Western Bill on the strength of the opposition of the Eton masters. However the Great Western blamed Lord Morpeth, the Commissioner for Woods and Forests for losing them their Bill. On being asked by Counsel whether one railway would be better than two, his Lordship had replied, 'I think one would be preferred'. Later he was asked as to which of the two railways preference should be given. Lord Morpeth answered, '. . . I have no hesitation in saying that taking the whole scheme together they (the Crown) prefer the adoption of the South Western line'.

The GWR made representations at Buckingham Palace following the loss of the Bill which resulted in Lord Morpeth being sent for. He expressed regret for the statement he had made, which he claimed had been made inadvertently, 'under some excitement'.* It had been the Crown's intention that both Railway Bills and the Town Improvement Bill should be dealt with together, the railways in fact paying the whole of the cost of those improvements. The failure of the GW Bill led to the withdrawal of the Town Improvements Bill. The South Western Bill however was passed on 25th June, 1847 (but with its terminus at Black Potts) and that railway company committed itself to paying the Crown £60,000 towards the town improvements.

After a summer of recriminations, meetings between the Commissioners for Woods and Forests and the two railway companies separately took place in October 1847. Agreement was reached with the Great Western and the Crown pledged support of the GWR branch line upon payment of £25,000 towards the town improvements. Payment would be in three instalments, the first, of £8,000, to be paid within three months of passing of the Act. The following month saw an agreement drawn up between the 'Woods and Forests' and the South Western Company for the latter to pay its £60,000 in £10,000 instalments. (In Parliament, the following June, F. Scott, a Director of the South Western Railway admitted that there was not much difference between the payments [£85,000] and a 'bribe'!)

In the period between autumn 1847 and the following spring when the Great Western Bill† came before Parliament, the Eton masters' opposition remained as strong as ever, despite Lord Morpeth's effort to obtain their approval. Edward Coleridge, Senior Assistant Master, was described by Lord Morpeth as being implacably hostile, and Dr Hawtrey, the headmaster, although concerned that he did not appear disloyal to the Crown, would, it was felt, be carried along by Coleridge's opposition. Those actually in charge of the College, the Provost and Fellows, supported the Bill.

At the same time the Commissioners for Woods and Forests tried to get the two railway companies together so that there would be only one terminus; in

---

*The GWR Brief stating this is marked 'This is only for the information of Counsel and must not be referred to as it is of too delicate a nature'.

†Technically it was again promoted by the Windsor Railway, but with an inbuilt agreement that the railway was to be built by, and incorporated in, the GWR.

fact the agreement between 'Woods and Forests' and the South Western dated 10th May, 1847 expressly required the latter railway company not to object to any line from the Great Western at or near Slough running into the South Western terminus at Black Potts (north of Dachet).

But neither company wanted this arrangement; the Great Western would have no dealings with the South Western and for its part the latter put up a Windsor, Staines and South Western Bill (Slough Extension and Deviations etc.). This Bill was opposed by both the Great Western and the Crown and was rejected by a Parliamentary Committee on 2nd June, 1848 in favour of the alternative Great Western Bill. At last, after more than 13 years, might the scene be set for a Great Western branch line to Windsor?

TIDAL WATERS, AND NAVIGABLE RIVERS.

APPLICATIONS TO PARLIAMENT FOR LOCAL BILLS.

Great Western Railway

BRANCH

FROM SLOUGH TO WINDSOR.

NOTICE.

I, GEORGE HURWOOD, of Ipswich, in the County of Suffolk, Civil Engineer, having been appointed by the Lords Commissioners for executing the Office of Lord High Admiral, Surveying Officer under an Act passed in the 10th year of the reign of Her present Majesty, intituled "An Act for making preliminary Enquiries in certain cases of applications for Local Acts," in so far as the said Act relates to an intended application to Parliament for an Act in relation to making a *Railway from the Great Western Railway near Slough to the Town of New Windsor, in the County of Berks.* DO HEREBY GIVE NOTICE, that I shall attend on Wednesday, the 2nd day of February, 1848, at the Town Hall, at Windsor, at the hour of Ten o'clock in the Forenoon, for the purpose of making such examination and survey of the Locality which the proposed Act will affect, and of making such enquiries relative to the provisions of the said proposed Act, and of investigating such other matters relating thereto, as the said Lords Commissioners have by their Order directed me to make and investigate. AND I DO HEREBY REQUIRE the Promoters of the said intended Work to appear before me at the time and place aforesaid, and to produce all such surveys, plans, sections, estimates, documents, and evidences, as will be necessary to support such intended application.

I DO HEREBY FURTHER GIVE NOTICE, that all persons desirous of being heard in opposition to such intended application, do appear before me, with witnesses, plans, sections, maps, books, or other documents relevant to the said enquiries.

As Witness my hand this 15th day of January, 1848.

GEORGE HURWOOD,
Surveying Officer.

Notice of the Inquiry to be held on behalf of the Admiralty, 2nd February, 1848.
Great Western Trust, Courtesy Laurence Waters

Chapter Three
The Final Hurdles

With the agreement between the GWR and the Commissioners for Woods & Forests in its corporate pocket, the Board of the GWR must have known that it would be only a matter of time before broad gauge rails reached Windsor. But there were still several hurdles to cross.

First came an Inquiry by the Admiralty as to whether the proposed bridge at Windsor would interfere with the current or obstruct free passage of boats, also whether sufficient provision had been made for the escape of flood water. This Inquiry took place in Windsor Town Hall on 2nd February, 1848 and concluded that 'upon the whole . . . the proposed bridge will not objectionably interfere with the River . . .' However the document recommended that part of an islet crossed by the bridge be cut off to afford a freer passage of water and this the GWR agreed to do.

The Bill came before the House of Commons for its second reading on 24th March. Gladstone, old Etonian and MP for Oxford University, took the lead in opposing it in the interests of Eton. The *Windsor Express* had, by now, completely changed its attitude to the Great Western and wrote in a report of 25th March, 1848:

> We give in our parliamentary intelligence a brief report of the debate on the second reading . . . and call the attention of our readers to the jesuitical attack made upon it by Mr Gladstone on the part of the assistant masters of Eton. From what the Hon. gentleman stated, it might be inferred that there were claims of the two companies founded upon some equal right, instead of the absolute fact that the GW had been unjustly deprived of their Bill last autumn by a company who, in reality, had no previous right to the occupation of the district, and who have utterly failed in giving the communication either to Windsor or Eton which they undertook to do (a reference to the proposed terminus near Dachet).
>
> There is, then, we are glad to see, every prospect of the Bill passing into law this session; and . . . that it will be a great boon to Windsor, reduced – as it is now – to the lowest possible condition, in a commercial point of view.

A remarkable change from the sentiments expressed at the time of the 'packed' meeting.

The Bill went to a Commons Select Committee on six days between 22nd May and 2nd June. On 23rd May the GWR was able to announce to the Committee that it had the signed agreement of the Provost and Fellows of Eton to the building of the line (*see illustration*). In fact several GWR witnesses, including Brunel, pointed out that the Eton authorities had selected the line of route in the Eton area and it was now completely 'out of (Eton's) bounds'. The station site at Windsor had been suggested by the Commissioners for Woods & Forests and it would, in Brunel's words, 'clear out one of the lowest, dirtiest, worst drained and ventilated streets in Windsor'.

The Very Revd G.H. Greville, Dean of Windsor, stated that, in his opinion, the railway 'will be the greatest possible advantage to the School . . . also of the greatest benefit to Windsor'. Another glowing reference came from Revd Thomas Carter, Fellow of Eton, Magistrate and Rural Dean and previously an opponent of the GWR, who conceded that 'the evils which he anticipated (from the building of the GWR) have not taken place (and) that the greatest evil now existing is the perpetual passing and repassing of vehicles . . .

The written agreement of the Provost and College of Eton to the making of the GWR branch from Slough to Windsor, 17th May, 1848; and the final route of the Windsor branch.

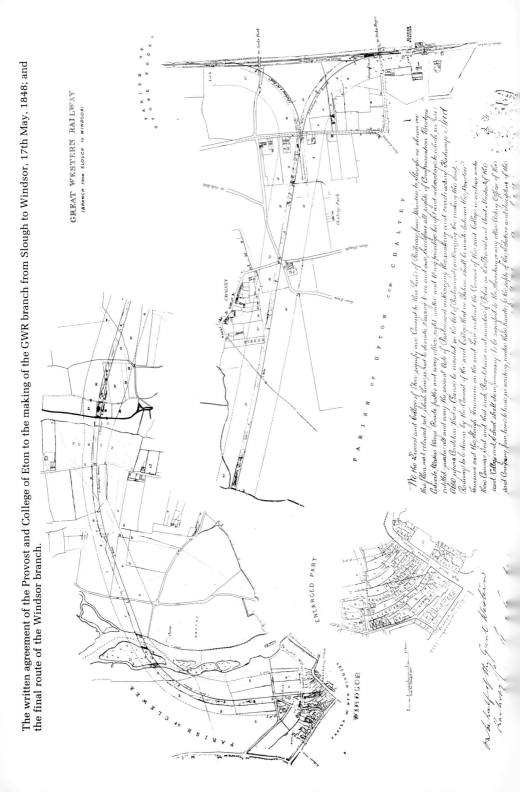

GREAT WESTERN RAILWAY

(BRANCH FROM SLOUGH TO WINDSOR)

through the College in the midst of the boys'. The College's consent had been given 'because a railway was found to be strongly called for and that was deemed the best for Windsor because it had a terminus in the centre of the town and was not objectionable'.

I.K. Brunel, Engineer to the company pointed out that all the objections raised in 1847 had been taken into account; in particular the viaduct on the approach to Windsor which previously had only extended to the first road north of the Thames, but now had been lengthened to 1965 yds long so that the boys could pass under the line to reach their bathing places and could rove over the fields without danger or inconvenience. The station would be constructed 'with an elevation to harmonize with the Castle'.

The GWR's Counsel brought out several key issues during the hearing:

– the company had made repeated overtures for constructing a railway to Windsor but had respected the wishes of the Court not to press the matter until such a proceeding was inevitable. The company had a just claim to the Windsor traffic.
– a frequent traffic was occasioned by the Ministers of the Crown going to and from HM's Councils
– the traffic between Slough and Windsor during the Races was quite astonishing
– during the summer season vast numbers of persons were compelled to walk from Slough to Windsor and back
– the time consumed in travelling between Windsor and Slough by omnibus was as great as that taken by travelling the 18¼ miles from Slough to Paddington by train

Several petitions 'against' had been entered including the inevitable one from the masters of Eton. Amongst the points this made were the following:

– would interfere with the playing grounds of Eton
– injurious to petitioners' property rights
– the estimate for building the line was insufficient
– would be better if line diverted to join the Windsor, Staines and South Western line

The GWR, at the request of the House of Commons' Committee, made two attempts (on 31st May and 1st June) to meet the wishes of the masters of Eton, but both approaches were rebuffed by Dr Hawtrey. The masters and several old Etonians, including William Gladstone, spoke at the Committee. But this time the Bill was approved and passed for its third reading.

Some fairly strict safeguards had been included to protect the College, permitting the Provost or Head Master etc. to visit stations to check that boys were not using them (this privilege was never exercised), the provision of police officers to keep boys away from the line and provision for the privacy of the bathing place at Cuckoo Weir (in the end the screen was never erected). No intermediate station or stopping place was to be built on the line without Eton's consent. By the agreement with the Commissioners for Woods & Forests the GWR was prevented from 'the manufacturing or repairing of steam or other engines or carriages of any description', probably

explaining the absence of an engine shed at Windsor, somewhat unusual for a branch line terminus.

Of the provisions for the patrolling of the line to keep boys away, R. Neville Grenville who was at Eton from 1858 to 1864 wrote as follows:

> . . . the authorities of Eton College compelled the GWR to have a watchman on the railway in the neighbourhood of Eton to prevent the boys from going on the line. I remember him, a weird looking old gentleman with blue swallow-tail coat and a very tall hat. His name was Bott and he was reputed to have fought at Waterloo.

In 1878 the watchman's wages amounted to about £40 per annum. The GWR finally obtained permission from Eton College to withdraw this watchman in 1886!

Later that month (June) the Bill received its third reading in the House of Commons. Despite a lengthy oration opposing the Bill from Benjamin Disraeli, recently elected to a Buckinghamshire constituency (Beaconsfield) that included Eton, which called into question the good faith of Lord Morpeth,* stoutly defended by the latter, upon the vote being taken a majority of 127 supported the Bill.

Having received an unopposed second reading in the Lords on 4th July, the Bill was passed to the Lords' Committee, where it was examined between 18th and 20th July. Six petitions had been received against the Bill, three of which the GWR dismissed as irrelevant. Petition No. 4 was from the Eton masters and some 200 residents of Eton purporting to be 'Resident Householders Commoners of the Manor of Eton other Owners lessees and Occupiers of land etc'. The GWR showed that only two of these were *owners*, the remainder being Commoners, whose rights were provided for by the Lands Clauses Consolidation Act. Petition No. 5 was from two or three owners of ruinous property in Windsor and Petition No. 6 came from the Windsor Staines & South Western Railway. Counter to these petitions 'against', which included only two inhabitants of Windsor was a petition in favour signed by 780 of the ratepaying inhabitants of Windsor, including the Dean and the Mayor.

The petition from Eton mainly concerned property rights, commoners' rights, injury to the trade of Eton, injury to the College, flooding etc. etc. Evidence against the Bill was given once more by the masters, W.E. Gladstone MP and Robert Stephenson (son of George Stephenson); the latter favoured the extension of the South Western line into Windsor, thus cancelling the need for the GW line, in his opinion.

When Lord Morpeth gave evidence he conceded that if the GW Bill was passed it was inevitable that the South Western line would be allowed to come from Dachet through Home Park into Windsor. However, the Crown would not allow this to happen unless the GW and Town Improvement Bills were passed.

I.K. Brunel pointed out that whereas the limits of deviation of the 1847 alignment passed through the 'Brocas Clumps' (of trees, a well known landmark) to which Eton had objected, this had been altered this time. He added that Slough would be the location for spare carriages and engines for working the Windsor traffic.

*On the basis of what he had said in May 1847 (see page 27), accepted £60,000 from the South Western Railway and then entered into a similar arrangement with the GWR on payment of £25,000.

Following the hearing of all the Evidence, the Committee approved the Bill which received its third reading on 24th July, announced to the citizens of Windsor by the ringing of the bells in Windsor parish church. Following Royal Assent on 14th August, 1848 (the Town Improvement Bill was also signed the same day) work began immediately on building the line. Charles Saunders wrote to Thomas Batcheldor, Registrar of Eton on 18th August '(we are) ready now to commence our works, almost immediately, to the discomfiture, I apprehend, of our various numerous Foes . . .' Great must have been the celebration in the Great Western Board Room at Paddington – after more than 15 years, Windsor, the town between which and Slough over half a million passengers travelled annually by road, was at last to come into the GWR fold. The Windsor Railway promoters would receive two £20 GWR shares in place of three Windsor shares of £20 each, dividend to be paid only on completion of the line.

On Wednesday, 29th November, 1848, while labourers were at work in a cutting near Chalvey Park 'the sidings suddenly fell in' and completely buried three of them (presumably this means the sides of the cutting). Their fellow workmen quickly extricated them and Mr Champneys, the Surgeon to the union-house, soon arrived. One man escaped with only severe bruising but both the others had a broken right leg and other injuries, necessitating their removal to Eton union-house.

In March 1849 the *Railway Chronicle* reported:

> The branch line from the Great Western, at Slough, is rapidly progressing. A great portion of the viaduct, nearly a mile in length, supported by iron columns (on the Slough side of the railway bridge across the Thames) has been erected; and the cutting and embankment from the main line to Chalvey fields at Eton, nearly completed. The castings of the bridge are all prepared for its erection, as soon as the brick and stone work for the support of the structure are in readiness.

The bridge, of wrought iron, was built by Hennet's of Bristol and weighed 450 tons. To move it to Slough (by rail) it had to be made in pieces weighing about 15 tons each and placed 'on exceedingly strong and heavy carriages'. The *Windsor Express* for 7th July, 1849 reported that 'the several parts of the iron bridge have found their way perfectly safe to Slough'.

The Engineer's report for August 1849 reads:

> Upon the Windsor branch the works have proceeded rapidly, the whole of the viaduct and the rest of the line, with the exception of the bridge across the Thames is finished, ballasted and the permanent way laid: a temporary bridge has been for some time past constructed across the River and arrangements might have been made for opening the Railway with such contrivance a month or six weeks ago. The permanent bridge which is a work of some magnitude, being of a single span of 200 ft, is in a very forward state: two of the three ribs or arches of which it consists being in place, and the third, which has been entirely completed and proved at Bristol is in the course of delivery on the spot: in a few weeks it will be quite finished.
>
> The completion of the station will govern the opening of the line: every endeavour has been made to advance this . . . I should hope that in the course of the next month it will allow of the opening of the railway.

The two rival railway companies were each striving to be the first to reach Windsor. The South Western line had opened to Dachet on 22nd August, 1848 and almost a year later the short extension to Windsor was awaiting the Board of Trade inspection when disaster struck. On 14th August, 1849 a cast iron girder of one of the bridges across the Thames at Black Potts snapped because of the sinking of one of the piers. The Engineer, Locke, had built the piers of cast iron cylinders, a method he had never employed before, because of the pressure on him to complete the job quickly. As a result the GWR was able to complete its line first.

On 20th September, 1849 the townspeople of Windsor were surprised and excited by the appearance of the first engine to be seen in the town. The engine arrived just after 8 am accompanied by Mr Brunel 'after a most satisfactory transit over the bridge which, although the supports were removed did not exhibit the slightest deflection. The engine was a newly constructed one, having a tender over the boiler' (*Windsor Express*). Sadly, the day before, James Moyser, a riveter working on the bridge fell off and was drowned.

The following week the *Windsor Express* allowed a little excitement to enter its progress report:

> The works on the branch line from Slough to Windsor are still progressing rapidly, the loaded wagons used on the works have been drawn by engines up to George Street during the week, and the new station, erected as if by magic, in a room of squalid tenements and opening a smiling scene of the wooded uplands in perspective bids fair to be an ornamental feature of the town. The works and railway line and bridge exhibit that substantial completeness and workmanlike finish which characterises all the undertakings of the Great Western Railway company. It is now stated that the opening of the line will take place on Monday week instead of Monday.

Captain Simmons inspected the line for the Board of Trade on 5th October, 1849 and passed it as perfectly satisfactory. The bulk of his three page report deals with the construction of the river bridge at Windsor, such description felt to be necessary because it was 'new in construction and design'.

The public opening took place just three days later on Monday 8th October, although Windsor station was not completed until 1850, having been delayed by bad weather. The first train left Windsor at 8.05 am and there were ten other departures up to 9.20 pm. Because the service comprised trains between Windsor and London, rather than a shuttle to Slough, there were a couple of gaps which necessitated a horse omnibus leaving Windsor to meet the 11.45 am arrival at Slough from Paddington, and another to take passengers to the 1.25 pm departure from Slough. Down trains arrived at Windsor at 8.30 am (7.05 am (slow) and 7.45 am (fast) ex-Paddington, combined at Slough) and thereafter there were a further nine trains up until 9.40 pm. Several trains were 'express', running non-stop between Slough and Paddington. On Sundays six up trains left between 9 am and 9.10 pm (plus a horse omnibus to connect with the 12.30 pm ex Slough) and seven down trains arrived between 8.20 am and 9.40 pm. Altogether a most reasonable timetable for the opening of the line.

The *Windsor Express* carried an interesting report of the opening day's events and the first Royal traffic over the line:

Opening of the Great Western Branch Railway to Windsor – The opening of the Great Western extension line from Slough to Windsor took place on Monday, in conformity with our statement in Saturday's *Express*. On Sunday the public were allowed to traverse on foot the whole line from Windsor to Slough, and a large number of promenaders of both sexes availed themselves of the privilege who appeared much delighted at the construction of the bridge and the line altogether. On Monday several of the inhabitants of Windsor, and others interested in the undertaking, proceeded to Slough by the first train from Windsor, at five minutes past eight, in order to pay due honour to so memorable an event. The actual transit from Windsor to Slough and vice versa occupied about six minutes. The first train left the Paddington station at 7.05 am, reaching Slough, the junction point, 18 miles, soon after eight, and Windsor, 21 miles, at half-past, under the superintendence of Mr Seymour Clarke, the manager of the line, Mr Gooch the locomotive superintendent, and others. This was a 3rd class train; the other trains perform the distance in much less time, as will be seen by the timetable. The line proceeds out of Slough through a cutting of a quarter of a mile in length. It then runs for nearly the remainder of the way, or to within about a quarter of a mile of Windsor, on an embankment, where an elegant viaduct* carries it, by a continuous curve, into the centre of the town. This viaduct is between 5,000 and 6,000 feet long, and in the middle of it is the bridge designed by Mr Brunel, with a span over the Thames of 167 feet, so as to give, in conformity with the requirements of the Admiralty, headway enough to allow of vessels passing in sail.

The principle of the bridge, known as that of the arch and tie, the ends of the arch being connected by strong metal ties, has been severely tested and has been found to exhibit no perceptible deflexion; its foundations are on hard gravel below the bed of the river. In addition to the new line the company have constructed a diverging branch, by which Royal and express trains may run up to Windsor without being detained at the junction at Slough. Additional interest was created in Windsor on the opening of the line by the report that her Majesty would, on her return from Osborne, on Wednesday, come by it; and during Monday and Tuesday, some of the Royal carriages, luggage vans and horses arrived by the line. During Wednesday, also, active preparations were made at the station, a carpet being laid down on the platform &c, for the reception of the Queen and her Royal Consort and court. On Wednesday, however, about noon, Colonel Bowine arrived from Osborne and countermanded the order for the carriages meeting her Majesty at the station at five o'clock, as the Royal visit was postponed; and the cause of which may be seen by the following announcement from Wednesday's Court Circular – 'Her Majesty's departure for Windsor, which had been fixed for this day, has been postponed, upon the recommendation of the Board of Health, in consequence of the number of new fatal cases of cholera that have occurred in that town . . .'

In the event the Royal journey was postponed until the Saturday and then rail was used only to Slough, the last part of the journey being made by road.

The first Royal use of Windsor station came just over a month later and began a tradition at Windsor that was to last nearly 120 years and involve many hundreds of journeys, until it became almost commonplace. On 23rd November, 1849 the GWR laid on a Royal train to Basingstoke for the first part of Queen Victoria's train and ship journey to Osborne House in the Isle of Wight. Bought by Prince Albert in 1844 and rebuilt in 1846, Osborne

*The viaduct was built of wood but was replaced by a brick-built structure between 1861 and 1863.

became the holiday destination of the Queen two or three times each year. On this occasion the train pulled out with Daniel Gooch driving the engine and the 'top brass' of the GWR in attendance, Brunel, Saunders and Charles Russell the Chairman.

To complete the story of the events leading up to the branch opening, it is necessary to record that the South Western line finally opened to traffic on 1st December, 1849.

Copy.   Great Western Railway,

                              General Manager's Office,

51654   Paddington Station, London. W.

                                    October 30th. 1886.

Sir,

        I submitted your letter to the Directors at their meeting on Wednesday and they gave instructions for the Watchman upon the Line between Slough and Windsor to be removed, at the same time expressing their willingness to replace him if in the opinion of the College Authorities his services are required.

        Thanking you for the trouble you have taken in the matter

            I am,

                Your obedient Servant,

                    (Sgd) J. Grierson.

The Revd. J. J. Hornby D. D.

        The Lodge,

            Eton College.

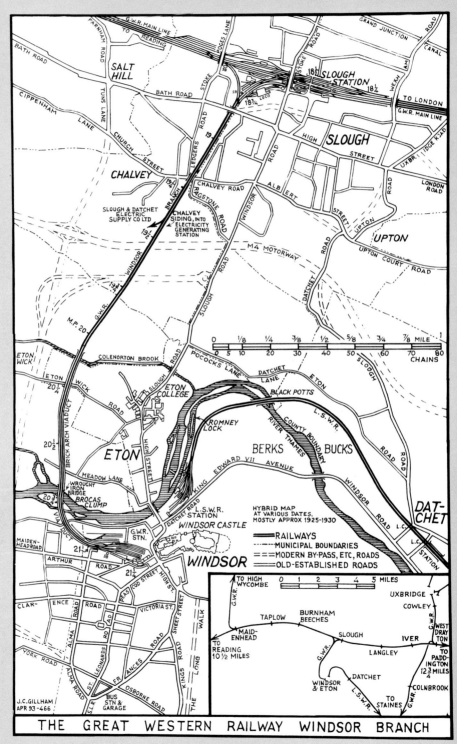

THE GREAT WESTERN RAILWAY WINDSOR BRANCH

Courtesy John Gillham

Chapter Four
A Royal Branch Line

THE GWR'S ROYAL VEHICLES

Prince Albert had travelled from Slough to Paddington by GWR train as early as 14th November, 1839, before his marriage to Queen Victoria on 10th February, 1840. In that year, the GWR anticipating the patronage of the Queen, had their first broad gauge saloon built by David Davies & Co., coach builders of Wigmore Street, London. In appearance it was not unlike an elegant road coach on an underframe with four wheels. Some 21 ft long it was divided into three compartments, the two end ones being 4 ft 6 in. long and 9 ft wide (these for Equerries and attendants), while the centre saloon was 12 ft long, 9 ft wide and 6 ft 6 in. high. It was painted brown and at each end was a large window 'affording a view of the whole line'. The saloon had been decorated with hanging sofas and the walls were panelled and fitted up with rich crimson and white silk, the work carried out by Mr Webb of Old Bond Street. However the Queen did not use it in this form and, in January 1842, following complaint of roughness of running from either Prince Albert or the Dowager Queen Adelaide, the vehicle was converted to run on eight wheels, one of the first vehicles in the country to be a multi-axle carriage.

Finally, some two years after it had been completed, the orders came for its use to convey the Queen and entourage from Slough to Paddington, in two days time, on 13th June, 1842. A Royal train was hurriedly put together comprising a second class brake, a posting carriage, the Royal Saloon, another posting carriage and three carriage trucks for the Royal horse-drawn vehicles. The train was drawn by *Phlegethon*, a brand new 7 ft single express locomotive built by Daniel Gooch and completed only one month before.

Arriving at Slough station just before noon, the Queen took advantage of the time taken to load the road vehicles to carry out an inspection of the Royal carriages and the arrangements generally, asking many questions of Charles Russell the GWR Chairman. Promptly at 12 o'clock the special left the station, the engine being driven by Daniel Gooch who was accompanied on the engine by I.K. Brunel. Exactly at 12.25 the train entered the Paddington terminus where the Queen 'was received with the most deafening demonstration of loyalty and affection!' So pleased was the Queen with her first experience of rail travel that she returned to Slough by train on 23rd July, incidentally giving the future King Edward VII, then 8 months old, his first railway journey.

The original saloon was stabled at Paddington and was used until 1850* when a new and enlarged saloon with wooden wheels (to minimise noise) was built, again by David Davies. Its dimensions were 28 ft 8 in. long, 9 ft wide (the Queen's compartment, 10 ft wide) and 8 ft high. Broad gauge and on eight wheels, it had a large state compartment and a smaller attendants' compartment complete with small disc and cross bar signal on the roof. This latter was used to signal the Queen's wishes regarding the speed of the train to the driver! At the other end of the vehicle was an ante room containing what was probably the first train lavatory in Great Britain. The replaced (1840) saloon was converted into an ordinary passenger carriage and subsequently condemned in 1879.

---

*GWR Historical Notes at PRO Kew (RAIL 1005/41) based on 'Board Book No. 1' say 1850 but MacDermot says the new vehicle was built in 1848 (see Revd Edition vol. 1 page 444). The Historical Notes give the dimensions shown above, MacDermot gives the length as 30 ft 8 in. and the height as 7 ft 7 in.

The Queen's broad gauge saloon built in 1850. It had wooden wheels (with metal tyres) to deaden the noise, note the roof-mounted signal.
British Rail

The 1850-built Queen's saloon. The reverse of the photograph is marked 'Queen's Broad Gauge Saloon as altered 1887: new bogies and vacuum brake, oil boxes etc.' Two years later in 1889, it was converted to standard gauge.
British Rail

Following a request from Her Majesty in October 1853 that the springs of the vehicle should be altered to reduce movement at 'high speed' (the Queen's objection to speed over 50 mph is, however, well known!), an additional plate was added to each spring to remedy the defect. Further alterations to the vehicle were carried out in July 1858 and in July 1870 the saloon was relined, and new wheels and axles incorporated at a total cost of £566.

The (1848 or) 1850 carriage was replaced in 1874 by a new standard gauge saloon, after which it was kept at Swindon for possible broad gauge journeys west of Exeter. The former vehicle was converted to standard gauge in 1889 (the Windsor branch had been 'narrowed' on 1st July, 1883) and in February 1890 the vehicle was moved to Slough and kept there for possible use until 1900 or 1901 when it was returned to Swindon. It had then been intended to alter the vehicle into a travelling saloon for the General Manager, but the early death of Sir J.L. Wilkinson caused that idea to be abandoned and the vehicle was broken up in 1903.

The new Royal Saloon was somewhat longer than its predecessor at 43 ft and again 9 ft wide (Macdermot '8 ft 10 in.') with a bulge in the middle, with three compartments, that for the Queen in the centre, and each with their own lavatories. The Queen became so fond of this vehicle that, when the GWR approached her with a proposal for a new complete Royal train to celebrate her Diamond Jubilee in 1897, she insisted that this carriage be retained. And so it was, lengthened to 54 ft and with the ante-chamber and entrance doorway widened to enable the Queen (who by now had to be supported by attendants) to enter more easily.

For a description of the new Royal Train, an article from *The Manchester Guardian* of 8th June, 1897 (slightly abbreviated) can hardly be bettered:

> The train consists of six vehicles, and is about 360 feet long over the buffers, or including the engine nearly 400 feet long. The carriages weigh 150 tons when empty, and the engine and tender 81 tons 10 cwt. in working order. The Queen's carriage is not entirely new, because Her Majesty commanded that the saloon which she had used since 1874 should not be altered, and therefore the body of the carriage has been lengthened from 43 ft to 54 ft without interfering with the Queen's own saloon. This difficult operation has been so skilfully performed that it is impossible to distinguish from the outside the new parts from the old. The Queen's saloon is 15 ft 9 in. long by 9 ft wide, and has a high-domed ceiling 8 ft 3 in. above the floor. It contains, besides the Queen's own chair, a sofa and three other easy chairs and a beautiful satinwood table. It is upholstered with fine corded silk of the lightest possible shade of grey, almost white. The curtains and blinds are of green silk, and the laces, trimmings, tassels, etc. are of green and white silk. The ceiling is handpainted. The floor is first covered with thick kamptulicon to deaden the sound, and then with a thick Axminster carpet having a white ground and a small, undefined pattern in green. All the fittings are silver-plated. In the centre of the ceiling there is a ground-glass globe containing six incandescent electric lights, which may be all or half on as required. The doors and panels are of satinwood. Adjoining this saloon is the toilet-room, 4 ft long, and immediately beyond is the compartment, 9 ft 6 in. long, for the Queen's dressers. The other end of the Royal saloon opens into the entrance vestibule (5 ft 10 in. long) which is provided with double doors six feet wide, so that Her Majesty may enter the coach without leaving the arm of her attendant. The lower inside panels

The 1897-built Royal Train, seen here headed by '3031' class 4–2–2 No. 3041 The Queen, consisted of full brake, 56 ft first corridor, 58 ft saloon, the extended 1874-built Queen's saloon (the fourth vehicle in this posed picture), 58 ft saloon and full brake. The two brakes each included a 20 ft compartment for guards and travelling staff.

British Rail

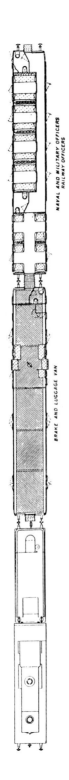

NAVAL AND MILITARY OFFICERS
RAILWAY OFFICERS

BRAKE AND LUGGAGE VAN

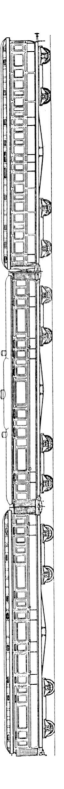

OBSERVATION COMPARTMENT

DIRECTORS AND OFFICERS

THEIR MAJESTIES THE KING AND QUEEN.

LADIES IN WAITING.

GENTLEMEN IN WAITING.

A plan of the 1897 Royal Train, as it was when used to take the King and Queen to Dartmouth on 7th March, 1902.

Engineering

of these doors are filled with fine carvings of the Royal arms. On the other side of the vestibule is the compartment (9 ft 6 in.) long reserved for the Queen's secretary. The Queen's carriage is the fourth vehicle from the engine. The third and fifth vehicles are Royal saloons, exactly similar to each other. They are 58 ft long, 8 ft 6 in. wide, and 8 ft 3 in. high to the top of the clerestory roof, with which all the carriages except the Queen's are fitted. These carriages are divided into two main saloons, each 15 ft 6 in. long, one upholstered with cream-coloured morocco leather, and the other with figured silk tabaret, and one small compartment, with four seats at the end of the coach. The second vehicle is a first-class corridor carriage, 56 ft in length. Accommodation is provided elsewhere for the Company's officers travelling with the train. The first and last vehicles are vans, divided into a large baggage compartment, 30 ft 10 in. in length, and a compartment of 20 ft 4 in. for the guards and staff. The seats are fitted with lockers, in which tools and gear are stored. Both the vans are provided with small gas cooking-stoves, and are lighted with compressed oil gas. The other four carriages are all fitted with the electric light, each vehicle being provided with a dynamo driven by means of a belt from one of the axles, but inasmuch as the Royal train has often to stand a long time at a station, accumulators which will store sufficient electricity to light the carriages for ten hours are also provided. The decorations of the three carriages harmonise with those of the Queen's saloon, for while the materials vary, the colours, white and green, do not.

In the Queen's coach, the mouldings are American walnut and the panels of sycamore. The panels above the seats and elsewhere are filled with coloured photographs of some of the many beautiful places which the Great Western Railway serves. Gold has been freely used on the mouldings. The roofs are of white Lincrusta-Walton, the pattern picked out with gold. There are mirrors in all the carriages, but not too many of them. The side lights in the clerestory of the roof are filled with glass panels having polished bevelled edges and a polished pattern of the rose, shamrock, and thistle on a dull ground. The effect is most brilliant. Electric communication with the guard is provided throughout, and the compartments are fitted with an indicator. The carriages likewise contain a steam heating apparatus for use when required. A feature of the train is a sliding door that is not an abomination. It is used in the corridors to close the compartments, and at the ends of the carriages to close the gangway passages. These doors do not run on rollers at the bottom, but hang from a grooved rail at the top on wheels which run in ball bearings, so that they can be moved with the greatest ease. Moreover, they slide into padded pillars, and are consequently draught-tight. The side doors throughout are 2 ft 6 in. wide, or 6 in. wider than is usual. Mahogany has been used for the framework and outer panels of the carriages.

The external appearance of the train is very handsome. The lower panels only are painted the usual Great Western brown colour, and the upper and long 'waist' panels are cream colour. The under-frames and buffer are lined with gold, and the royal arms are painted on by hand, while the varnishing is most brilliant. The door handles and handrails are heavily gilt, the former being ornamented with lions' heads. All the windows are surrounded with a heavy polished mahogany moulding, fixed from the inside, so that there are no screw heads to catch the dirt.

The bogies, which are all four-wheeled, and have a wheel base of 10 ft are of the pattern peculiar to the Great Western system. The smooth and noiseless running which is so noticeable a feature of Great Western travelling is almost if not entirely due to its use.

It is interesting that this and other reports written only a few weeks before the train came into service say that the Queen's saloon was lit by electricity. Hamilton Ellis and various other respected authorities state that the Queen

Great Western Railway.

[Circular No. 1746.]

GENERAL MANAGER'S OFFICE,

Paddington, 14th April, 1897.

HER MAJESTY'S DIAMOND JUBILEE.

The 22nd. June next having been set apart as a general holiday in commemoration of the 60th year of the reign of Her Majesty the Queen, the Directors have authorised a day's holiday being granted, without deduction of pay, to the whole of the Staff throughout the line who are regularly employed in the service of the Company at weekly or daily wages, and who can be spared from their duties on that day.

Those persons whose duties prevent them from taking a holiday on the 22nd. June will be granted a day's leave of absence on the same conditions on a later day; and arrangements will, as far as practicable, be made for the holiday to be granted on the day most convenient to the individual members of the Staff, or for adding it to their annual leave if they desire it.

J. L. WILKINSON,
General Manager.

Copies sent to
Brit Forth ¼/97.

A notice to staff advising them that the Directors had granted a day's holiday to celebrate the Queen's Diamond Jubilee.

GREAT WESTERN RAILWAY.

GENERAL MANAGER'S OFFICE,

PADDINGTON, *June 10th. 1860.*

(Circular. No. 1693.)

On the night of March 19th several Goods Trains were detained at Paddington, although ready to start at the proper times, waiting for the departure of a Special Royal Train that was considerably behind the time for which notice had been given for it to leave.

The delay to the Goods Trains caused thereby contributed to an accident, near Hanwell, to one of the Trains which had been stopped to pick up a tool chest that had fallen off the engine.

The Goods Trains had been detained under the impression that Special Trains for the conveyance of any members of the Royal Family were, even when not ready to start at the fixed time, to take precedence of the ordinary Passenger and Goods Trains.

In order to remove this misunderstanding, the Directors wish it to be understood that, except in the case of a Train for the personal accommodation of the Queen, the running of Special Trains is to be considered as secondary to the regularly appointed Passenger and Goods Trains.

In future, therefore, when a Special Train is not ready to start at or about the proper time, the ordinary Trains are to be run in their appointed order, until such time as the Special Train is ready to start; the object of this arrangement being merely to prevent, as far as possible, any such interruption of the traffic as might arise if the regular Trains were unduly kept waiting for Special Trains.

J. GRIERSON,
General Manager.

An early notice reminding staff that timetabled trains were not to be delayed for a late running 'Royal', except that conveying the Queen.

insisted the carriage retain its oil lamp for illumination so it would seem that the GWR had to make a modification at the last minute.

The train was first used to convey the Queen to Paddington on 21st June, 1897 to celebrate her Diamond Jubilee. Just prior to this on Saturday, 19th June, the train made a trial run from Paddington to Windsor and back hauled by the locomotive *The Queen.* On board were all the top brass from the Chairman down to the superintendent of the line. The select company inspected the new Royal waiting room at Windsor, which would also receive its Royal 'christening' the following Monday.

On the Monday, Queen Victoria left Windsor just before noon. *The Times* much enjoyed the preparations to receive her at Paddington:

> Some amusement was caused during the period of waiting by the efforts to erect and test the temporary gangway which it is customary to provide Her Majesty when she moves from a railway carriage to her own carriage. From a point of view of trustworthiness the tests were certainly adequate. To be plain, the heaviest Directors jumped on the gangway. But unfortunately, when the Royal Train really arrived the whole arrangement was found to be at the wrong level, and the preparations and testing had to be done over again. To prepare a more substantial gangway fitted with a handrail and accurately fitted would hardly, it may be suggested, pass the wit of the engineer.

The Queen returned to Windsor in her new train on 23rd June and on 1st July the GWR lent it to the South Western Railway to convey HM and guests from Windsor to Farnborough and back.

The Queen's own vehicle (built in 1873) was last used, it is thought, to convey King Edward VII's body to Windsor in 1910. The coach body was scrapped in 1912 but the underframe lived on, being used for a new inspection saloon which was fitted out with some of the furnishings from the former Royal Saloon.

The splendid Diamond Jubilee train was sent to Darlington for the Railway Centenary Exhibition in 1925 but soon thereafter was withdrawn. GWR records note that the coaches were converted for everyday passenger use and put into ordinary traffic on 2nd March, 1927. Thereafter the GWR used other companies' Royal trains when necessary.

One of the former Royal saloons is pictured in *The Railway Gazette* of 7th June, 1935 being taken by road to Aberporth in Cardiganshire to begin a new career as a seaside bungalow. Two went there and one, No. 9002, came back in 1982 to be restored to form part of the Royalty and Empire exhibition, opened at Windsor in 1983. Here it remains, some 96 years after it was built!

ROYAL JOURNEYS

Things did not always go as they were supposed to – even for the Queen. On 1st December, 1852 Charles Saunders the GWR's Secretary had to write a rather grovelling letter to the Palace officials after something went wrong on a journey from Windsor to Gosport (for Osborne).

> I must ask you to have the goodness to explain that . . .there was not on the part of this Company a moment's delay in the arrival of Her Majesty's Vans and Carriages at their destination – for although the great weight of them loaded with luggage and the difficulty of getting the pole out of one of them, occasioned some

delay in leaving the Windsor station, they reached Basingstoke in good time to be taken off our tracks and placed on those of the SW Co. before the train of that Company arrived at Basingstoke which was to convey them to Gosport.

(The South Western train from Basingstoke) being on that occasion behind its time by a few minutes may have delayed the due arrival of the Carriages at their destination. I had given very strict orders to employ the additional men . . . and we sent to Windsor and to Basingstoke for Her Majesty's Service extra . . . porters and policemen. I attended personally to see that everything was done to move the carriages at Basingstoke from the broad gauge to the narrow gauge tracks, which was principally effected by our *own* men and I did not leave the station until I had seen them transferred . . .

I beg to repeat that nothing should be wanting which can be foreseen to carry out the orders we may receive for any future removal with the utmost expedition and punctuality.

On 10th March, 1863 Edward, Prince of Wales married Princess Alexandra of Denmark and brightened, for a while, the gloom which had surrounded the Queen since the death of her beloved Albert in December 1861. Unfortunately what should have been a joyous occasion was marred for the GWR by a strong letter of reproof from the Lord Chamberlain's office afterwards. Two complaints were made: of delay in reaching Windsor from London in the morning and of congestion and disruption in the return arrangements.

The GWR, as usual, went into these complaints in very great detail and was able to show that the circumstances complained off were quite outside their control. In the morning thick fog had come on suddenly (possibly the Lord Chamberlain hadn't noticed!) and there had been delay in forming the trains at Paddington, and in running, stations having to be approached more slowly than usual. Such things were unfortunate, but, the Great Western politely informed the Lord Chamberlain,

Security for the public ought on this, as on all other occasions to be the predominant care and duty of all who are responsible for the arrangement of the Railway and that no consideration of mere convenience can be allowed to interfere with that of safety.

The complaint about the evening return arrangements was somewhat more complicated to deal with and here it is better for the GWR's words to speak for themselves:

With respect however to the *return* journies of the irregularity of which your letter more specially complains, the Directors desire me, to remind you that all the previous arrangements with your Department had been founded upon the principle of one return train only to London preceding the departure of the Prince & Princess of Wales, which had been fixed for 3.30 pm and the two other trains following at intervals of half an hour each, *after* the departure of the Royal Train for Basingstoke and Southampton.

These arrangements were most unfortunately but unavoidably neutralised by commands received from the Castle, almost at the last moment, to postpone the departure of the Prince & Princess of Wales from 3.30 until 4.05; and they duly started finally at 4.10 [Daniel Gooch drove]. That train was formed and in waiting at the very platform from which the Lord Chamberlain's two later special trains had been appointed to start.

It cannot of course be supposed that the commands so received, could have been disregarded.

The consequence of that change led to the accommodation of the Public within the Station during the interval, upon the one usual Departure platform; instead of being divided so as to admit of the invited guests leaving Windsor from the other platform, and although a train was started from the station after the 3.15 train it was impossible, in the excitement of expectation to see the Royal Party, to induce many passengers whether guests or the public waiting on the platform to take their departure on that train. The accommodation of passengers at that time within the station rendered it impossible to keep the Special Trains which had been arranged for the Lord Chamberlain's service separate from the other trains which had been delayed by the like cause, nor could the invited guests at that time be separated onto the other platform.

Notwithstanding all these difficulties ascribed to the change of time by orders from the Castle, and not by neglect of Regulations or disobedience of orders at the Railway, a train did leave for London within twenty minutes of the departure of the Prince & Princess of Wales followed by other trains at very short intervals.

The Directors think it their duty to add that the services of from 15 to 20 Metropolitan Policemen had been requested for the Railway Station at Windsor upon that occasion but unfortunately although that number had been arranged for, not more than 6 or 7 did attend for the purpose.

The Metropolitan Superintendent has since informed the officers of this Company that his men were required elsewhere on that day where the crowd appeared to him to be the greatest. This circumstance rendered it necessary to divide the Railway Police Force intended to be employed exclusively within the Windsor Station and for which it would have been ample.

Trusting that the explanation thus given will remove the first impressions of his Lordship, as communicated in your letter.

I have the honour to be, Sir,

Your faithful servant

(signed) Charles Saunders

Secretary

A second explanatory letter was necessary, despite receiving 'more favourable sentiments' from the Lord Chamberlain, because Supt Walker of the Metropolitan Police was putting the blame on the GWR for the lack of control at Windsor. The GWR's own superintendent of Police, however, submitted a report which indicated that the Metropolitan Police had promised help and as the GWR pointed out, very carefully, '... without attributing to him (Walker) any intentional mis-representation that in the various important matters engaging his attention at the time he may have forgotten or misunderstood all that occurred upon one branch of his business'(!)

The Prince of Wales's name was 'before the Board' for quite a different reason some 12 years later. The Prince, Princess and children came down from London to visit the Queen on 11th May, 1875, prior to the Queen's spring visit to Balmoral, due to take place in four days time. The Royal party came down in the Queen's broad gauge saloon, conveyed in an ordinary train, it is assumed, as the train does not appear in the list of Royal trains for 1875. At about 3.30 pm as the train passed over the viaduct near Eton Wick, a boy in the meadow below fired his catapult at the train and a stone crashed into one of the large plate glass windows in the Royal saloon. Although these windows were ¼ in. thick a pea-sized hole was made in the window and some glass splintered through inside, fortunately without injuring the occupants.

The attempt on Queen Victoria's life by Roderick Mclean, 2nd March, 1882, as portrayed in the *Daily Graphic*. In the lower view (a) and (d) are Mclean, (c) is Supt Hayes who arrested him and (b) is the route taken by the bullet which struck a tarpaulin on a goods truck opposite, and dropped to the ground.

(Both) Colin Maggs Collection

The GWR's divisional superintendent, Alfred Higgins, and an Inspector of the Company's police, Mr Noble, were travelling on the train but were unaware of the incident until arrival at Windsor at 3.35 pm, when the Prince stepped out of the train holding the piece of broken glass and said 'Some of the boys had thrown a ball'. Suspicion fell on the boys of Eton College and Mr Noble and Superintendent Dunham of the Bucks Constabulary visited Dr Hornby, the Head Master, in an endeavour to apprehend the perpetrator.

Next day Queen Victoria sent a messenger to the station to enquire if the culprit had been caught. However, two Eton college boys had 'admitted throwing at the train, but not at the precise spot named. The inquiry is still proceeding, and the school captains have taken up the matter in earnest' (one can imagine).

The local paper reported that, following several other 'outrages' at this time, the GWR had stationed a watchman at the end of the viaduct to prevent any recurrence of these attacks.

An event of a somewhat more serious nature occurred on 2nd March, 1882, when an unemployed man named Roderick Mclean, aged 27, fired a pistol at the Queen as she left Windsor station in a coach en route to the Castle. The Queen had travelled from London in the Royal Train leaving Paddington at 4.50 pm and arriving at Windsor at 5.25 pm. The shot missed, the assailant in fact claimed that he had deliberately fired at the wheels, and Mclean was set upon by the crowd and had to be rescued by the police. Mclean said that he had fired the shot to draw attention to his straitened circumstances. From the details of the prisoner's character revealed by his father, it would appear that Mclean suffered from a split personality and was subject to all sorts of fantasies and delusions. In 1874 he had been charged with inciting a schoolboy to wreck a train on the London, Chatham & Dover Railway but the charge was dismissed, on the grounds that inciting a person to do what he was unable to perform was no offence. Among the many column inches of the report in the Windsor & Eton Express is a statement from Frank Potter, clerk at Windsor station who was returning to the station from his tea and witnessed the attack. Frank Potter later became General Manager of the GWR.

The paper also revealed that this was the sixth attempt on the Queen's life, earlier attacks having been made in 1840, 1842 (two), 1850 and 1872. At his subsequent trial Mclean was acquitted on the grounds of insanity but ordered to be detained at Her Majesty's pleasure.

Details of Royal journeys made between Windsor and London by Queen Victoria during the period 1870–1888 are preserved at the Public Record Office. It is interesting to see how frequently she used the GWR for these short journeys, the average number of such trips being between 8 and 9 per annum during this 19 year period. In addition she made several longer journeys each year (including the two to Balmoral), details of which are shown in Appendix Three. Details of a typical local journey, together with the special measures taken for the Queen's security, are illustrated.

Marie Adeane, Maid of Honour to Queen Victoria wrote descriptively of the 'manifold perils and luxuries of a Royal journey' (actually the return from Balmoral on 15th November, 1888):

RAILWAY.

Amended Notice

NOTICE OF ROYAL TRAIN,

WITH HER MAJESTY AND SUITE.

FROM WINDSOR TO PADDINGTON AND BACK.

On *Saturday* the *12th* of *July* 1884

TIME TABLE. UP JOURNEY.		NOTES.
WINDSOR	dep. at *4* 40 ʄm.	The 4.0 ʄm or 4 Paddington to be kept on the P.R.I for
SLOUGH	pass at 4.47 ʄm.	the Royal train to pass left,
PORTOBELLO JUNC.	pass at 5.11 ʄm.	and the 7.30 ʄm or oxford
PADDINGTON	arr. at 5.15 ʄm.	must be kept on back at that side

TIME TABLE. DOWN JOURNEY.		NOTES.
PADDINGTON	dep. at 6.40 ʄm.	The 6.52 ʄm or West Drayton
PORTOBELLO JUNC.	pass at 6.44 ʄm.	to be kept back
SLOUGH	pass at 7.8 ʄm.	
WINDSOR	arr. at 7.15 ʄm.	

SPECIAL INSTRUCTIONS.

1. Station Masters and others in charge of Stations must be on duty to see the Royal Train pass.

2. Goods, Mineral or Cattle Trains must not be allowed to leave any Station or Junction to proceed over the Line on **which the Royal Train has to run,** unless they can arrive at the next Shunting Station at least 15 minutes before the Royal Train is due.

3. At all **Level Crossings** at which Policemen or Gatemen are stationed, the men in charge must be on duty; and at all Level or Occupation Crossings at which no men are regularly stationed Platelayers must be placed to see that there is no obstruction. The Gangers will be responsible for seeing that this is done. Nothing must be allowed to cross the Line at a Level Crossing within 15 minutes, and at an Occupation Crossing within 30 minutes of the time the Royal Train is due to pass.

4. Station Masters must arrange for all **FACING POINTS** to be examined 15 minutes before the Royal Train is due to pass.

5. **The Flagmen must have Special Instructions to be at their posts if there is the slightest appearance of a Fog coming on.**

6. **Where the Block Telegraph System is in operation,** the Royal Train is to be signalled in the same way as an Ordinary Passenger Train, except that immediately after the "Train on Line" Bell Signal has been given the letters "**H.M.**" are to be sent on the Single Needle Instrument, and which must be returned by the Signalman receiving them to show that they are understood, see Block Telegraph Instructions.

7. **Between Slough and Windsor, where the Block Telegraph System is not in operation,** the persons in charge, immediately on the departure or passing of the Royal Train, must inform the Telegraph Clerk of the time at which it left or passed, who must instantly signal to the next station in advance, thus, "Royal has passed at......" immediately after the arrival or passing of the train, and must be sent back to the Station in the rear that the Royal Train has passed the next, thus, "Royal has passed," and until the Royal Train has been telegraphed as having arrived at or passed the Station in advance, no Train or Engine may be allowed to follow.

8. Two **Guards** will be sent from Paddington to work the Royal Train; one will ride in the Brake Van in front of the Train, and the other in the Van at the rear of the Train, and they must note the number of passengers travelling by the Royal Train Up and Down, and give the information on their Reports, a copy of which must be sent to the Divisional Superintendent, as well as myself, immediately after the journey is completed.

9. **The Empty Train** will leave Paddington for Windsor at 3.5 ʄm, and when the return journey to Windsor is completed, will return immediately to Paddington.

NOTE.—Station Masters and Heads of Departments must read this Notice carefully, and immediately instruct the Staff to act up to the Instructions. No excuse of want of knowledge of these instructions can be admitted for any failure or neglect of duty.

PADDINGTON, *July 12* 1st *84*

G. N. TYRRELL, *Superintendent of the Line.*

Per E. Woodley

Mr. *Higgins* ✗

Mr. *Flitt* ✗

✗ Mr. *Palmer* ✓

Mr. *Wooding* ✓

✗ Mr. *Spinale* ✓

✗ Mr. *Cook* ✓

✗ Mr. *Shapsnelle* ✓

✗ Mr. *Linke* ✓

Mr. *Saunders* ✗

✓ Mr. *Saunders*

✓ Mr. *Grierson*

✗ Mr. *Inspector Melbourne P.K* ✓

✓ Mr. *Signalman West Drayton* ✓

✗ Mr. *Master Acton*

✗ Mr. *Engine Ealing* ✓

✗ Mr. *Polisse Castle Hill* ✓

✗ Mr. *Inspector Hanwell* ✓

✗ Mr. *Forman Southall* ✓

✗ Mr. *Adams Hayes* ✓

✗ Mr. *Graig West Drayton* ✓

✗ Mr. *Richards Langley* ✓

✓ Mr. *Reave Slough*

✓ Mr. *Turen* "

✗ Mr. *Radle* "

My dear, I can't tell you how much food we were provided with. There were three large hampers stuffed with every kind of cold meat stuffed rolls, grouse and enough cake and biscuits to set up a baker's shop, then we had bottles of hot tea, cream, claret, sherry, seltzer water and finally champagne! But this was not evidently deemed sufficient to support life, so we had a hearty tea at Aberdeen, where royal footmen rushed about wildly with tea-kettles gazed at by a large crowd, and a huge dinner at Perth, with six courses, the table was beautifully decorated with orchids, which were pressed into our hands at parting, and at 11.30 pm on our arrival at Carlisle, we partook of tea and juicy muffins . . . I send you a paper of the train. Our names were painted on tin and hung on the doors of the carriages to prevent mistakes.

For over a century the Windsor–Slough branch was the starting or finishing point for Royal trains and those for which details exist are listed in Appendix Three. This has been compiled from four different sources and is as comprehensive as circumstances allow, but cannot be guaranteed to be complete. The apparent gaps between 1918 and 1924 and 1927 and 1936 may have seen some Royal journeys on the branch, but, if so, details do not exist at either the Royal Archives, PRO, Kew or in BR's own records.

The precautions taken for Royal journeys were all-embracing and for that reason Royal Train notices extended to many pages. Additionally various subordinate notices were published by District Officers setting out even more detail. The 8th June, 1889 edition of *The Railway News* gave some interesting information of the precautions surrounding Queen Victoria's journeys; the journey in question took place on 6th June.

THE QUEEN'S JOURNEY NORTH – THE ROYAL TRAIN
    Her Majesty and suite left Windsor on Thursday night at 8.20 and reached Ballater at 2.30 pm on Friday, driving thence to Balmoral. It may not be generally known that the precautions taken in this peaceful country to secure her comfort and safety, though not so strict as those in force when the Czar moves about, are, nevertheless, numerous, and of a very complete kind. Thus a pilot engine clears the way for, and is always fifteen to twenty minutes in front of, the Royal train, so that the line may be in order.

    No trains are allowed to run on the main line in the direction in which the Royal train is going for half-an-hour before it passes, and none but passenger trains are permitted to come in the opposite direction after the pilot has passed, and they must reduce their speed to about 10 miles an hour when passing the Royal train. Those in charge of trains shunted into sidings, &c., must on no account allow their engines to whistle or blow off steam. Platelayers patrol the whole extent of the line to be traversed to see that nothing obstructs the rails and that road crossings are secure. There are two vans on the train, and the guard in the one in front must keep constantly looking to the rear of the train, and be on the alert for signals from other officials in the train to be communicated, if need be, to the driver. Level crossings not guarded by a gatekeeper are locked for an hour before the Royal train passes, and all facing points to be passed over are securely padlocked or bolted. Special coal is always used, and the most reliable drivers are selected for the pilot and train engines, and to have driven the Queen is something for the men to remember with pride.

    Generally, the locomotive superintendent travels on the Royal engine, and an assistant on the pilot, over their respective lines, and a few of the directors and other officials travel in a couple of carriages, set apart for them in the Royal train.

But this is not all. The train is also accompanied by a complete squad of artisans, to be called into action in the event of a mishap. Their duty, while the train is running, is to keep a look-out in all directions, so as to discover at the earliest stage anything that seems to be going wrong with the carriages.

It will be seen that no precaution is wanting when we mention that a staff of competent telegraph men are also in the train, equipped with all the necessary appliances to enable a communication being established at any point should necessity arise.

When at stations, the railway servants perform the necessary duties noiselessly, and after the vehicles are examined and greased, the guard in charge must assure himself that every member of the suite is seated before giving the signal to restart.

In November 1883, on the eve of the Queen's return journey from Ballater to Windsor, the Government was warned that an attempt to wreck the Royal train would be made by Fenians, who had been perpetuating outrages in support of their cause for some three years. The Queen decided she would still travel so the Home Secretary passed on the threat to the General Manager of the LNWR, Sir George Findlay. In his book *British Railways and the Great War* Edwin Pratt describes the action taken:

In effect, Sir George called out some thousands of platelayers and other of the company's employees who not only watched and guarded every bridge and viaduct *en route* until the Royal train had passed, but, for some time before the train was due, formed a continuous line of sentries, watchers, and permanent-way examiners, remaining within sight of each other, and looking closely at every yard of track, for the entire distance (in co-operation with the Scottish companies) of nearly 600 miles between Windsor and Ballater. In the result, the Queen's journey was in no way interrupted, while Sir George Findlay gave a striking proof of what his company could accomplish in the taking of an emergency and precautionary measure.

Many interesting facts about Royal journeys in Queen Victoria's time can be found in *Railway Reminiscences* by G.P. Neele, who, as superintendent of the line for the LNWR escorted the Queen as Officer-in-Charge of the LNWR Royal train on no less than 112 occasions, including most of the long distance journeys from and to Windsor between 1863 and 1895. In his book George Neele describes the routine at Windsor, both outward and return. The details, of course, refer to Windsor Station before rebuilding in 1897:

OUTWARD JOURNEY

Arriving at Windsor, our first care would be to ascertain that the train had been brought to the station platform in good time, that the vehicles corresponded in position to those indicated on the approved diagram, and that the temporary labels attached to each of the coaches, indicating the passengers for whom the respective vehicles were intended, were properly affixed (an important point in guiding the sergeant-footmen, and other servants in dealing with the innumerable articles of impedimenta that accompanied the travellers), and a copy of the carriage diagram and the time table for the journey placed in all the compartments, not forgetting special copies for the Queen's use in both her night and day saloons.

It was by no means uncommon, an hour or two before the time for starting, to find some of the gentlemen of the Court on the platform with a special enquiry or request as to accommodation. General Grey and Lord Charles Fitzroy were always early visitors, and so was Sir Henry Ponsonby, anxious that special wishes, as to lighting, or warming, or cooling the Royal carriage, should be fully met.

As time drew near, the officers of the Great Western Company would come upon the scene – Mr Armstrong of Swindon, and his junior, Mr George Armstrong, of Wolverhampton, proud of their massive locomotives, though they might be of the narrow gauge. Here, also, is Mr Tyrrell, who will accompany us through to the limit of the Great Western Line, and Mr Alfred Higgins, the divisional Superintendent of the London district, is also in attendance; the General Manager of the line is but seldom seem on these occasions at Windsor, it being a recognized part of the duty of their Superintendent of the Line to receive Her Majesty.

About half-an-hour prior to the time of departure, there commence to arrive, one after another, carriages from the Castle, bringing contingents of the household – the pages, the upper servants, the dressers, the ladies' maids, the sergeant-footmen, the Queen's dressers; each settling down into the allotted place, or seeing that the travelling articles of their respective masters are put into the marked vehicles on the train. Shortly after, the Ladies of the Household, and the Gentlemen of the Court, the Equerries, and the Lords-in-Waiting, put in their appearance. A few moments later the approach of the junior members of the Royal family will be announced, and then the clatter of horse hoofs, and the rapid entrance of the well-known equipage, tells us the Queen has arrived.

From the carriage, in hot haste, both John Brown and Francis Clark descend, and are at the door of the vehicle without a moment's delay, assisting Her Majesty to alight.

Her saloon is marshalled, as nearly as possible, opposite to the Royal waiting room, so as to entail the least distance for walking; the vehicles for the ladies-in-waiting generally in front of, and those for the gentlemen of the suite, behind the Royal saloons; but the platform is somewhat curtailed, and it is necessary, when the Queen is seated, for the train to be drawn forward, and for the rear portion to be attached outside the station, a special stoppage being made for the purpose. The rear portion includes the Queen's 'fourgon' as well as the carriages allotted to the Directors and officers; it was my lot, generally, to travel with Mr Tyrrell or Mr Burlinson in this part of the train; while our carriage Superintendent, Mr Bore, was accustomed to ride in the front portion, usually accompanying the chief officer of the household police, Mr Superintendent Fraser, who was for many years an unfailing traveller with these Royal trains.

The attaching of the two portions outside the station naturally caused some little delay. There was the screw coupling to be first seen to, then the side chains, the cord communication, the two electric couplings, the brake coupling, and the test to be given to prove all was complete with the connections. Two minutes generally sufficed, and the train then made its actual start. It was curious to watch the regularity with which the sentinel in charge of the flagstaff on the Castle-Keep hauled down the Royal Standard as soon as the train crossed the Thames. Royalty had left the sacred boundary of the Castle, and Balmoral, instead of Windsor, would be entitled to the honour of displaying the standard of the Sovereign of the Kingdom.

RETURN JOURNEY

The limited platform space at Windsor Station necessitated a special mode of dealing with the Royal train. The train engine and three or four of the leading vehicles were detached and taken forward to a side line adjoining the platform appointed for our coming, which was the platform in general use for up trains, the one on which Her Majesty's waiting room existed. Another engine stood in readiness to draw the rest of the train forward, the vehicles being so 'cut' as to bring the Queen's saloon as nearly as possible opposite to her waiting room. The Ladies-in-waiting were generally in the vehicle next to this second engine, and were thus in a very convenient position for alighting before the Queen and taking up their place near the exit, so as to make their courtly courtesies to Her Majesty as she passed to her carriage.

HER MAJESTY'S

JUBILEE FESTIVITIES

AT WINDSOR.

On Wednesday and Thursday, June 22nd and 23rd,

A

LATE SPECIAL TRAIN

WILL LEAVE

WINDSOR

AT 12.0 MIDNIGHT, FOR

SLOUGH   GREAT MARLOW

MAIDENHEAD   HIGH WYCOMBE

AND ALL INTERMEDIATE STATIONS,

For the convenience of Visitors witnessing the Jubilee Festivities at Windsor, and wishing to remain to see the Illuminations, &c.

First, Second, and Third Class Ordinary Tickets will be available by this Train.

GRIERSON,

General Manager.

Poster advertising a late special train from Windsor run during Queen Victoria's Golden Jubilee celebrations (1887).
Royal Borough Collection

GREAT WESTERN RAILWAY.

(For the use of the Company's Servants only.)

NOTICE OF A SPECIAL TRAIN

WITH H.R.H. THE PRINCE OF WALES' HORSES AND CARRIAGES,

WINDSOR & ETON TO BALLATER,

WEDNESDAY, AUGUST 19th, 1908.

	Arr. p.m.	Dep. p.m.
WINDSOR & ETON		M 2 30 L / 2 30
Slough, West Curve		
Maidenhead		2 49
Twyford		2 59
Reading		3 10
Didcot		3 34
Oxford	3 55	4 5
Banbury		4 43
Southam Road		5 8
Leamington		5 18
Lapworth		5 34
Birmingham (Down Middle)		5 53
Wolverhampton	6 13	6 17
Wellington		6 47
Nantwich		7 30
Crewe	7 40	—
BALLATER	arr. 8 0 a.m.	{ Thursday morning.

GENERAL INSTRUCTIONS.

For General Instructions to be observed in connection with the running of Special Train shewn in this Notice, see "Revised General Appendix to Book of Rules and Regulations," 1st January, 1905

Acknowledge Receipt to Head of Department on the enclosed form immediately on Receipt of the Notice.

J. MORRIS,

Superintendent

10TH August, 1908.

This notice reminds us that when the Royal family made journeys to Balmoral and Osborne, separate trains were required to move the horses, carriages and servants.
David Castle Collection

On one occasion the Great Western officer in charge of the Windsor district 'cut' the train in the wrong place, with the result that the saloon conveying the ladies-in-waiting was taken to a platform remote from the Queen's waiting room, and they were unable to find their way back in time to take up their expected places. There was considerable wonder expressed at their absence, and such an impression was made that even twelve months afterwards I was reminded by the ladies of the *contretemps*.

The Mayor of Windsor, wearing his gold badge of office, was generally on the platform, and took his place near to the exit on the opposite to the ladies, grouping himself with the railway officers, who made their final obeisance as Her Majesty passed out. Sometimes, but infrequently, 'a pleasant journey' was mentioned; but it was generally reserved for the equerries to express their remarks to this effect.

Some appreciation of the precautions that used to be taken for the passage of a Royal train may be gleaned from abbreviated details from a notice dealing with a Royal Train from Windsor to Shirehampton on Tuesday 7th September, 1915, conveying the King and Queen:

STANDARD INSTRUCTIONS
1. The Royal Train (RT) must be accompanied by Artificers . . . with all needful material and appliances . . .
2. Special head code (four lamps)
3. Telegraph men accompany the RT
4. Not less than two clear block sections between RT and next train on the same line, both in advance and in rear
5. Fog signalmen must be in position 30 minutes before RT due (but only carry out their duties in fog or falling snow)
6. All signal boxes normally switched out must be open and signals lighted
7. No train to foul the line on which the RT will run for at least 15 minutes before train due. No train movements in same direction on adjacent line. Shunting to be suspended 20 minutes before RT due.
8. Only passenger trains travelling in the opposite direction are allowed to pass the RT
9. All engineering work to be suspended 30 minutes beforehand
10. All station masters to be on duty
11. All facing points to be clipped and a man to be present 30 minutes before
12. All level crossings to be guarded and no road movements over them for 15/30 minutes beforehand (depended on type of crossing)
13. Special precautions to prevent a rail overbridge being used when RT underneath
14. All tunnels to be inspected and a competent man to be placed at each end

SPECIAL LOCAL INSTRUCTIONS (BRISTOL DIVISION)
1. Three pages of special signalling instructions to cover 'Is Line Clear', 'Train out of Section' bell signals and short section working
2. Arrangements re special opening of boxes and setting of points at junctions
3. A spare engine to be available at Swindon, two engines at Shirehampton and one at Bristol in the evening
4. Special working arrangements Shirehampton–Horse Shoe Point
5. Lists 40 locations where men required at facing points
6. Lists 101 level crossings to be protected
7. Describes precautions at four tunnels (twenty men involved in protection arrangements)
8. Breakdown van trains to be available at Swindon and Bristol
9. Nine inspectors located at nine key locations

From all this it will be gathered that Royal trains were certainly not a financially attractive proposition to a Railway company as the fares received did not cover all this! However, in the days when railways were the main form of land transport, the prestige of carrying the Royal family was probably worth a year's advertising on station posters or in the press.

Although BR singled the line from Slough to Windsor in 1963, this did not immediately affect the running of Royal trains because the Windsor layout of four platforms was left untouched, as was the signal box. However in 1968 it was decided to reduce the layout to one platform, and close the signal box and this meant that Royal trains would no longer be run unless branch trains were cancelled, an arrangement the Queen did not favour. However, the distance by road from Windsor to Slough being very small, the Queen agreed that Royal trains could run to and from Slough in future. Accordingly the last Royal train to use the Windsor Branch ran on 10th May, 1968 leaving Matlock at 19.00 hrs and arriving Windsor, platform 4, at 23.00 hrs. The train, conveying HM The Queen, was hauled by type '2' locomotives Nos. D5223 and D5226 in multiple. The empty coaches were booked back to Wolverton via Acton at 23.27 hrs and the departure of the empty train brought to an end nearly 120 years of special Royal trains on the Windsor branch. That a Royal train may run again over the line is not impossible, but it would only be in connection with a major event and the line would have to be closed to all other traffic for the duration.

GREAT WESTERN RAILWAY.

ROYAL TRAIN,

BUSHBURY JUNCTION TO WINDSOR,

NOVEMBER 29th, 1873.

As Fogs are very prevalent at this season of the year, and as they come on very suddenly, the Fogmen must be out along the Line between Bushbury and Windsor an hour before the Royal Train is due, whether there is any Fog at the time or not.

Station Masters will see to this, and will themselves be at their Stations an hour before the Train is due, and see that the Line is kept clear for the Royal Train.

J. GRIERSON,

Paddington, *November 29th, 1873.*   General Manager.

Precautions in the event of fog, 1873.   *Public Record Office, Kew*

Windsor station as it was when built in 1850; Windsor Castle in the background.
British Rail

Chapter Five

Windsor Station in the 1870s

The GWR in the mid-19th century was a very different railway from that which those still alive who have memories of it recall with nostalgia. Few people alive today (1993) will have memories any earlier than that of the Grouping (1923) when the GWR, recognised as a first class concern, was able to claim in a cartoon, proudly, 'Hooray, never even blew me cap off', a reference to the fact that alone of the larger companies, it had retained its name and territory, after the Grouping.

Unfortunately there are very few contemporary records available to give a flavour of the life of a Great Western railwayman in the 19th century. George Gibbs left his diary of events at the very beginning of the company (1835–1840) and Sir Daniel Gooch left a much more comprehensive diary of his long service with the company (1837–1889), but both these men were Directors employed to make the business and policy decisions. Neither got involved in the day to day 'slog' that kept the trains running, involving long hours and very low pay for the men so employed (although Sir Daniel in his early days as locomotive superintendent did get his hands dirty keeping his primitive machines on the road, and often driving them). Between the Directors' lives and the workforce's toil there was an enormous gap.

However we do have one lively account of what it was like at ground level on the Great Western in those days. Hubert Simmons joined the GWR as a clerk at Wallingford Road in 1861 (aged 21) and spent 15 years with the company, earning his final promotion as station master at Windsor in 1867 and resigning from that post some nine years later. His story is written with a certain amount of bitterness and, because it was long after some of the events described (his memoirs were first published in 1879/80*), some is distorted and the chronology is suspect. When Volume One of his book was reprinted in 1974,† this is what Professor Jack Simmons had to say about its author:

> How seriously can we taken what he has to say? On matters of fact he is unreliable. He was writing a good time after the events he describes, and it seems plain from memory . . .
> It is more difficult still to accept his estimate of persons. His portraits of the senior officers of the Great Western Company, of Gooch, and even more of Grierson and Spagnoletti are caricatures . . . The value of what he has to say lies in his point of view. The members of the Board of a railway company *were* the uncontrolled arbiters of the destiny of the men they employed . . . He speaks for thousands of his fellow railway servants when he attacks individual Directors and senior officers for stupidity, prejudice and arrogance. They may not have been, in fact, stupid or prejudiced or arrogant; but that we can feel tolerably sure, was how they often looked.
> Simmons gives us the sense of what the ordinary railwayman of his standing felt. For the railway service was a hierarchy . . . Every Victorian railwayman knew his place in that chain. If, like Simmons, he was somewhere near the middle of it, he was apt to be particularly conscious of his dignity. Simmons gives us no sense that he was overbearing towards those under him. But he was acutely touchy with his superiors, always jealous of his personal position and affronted by the least

---

Note: because Hubert Simmons' work has been out of print for over 100 years I have quoted at length from this unique record, rather than précis his humorous writing in my own words. I hope the reader will agree with this approach.

Ernest Struggles, or the Life of a Station Master
†*Memoirs of a Station Master* (Adams & Dart, out of print)

slight, real or supposed that was put upon it . . . He was a man of some education
. . . in that respect at least the equal of Daniel Gooch . . . All this can be detected in
Simmons' narrative, and it must be given its due weight in assessing the value of
what he has to say.

We cannot take the dialogue in his book literally . . . but much of it carries the
stamp of truth and is both consistent and credible.

Under the shadow of the law of libel, he unfortunately felt compelled to disguise
the names of people and places under pseudonyms . . . by the use he makes of this
expedient Simmons does himself an injustice. He appears, inevitably, to be writing
a work of fiction.

The book is not that, however. Its value lies in its fundamental truth; a truth not
of fact but of feeling.

His story, as published, is split into two. Volume One deals with his life at
Wallingford Road and Didcot as a clerk, and then, from 1863 onwards, as a
station master at variously, Aynho, Thame, Twyford and Bilston (March
1866). Then in November 1867 he was appointed to what was regarded as a
most important station, Windsor, at the princely sum of £110 per annum (at
this time, according to Simmons, his superintendent would be earning £500
p.a. while the General Manager received £4,000!). His time at Windsor fills
the whole of Volume Two, which, unfortunately, has never been reprinted
since its original publication in 1880 and few copies exist. Fortunately there
is one in the Clinker Collection at Brunel University so it is possible to
illustrate, by some extracts, a flavour of railway life at Windsor at this
period. This is all the more worthwhile because a later Windsor station
master also left a diary (see Chapter Seven) and the two diaries give an
impression as to how things had changed in the intervening 25 or so years.

Struggles' (to give Simmons' pseudonym from his memoirs) journey from
Bilston to his new station involved a change at 'Jam Junction' (Reading)
where he came across his former governor (and adversary), the station
master at Didcot, now promoted to a similar post at Reading. In real life
Mr Peach, the book renames him Mulberry. The latter offers Struggles any
assistance he can give but also these words of warning:

> "'By the bye', continued Mr Mulberry, 'I am sorry to tell you that it is no
> 'bed of roses' that you are going to; and I only know of one Station Master
> who ever did any good at that Station, and that one was promoted by
> influence, and not merit.'"

Reaching Plough Junction (Slough), Struggles changes for 'Flinter'
(Windsor) and meets Inspector Biggs, 'an enormous railway inspector
dressed in a long, tightly fitting coat, with bright buttons down the centre.'
Biggs' only real task seems to be to call out 'Plough! change for Flinter!' in an
extremely loud voice, or mystifying the passengers by such statements as
'Down train coming in . . . Passengers for the down train go forward!
Passengers for the branch behind' (At this time Slough was a single-sided
station with both up and down platforms served by the same line.)

Almost until the end of its use of the broad gauge (1883), the Windsor
branch ran trains of mixed gauge stock, but very little has been written about
this and how regular or frequent the practice was is not really known. The
working timetable said rather mysteriously 'The gauge of the Windsor

Branch is uncertain' (meaning the gauge of the trains on it rather than the track itself, which was of mixed gauge). So it is worth including a humorous extract from Simmons' book describing his first journey from Slough to Windsor, which does throw a little light on the practice:

"When the engine came to take our train, it was a narrow gauge engine, whereas the carriages were broad gauge.

Inspector Biggs called lustily 'Where's the Dummy! Pretty thing, pretty thing, pretty thing; some of you will have to answer for this, but if it will do for Mr Badger, it will do for me.'

The men all looked astounded – I, too, although a Railway man was equally astonished, as I did not know what he could mean. 'Well, well, well,' continued the Inspector. 'Nice boys, fine heads, no dummy, no train, board job certain, but if it will do for Mr Badger* it will do for me. Hah! Hah! Hah!.'

'When are we going on to Flinter, Mr Biggs?' enquired a passenger.

'Going on, sir-going on, sir-why you can't go on. These Harlequin Devils have forgotten to bring the dummy up from Flinter.'

Addressing the engine-driver Inspector Biggs said – 'There, be off with you to Flinter to fetch the dummy,' and the driver then put on steam and was soon out of sight.

'What on earth do you mean by the dummy?' enquired the passenger of Mr Biggs.

'It's a railway term, sir – a railway term, sir.'

'Are you gone mad further?' enquired the passenger.

'Me gone mad, sir; no sir, and I will trouble you to take your seat. I shall certainly report the case to the Station Master when he comes. The public expect every civility from us – but we must put up with all sorts of insults, but if it will do for Mr Badger it will do for me,' and so saying Mr Biggs swung himself round and walked off.

The passenger looked bewildered and said to me –

'Certainly he is "no dummy", but what does he mean?'

One of the porters then came up and explained that the dummy was a broad gauge carriage with dummy buffers made to fit in between a narrow gauge train and a broad gauge engine, and vice versa, without which a mixed gauge train could not run.

Whilst waiting for the dummy I walked round the station. It was a one-sided station, both up and down trains having to come in and load and unload on one side. This my experience teaches me is a most objectionable practice, necessitating all trains to cross each other's path, preventing more than one train coming in at the time, and it occasions delays to both trains. It is the frequent source of accident, and ought to be abolished.

In twenty minutes the dummy carriage arrived, and we were packed off to Flinter."

Windsor could hardly have been more different than industrial Bilston and Simmons writes rather disparagingly about its tradespeople:

---

*'Mr Badger' was Mr Higgins the divisional superintendent

"The difference between the Station I had recently left, and the one I then took charge of was very great, for I found myself in a very pretty town, amongst wonderfully polite people. Nothing but bowing and scraping from one tradesman to another; and I should think they would sooner go without food all day, than be seen to carry a pail across the street."

Simmons comments that he had quite a small staff for there was little goods traffic, 'and there was no manufactory in the town.' But the lack of goods traffic was more than made up for by the frequent passenger train service, 'in and out from 7 am until past midnight' and the station master was expected to be in attendance for all of them.

Unfortunately for Simmons no less than three Directors lived in Windsor, amongst them the Chairman, Sir Daniel Gooch and Capt. Bulkeley who had been much involved with the GWR in Windsor for over 20 years. Because of this and the presence nearby of the Queen and the need for Ministers of State and other important people to visit her at the Castle, Simmons 'patch' was endlessly inspected and criticised by Superintendent Higgins or one of an army of petty officials paid to make sure the superintendent's backside was protected in case of complaint from the company's Directors or important passengers. He got very little in the way of help, was expected to solve his problems by himself and if he got things wrong then a trip to the Board Room to explain himself before the Directors was likely to be his only reward.

It was not long before his first test came:

"There were cavalry and foot soldiers stationed in the town, and I was first made aware of the fact by an officer walking into my office, and asking if he could have a special train to Plough Junction, to take 100 men to Snorum, [Oxford] to quell a bread riot.

'How are you going to get the men from Plough to Snorum?' I enquired.

The officer was under the impression that the Company would stop the express if I telegraphed to London, and on my telling him that it was very doubtful, he lost all patience, would not charter the train beyond Plough; telegraphed on his own account to Mr Justice, [G.N. Tyrrell the superintendent of the line] and on my assurance that the train should be ready in 10 minutes, and that he had not a moment to lose, in case the train mentioned should stop at Plough, he galloped off for his men.

Our spare engine was full of steam, I found the stoker in the porter's room eating his dinner, and the driver asleep on a settle in the nearest public house, but I could not find [guard] Bomer.

He had gone to his dinner, although he must have heard what the officer said, for my office door was open. I therefore hooked on the engine to the carriages, put a special tail lamp on behind, telegraphed to Plough that I was coming up with special to join on to the express in case she stopped; and securing some flags and detonating signals, I worked the train up as guard myself, leaving Bomer to enjoy his dinner at his leisure.

We arrived in very good time, and the express was not due for some minutes.

The officer in command was the same who ordered the train, and he immediately made enquiry of me as to whether the express train was going to stop for him and his men. I could not inform him as I had not received any reply, although I had myself telegraphed Mr Justice, telling him I was going up with the men to await his instructions at Plough. Further I had no power away from my own station, and I reminded the officer that I was only the guard, and that he had better apply to Inspector Biggs, who was in charge of that station.

Thus, it happened that Inspector Biggs, who had been thirty-five years in the Company's service, calling out 'Plough! Change for Flinter', was, as I thought, in charge of the station.

I followed the officer, who addressed him. Inspector Biggs heard all he had to say, and then quietly replied: 'I can't interfere, sir.' 'Hang it man! you can,' said the officer. 'You can put the signals on against the express and stop her.'

Inspector Biggs pointed to the booking clerk, who then emerged from the office, and saying: 'That's the young person in charge, sir,' betook himself off to an up train to call out 'Plough! Change for Flinter!' in his usual stentorian voice.

'Are you in charge of this station?' said the officer.

'I am,' said the clerk.

The clerk had evidently not seen my telegram, so I explained the whole thing, and left them to settle it, little thinking that he would be persuaded to put the signals against the express, which slipped three coaches at Plough.

Presently the officer returned, and informed me that he had prevailed on him to do so.

There was no time to correct the error, for I could see the signals turned against the train, and the train coming, so I ran towards it and waved it on; for it is a very dangerous thing to stop a train after she has slipped her coaches.

The coaches are slipped a long distance, quite a mile, sometimes two miles, according to the gradient to the station for which they are intended to stop, and they then have a sufficient impetus to allow them to run home; so that should the train in front pull up before it has passed that station, and after it has slipped the carriages, the hinder ones are bound to run into the stopping ones with all the power they have left; and if you, gentle and benevolent reader, happened to be seated in either, and faced a fellow passenger, whether that fellow passenger were a dear friend, or a most objectionable person, you would most assuredly rub noses, and in a manner that would partake of the character of acute electricity.

The clerk roared out to me 'What are you at? Can't you leave me to manage my own station?'

I, however, ran on, and waved my flag; but whether the driver remembered about the slip coaches, or whether my waving reminded him, he, like a good sensible man, drove on through the station and stopped just beyond to see if we had all gone mad.

The object of the officer was, however, achieved. The coaches with the soldiers were all tacked on to his train, and there was, for a time, an end to that little matter, which came off without an accident – more possibly by luck than by judgement."

The same evening a letter was received at Windsor calling Mr Simmons 'before the Board' at 11 am the next day for an 'enquiry'. However after hearing the booking clerk's story the Board reprimanded the latter and told him a mark would be made against his name, effectively stopping him from receiving any promotion. However as the clerk was within a week of the expiry of his four weeks notice following his resignation he was not over-concerned!

Despite its frequent Royal usage the station at Windsor was in very poor shape. Simmons writes,

> "My office was unfinished, that is to say, it had no carpet, a broken washstand, no fire irons, and it required papering. As Her Majesty was about to pay us a visit, I strove to make some preparation to appear decent, and I had recommended that the station should be painted, and an unused waiting room set apart for the royal visitors. My persistence in these matters and my having spoken to the Captain [Bulkeley] at last resulted in an enquiry from Mr McLion [J. Grierson, the General Manager], who sent for me."

The visit however proved fruitless and Simmons was told to mind his own business and leave these things to the engineers. However, the Directors *did* decide the station needed some attention, but,

> "They, however, were persuaded to try a new inexpensive colouring which could not be laid on until all the paint had been scraped from the wood. The consequence of this economy was that in six months our station was in a worse plight than ever, and devoid of paint altogether as the colouring all fell off.
>
> The day before the Royal train was to arrive saw great preparations at Flinter. The Railway itself was scraped over by the permanent way men, and the road round the Station was swept. Two trucks of gravel were sent, and the gravel was spread about in the morning to make the road and the lines look smart. Six trucks of coal, two horseboxes and a carriage truck were taken to Plough Junction to make more room. A bundle of flags was sent down from London to be distributed and suspended from the blackened roofing, which certainly formed a very strange background, and about three hours before the Royal train was due, Mr Badger arrived with ten railway policemen to keep order."

After the arrival of the Queen, and after she had negotiated her way through the party of railway officials who had encircled her carriage in order to greet her arrival, Simmons has some interesting details of the Royal carriage then in use for long journeys:

> "The royal carriage is, in reality, two railway carriages. That is to say, that it is composed of two distinct carriages which are as long as it is considered wise to make them to run safely round the curves and other particular spots on the journey. These two carriages are made into one, so far as the occupants are concerned, by means of an india-rubber passage from the end of one carriage to the end of the other, a door-way being made in both of them. By this means there is sufficient length to enable

Her Majesty to have a complete suite of rooms. In the centre are three distinct compartments of rooms for Her Majesty's use; consisting of a sitting-room, a lavatory, and a bed-room; all the rooms are carpeted with Brussels carpeting. The sitting-room is furnished with a couch on either side, two chairs, and a table. The chairs and two couches are covered with silk, and the table is a plain polished one. The windows to the carriage are very large, and are furnished with blinds to exclude light, sun blind, and a fine wire dust blind. The lamps to the carriage are fixed to the roofing, and there is a green hood covering to each, by means of which Her Majesty can diminish the light in the carriage. All the furniture is screwed by its legs to the floor of the carriage, in case it should wish to dance to Her Majesty on the journey. There are also fixed bells of communication for Her Majesty's use, both in the sitting-room and in the bed-room. One is a telegraphic bell, above which is printed 'To the Directors.'"

The station master at Slough having resigned, or been forced to resign, (a seemingly frequent occurrence at this period according to Simmons' book) a much cheaper one had been installed but unfortunately an elementary mistake meant he did not remain in the post very long:

"Mr McLion wished to keep him if he could possibly be made to answer, but the following little mistake sealed his fate and he was moved.

A particular train came from London to Plough Junction, where it had to be divided, half of it going on to Byfield [Twyford] and Snorum and the other half containing passengers for Flinter. Our half of the train came in at Flinter, but no one got out.

'Well, this is a rum lot of passengers' said porter Bass. 'Not one of them will get out. What's up with them? They must be struck moonblind.'

'When are we going on?' enquired one of the passengers.

'Never!' said porter Bass.

'Where are we, then?' said another.

'Why don't you start the train?' said a third.

No one was for Flinter. The people at Plough Junction had sent the wrong half of the train into us, and my passengers had gone down the line, goodness knew where.

I lost no time, but popped the engine on the other end and ran the train back to Plough Junction, where stood Inspector Biggs, bigger than ever."

After some three years at Windsor, Simmons applied for a rise 'and with very great difficulty my salary was increased from £110 to £125, but I was given to understand that I should not have received the increase of salary had not Captain Boldway [Capt. Bulkeley] fought my cause in true style.' Simmons continues,

"I was much disappointed at the amount for I had managed the station at a considerable saving in the expenses year by year for three years, had personally superintended economy in the use of gas, and in all matters of stores I had effected a saving, and was even doing the whole of the goods work with a lad clerk, whose salary was £20 per annum only, on

Mr McLion's ladclerk scale. Nevertheless, I had had no accident, and no claim of any amount, the trains were nearly fifty in number, and with the aid of two clerks, I managed everything without a railway policeman or an Inspector to parade the platforms.

It would not have mattered so much had I been able to do as some station masters did, viz, swell about myself all day, and then retire to a cottage home to take my meals, and to find my wife and family in a suitable home for an income of £100 per annum. But our house being part and parcel of the station, there was no disguising the fact that the occupants were the wife and offsprings of the station master, and I could not see them unsuitably clad or tutored to clash with my position.

For the first few months we managed without a servant, but directly the gentry and others made my acquaintance they no longer inquired for me at the station, but at my residence, and I constantly went to the relief of Mrs Struggles, who had left off her bed-making or her pastry-rolling to answer the everlasting knocks at the door.

'Ernest,' said my wife one day, 'I will do no more of this station work, the knocks at the door occupy nearly all my time, besides the unpleasant necessity of having continually to come forward in dishabille.'

A servant was therefore engaged, and the cost of that addition to our household entirely cancelled the advance in salary."

Unfortunately written so long after the event, many interesting incidents are undated but it is possible to date the following mishap, and the official version is given in Chapter Twelve. The date of the incident was 9th November, 1871. Some of the details given are wrong but Simmons's version is basically correct and written in his usual rather cynical style.

As the first mile out of Windsor runs continuously on a viaduct it is apparent that fortune smiled on the Great Western this day because the mishap could so easily have been a disaster:

"Now, the train by which the Directors arrived was due at seven o'clock, and we had a train due to start at the same time. It was therefore obvious that I could not attend to both, and, wishing to see the Captain, I was waiting for his train on the opposite side of the line, when the whistle of the starting train sounded.

No sooner had it started than my accustomed ear caught a discordant sound in the movement, and I ran forward to ascertain the cause. It was one of the wheels of a carriage, and as the train passed me, for it was getting into full swing, I could see that the lumping proceeded from the irregular revolution of the wheel. The wheel was a patent one, the centre being of wood and the outer portion of iron. It was already quite out of place, and, as it revolved, the grease-box acted as a turning lathe, and the shavings from the wheel flew onto the line. In this carriage were several people, and looking from a first-class window was Mr Darwin,* our chief solicitor.

Now, if there is a class of people more nervous than another, whilst travelling in a railway train, it is the legal gentlemen. Although they are very fond of briefs, they don't like the idea of a brief notice of exit on a

*Mr Darvill

railway, and Mr Darwin had already got his head out of the carriage on my side.

'What is it, Struggles?' said he.

'The wheel!' was all I could say.

'Stop the train! Stop the train!' shouted the lawyer, and he waved frantically, shouted at the top of his voice, opened the door, and got out on to the step of the carriage as it lumped along. Fortunately, he did not decide on jumping or he would have certainly spoilt the look of his sleek well-nourished body.

It was always a rule with me when I had started a train and again wished to stop it, to run up to the driver, and if he failed to notice my signal to stop, either by reason of the noise of the steam blowing off, or under pretence or inattention, I simply jumped on to his step and put my hand on his shoulder.

The drivers, however, soon know their customer, and they rarely disregarded my 'Hold on!' although it is annoying to a driver to have to pull up when once he has put his powerful steed in motion. In this case, however, the train had the start of me, and all that I have related occurred in a much briefer space of time than it has taken you to read it. All I could have done would have been to have jumped on to the footboard of a guard's van, but then I had no power to communicate with the driver, who had got full steam up and was puffing away unmindful of Mr Darwin, who was at the moment extending his pocket handkerchief tied on his umbrella from the window of his carriage. Doubtless, it will be said 'But what about the cord communication between the driver and the guard?' Yes! what about that? I think I cannot better explain the usefulness of this communication than by stating that once a Railway Director borrowed a piece of the cord of me to tie a parcel with, and he then said, 'Struggles, this is the first time I ever knew this cord to be of any service.' Besides, who would think to put his hand out of window to feel on the roof to pull it, and if you did pull it, the chances are it would be tied to anything but the engine driver's bell.

Here then was a train under weigh [sic] which the guard, the passengers, the station master and the signalman (for I shouted to that officer, 'Stop the train') all knew was going to certain doom. Yet we were all powerless to attract the attention of the driver. The signalman frantically turned and re-turned his distant signal, which was then still ahead of the departing train, but which signal of course was only for the direction of incoming trains, and as I took a last view of the train as it rounded a curve a mile and a half ahead, I could see Mr Darwin in his shirt sleeves waving his coat. He had lost his umbrella and his hat.

I ran to the telegraph office and telegraphed the next station to stop the train, 'Wheel broken,' and returned to listen for the smash. I could already imagine myself dragging poor Mr Darwin from the ruins, but better news was in store for us, for the signalman came running to say, 'She has stopped just round the corner, two miles distant.'

Beyond the damage to a carriage and to a bridge no one was injured, but it was a very near thing, and poor Mr Darwin was in a dreadful state. It took two seltzers and brandy to get him at all round."

The final extract from Simmons extremely interesting book (again undated, but from Appendix Three we can establish this as 24th June, 1873), is
a long one but it is so full of interest and reveals details of matters not dealt
with elsewhere that it is worth retelling in full. Remember that at this time
the station consisted of just two short platforms!

"'Struggles,' said the Captain, 'the Shah of Persia is coming to visit the
Queen, and I want everything in order, write to the admiralty for flags,
arrange for shrubs and flowers for decoration, fresh gravel the roads, get
rid of your trucks to make room, and see how smartly you can do the
thing when he comes.'

It may interest some of my readers if I give a short account of that
twenty-four hours' work.

At 4 am I rose, hoisted flags, placed flowers, evergreens and gravel,
superintended the general cleaning and sweeping of the station, and
telegraphed for an engine to clear the sidings of trucks. With the daylight,
two miserable little girls, with scarcely rag or shoe, crept into the station
and picked up the knobs of coal that had fallen from the trucks, and with
their hands, raked over the ashes that were thrown out on the dust heap
after they had been collected from the office and waiting room fireplaces.

It was true these little starvelings had no business there, and that the
night porter should have ordered them off, but as he said, he knew I
should not forbid them taking what would otherwise be wasted, and he
also knew that the children's owners (he couldn't call them mothers)
invariably thrashed them if they did not collect fuel and boil the kettle by
the time they awoke from their drunken revelries of the previous night.

All the flags were up except one, and that was the Union Jack – 'Where
shall we hoist this one?' said one man.

'What trucks shall we take with this engine?' said another.

Having given instructions as to the trucks that were to be moved, I
turned my attention to the fixing of the flag, and selected a post on which
was written 'No Thoroughfare,' and which could be up-ended as a suitable pole whereon to fix the Union Jack.

The two little ragged girls watched the pretty flags with childish joy,
and ceased their pickings. As the flag was hoisted I heard a shriek – it was
one of the poor little things knocked down by the goods trucks, run over
and killed!

By the direction of the other child, the porters carried the corpse to the
pigstye of the mother.

It was true it was a room, and still in clothes that were daubed in last
night's mud lay her drunken mother, senseless and filthy.

Slowly the truth of what had occurred dawned upon the wretch, who
gave way to the most fearful oaths; and if the poor child was destined to
follow in the steps of her mother, death was the best thing that could have
overtaken her.

This was not a good beginning for a hard day's work, but in the bustle
that followed, no time was allowed to me to reflect on what had occurred,
but the child's shriek would sometimes flash across my memory.

At 8 am I had performed my usual toilet and partaken of a light break-
fast, for the scene at the child's mother's was almost too much for an

empty stomach, and although I had only to cross the road to be at home, I never succeeded in getting there again until 4 o'clock the next morning. The number of my passengers on that day at the small station was estimated at 15,000, so that doubling that number, for all returned, I had 30,000 passengers to deal with in one day. Train after train of soldiers and civilians arrived, carriages and horses *ad libitum*. Then came trains with Ministers of State and Royalty, and lastly a batch of Great Smash [Great Western] officials. Mr Badger hurried off to the Review, but Mr McLion remained and conversed with Mr Gabriel Gouge [Daniel Gooch] as to the day's traffic.

'How in the world are you going to get all these people away again, Struggles?' said Mr McLion.

Now this was what I had been considering. I had got through many hard days, on Bank Holidays, and other occasions, and I had found out the only way to work the terminus without a block, but I knew very well that my proposal would be sure to meet with Mr Badger's objection, for we rarely agreed, so I made bold to go to the point at once.

'There will be no difficulty about it,' I replied, 'if for once you will allow me to have my own way.'

'What do you call your own way?' snappishly enquired Mr McLion.

'Why, for you to send back about ten superintendents who will be here to interfere presently, and to determine whether Mr Badger or myself shall manage the station for the day.'

'You are not altered, I see, Struggles,' said Mr McLion with a sneer on his countenance.

'He is quite right,' said Mr Gabriel Gouge, 'if one man cannot manage a big thing like this, twenty cannot do it. Struggles is the better acquainted with the station. Why not let him manage, Mr McLion? How do you propose doing it, Struggles?'

'Well, you see, sir, directly the people begin to return they will be as a torrent of water, there will be no stopping them, reasoning with them, or dictating to them. The only thing to do is to get rid of them. I propose letting all the engines take water and form up, say, three miles of continuous trains on the down line, the first train to stand in the platform. After a few trains have been dispatched, there will be no shunting a train to get the engine at the right end, as our trains run to a dead end, so I propose having a spare engine in readiness always to put on to the other end of the train when it stops, to cut off the engine that brings the train and make that end of it the tail end. All lamps can be removed in readiness for this, and the trains will be loaded almost before the engine is cut off.'

'But what about your ordinary stopping trains, Struggles?' enquired Mr McLion.

'Why, sir, it will be impossible for me to start any but London trains, for which station nineteen out of twenty are bound; but all trains must stop at the junction, and the stopping trains can be formed there. They have room to do it.'

'Nonsense,' said Mr McLion.

'He is quite right,' again interposed Mr Gabriel Gouge. 'McLion, you let him carry out his ideas.'

'How many men have you to help?' enquired McLion.

'I have a large number, sir, but men will be useless to me. One hundred men cannot control one thousand people. You must let them in and start them, they will do all themselves.' – And they did.

Talk about English manners, where were they in a crowd? The passengers were, for the most part, well dressed people, and very many of them first class, but no regard was paid to sex or position. It was save himself, or rather train himself who can. You would see a lady stripped of her outer garments trying to get into a carriage, and some burly brute in a black frock coat, who claimed to be a gentleman at home, thrusting his elbows into her bosom and take the seat she had hoped to secure, then pushing her down between the train and the platform. I rode in with every train, cautioned the people to stand back, and I rode out with every train, moving it as steadily as steam would allow, until it was clear of the station, when we pulled up, shut the doors, and started it. I wanted no other help.

'Oh! you are here. I've been looking for you everywhere,' said Mr McLion. 'How are you getting on?'

'First rate, thank you, sir, only I see they are not getting the trains away from the junction. I can count seven trains now that I have dispatched, and which are still standing ahead there round the corner for the want of a signal from Plough Junction to proceed.'

'I must go there immediately, Struggles. Have you an engine?'

'Yes, sir, but you cannot get half way for the trains you see standing.'

'Then call a cab.'

'No such thing for love or money, sir.'

'Then how am I to get there?'

'Walk, I am afraid, sir.'

Mr McLion started, and I was very glad of it.

My trains soon told on the passengers, and when Tom Burley the foreman, in his honest thoughtful manner came round and said, 'Can't I help you a bit, sir?' I was glad to place him in charge of the passenger trains, and to go and see how the matter of horses and carriages was proceeding.

As I have said before there were plenty of men, and I had scarcely set them to work to load up all the horses and carriages, when Mr Badger put in an appearance.

'What are you at?' was his first enquiry.

We explained.

'I will have nothing of the kind done, said Mr Badger; 'First start all passengers, and then see to the horses and carriages.'

'But, my dear sir,' said I, 'what harm can there be in the men loading the carriages and horses? The coachmen will be relieved of their horses, and the carriages will be ready to start when the line is clear to make up a train of them.'

'I will not have it done,' said Mr Badger, emphatically, and the men left the work.

I could not help at that moment referring in my mind to Mr Blow-broth's* suggestion, viz., that the Company would be in pocket if they gave Mr Badger £1,000 per annum to mind donkeys on a common; but after all, perhaps, it was his misfortune that he had left the drapery and embraced his brother's occupation without having the necessary capacity. So I went on with the other work, and when the line was tolerably clear for a train to take Mr Badger to his home, he did me the honour to go.

It was very soon apparent that we should be short of horseboxes. Had we proceeded with the loading, two trains would have been despatched, and the stock would have worked back at once from London, but owing to Mr Badger's interference we were waiting about all night, and it was 4 am before all were despatched, the last train containing horses belonging to the Duke of Cambridge, who did not forget to complain about it.

A telegram had the effect of fetching first one leg out of bed, then the other, and finally by body. It ran thus:–

'FROM Mr McLion,   To Struggles.'

'Attend Board Meeting at 12 o'clock today. Bring all times of arrival and departure of trains yesterday, and when the Duke of Cambridge's horses left.

Now I had not been running up and down to Plough Junction all night without asking how they, too, had fared under the general supervision of our Railway Masters. Mr Barber, the new Station Master at Plough Junction, had been twenty years in the Company's service. He had worked his way up from the porter ranks, and had been an Inspector at a station, dressed in the Company's livery studded with buttons, before ambition had prompted him to seek the post of Station Master at Plough Junction. Unfortunately, his education did not enable him to dispose correctly of his h's, his has's, and his as's, and his clerks were apt to ridicule the compositions which he called letters. Nevertheless, Mr Barber was a thoroughly practical outdoor man, and a valuable servant to the Company.

From the day of his taking charge of Plough Junction he complained of the insufficiency of the staff for the safe conduct of the Station, but it was not until he had resigned his post of twenty years' standing, and thus lost the work of his whole life, that the Company took the slightest notice of his complaints. They then selected a youth from a Parcels office as Station Master, at a higher salary, and gave him even more additional staff than poor Barber had asked for.

Mr Barber, unlike myself, had allowed all authority to go from him on this 'Shah's Day,' and had merely walked about the station like a dummy, ready, however, to be the scapegoat if anything untoward had happened, and a Station Master should be wanted for the Government Inspector.

I questioned him as to what Mr McLion did when he walked up from the station on the day of the Review.

'Oh!' said Barber, 'he was in a passion. After abusing us all as a lot of blockheads, for not getting the trains away faster, he went to Mr Justice,

*A Windsor trader.

the Traffic Superintendent, and told him to take the block telegraph signal off.'*

'And did he do it?' I enquired.

'No,' said Barber. 'The old gentleman pulled himself together, and at once asserted his position by saying: "I do not receive my salary from the Great Smash Company in order that I may be hanged, thank you, Mr McLion!" Mr McLion then sent the Train Time Inspector half way between here and London, and took the block telegraph off, and the trains accumulated there. They very soon reached all the way back to the next station, and if there had been an accident, by George wouldn't there have been an enquiry!'

Before 12 o'clock I was in the passage outside the Board room, and many of the chief clerks who were running about under orders from Mr McLion and others, had exchanged salutations with me, such as 'Good morning, Mr Struggles – Why you are getting quite a familiar visitor at the Director's table!' They did not say it in an unkind manner, for I am certain that many of them knew that I was at cross purposes with the Managers, and they sympathized with me.

Mr Justice, too, came forward and shook hands. 'Good morning, Mr Struggles,' said he. 'You got your trains off in first-rate style yesterday. We could not deal with them fast enough at Plough. How ever did you manage it?'

'Very simply, sir,' I replied. 'You could take all the people round the World in that fashion, if you had trains and carriages sufficient, and I explained the system.

'And got through 30,000 people without an accident, I hear.'

'No, sir, we killed a little girl at 6 o'clock in the morning,' and I told Mr Justice all about it.

'Well, well,' said he. 'She was not a passenger, and it is hard to say whether you were right or wrong in letting her come into the station. Do you know, Struggles, I always say there is sufficient coal ground into powder by carts and by trucks in the coal yards to keep all the poor warm, if it was picked up; and enough good food given to dogs and thrown into hog tubs by servants, to keep them all, if it was only saved; but then comes the question – who are the deserving poor? I say – better not be poor at all, Struggles! I will go and see if the Directors are ready to see you.'

As I walked in some one whispered in my ear, 'Pluck up courage, Struggles, let them have it in your old style.'

It was Mr Campwood, Mr Justice's chief clerk, as goodhearted a man as ever held a railway pen. He sat himself down to take minutes for Mr Justice, and again I stood 'before the picture.'†

'Struggles,' said the Captain, in his usual deep voice, 'We have not sent for you to blow you up, for you seem to have got the trains away from your station all right; but some of them lost three and even four hours on the journey. The Prince of Wales' train was two hours and a half longer than we timed it at on the backward journey I see, and the Duke of Cambridge's horses were about all night. Can you tell the Directors how it

*i.e. let the trains follow one another instead of being controlled by the block telegraph system.
†The picture on the wall of the Board Room is described in Volume 1 of Simmons' memoirs.

all happened, as we don't seem to have anything very satisfactory before us at present.'

Mr Badger rose from his seat at the Directors' table, and addressing Captain Boldway said,

'I beg your pardon, Captain Boldway, but with regard to the horse-boxes, hum, if you will allow me, hum, to suggest that this should be taken as a separate matter, hum, I think I shall be able to prove to your satisfaction, hum, that it was a matter entirely beyond the control of Mr Struggles, hum, and rests entirely with the truck inspectors.'

Mr Badger was evidently going to shift what belonged to his interference on to the backs of the truck inspectors, and as the truth, or at any rate my view of the subject, would have been out of place I did not proffer it.

After I left, Mr Badger and the Truck Inspector fought this matter out before the Directors, but as the chief Wagon Inspector was apt to muddle his brain with sundry glasses of beer before dinner, Mr Badger beat him and his men into ribbons.

'Very well,' said the Captain, 'we will leave the horse-box enquiry until last. Now, Struggles, can you tell the Directors why these trains were so long on the road?'

'Yes, sir, I can.'

'Very well, then, do so, for we are quite in the dark at present.'

Mr McLion was going to say something, and he looked daggers at me, but Gabriel Gouge stopped him, and all the Directors waited patiently for my statement.

I produced my list of the running of the trains, not only from my station, but from Plough Junction, and commenced by saying,

'I think, gentlemen, if you are satisfied at the way in which the trains were despatched from my station, you will allow me to begin dealing with them at Plough Junction.'

'You have nothing to do with Plough Junction,' interposed Mr McLion.

'That is just where we want to begin,' said the Captain. 'We have heard several from Plough Junction already, and are none the wiser. We want to know why these trains were delayed. Go on, Struggles!'

Mr Campwood winked at me and smiled. I re-commenced.

'If you examine the block telegraph system between Plough Junction and London (Mr McLion looked daggers), you will find that it works out an average of ten blocks, each of which could be cleared by a train in six minutes, if no obstacle prevented, and thus ten trains could pass along in the hour. Now if you refer to the signalman's train book at Plough Junction, of which this paper is a copy, you will find that when I began to start my trains thickly, no less than fifteen trains arrived at Plough Junction on the main line and from my branch during the first hour, five of which were necessarily left behind at Plough Junction, because the block telegraph would not permit of their passing. At the end of the next hour you will find that no less than twelve trains were standing at Plough in the same way, and when Mr McLion sent the Time Inspector to one of the stations to take off the block telegraph, the trains only accumulated there instead of at Plough ...

'To do what?' shouted the Captain.

'To take off the block telegraph,' I replied.

'Is that a fact, Mr McLion?' enquired two Directors simultaneously.

'Yes, replied Mr McLion, 'I will explain it presently.'

'That explains the mystery,' said the Captain.

'Now, Struggles, one more word before you go back to your station. Do you know of any means of preventing this same block if a similar catastrophe should occur?'

'I do, sir.'

'What is it?'

'Double the length of your trains, and put two engines on. You would thus halve the number of trains to clear the block, and so long as the couplings did not break there would be no danger in it.'

'It is not practicable,' said Mr McLion, 'Our platform could not receive the trains, they are not long enough.'

'Better to let the people walk a hundred yards than to keep them four hours in a train, said the Captain. 'Struggles, you can go back to your station.'

I needed no second permission, and was very soon there, but I felt that I had earned some recognition of extra service, and not received it. In fact, I was like the railway porter, who said to the passenger, 'Beg your pardon, sir, but if you gave me anything, I have dropped it.'"

Simmons resigned his position in 1876 and the above details were printed in 1880. It is interesting therefore to find a report in *The Railway News* for 30th July, 1881 which describes a similar situation when the GWR had to carry 26,000 troops to Windsor for a Volunteer Review. A very similar method of working was carried out, thus validating Simmons' account. The details can be found in Appendix Five.

Ultimately disenchanted with the 'Great Smash Company' (and surely readers will agree that life on the GWR in the second half of the 19th century, as Simmons paints it, is entirely unlike the rosy picture of the GWR in the 20th century which one has come to accept), Simmons resigned after some 9 years at Windsor and 15 with the company. Still on a salary of £125 p.a., his final humiliation came when the GWR refused to return his super-annuation payments, amounting to £30, on the grounds that he had paid them for 9½ years and 'the Directors do not consider any application unless the applicant has paid for 10 years and over'! Simmons became a farmer, his father's former occupation, and as well as writing the two volumes 'Ernest Struggles', also wrote 'Stubble Farm', described as illustrating 'the rise and fall of the English Agriculturist', and two novels. It is thought he died in 1895.

Chapter Six
A Station fit for a Queen

Although the branch line opened on 8th October, 1849, Windsor station was not ready until 1850, its completion having been delayed by wet weather during the intervening winter. The station had two platform lines and a middle siding, but the well-known illustration of the first Windsor station with its train shed (overall roof) is not clear as to whether the middle siding was there from the beginning.

By 1880 the station consisted of a down platform about 460 ft long, a shorter up platform only about 264 ft long and a middle siding. This latter continued between the two main lines to the station throat. On the up (south) side of the station there were three short sidings, two of which had end dock loading facilities and contained wagon turntables connected with the up main line. These would have been used principally for loading carriages etc. Beyond this were three longer sidings for goods traffic, one of which ran through a short goods shed. At the back of the up platform at its east end lay the Royal waiting room.

The first major alteration took place in 1880. On 23rd December of that year the GWR wrote to the Board of Trade:

> I have to inform you that at Windsor station (which at present is on the mixed gauge) in order to enable narrow gauge carriages to be drawn close to the side of the up platform,* a change of gauge has been made for a few yards distance . . . and the crossover points have also been slightly altered . . . and the [up] platform has been extended on the opposite side of the line. [*This was an error; the plan and the inspecting officer's report indicate it was actually the down platform.]

To enable the up platform to be extended to about 460 ft in length, one of the three short up sidings (the one without end dock or turntable facilities) had been removed. The two remaining short sidings of course no longer had turntable connections with the up main line as the platform was now in the way.

Major Marindin inspected the layout on 3rd January, 1881, and, while approving the arrangements enabling narrow gauge carriages to use the west end of the down platform went on to say this:

> . . . the approval of this alteration must not be taken as a general approval of the arrangements at this station, which are far from satisfactory inasmuch as the points and signals are not interlocked, the facing points are not provided with interlocking bars and facing point bolts, there is but one starting signal and one arrival signal for the two platform lines, which are used indiscriminately for arrival and departures, and there is a length of about 50 yds of line which is practically worked as a single line (the middle siding), the two outside lines being as a rule used for carriage sidings or shunting purposes.

Despite this rebuke and a collision between a passenger train and a shunting movement at Windsor in 1885, directly arising from this misuse of the layout (see *Chapter Twelve*), the GWR declined to act until 1888/9, when at last a properly interlocked layout, controlled from a new signal box, was provided. Colonel Rich inspected the new arrangements, reporting on 23rd May, 1889, as follows:

> The entrance to the station has been widened, the platforms have been lengthened, and an additional Dock line has been constructed at the back of the old up line

platform so that now the Station has two platforms that can each be used for trains arriving or departing, and a third platform which is to be used solely for trains leaving Windsor station.

The points and signals have been interlocked, and are worked from a new cabin, which is placed at the west [south] end of the Railway and contains 50 working and 3 spare levers.

Apart from wanting some minor locking alterations and a clock at the 'south' [east] end of the station, Col Rich recommended the works be approved.

Traffic dealt with continued to increased and, at last, in 1895, the GWR decided that only a complete rebuilding would suffice, and with the Queen's Diamond Jubilee coming up in 1897, what better time to do it. The General Manager made a comprehensive report to Traffic Committee, which approved, as did the Board on 23rd December, 1895:

> The General Manager stated that for a considerable time past it has been felt that the accommodation at Windsor station is inadequate to meet the requirements of the traffic but that, owing to the necessity for dealing with more urgent works at other places and the large expenditure involved, the scheme for improving the accommodation at Windsor has been held over. The time has, however, arrived when, having regard to the attention which has been called to the subject by Her Majesty, and other members of the Royal Family and to the increasing traffic, the work should be taken in hand and he submitted plans showing the scheme which it is recommended should be carried out, together with an estimate of the cost amounting to £41,788.
>
> The scheme provides for the widening of the viaduct on the north side and the removal of the mileage traffic and the east depot to the Low Level, the goods shed, however, being retained at the High Level. The space thus gained will enable three platforms to be constructed which will be served by four lines of rails and will be available for either arrival or departure purposes. A more central and convenient site is provided for the Royal Waiting Rooms and the approach thereto will be constructed so as to offer ample accommodation for carriages, escort, etc. on state occasions.
>
> In connection with the improvement of the approach it will be necessary to remove the Station Master's house and in place thereof, rooms will be provided for his use in the new station buildings.
>
> The proposed Low Level yard has been laid out with the view not only of providing sufficient room for the present requirements of the goods traffic but also of allowing for extensions in the future should the need arise.
>
> The alterations will necessitate the acquisition of 1 acre 3 rods 31¾ perches of land which it is estimated will cost about £1,200.

Chief components of the £41,788 expenditure were:

Widening the viaduct	£10,975
New platforms	£3,310
New buildings	£8,354
Platform coverings and verandah	£7,571
New royal waiting room	£686
Additional platform lines	£1,846
Low level goods yard	£6,595
Signalling	£1,168

Later (in 1897) the vote was increased by £6,880 to £48,668, this increase to include a wider approach to the station, a larger roof, an additional £1,600

The imposing archway over the road leading to Windsor station, c.1901. In this view only the condition of the roadway is not up to the standard of the station facilities.

British Rail

The interior of the booking hall, soon after rebuilding.   *British Rail*

This could be a major terminus, but in fact it is platform 1 at Windsor, soon after rebuilding, 1901. *British Rail*

Windsor station frontage in 1967. *British Rail*

The magnificent glazed roof over the Royal room and roadway, after completion, c.1902. Platform 4 is to the right. The gentleman who owns the wheelbarrow in front of the Royal room is lurking in the shadows at the end of the brick wall on the left, doubtless moved by the photographer.

British Rail

What a splendid array of station signs and posters are on display in this April 1901 view. Doubtless the GWR built it to last for at least one hundred years, but less than seventy years later, only a fraction of these facilities were needed.

British Rail

British Rail

..., 1884. Note the separate entrances to 1st and 3rd class booking offices.

A view of the interior of the Royal rooms at Windsor station, c.1897. *British Rail*

A closer view of the Royal rooms at Windsor station.   *British Rail*

An unusual part of Windsor station to be photographed, and a hive of activity although a good number of people in evidence are staff! This undated view, probably from the first decade of the 20th century, is taken from an old postcard. There is a 2-lever ground frame at the foot of the steps. *Lens of Sutton*

An interesting postcard dated 19th August, 1909 (the halfpenny stamp is under the postmark) showing the impressive entrance to Windsor station and a couple of early buses. *Lens of Sutton*

for the Royal waiting room, and the 'provision of more important architectural features on the station buildings generally' (extra £2,800). Perhaps it was at this stage that the Queen's Jubilee was recognised and the plans for the station enhanced.

The various contracts were distributed as follows:

Widening the viaduct and construction of new yard	A. Jackaman & Son (of Slough)	tender £9,223 14s. 8d.
New platforms	A. Jackaman & Son	tender £2,678 15s. 0d.
Foundations	A. Jackaman & Son	tender £2,629 13s. 2d.
Buildings	W.J. Bloxham (Banbury)	tender £14,897
Station roof and verandahs	A. Handyside & Co. (Derby)	tender £4,648 13s. 5d.
Platform roof and verandahs	A. Handyside & Co.	tender £5,182 2s. 9d.
Royal waiting room	H. Lovatt (Wolverhampton)	tender £2,530

The order for the Royal waiting room, dated 3rd March, 1897 required the work to be finished by 1st June, and indeed the room was first used by Queen Victoria on 21st June, 1897. But the other work took rather longer; the order for the buildings is dated 31st December, 1897, and for the platform roof and verandahs 6th January, 1898.

Before the new station was completed Queen Victoria died. On 28th October, 1901 King Edward VII travelled by the 10.10 am ordinary service from Paddington to Windsor and on arrival there inspected the station roadway to the Royal waiting room. This roadway had been lowered in the vicinity of the Royal room at the request of the late Queen to facilitate her movement to and from her carriage. The King asked that the roadway now be restored to its proper level. At the same time the King expressed his opinion that the Royal room was 'very small for exceptional occasions'. In addition, it had no separate accommodation for gentlemen, having only one Reception room (plus toilet) for Ladies. The King indicated that he anticipated 'a very considerable user for Royal purposes of the Company's station at Windsor' and hoped that the suggested improvements could be made by next year (1902).

This matter was rushed through the 'usual channels' and the Directors authorised on 13th November, 1901 the provision of a 'new and additional saloon 14 ft × 18 ft to the Royal waiting room with lavatory accommodation for Gentlemen'. This work, together with the raising of the roadway and a large new gate at the entrance to this part of the station cost £1,952. Messrs Kirk & Randall of Woolwich got the contract to do the work, the order being dated 29th January, 1902. Excluding the (1902) extension to the Royal rooms, the grand new station eventually cost £67,558 and 5d. when the books were closed in 1906, the over-expenditure included £7,649 for contracts in excess of estimates and £10,225 additional agreed expenditure for which no details are given.

The remaining works being ready, the General Manager wrote to the Board of Trade on 9th January, 1902 stating that the station was ready for inspection. Colonel Yorke inspected the station on 27th February, 1902, and found everything in order. The four passenger platforms, reading from north to south (No. 1 to No. 4) were 636 ft, 636 ft, 611 ft and 680 ft in length respectively. After the provision of an additional siding holding 22 wagons

NOTICE No. E:15.

GREAT WESTERN RAILWAY.

(FOR THE USE OF THE COMPANY'S SERVANTS ONLY.)

Notice to Enginemen, Guards, etc.

Sunday, March 7th to Tuesday, March 9th, 1937.

SIGNAL ALTERATIONS

WINDSOR AND ETON

Between the hours of 7.30 a.m. Sunday, March 7th and 5.0 p.m. Tuesday, March 9th, the Signal Engineers will be engaged in bringing into use the following New Signals and Connections.

FORM.	DESCRIPTION.	POSITION.	DISTANCE FROM BOX.
2 3	1. Down Main Intermediate Home. 2. Down Main to Loop Intermediate Home. 3. Not in use.	Down Side of Down Main.	254 yards.
	Backing from Up Main. Route Indicating. Up Main. Down Main. Loop.	Up Side of Up Main.	260 yards.
	Up Main Starting.	Up Side of Up Main.	184 yards.

The following existing signals will be taken out of use :—
Down Main Intermediate Home ; Up Main Starting ; 3-arm Backing signal from the Up Main.
New connections will be brought into use in accordance with the sketch appended.
Occupation of the locking frame will be required for the purpose of altering and testing.

All arrangements for the safe working of the Line (including the appointment of Handsignalmen), must be made by the District Inspector in accordance with Rule 77.

PADDINGTON STATION,   C. T. COX,
February 25th, 1937.   Divisional Superintendent.

The receipt of this Notice to be acknowledged by first Train.

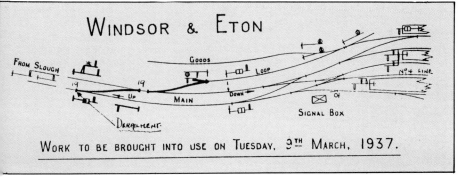

Part of the resignalling work involved in 1937 to enable longer trains to be handled at Windsor. This particular copy has been used to indicate the site of a later derailment!

in 1905, the low-level yard held 170 wagons. The goods shed was at the same level, and south of, the passenger platforms; the goods shed siding accommodated 16 wagons and two 2 ton cranes were available for lifting heavy items.

In 1908/9 the roof over the island platform was extended at a cost of £1,418 16s. 0d. and in 1912/3 the platform lines were track circuited at a cost of £334 1s. 8d.

Sadly after the death of King George V in 1936, the Royal waiting rooms were only once again used as intended and in 1951/2 the building was converted to office accommodation for the Area Chief of Police (British Transport Police) at a cost of £1,687.

The last major improvement at Windsor was authorised by the GWR Board on 18th December, 1936. The sum of £4,480 was authorised to alter the crossovers and connections in the approach to the platforms and extend platform 1 by about 60 ft. This was needed because 'a number of long trains have to be dealt with at Windsor & Eton station, but the present layout does not permit of more than one being accommodated at a time, and difficulties arise'. Extensive alterations were necessary to the gas and water mains, as well as the position of signals. The work was carried out in 1937 and the final cost was £4,234 (less than the estimate).

For details of the demise of the comprehensive facilities at Windsor, so carefully built up by the GWR, please see page 175.

A 1960s view of Windsor station before rationalisation set in.   *Photomatic*

Chapter Seven
Samuel Maun, Windsor Station Master
1903–1925

Samuel Thomas Maun went to Windsor as station master in 1903. He had begun work with the GWR as a booking clerk at Ironbridge & Broseley in 1875, later moving to Bridgnorth (his birthplace) as chief goods clerk in 1880. In 1888 he was offered his first station mastership, the position at Chipping Campden on the Oxford–Worcester line, and this he held until 1899. In the latter year he was selected for the post of station master at Uxbridge, west of London, the terminus of the branch line from West Drayton. After the accession to the throne of King Edward VII, the latter made frequent visits to Uxbridge on his way to the home of the Earl & Countess Howe and this doubtless helped Samuel Maun prepare himself for his subsequent post at Windsor, where the reception of royalty was an almost everyday event.

After three years and ten months at Uxbridge the position of station master at Windsor became vacant. Maun had never had to apply for a station master's post, in each case he had received an offer of the job. And so it was with Windsor; in his mail one morning he received an invitation to see the Chairman of the GWR (Earl Cawdor) and the General Manager (Sir Joseph Wilkinson) at Paddington for interview. A few days later he went to Paddington and, after some talk, Earl Cawdor said, 'You will do for Windsor' and he had been appointed!

In those days an official transfer of responsibilities between the outgoing and incoming station masters took place with the divisional superintendent, or other high official present; this duly took place at Uxbridge on Thursday 31st March and Maun went to Windsor the next day expecting himself to be 'transferred in' there in the same way. However, no official appeared, but on the Saturday the Superintendent came down and said he had not come on the Friday as he was a little superstitious, and that he would come on the Monday, if that was all right! As Monday 3rd April was Maun's birthday he was quite in agreement, considering it a fine birthday present.

Samuel Maun was destined to be at Windsor for 22 years, eventually retiring there in 1925 after 50 years railway service. In that time nearly all the crowned heads of Europe visited Windsor Castle, some of them two or three times over, as well as three French Presidents, the King of Siam and the Archduke of Austria, whose murder bought about the start of World War I. In his time there were three Royal weddings at Windsor, those of Princess Alice, Countess of Athlone, Princess Margaret of Connaught and Lady Helena Cambridge. There were also six Royal funerals, those of King Edward VII, Prince Francis of Teck, the Duchess of Connaught, Prince Christian, Lord Leopold Mountbatten and Princess Christian.

Samuel Maun was well placed to observe the comings and goings of those in charge of his country's affairs for almost a quarter of a century and, fortunately for posterity, recorded the highlights of his observations in a diary which he wrote after many years of retirement, in 1941. Probably because it was written so long after the event some of the dates of the Royal visits are wrong but it has been a simple matter to correct these by checking the list of Royal trains on the branch (see Appendix Three) and his dates have been altered where they are wrong. The diary is now in the Royal Borough Collection and, thanks to the kindness of the Curator, I was allowed to see a copy, and this forms the basis of this chapter.

The first major Royal event with which Maun had to deal was the state visit of the King and Queen of Italy in November 1903. These visits entailed a lot of extra work for the station master and almost round-the-clock working for the branch. During this visit a state banquet was held on one night and a theatrical performance on the next. For the banquet two special trains ran, one with guests and the other with Yeomen of the Guard (the Beefeaters) who stood round the tables. Both these returned between 1.30 and 2 am the next morning (Maun would have remained on duty to see these away). For the theatrical performance of 'A pair of Specticals' [sic] with Sir John Hare, a special train took the company back at 2.30 am. At the end of the visit Maun received the first of many presents he was given over the years: a beautiful diamond tie pin with the King of Italy's initials 'V.E.' in blue enamel in the centre and a gold crown on the top.

In February 1904 came the next major Royal event, the wedding of Princess Alice (the King's niece) to HSH Prince Alexander of Teck (afterwards the Earl of Athlone) on 10th February, 1904 in St George's Chapel. There were several specials trains for visitors but the thing that Maun remembered most was that after the service Lady Mount Stephens found she had lost her £2,000 pearl necklace. In Maun's words:

> St Georges Chapel was searched and then the station yard but it not found and posters were issued offering £50 reward and detectives were making enquiries and King Edward constantly asked if it had been found. We felt sure that if it had been lost in the station yard someone would have found it as the large gate was closed and no one but officials in the yard when the visitors arrived. Some weeks afterwards when I was in the Royal Room waiting for Princess Christian to arrive one of the porters came to me and said, 'You have been making enquiries for a pearl necklace'. I said, 'Yes what about it?' He replied, 'I found it on the day of the wedding and thinking it was a cheap one I gave it to my girl in London.' After seeing HRH to the saloon I told him to get in the train and fetch it. I then phoned my Supt at Paddington and told him and asked for someone to go with him to get it, this he did, and it was brought back to his office, he then took the man to Lady Mount Stephens' town house and she being there it was given to her. She gave the porter the £50 reward and asked what would be done to him, the Supt replied that he would be dismissed and then she said she would find him something to do, he was a smart young man and could drive a car so she got him the position of chauffeur to Lady Burnham where he was for a long time and perhaps is now, he called several times to see me.
>
> When it was examined it was found the diamond clasp had given way as she was entering the carriage and one pearl was missing, all the staff searched the yard as she offered £5 reward for it, but there was no luck, so I sent to his landlady and asked her to search her rooms and one day she said she was sweeping the kitchen and found it, but said nothing until she had taken it to Lady Mount Stephens and received the £5. When she came back she told me and I asked when she found it and she said after I sent to ask her to search, so apparently the kitchen was not swept very often or she had found it before. The jewellers who made the necklace told me they had two packs of pearls to match them – and so that was the end of that excitement.

The invited guests stream towards one of the special trains from Paddington that will take them to the Garden Party at Windsor Castle in 1908. *British Rail*

An unusual view of the upside of Windsor station, looking towards the buffer stops. Platform 4 (*left*), line leading to high level goods sidings (*right*). Photographed in 1919. *LGRP*

Not much more than a year later there was another Royal wedding, that between Princess Margaret of Connaught (another niece) and Prince Gustavus Adolphus of Sweden and Norway on 15th June, 1905 in St George's Chapel. Maun received two tickets to the ceremony and his wife and sister attended the event. The following week the King had a garden party at the castle to which 10,000 guests were invited. No less than 12 special trains were despatched from Paddington in an hour, and they arrived like clockwork every 5 minutes! Even with its four platforms, Windsor must have been hard pressed to clear the trains quickly to allow subsequent trains to arrive without delay. The empty coaches would need to be removed to Slough once the commodious goods yard had been filled up with stock. The return specials began at 6 pm.

Samuel Maun mentioned in passing that on one occasion Mark Twain the celebrated American author was invited to a garden party. Maun put him in a carriage to the Castle, but chancing to come to the front of the station about half an hour later, saw Twain still sitting in the carriage. Maun asked if he had been to the Castle, to which the American replied, 'Oh yes, but they sent us back for another run round!' Later Maun ascertained that because of the punctuality of the special trains bringing the visitors, the Castle staff had been unable to unload the horse drawn vehicles quickly enough and had sent some back to make room for others.

On another occasion a garden party coincided with Windsor races and the times of the races were advanced so that all the return race specials could leave before the garden party guest trains were due to return. Unfortunately at about 4.30 pm it began to rain heavily and many of the guests at the garden party made a dash to the station 'and so got all amongst the racing people and I am sorry to say many lost their tiepins and watches'. The station master was forced to listen to numerous complaints but pointed out to these people that they knew the time the King had ordered their special trains to leave and that they shouldn't have come to the station early! This may well have been 20th June, 1908, on which date the GWR Magazine records that eleven special trains ran for 4,000 guests as well as four special trains for 2,000 race-goers (see Chapter Nine).

The boys of Eton College were also regular users of the branch. When they were going away for long leave or at the end of term two special trains were provided for them. Another occasion when the boys needed special transport was the annual Eton and Harrow cricket match held in London. On 4th June each year there was a 'great celebration' [to celebrate King George III's birthday] at the College, speeches in the morning, cricket in the afternoon and 'a procession of boats on the river about 6.30 pm, the cox in each boat being dressed as an Admiral, the others being in fancy dress'. Great crowds of parents arrived by special trains in the morning; the celebrations concluded with fireworks after dark and two special trains returned to London with weary guests between 10.30 and 11 pm, or later if it was a very light evening.

November 1907 saw the arrival of the Emperor (Kaiser) and Empress of Germany for a state visit. During their stay there was a state banquet one evening, a theatrical performance the next night and the following day the

GREAT WESTERN RAILWAY.

Circular No. 1965.

GENERAL MANAGER'S OFFICE,

PADDINGTON STATION,

LONDON, W.,

5th September, 1904.

ALTERATIONS IN NAMES OF STATIONS.

The name of Windsor Station has been changed to

"**WINDSOR & ETON**"; and from *October 1st* the name of Dynevor

Station will be altered to "**SKEWEN.**"

All letters and invoices must be directed, and all trucks

labelled accordingly.

Acknowledge receipt to Head of your Department.

JAMES C. INGLIS,

General Manager.

Windsor station was renamed Windsor & Eton in 1904.

CRICKET MATCH

AT LORDS

A great social occasion – as well as a cricket match – the annual
Eton v. Harrow Cricket Match at Lords.
Courtesy Modern Postcards Wholesale, Hounslow

Llanelly choir, 200 of them, arrived in a special train to sing before Their Majesties in the evening. Returning to South Wales the next morning they were at the station in time to greet the Empress of Germany who was off to London to visit the German Hospital. As she passed by on her way to the train, the choir sang 'Land of my Fathers' which pleased the Empress greatly and she waved to the Welshmen as she went by. Afterwards Mr Maun had some difficulty getting the choir into the train as they were singing in groups on the platform!

A couple of nights earlier, after the State banquet, the guests' special was about to leave at 1.30 am (another long day for the station master) when Lord Roseberry called Maun to the train and asked him if he had seen the German Ambassador, to which Maun replied 'No'. 'Well', said Roseberry, 'there he is in the corner and if you keep this train so hot, there will only be his bones when we reach Paddington!' Maun had the steam pressure reduced but as he remarked to his diary ruefully, 'One would have thought that on a cold morning they would have been glad of a warm compartment, but I suppose they had something at the Castle that warmed them and they were smoking cigars.'

At the conclusion of the Kaiser's visit Samuel Maun was presented with the Order of the Royal Crown by the Kaiser in the Royal waiting room. This was a gold cross with a crown in the centre surrounded with a thin band of blue enamel on which were the words 'God and my right' (in German).

The Royal Family's routine at this time was to use Windsor at Easter and for a garden party in the summer and again in November if there was a state visit. Whilst the Royal Family were at Balmoral one autumn, a foreign Queen paid a private visit to see over the Castle. Returning to the station somewhat exhausted, she asked if she could have some biscuits to eat, which Maun dutifully obtained from the Refreshment Room. Unfortunately she did not offer to pay for them so the station master had to stand the cost!

The November 1909 state visit was by King Manuel of Portugal, at the conclusion of which the latter presented Samuel Maun with a diamond pin with the initials 'M' in its centre in diamonds and a diamond crown on the top. This, sadly, was the last visit to Windsor by King Edward VII, who died in May 1910. Some details of the funeral, as described by Maun, appear in the next chapter. Before the coronation of King George V, the new King, while on his way from Windsor to London, summoned Mr Maun to the Royal waiting room and presented him with the medal of the Royal Victorian Order to acknowledge all the work he had done on his father's behalf.

Princess Alice regularly travelled to London by train and on one occasion Maun had shown her to her reserved compartment when she called him back because there was a large moth in the compartment. In Maun's words:

> I said I would catch it and went in the compartment; it was flying about as I was striking at it, when she said, 'Here it is' and I went to strike at it and she moved her head on one side and instead of hitting the moth I caught her slap on the cheek. She laughed and said it was her fault, but we caught it afterwards. She never forgot it and often said afterwards, 'No moths this morning'. She was a charming lady and used to send me a present each Christmas and a card enclosed on which was written 'From Alice'.

Princess Alice was obviously a great favourite with Maun; she died aged 97 in 1981.

The November 1913 state visit was by the Archduke Ferdinand and the Archduchess of Austria. This proved to be the last state visit for several years because the following summer the Archduke was assassinated at Sarajevo which led to the start of World War I.

The State visits may have ceased but the King made several journeys by train each year on visits of inspection of the troops. On these journeys the LNWR Royal train of 14 vehicles was used because it had sleeping accommodation. Maun was kept busy because whenever there were Zeppelin air raids at night he was called out, sometimes being called up on two or three occasions in one night (the station master's house was on the first floor of the station building). In those days trains were completely stopped during the warning period, and delays could be substantial:

> When there was a raid on the trains they had to stop where they were, and on one occasion Sir Douglas Barry had been to a meeting in Windsor and came to catch the 9.52 pm train but as I had heard the warning I could not let it go, and after some time, he said to me, 'What am I to do?', I said, 'You can come and sit in my office. I have a fire but no light'. We sat there until after midnight when I went in the house and fetched some whisky and biscuits. We then refreshed ourselves and sat chatting until 4.30 am when I had the 'All Clear' and started the train. The next day his wife wrote me a nice letter of thanks for looking after him and he sent me a silver cigarette case with the inscription
>
> 'S.T.M. from D.H.B.
> A friend in need is a friend indeed
> Windsor Station
> March 31st to April 1st, 1916'

A friend of mine sat with us as he had come to meet his sons from London, he waited until 5.0 am when the train arrived; it had been stopped at Langley, two stations away and they had got out and walked home, and when he got there he found them safe in bed, we often joked him about it being April 1st and he sitting up all night.

Towards the end of the War the order to stop all trains was relaxed and they continued to run, but in complete darkness.

On 11th November, 1918 Maun had just started the 8.47 am train and on going back to his office found HRH Princess Alice standing at the door. She said, 'I have some news for you; the Armistice was signed in a railway coach at 6 am but it is not to be made known until 11 am. I was sure you would like to know, so don't tell anyone until then!' At 11 am the news was announced by the Mayor from the Town Hall.

In 1919 the British aviators John Alcock and Arthur Brown who were the first to fly the Atlantic, came to Windsor to receive their knighthoods from the King. The streets were full of crowds and on the way back from the Castle to the station the carriage was surrounded by Eton Boys, who in their enthusiasm to meet the pair, wrenched the door off the Royal Carriage! Maun relates that Alcock and Brown made good their escape from the other side of the vehicle, ran up No. 1 platform and across the line to No. 4 platform where their train was standing and thus away from the press of well-wishers. Sadly, only months later, Alcock was killed in a flying accident.

As station master Maun had to be prepared for all eventualities and be able to deal with them. These ranged from dealing with tricksters, to turning a blind eye to the odd indiscretion and, rarely, the bad behaviour of people who should have known better. Here are three examples from the diary:

> I had many strange experiences during my time at Windsor, it was surprising the number of people who came to ask me to let them have a ticket to London with all sorts of excuses, in some cases I did, and others I had to say 'No', but I may say I did not always have the money sent as so faithfully promised. I remember one occasion a gentleman came to me just before the train was due to leave and said, 'Station master will you let me have a First Return ticket to London and I will pay you when I return this evening, I am staying at the White Hart Hotel, and have come away without any cash and there is not time to go back for it.' He took out his silver card case and said 'This is my card', so I let him have the ticket, I did not see him return but the next morning I saw him passing the station and he said 'I was late last night in returning but my servant will bring you the cash for the ticket (8/6d.)' but no servant arrived and the next day I went to the Hotel and enquired but he had gone and not paid them and he had no servant with him. I then wrote to the address on the card but my letter was returned 'Not Known' so that 8/6d. was gone. A few days afterwards a detective came to my office and gave me a description of the man he was enquiring for and asked if I had seen him. I then took his card and the returned letter from my desk and gave them to him. He said, 'Yes, that is the man'. He had been to a jewellers shop and asked for some silver cases to be sent to the White Hart for him to choose from, this was done but he made off with them and as I have said without paying his bill. The detective took the card but I don't think he was found.

Maun's sense of discretion was such that when he described the next incident in his diary, possibly 20 years after the event, he did not identify those involved:

> One evening Lord . . . came from London and I saw he was looking for someone and as I knew him I said, 'Are you looking for someone', and he said, 'Yes, do you know if there is a car to meet me', and I sent my Cab Inspector to see if there was one, but there was not. I then asked if I could do anything as I knew the lady he was expecting and he said, 'Can you ring up Mrs D. . . and ask if she is sending the car for me'. I asked him into the office as it was a cold January evening whilst I went to the phone. I got the lady and asked if she was sending the car for Lord C. . . but she said 'No, tell him to get here the best way he can'. I did not like to give him this message so I said, 'She is not sending the car, will you take a taxi?' This he did and when he returned he thanked me for the trouble I had taken, but Mrs D. . . afterwards became Her Ladyship – he was a very important person in the Government.

Finally, and probably unusually, because it is the only such incident recorded in the diary, some rather undeserved treatment from an unexpected quarter:

> An incident happened on the evening of one Fourth of June, a Royal Duke and Duchess and family came down in the morning for the celebrations at Eton College and when they arrived he asked me to reserve a compartment for them on the first special in the evening. I said I would on the 10.30 pm (we had three specials after the fireworks at 10.30 pm, 10.40 pm and 11.00 pm). In the evening they dined with

his brother at Henry III Tower, Windsor Castle, and when it was time for the train to start there was no sign of them and the train was full. I held it until 10.35 pm and then I started it and just as it left the platform they came running up and he said 'Is that the train going out?' and I said 'Yes I could not keep it any longer', and he shouted out 'Oh you B.F., you ought to be shot'. I said 'Thank you, but there is another train in five minutes' and I took them to the compartment I had reserved. When they were in he said 'I will write to the Chairman (Lord Churchill) about you'. Just then I saw my Superintendent from Paddington was near and I called him and said to the Duke 'This is my Supt perhaps you would like to speak to him?' – My Superintendent said, 'The Station Master could not keep the train any longer it was quite full'. The Duke replied 'Oh you B.F. you ought to be shot, I will write to the Chairman about you'. My Superintendent took out his card and said 'Please attach that to your letter and he will know who to enquire for'.

This was a Saturday and in the Sunday papers was, 'Who was the Cavalry Officer who used such insulting language to the Station Master on Windsor platform last night?'. The Duke was a Colonel of the Life Guards.

He evidently wrote to Lord Churchill the same night while he was feeling furious for his Lordship came down to see me about it on Monday. He said that the Duke had written to him the same night, but the next morning when he had thought over what he had done he wrote him another letter asking if he could see me, and ask me to forgive and forget it all as he was quite in the wrong. I said I would, and his Lordship said he was sure the Duke was very sorry. When King Edward saw it in the Sunday paper I was told he was very furious and I expect told the Duke so.

The Duke came down a few weeks afterwards and on the platform he put his hand on my shoulder and said. 'I am sorry, forgive and forget it all'. I told him that I would and we were good friends afterwards. The Duchess took some little time before she would speak to me and we had been good friends before, and when they were living at one of Towers she used to send for me to go and see her to arrange journeys for herself and the children, but she became alright [sic] in time.

On 3rd April, 1925, exactly 22 years after his first day at Windsor, Maun became 65 and had to retire. As might be expected after such a long tenure he was well known in the town and received many presents. From the townspeople he received a handsome cheque and a 'beautiful illuminated album with an address' presented by the Mayor. The Colonel and officers of the Royal Horse Guards presented a drawing room clock, the Rectors of Beaumont College made a gift of some silver vases and from Eton College he received another generous cheque and a letter of thanks for all his help over the years. His own staff at Windsor station gave him a Sheraton clock.

In June when the Royal family returned to Windsor for Ascot Races he was summoned to the Castle and there King George V presented him with a gold tiepin with 'G.V.' in blue enamel in the centre, and a gold crown on the top surrounded with pearls. He had 'a long chat' with the King about past days. As a sign of how, even then, things were beginning to change and the railway was no longer the sole means of getting from 'A' to 'B' quickly, the King made a telling comment:

'When I first came here I had to drive to Paddington, train to Windsor, and drove to the Castle. Now I get in my car at the front door and am at Buckingham Palace in 45 minutes. Don't you think it is more convenient?' I replied, 'Yes, sir, although I am a railway man it does seem so'.

Maun remarks that after his retirement the Royal waiting room was little used as the Royal family tended to travel by car more often, at least for the short journey to London.

A year after his retirement the General Strike took place and Samuel Maun was asked to return, briefly, to his old command to enable the present station master to work the signal box. All the staff were on strike apart from the foreman, so with him and a supernumerary from the town Maun kept the service going. He says, 'We had some young men who could drive cars and they took on the engines and they managed very well, indeed without any mishaps'.

It has only been possible to give a flavour of Maun's diary in this chapter. The document itself translates into 35 typewritten sheets of A4 size paper, so it is a lengthy piece of work. However it must be said that it does not describe in much detail the ordinary work of the station or those who manned it. Most of it is taken up with Maun's involvement with Royal occasions, but written so long after the event possibly these were the events best remembered. In any case it is a valuable historical document and we must be grateful to Samuel Maun for recording matters which otherwise would have been lost for ever. He died in 1948.

Windsor Castle, Norman Gate.   *British Rail*

Chapter Eight
Four Royal Funerals

Windsor station has been the scene of many momentous happenings, many happy, some sad; some are described in station master Maun's diary. Because of the proximity of Windsor Castle there were the great Royal events, the State visits, the Weddings, Queen Victoria's constant use of the train. Garden Parties at the Castle brought the rich and famous to the town, Ascot races brought thousands of others who would be rich! Eton scholars used the trains at the beginning and end of term, for the annual Eton v. Harrow cricket match and their parents arrived by train for Founder's Day, on 4th June each year. The importance of the station master here, in the Director's eyes, probably ranked only slightly below that of Paddington – in fact the station master before Maun went to Paddington on promotion. It was truly a 'top hat and tails' job and in the days before road vehicles provided personally-tailored journeys, there cannot have been many days without a VIP at Windsor.

Of all the events with which the Windsor S.M. had to deal, perhaps the most important were the Royal funerals. When Queen Victoria died in 1901, having been on the throne since 1837, the railway had not previously been involved in the conveyance of a body of a dead Monarch to its last resting place. Sadly only nine years later, in 1910, the event was repeated when King Edward VII passed away. The administrative work involved in planning the events was colossal, due protocol and pomp having to be observed in full measure. However the GWR rose to the occasion three times before it was nationalised in 1948 and British Railways, Western Region was able to draw heavily on the GWR records of the 1936 funeral when it was called upon to convey the body of King George VI to Windsor in 1952. It would be impossible to replicate these comprehensive arrangements, involving five or six special trains, nowadays, with the branch reduced to a single line and one platform at Windsor, although a *much* simpler operation would still be possible. For that reason this chapter sets out, in some detail, the railway's involvement in four solemn occasions in the first half of the 20th century. It is rather strange that three out of the four events took place at the same time of the year, a period little more than a fortnight long at the end of January to the middle of February.

1901

Queen Victoria died at Osborne on 22nd January, 1901. The remainder of the Household and the Horses and Carriages returned to Windsor by special train at 12.38 pm from Southampton on 30th January, 1901. Running via the West Curve at Slough the train arrived at Windsor at 3.02 pm. The Queen's mortal remains were brought to Gosport in the Royal yacht on 1st February and a special train left there at 8.53 am (8 minutes late) on Saturday 2nd February, 1901. Arriving at Victoria just before 11 am, the coffin was carried on a gun carriage in procession to Paddington, while the funeral coach itself, the late Queen's (GWR) Saloon No. 229, was transferred via Battersea, Addison Road (Kensington), Uxbridge Road, Westbourne Park to Paddington, where it was placed in the GWR Royal Train.

Paddington, 'spacious, substantial and with a solemn dignity of its own', as *The Times* described it, had been prepared for its important role but,

GREAT WESTERN RAILWAY.

TIME TABLE

OF

ROYAL TRAIN

CONVEYING

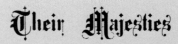

THE

KING and QUEEN

And their Imperial and Royal Guests,

FROM

PADDINGTON to WINDSOR

AND BACK,

IN CONNECTION WITH THE FUNERAL OF

Her Majesty Queen Victoria,

ON

Saturday, February 2nd, 1901.

WYMAN & SONS, Ltd., Printers, 63, Carter Lane, Doctors' Commons, E.C.

The timetable for the Royal funeral train, 2nd February, 1901.

The Public Record Office, Kew

TIME TABLES

SATURDAY, FEBRUARY 2ND, 1901.

DOWN TRAIN.

Miles distant from Paddington. M.	C.	STATIONS AND SIGNAL BOXES.		Via Main Line Subway Junction to Slough. About P.M.
...		PADDINGTON ...	dep.	1 0
	38¼	Westbourne Bridge *	pass	—
	51¾	Lord Hill's Junction	,,	—
	71¾	Subway Junction	,,	1 6
1	12½	Green Lane	,,	—
1	30¼	Portobello	,,	—
1	66½	Ladbroke Bridge	,,	—
2	64	West London Jct. East ...	,,	1 8½
3	18¼	West London Jct. West ...	,,	—
3	53	Friars Junction	,,	—
4	13¾	Acton, East	,,	—
4	25¼	,, Middle	,,	1 10½
4	61	,, West	,,	—
5	48	Ealing	,,	1 12
6	47½	West Ealing	,,	1 14
7	24	Hanwell	,,	—
8	58½	Southall, East Junction ...	,,	—
9	2	,, East	,,	—
9	15½	,, Middle	,,	1 17
9	42	,, West	,,	—
10	70½	Hayes	,,	—
12	2¾	Dawley	,,	—
13	10	West Drayton East	,,	1 22½
13	33¼	,, ,, West	,,	—
15	3¼	Iver Box	,,	—
16	17	Langley	,,	—
17	25	Dolphin	,,	—
18	30½	Slough, East	,,	1 29
18	44	,, Middle ... ... * ...	,,	—
18	59½	,, Bath Road	,,	—
19	71	Eton...	,,	—
21	10	WINDSOR	arr.	1 35

REMARKS.

PILOT SERVICE.—The Special Train from Paddington to Windsor, starting from No. 9 Line about 10 minutes in advance of the Royal Train will act as "Pilot" to that Train, and must occupy the same time in running between Stations as shewn for the Royal Train. The "Pilot" will be distinguished by Special Head Signals as specified in Clause 14 of the Special Instructions.

THE ROYAL TRAIN.—The Royal Train will start from No 8 Platform, and pass over the Empty Engine and Carriage Lines to Subway Junction, as shewn in Clause 1 of the Special Instructions.

The exact starting time of the Royal Train is somewhat uncertain, but at whatever time it starts it must occupy the same time in running between Stations as shewn in the Time Table.

* The time allowed at this point of the journey provides for the necessary slackening of speed in accordance with the special and standard instructions.

RETURN TRAIN.

Miles distant from Windsor. M.	C.	STATIONS AND SIGNAL BOXES.		Via Main Line from Slough. About P.M.
...		WINDSOR	dep.	3 30
1	19	Eton	pass	
2	30½	Slough, Bath Road	,,	
2	46	,, Middle .. * ...	,,	
2	59½	,, East	,,	3 36
3	65	Dolphin	,,	—
4	73	Langley	,,	—
6	6¾	Iver Box	,,	
7	56¾	West Drayton, West ...	,,	
8	0	,, East	,,	3 42
9	7¼	Dawley	,,	—
10	19½	Hayes	,,	—
11	48	Southall, West	,	—
11	74½	,, Middle	,,	3 46½
12	8	,, East	,,	—
12	31½	,, East Junc. ...	,,	—
13	66	Hanwell	,,	—
14	42½	West Ealing	,,	—
15	42	Ealing	,,	—
16	29	Acton, West	,,	—
16	64¾	,, Middle	,,	3 52½
16	76¼	,, East	,,	—
17	37	Friars Junction	,,	—
17	71¾	West London Junc., West ...	,,	—
18	26	,, ,, East ...	,,	3 55
19	23½	Ladbroke Bridge	,,	—
19	59¾	Portobello	,,	—
19	77½	Green Lane	,,	3 57
20	18¼	Subway Junction	,,	—
20	38¼	Lord Hill's Junction.. ...	,,	—
20	51¾	Westbourne Bridge ...	,,	—
21	10	PADDINGTON	arr.	4 0

REMARKS.

PILOT SERVICE.—Either a Pilot Engine, or one of the Return Specials acting as "Pilot" will start from Windsor for Paddington, about 10 minutes in advance of the Royal Train, and must occupy the same time in running between Stations as shewn for the Royal Train. The "Pilot" will be distinguished by Special Head Signals, as specified in Clause 14 of the Special Instructions.

ROYAL TRAIN.—The exact starting time of the return Royal Train is somewhat uncertain, but at whatever time it starts it must occupy the same time in running between Stations as shewn in the Time Table.

* The time allowed at this point of the journey provides for the necessary slackening of speed in accordance with the standard instructions.

The enclosed Form of Receipt for this notice must be forwarded to me in a foolscap envelope **BY NEXT TRAIN,** and the envelope marked outside, in red ink, "Receipt for Royal Train Notice," and the Guards must be instructed to personally deliver these letters immediately on arrival at Paddington.

An acknowledgment BY WIRE must also be sent, immediately the notice is received.

T. I. ALLEN,
Superintendent of the Line.

PADDINGTON, *February 1st*, 1901.

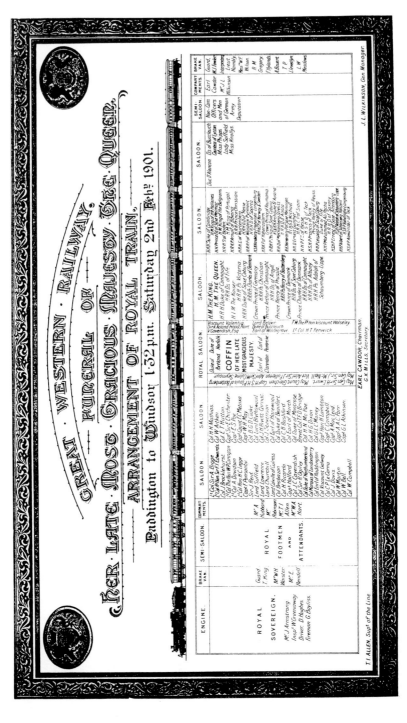

The seating plan for the Royal Train, 2nd February, 1901.

Madame Tussaud's Collection

With a wise discretion, the draping of the station was not carried very far. The utilitarian severity of this busy centre of traffic would have been rendered incongruous rather than impressive by a too ambitious attempt to change its natural aspect.

The main arrival platform of the station was used for the Queen's last journey, for as *The Times* explained:

> ... though the ordinary departure platform of the GWR affords an admirable approach and exit, the offices and waiting rooms which stand between the approach and the platforms present obvious disadvantages for the proper ordering of solemn offices. It was, therefore, decided that the departure should take place from the arrival platform (No. 8) to which access is given from Praed Street by a broad carriageway extending the full length of the platform and passing out at the other end of the station into Bishop's Road.

The platform was covered with a thick crimson carpet, 'upon it . . . arranged two very beautiful patterns of white flowers, backed by palms and evergreens.'

Special trains for guests and officials were timed to leave Paddington for Windsor at 12 noon, 12.10, 12.30 and 12.50 pm, the last acting as 'Pilot' (i.e. proving the line was clear) to the Royal Train which was expected to leave at 1 pm.

At half-past 12 the head of the Royal procession entered the station from Praed Street. At its head were the trumpeters and bands of the Household cavalry, followed by detachments of many regiments which marched past the Royal Train, continued on and left the station by the Bishop's Road exit. Eventually, preceded by massed military bands playing Beethoven's 'Funeral March' the gun carriage holding the coffin, hauled by eight horses, entered the station and halted opposite the carriage which would convey it to Windsor. Every eye gazed upon the sad spectacle, so much so that at first no one noticed the arrival of the King, the German Emperor and 'the brilliant company of Kings, Princes and Royal dukes which followed behind them'. Finally six more carriages drove in, containing the Queen, the other ladies of the Royal family, the King of the Belgians and others.

The Royal Train, hauled by the 4–4–0 locomotive *Royal Sovereign* (actually No. 3373 *Atbara* in disguise), consisted of eight 8-wheel coaches: five saloons, the Queen's coach (No. 229) and two brakevans, most of which had been built as recently as 1897 for the late Queen's Diamond Jubilee. One of the carriages however, the previously mentioned No. 229, was a rebuild of a much earlier 6-wheel carriage which Her Majesty had a great liking for and was therefore retained, extended by 11 ft in length and with another pair of wheels added. Into this vehicle, draped in purple and white satin, the Queen's coffin was loaded for its journey to Windsor. The engine driver was Mr David Hughes, Royal Train driver since 1891, who retired in 1907.

So time consuming had been the procession to the station that the Royal Train, the last in the procession of five special trains, did not leave until 1.35 pm immediately preceded by the special timed for 12.50 pm. An eye witness, who was adjacent to the funeral coach, told the *Railway Gazette* some 35 years later that after the GWR guard had locked the doors of the funeral coach he heard King Edward say to the German Emperor, 'Come

David Hughes, Royal Train driver photographed holding the timetable for the Royal funeral train; note the armband. *British Rail*

The locomotive allocated to haul the Royal Train on 2nd February, 1901; No. 3173 was renamed *Royal Sovereign* for the duty. *LGRP*

Queen Victoria's funeral procession leaves Windsor station for the Castle; King Edward VII is immediately right of the nearest gas lamp. *British Rail*

GREAT WESTERN RAILWAY.

FUNERAL

OF

Her late Majesty Queen Victoria

On SATURDAY, FEBRUARY 2nd, 1901,

The Train Service throughout the Great Western Company's system will be the same as on Sundays, with the following modifications, viz.:—

The 5.30 a.m. and 5.40 a.m. Newspaper Trains from Paddington will run as usual as far as Plymouth and Swansea respectively, with connections to the Weymouth Line, Torquay, Kingswear and Penzance, and also to Oxford, Birmingham, Wolverhampton, Dudley, Worcester, Malvern, &c.

The 12.0 night Train from Paddington to Penzance, and the 12.15 night Train from Paddington to Birmingham, Chester, Birkenhead and Liverpool will run as usual.

LONDON AND WINDSOR SERVICE.

The 1.0 p.m. Sunday Train from Paddington to Windsor will not run.

The 10.30 a.m., 10.35 a.m., 1.50 p.m. and 2.20 p.m. Sunday Trains from Paddington will not convey passengers to Windsor.

Windsor Station will be closed for public traffic from 11.0 a.m. until 2.30 p.m.

LONDON SUBURBAN SERVICE.

The following Trains will run as on Week Days in addition to the usual Sunday service :—

8.0 a.m. Southall to Paddington.
7.45 a.m. Windsor to Paddington.
8.0 a.m. Reading to Paddington.
8.50 a.m. Southall to Paddington.
8.53 a.m. Uxbridge to Paddington.

A Train will run from Southall to Paddington at 10.0 a.m., calling at intermediate Stations.

The 11.25 a.m. Sunday Train from High Wycombe to Paddington will be half an hour later at all Stations.

SAILINGS—NEW MILFORD AND WATERFORD.

There will be no Steamer from Waterford to New Milford on Friday, February 1st, nor from New Milford to Waterford on Sunday morning, February 3rd.

The issue of Week-end Excursion Tickets to Windsor and the Half-day Excursion Tickets to London will be suspended.

For particulars of any additional Local arrangements on other parts of the Line, see Special announcements issued locally.

J. L. WILKINSON, General Manager.

Paddington Station, January, 1901.

Wyman & Sons, Ltd., Printers, 63, Carter Lane, Doctors' Commons, E.C.

Poster notifying the public that a Sunday train service will operate on the day of Queen Victoria's funeral.   *Oakwood Collection*

along, hurry up, we are 20 minutes late already', whereupon the Royal party entrained with alacrity! (The same correspondent described the effect of the funeral music under Paddington's roof as 'stupendously overwhelming'.) Apart from the Royal travellers, on board were the GWR's Chairman, Earl Cawdor and Deputy Chairman; Mr Wilkinson, the General Manager and other high officials. Thirty-five minutes were allowed for the journey to Windsor which was reached at 2.10 pm.

Here, the Royal waiting rooms had been beautifully decorated by the Royal gardeners. Railway arrangements at this end were in the hands of Mr J. Morris the assistant superintendent and the station master, Mr S.F. Johnson. Non-commissioned officers of the First Grenadier guards carried the coffin from the train, to the gun carriage which was to convey the late Queen to her final resting place in Windsor Castle.

Then the unthinkable happened. One of the team of six horses pulling the gun carriage, already restive because of the delay and the intense cold, possibly frightened by the massed bands or the firing of guns became alarmed and, kicking out with its hind legs, became entangled in the draw-gear to which the horses were harnessed, eventually smashing it. It was decided to unhitch the horses and after raiding the station for ropes and even communication cords from the trains, a team of sailors took the place of the horses, hauling the carriage swiftly to the castle. As the *Windsor & Eton Express* said, 'surely all the history of royal funerals can show nothing to equal to this.'

After the service the King and Queen and many of their guests remained at Windsor, while the others returned to town after partaking of luncheon.

1910

Only nine years after the death of Queen Victoria, Windsor station again had the solemn task of receiving the body of a dead Monarch, on his last journey to burial in the grounds of Windsor Castle.

Friday 20th May, 1910 dawned bright and quickly became very hot in contrast to torrential rain earlier in the week. From nine o'clock Big Ben tolled every minute which was very effective in creating an atmosphere of solemnity.

The day had been declared a national day of mourning and the railways were running a Sunday service. Windsor station was closed completely to the public between 10.30 am and 1 pm. No ordinary *down* line passengers were able to arrive at Windsor between 10.30 am and 6 pm. However in the up direction, the Sunday service was planned to be withdrawn at 1.30 pm and a special service of *up* trains run as required by circumstances (fast trains to Slough, Westbourne Park and Paddington only, stopping trains calling at all stations to Paddington), after which the Sunday service would be restored. In the event this plan would have had to be modified because of the late start of the funeral service. To cater for local passengers the GWR's road motor service between Slough and Windsor was increased 'according to circumstances', but at a flat fare of 6d., any journey, and with buses terminating at the river bridge in Windsor.

King Edward's body had been lying in state at Westminster Hall and had been visited by an estimated 400,000 people, many standing in pouring rain for many hours before reaching the head of the queue – some never succeeding in gaining entry to the Hall before it closed each night. The royal procession left Buckingham Palace at 9.10 am, behind the King 'were no fewer than 17 lines of foreign Royalties, riding three abreast . . . over 50 of them in the procession'. In addition to the escort of Life Guards there were also 12 carriages including two closed carriages conveying Queen Mary and Queen Alexandra, the Queen Mother.

By the time the procession, now including the gun carriage containing King Edward's remains, left Palace Yard, Westminster the heat was intense and many onlookers and some soldiers lining the route, collapsed in the heat.

Ordinary traffic at Paddington Station was suspended at 10 am; at the King's command the station was entirely without decoration. At 11 am the advance guard of the procession entered the station by the roadway leading from Praed Street to platform eight; not until 11.30 however did the band of the Guard's Brigade immediately preceding the King arrive at the station.

Prior to the arrival of the coffin and the Royal family and Kings and Queens from other countries, a startling accident had occurred at the station. An unidentified person had mounted to the glass roof above the station (presumably for the purpose of photographing or just to obtain a private view) and had inadvertently put his foot through one of the glass panes, fragments of which descended upon one of the viewing stands below. Very fortunately no injuries were sustained in this mishap. Amazingly a similar incident had occurred at Queen Victoria's funeral.

Four trains conveying guests were despatched from Paddington at 11.00, 11.10, 11.20, 11.30 am; these trains conveyed 356, 302, 45 and 9 passengers respectively. A special train for those involved in the Procession left at 11.50 am, conveying 248 guests and hauled by 'Star' class 4–6–0 locomotive No. 4023 *King George*, less than a year old. The Royal Train, containing the coffin, the Royal family and the crowned heads of Europe, was timed to leave at 12 noon from platform 8, but actually left three minutes before that time, hauled by the almost new 'Star' class 4–6–0 No. 4021 *King Edward*.

As the Royal Train crossed the River Thames bridge at Windsor the Union Jack was lowered from its flagstaff on the Round Tower of Windsor Castle and replaced by the Royal Standard. A couple of minutes later, the train eased slowly into platform 4 at Windsor Station, which was closed to the public from 9 am–2.30 pm. King George V was the first to alight: while the coffin was being unloaded the King and the other mourners stood with bowed heads; while the procession from the station to St George's Chapel was being made ready the Royal ladies retired to the Royal Waiting Room.

Remembering the near catastrophe that had occurred at Queen Victoria's funeral, on this occasion it had been decided to exclude horses from the procession to St George's Chapel. A contingent of sailors pulled the gun carriage conveying the coffin, as had had to be so hastily arranged for the late Queen; everybody else in the procession marched or walked to the Chapel. Queen Alexandra, the Queen Mother, however, rode in a coach pulled by a pair of greys, immediately following the King. The procession left via High Street, Park Street and the Long Walk, followed for a short distance by eight carriages conveying Queen Mary and the other Royal lady mourners which,

GREAT WESTERN RAILWAY.

...TIME TABLE...

FOR THE JOURNEY OF

Their Majesties the King and Queen,

Her Majesty Queen Alexandra,

AND

Their Imperial and Royal Guests,

FROM

PADDINGTON to WINDSOR and ETON,

ON

FRIDAY, MAY 20th, 1910,

... ON THE OCCASION OF THE FUNERAL OF ....
HIS LATE MAJESTY KING EDWARD VII.

Paddington · · · ·	depart	12. 0 noon.
Windsor & Eton · ·	arrive	12.35 p.m.

JAMES C. INGLIS,
General Manager.

ACTUAL RUNNING TIMES:

Paddington (dep.)	...	...	...	11.57 a.m.
Southall (pass)	...	...	...	12.15 p.m.
Slough "	...	...	...	12.25½ "
Windsor (arr.)	...	...	...	12.32 "

GREAT WESTERN RAILWAY.

Circular No. 2195.

GENERAL MANAGER'S OFFICE,
PADDINGTON STATION,
LONDON, W.

14th May, 1910.

Friday, May 20th, being the day fixed for the Funeral of HIS LATE MAJESTY KING EDWARD VII, will be observed as a day of general mourning, and business throughout the country will be practically suspended.

The train services of the Company will accordingly be reduced within the smallest limits compatible with requirements, and as far as may be practicable the staff will be released from their duties.

JAMES C. INGLIS,

General Manager.

Notice informing staff that the day fixed for the funeral of King Edward VII would be a day of general mourning.

GREAT WESTERN RAILWAY.

TIME TABLE

OF

ROYAL TRAIN

CONVEYING

Their Majesties

THE

KING and QUEEN

And Their Imperial and Royal Guests,

FROM

PADDINGTON TO WINDSOR & ETON

AND BACK,

IN CONNECTION WITH THE FUNERAL OF

His late Majesty King Edward VII.

ON

Friday, May 20th, 1910.

☞ In cases where the supply of this notice is sent out direct by me a special form of receipt, printed on pink paper, will accompany the notice, and this receipt must be carefully filled up and forwarded to me **BY NEXT TRAIN.** The envelopes containing the receipts must be marked outside "Receipt for Royal Train Notice," and Guards must be instructed to personally deliver these letters immediately on arrival at Paddington.

In cases where this notice is distributed locally receipt must be acknowledged **without delay** to your Superior Officer.

J. MORRIS;

May 18th, 1910.   *Superintendent of the Line.*

The timetable for the Royal funeral train, 20th May, 1910.

The Public Record Office, Kew

TIME TABLES—FRIDAY, MAY 20TH, 1910.
FORWARD JOURNEY.—PADDINGTON TO WINDSOR & ETON.

Distance from Paddington.		STATIONS.		NOON	REMARKS.
Miles	Chains				
—	—	PADDINGTON ... ... dep.		12 0	The Down Royal Train will start from No. 8 Arrival Line, pass along the Down Engine and Carriage Line as far as Subway Junction, passing on to the Down Main Line at Subway Junction. The speed over this portion of the Line must not exceed 10 miles per hour.
	72	Subway Junction		P.M. 12 6	The working of the Permissive Block Telegraph on the Down Engine and Carriage Line between the Arrival Box and Subway Junction must be suspended from 11·0 a.m. until after the Royal Train has passed, and the Special Absolute Block Telegraph Working, as set out in clause 6, page 3, and in Notice No. 50 issued by the Divisional Superintendent, must be strictly observed.
					All catch points and facing points, except facing points No. 27, on the Down Engine and Carriage Line over which the Royal Train will pass must be clipped and padlocked at least half an hour before the Royal Train is due to start, and must be kept so clipped and padlocked until the Royal Train has passed over them. Facing points No. 27, leading from Up Relief to Down Engine and Carriage Line at Arrival Box, must be set, clipped, and padlocked immediately the 11·50 a.m. Special Train from Paddington to Windsor and Eton has passed from No. 9 Line on to the Down Engine and Carriage Line. The Train will run over the Down Main Line from Subway Junction to Slough Middle.
					No train or engine must be allowed on the Down Hammersmith Line between Bishop's Road Station Platform and the Junction with the Great Western Suburban Line West of Royal Oak Station while the Royal Train is running between Paddington and Lord Hill's Box. The 9.0 a.m. train from Bristol to Paddington must run via Relief line from Reading Main line East to Subway Junction, and must be held back at Westbourne Park Up Relief Line platform until after the Royal Train has passed on to the Down Main Line at Subway Junction.
2	55	L. & N.W. Railway Overbridge ...			See note (✠)
2	64	Old Oak Common East ... pass			
3	56	N. & S.W. Jctn. Rly. Overbridge...			See note (✠)
5	18	District Railway Overbridge ...			See note (✠)
9	6	Southall Station ... ... pass		12 17	
18	45	Slough (Middle Box) ... pass		12 28½	Speed not to exceed 10 miles per hour passing from the Down Main Line to the Windsor & Eton Branch Line at Slough Middle. Speed not to exceed 30 miles per hour at Bath Road Junction (Windsor Branch).
21	20	WINDSOR & ETON ... arr.		12 35	Speed not to exceed 10 miles per hour when passing from the Down Line to No. 4 Platform Line at Windsor & Eton.

Royal Saloon, No. 9001, which will be used as the Funeral Car, is to be taken out of the train after arrival at Windsor & Eton and sent specially to Slough, where it must be placed under cover in the carriage shed to await further orders.

RETURN JOURNEY.—WINDSOR & ETON TO PADDINGTON.

Distance from Windsor & Eton.		STATIONS.		P.M.	REMARKS.
Miles	Chains				
					The Train will run over the Up Main Line from Slough Middle to Paddington.
—	—	WINDSOR & ETON ... depart		0 00	Speed not to exceed 25 miles per hour at Bath Road Junction (Windsor Branch).
2	55	Slough (Middle Box) ... pass		0 06	Speed not to exceed 15 miles per hour when passing from the Windsor & Eton Branch to the Up Main Line at Slough Middle.
12	14	Southall Station ... ... pass		0 17½	
16	2	District Railway Overbridge ...			See note (✠)
17	44	N. & S.W. Jctn. Rly. Overbridge...			See note (✠)
18	36	Old Oak Common East ... pass		0 24	
18	45	L. & N.W. Railway Overbridge ...			See note (✠)
20	0	Westbourne Park Station ...			Speed not to exceed 30 miles per hour through Westbourne Park Station to Ranelagh Bridge.
21	20	PADDINGTON ... ... arr.		0 30	Speed not to exceed 10 miles per hour when passing over curves west of Bishop's Road Bridge to Paddington Station.

The return Royal Train will probably leave Windsor & Eton for Paddington between 4.30 and 5.30 p.m., and all concerned must be prepared to act promptly on receiving an advice from Windsor.

The Standard Instructions as shown on pages 3 and 4 of this Notice must be strictly carried out.
The time to be occupied on the journey must be as shown in the table.

(✠)   *The London and North Western, North and South Western Junction, and District Railway Companies will take steps to prevent any Train or Vehicle passing over their respective bridges during the time the Royal Train is passing underneath. Arrangements must be made to advise the staff on these bridges of the approach of the Royal Train.*

☞   *For Special Instructions to be observed in connection with the working of the Royal Trains see third and fourth pages of this Notice. Also the following exceptions :—*

With reference to paragraphs (a) and (c) of Clause 11 in the Instructions on page 3, no Engine, Train or Vehicle must be allowed to cross or foul or run upon the line upon which the Royal Train will run for at least 10 minutes before the passing of the Royal Train, EXCEPT the 11.50 a.m. (No. 5) Special Train conveying members of the Royal Suites who have been in the Procession, but Rule 6 must be strictly carried out as regards the Block Signalling of the Royal Train.

ENGINES AND TRAINS OF EMPTY COACHES BETWEEN PADDINGTON AND WEST LONDON, AND PADDINGTON AND OLD OAK COMMON DEPOTS.

With reference to the Instructions contained in paragraph (d) of Clause 11, and paragraph (a) of Clause 12, Up and Down Trains of empty coaches and engines between Paddington and West London, and between Paddington and Old Oak Common, may be treated as Passenger Trains and worked in accordance with paragraph (c) of Clause 12.

however, crossed the High Street to Castle Hill and entered the Castle by the King Henry VIII gate taking the direct route to the chapel. Station Master Maun records in his diary that great crowds lined the street of the funeral procession's route – some had been on the pavement since the previous afternoon, and many others had been there all night! 'Windows on the route fetched big prices, a friend of mine let his (a corner one) to photographers for £100'.

Maun who had been on duty since 5 am and in charge of the arrangements at Windsor had been exceptionally busy ('it was the busiest day I have ever had') organising the prompt clearance of the five preceding specials and their valuable cargo before the arrival of the Royal Train. However he still had to deal with the return trains following the funeral; only four guests specials were needed for the return journey, leaving at 3.07, 3.28, 3.52 and 4.15 pm. The Royal Train had been ordered for 5 pm and here Maun was in for an unpleasant surprise.

Quoting from his faithful record, his diary:

> When the Royals returned after the ceremony, the eight Kings were assembled in the Royal Room and we were nearly ready for the train to start, when a message came from Slough that an engine, owing to the heat, had struck the points and left the rails blocking the up road over which the Royal Train would pass. We then had to arrange single line working for the Royal Train to travel on the down road; this took some time as someone had to go to Slough to get the signatures of the Signalmen and all concerned and then of our own Signalmen. When at last we were ready I opened the door of the Royal Room for them to enter the train. They had been talking and not noticed the delay and when they were entering the saloon the Czar of Bulgaria started off up the platform. I went after him and said 'we are ready to start Your Majesty'. He replied, 'I want to see the engine' and walked round it onto the line. When he returned I opened the first door I came to and put him in. Whether he found his way along the corridor to the others I do not know, and owing to this King George asked what they had been waiting for and was then told all about it. If the Czar had got in with them nothing would have been asked.

One can imagine a police escort for the person initiating Single Line Working! But the train was away at 5.14 pm, arriving at Paddington at 5.42 pm. Station master Maun will have been on duty well over 12 hours before he was finally able to take his cap off and relax.

Although the GWR doubtless enjoyed tremendous publicity from its involvement in these events, the cost to the Company must have been enormous. The following is a list of additional staffing requirements at Windsor alone:

30 Metropolitan Police	1 telephone attendant for parcels office
2 clerks for station master's office	1 telephone attendant for station master's
1 booking clerk	office
2 telegraph clerks	1 telephone attendant for inspector's office
1 telephonist for signal box	2 shunters
3 inspectors	2 cloakroom porters
12 extra porters (from Tuesday	1 waiting room attendant
19th May–Monday 23rd May)	

In addition, all the intermediate signal boxes between Paddington and Windsor/Reading were required to be open between 6 am and 10 pm (unless their hours were already longer than this).

The scene at Paddington on 20th May, 1910. The coffin is being loaded into the Royal saloon (sixth from the rear). *The Illustrated London News*

Special train for the funeral of King George V passes Langley destined for Windsor on 28th January, 1936. The locomotive is probably No. 5006 *Tregenna Castle* on the 11.00 am from Paddington (or possibly No. 5008 on the 11.10 am train). *British Rail*

1936

London was again bathed in sunshine (although it did rain later) on 28th January, 1936 when Paddington and Windsor were again called upon to perform the most solemn of duties – the transport of the dead Sovereign's body to Windsor Castle for burial. The King had been at Sandringham when he died and the LNER transported the body to London. However, as the GWR Royal Train had been disbanded in 1927, arrangements were made with the LNER for their train to be used for the GWR portion of the journey.

As the coffin containing the body of King George V left Westminster Hall, 'a strange audible thrill, the like of which I have never before heard or seen, passed over the crowd like a wind over a vast field of corn' wrote the *Daily Mirror* correspondent. The procession over a mile long took 68 minutes to pass a point in St James' Street. At Paddington the entrance to the Arrival side of the station was heavily draped in purple, as was a portion of the roof, a large stand facing No. 8 platform and two other smaller stands. Midway along the platform was a huge wreath of laurels and Flanders poppies.

Soon after 10.30 am the Royal Train, which had left Old Oak Common just after 10 o'clock hauled by a pilot engine and with train engine 'Castle' class No. 4082 *Windsor Castle* attached at the rear was propelled into platform 8, the leading engine first having been removed at the Arrival Box inner home signal. The LNER train comprising nine vehicles all in varnished teak, except for the fourth vehicle, Funeral Saloon No. 46, which had been painted black, looked very impressive.

The Arrival side at Paddington (platforms 8–11) was closed for normal traffic from 10 am until 4 pm; Windsor & Eton station was closed from 10.30 am until after the last guest Special left at 3.30 pm (the last train from Slough to Windsor was just after 9 am according to the *Windsor Express*). The bus service between Slough and Windsor was supplemented by 15 extra buses. Windsor enjoyed a moment of excitement when a number of the Lord Chamberlain's officers, who had missed their train at Paddington, arrived at Slough by an ordinary train at 10.36 am and were taken to Windsor by taxi with police officers standing on the running boards! As the day had not been declared a National Day of Mourning, other normal services were maintained except that five down, and six up long distance and three up local trains were cancelled to enable the Guest trains to and from Windsor to run.

Five special trains had been laid on for guests at 11.00, 11.10, 11.20, 11.30 and 11.50 am, the last to convey guests who had been marching in the Procession and also act as 'pilot' to the Royal Train, which was scheduled to leave at noon. Possibly because of warnings in the Press of congestion, guests arrived at Paddington early and the first four specials actually left Paddington at (1) 10.40, (2) 10.55, (3) 11.15 and (4) 11.30 am arriving at Windsor at 11.09, 11.23, 11.44 and 11.58 respectively. Motive power for these trains was: (1) 'Castle' No. 5006 *Tregenna Castle*, (2) No. 5008 *Raglan Castle*, (3) No. 5038 *Morlais Castle* and (4) No. 5014 *Goodrich Castle*. A fifth 'conditional' special at 11.40 am hauled by No. 4090 *Dorchester Castle* was not required and was stood down. All the 'Castles' had been specially overhauled. These four trains only conveyed a total of 608 passengers between them; observers on Slough platform, which was not closed until

On a memorable visit to Swindon Works in April 1924, King George V, accompanied by Queen Mary, drove the engine *Windsor Castle* (built that month) from the Works to the station. In the top photograph HM Queen Mary smiles at the photographer, while in the lower picture the Royal Train, with King George V at the controls, leaves Swindon Works for Windsor. *Windsor Castle* was chosen to haul King George V's funeral train on 28th January, 1936.   *(Both) British Rail*

just before the passage of the Royal Train noted that the first two special trains appeared to be almost empty.

When the planning had been done for the event, it had been anticipated that the head of the procession would reach Paddington at 11.15 am. As things turned out, however, because of the crowds, progress was much slower and Paddington was not reached until 11.50 am. The carefully laid down timetable for the Processional Train and Royal Train was now quite impossible to follow; the coffin did not arrive at Paddington until 12.15 pm and the Processional Train did not get away until 12.26 pm (instead of 11.50 am). This left Platform 9 and ran via the Down Engine & Carriage line to Subway Jn. The GWR records state that 1,200 guests were conveyed to the funeral* so this train must have conveyed as many people as the other four specials put together! Motive power was 'Castle' class 4–6–0 No. 5004 *Llanstephan Castle*, and arrival at Windsor was exactly 30 minutes later, at 12.56 pm. The *Railway Gazette* reported:

> For five minutes there was complete silence and then the funeral train itself was signalled and slowly glided from the platform at precisely 12.33½ pm. Whole minutes elapsed before the last coach rounded the curve at the end of the station and passed from sight. The locomotive *Windsor Castle* was draped with the Royal Arms and bore the Royal crown-topped headlamps. It was in charge of Driver W.H. Sparrow and Fireman A. Miles.

A letter to Sir Robert Horne, Chairman of the GWR, the following day congratulated the company on a particularly skilful example of engine driving . . . 'the way the Royal Train *slid* out of the station . . .'

Meanwhile at Windsor, where the streets were estimated to contain 100,000 people, the first indication of the dead King's arrival to all except those few able to see the Royal Train come over the viaduct into the station, was the sight of the Union Jack being lowered from its position at half mast on the Round Tower, and its replacement by the Royal Standard. The Royal waiting room at the station had been equipped with 'Windsor Castle' note-paper, pens and pencils; flowers had been provided and even potted palms hired and placed there. The Royal Train arrived in platform 4 at 1.09 pm and stopped with the Funeral Coach adjacent to the Royal Waiting Room. (A railway 'post mortem' after the event decided that on future occasions this vehicle must be third, not fourth, in the train formation to enable it to be better placed and avoid a diagonal approach to the Waiting Room, also obviate the need to stop the train only 18 inches from the buffer stops.)

It had been intended that the Two Minutes silence at 1.30 pm should have been held during the lowering of the coffin into the vault of St George's Chapel. But with the event now running over ½ hr late it was necessary for the procession from the station to the chapel, past pavements on which people massed ten and twelve deep, to continue its slow progress during the Two Minutes silence.

After the funeral service, presided over by the Archbishop of Canterbury, the King and Queen Mary returned to Windsor station at 2.30 pm, rather earlier than expected but the Royal Train did not leave until the Procession-

---

*However, some other records at PRO, Kew state that 1,040 guests were conveyed. The cost of the special trains and refreshments was £607, for which an account was rendered to the Crown. However this was counterbalanced by the cost of the viewing stands erected at Paddington to accommodate 960 persons which cost the GWR £550.

al Train had left at 2.44 pm, the Royal Train following at 2.51 pm. Only three, rather than four, other guest specials were needed for the return journey and these left Windsor at 3.01, 3.11 and 3.30 pm. No less than 500 cars were assembled at Paddington to meet the King's guests, surely the largest collection of cars in one place up to that date!

The GWR, ever thoughtful, had arranged for six down long distance trains to call specially at Slough, as follows: 3.35 pm (Cheltenham); 3.50 pm (Plymouth & Truro); 3.52 pm (Birmingham & North); 4.15 pm (Carmarthen); 4.50 pm (Plymouth); and 5.05 pm (Worcester & Hereford).

After the event a report was submitted to the superintendent of the line regarding the working at Windsor. This commented that gravel had been thrown over the station yard and approach road – 'this looked very nice but after it had rained it turned slightly muddy and dirtied the boots of the guards of honour and also the trousers of some of the officers'. After the arrival of each down guest special it was backed out of the station and stabled at Slough. The processional train was held in No. 1 platform and the Royal Train in No. 4, except that it was first backed out for the Funeral Coach to be removed. The report commented that in future arrangements should be made with the Castle for the station to be advised when the Service is drawing to a close – 'I understand the Royal party arrived . . . before they were expected but fortunately everything was in order'.

Return arrangements were generally successful except that the report recommended on any future such occasion that tickets should be printed for those travelling on the Processional Train. There had been some difficulty on this occasion segregating the guests for the 'ordinary' return specials from those for the Processional Train, which left first.

1952

The King was at Sandringham when he died, just as had been his father 16 years earlier. So British Railways was able to draw heavily on the records of that earlier funeral as, in a way, history was repeating itself. The body of King George VI was brought from Sandringham to London for the lying-in-state, and then taken on to Windsor for the funeral service and burial, the ex-LNER train being used for both journeys, as in 1936.

On Friday 15th February the Funeral Procession left Westminster Hall at 9.30 am and made its solemn way along Whitehall, The Mall, St James' Street, Piccadilly to Hyde Park Corner, then through Hyde Park to Marble Arch, along Edgware Road, Sussex Gardens, and finally London Street and into Paddington Station passing under a wreath 'one of the simplest among all the magnificence of flowers a wreath of poppies . . . [8 ft in diameter] from the railway staff. Over it was inscribed on a purple drape: "The way of duty was the path to glory"'.

At Paddington four guest trains had been requested, to leave at 10.20, 10.30, 10.40 and 10.50 am. The Processional Train was initially ordered for 11.45 am and the Royal Train at 11.55 am. However, following a trial Processional March on Sunday 10th February, which took nearly 3 hours, these two trains were rescheduled to 12.20 and 12.30 pm, subsequently altered again to be 5 mins later. In the event the procession on the day was much quicker: the head of the procession arrived at 11.25, the gun carriage con-

FUNERAL OF HIS LATE MAJESTY
KING GEORGE VI

Friday, 15th February, 1952

ORDER OF FUNERAL PROCESSION

Bands of the Royal Air Force and Welsh Guards.

Detachments of :—

    Royal Air Force
    Colonial Troops
    Commonwealth Forces

Territorial Army

Infantry Regiments

Bands of Irish Guards and Coldstream Guards.

Detachments of :—

    Foot Guards
    Corps of Royal Engineers
    Royal Regiment of Artillery
    Royal Armoured Corps

Bands of Royal Artillery and Royal Marines.

Detachments of :—

    Royal Marines
    Royal Navy

Representative Officers of Foreign Navies, Armies and Air Forces

Representative Officers of Dominion Navies, Armies and Air Forces

Chaplains of the Services

Air Officers Commanding and Commanding in Chief

Inspector General and Marshals of the Royal Air Force

Air Council

Representative Colonels of His Late Majesty's Regiments

General Officers Commanding in Chief

Field Marshals

Army Council

Representatives of the Merchant Navy

Captains of Royal Naval Volunteer Reserve and Royal Naval Reserve

Commanders in Chief, Royal Navy

Admirals of the Fleet

Board of Admiralty

Aides-de-Camp to His Late Majesty

Drum Horse and State Trumpeters

First Division of the Sovereign's Escort

Band of Scots Guards and Massed Pipers of Royal Irish Fusiliers, Royal Scots
Fusiliers, The Royal Scots, Irish Guards and Scots Guards

The Earl Marshal

The Gun Carriage

The Sovereign's Standard

Her Majesty the Queen

The Royal Dukes

Members of Foreign Royal Families

Heads of Foreign Special Missions and High Commissioners

Officers of the Households

The King's Flight, Royal Air Force

Members of Foreign Governments

Second Division of the Sovereign's Escort

Other Members of Foreign Delegations and Delegations of Officers
of Foreign Armies, Navies and Air Attaches

Band of the Royal Engineers and Police Band.

Detachments of :—

    Police
    Fire Brigade
    Civil Defence Corps

NOT TRANSFERABLE
PRESS STAND
(No. 9 Platform)

BRITISH RAILWAYS (WESTERN REGION).
PADDINGTON STATION.

𝔍uneral of 𝔥is 𝔏ate 𝔐ajesty 𝔎ing 𝔊eorge 𝔙𝔩.

FRIDAY, 15th FEBRUARY, 1952.

Admit one representative of...
to Press Stand on No. 9 Platform.

Admission only by Approach Road, Departure Side (Hotel end of Station).

Holders of Tickets should be in their places not later than 10.0 a.m.

Issued to..

K. W. C. GRAND,
Chief Regional Officer

PADDINGTON STATION
Funeral of the late King George VI. February 15th 1952.

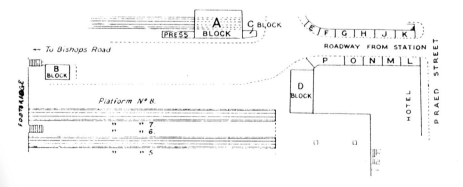

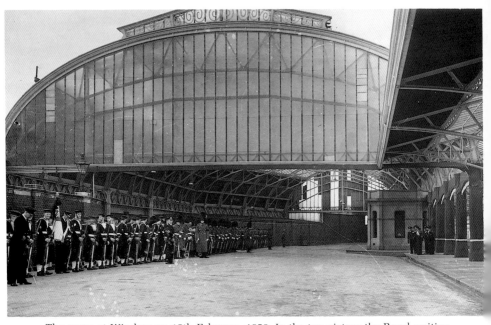

The scene at Windsor on 15th February, 1952. In the top picture the Royal waiting room can be seen on the right; note, in the lower picture, that the glass at the entrance has been covered by drapes, to which a wreath has been affixed. *(Both) British Rail*

TIME TABLE OF ROYAL TRAIN—
PADDINGTON TO WINDSOR & ETON (CENTRAL)—
FRIDAY, 15th FEBRUARY, 1952.

The Engine to carry **FOUR HEAD LAMPS**, viz. one at the foot of the chimney, one at each end of the buffer beam, and one in the centre of the buffer beam. (Important.—**See** paragraph 1 of R.E. Circular O RR, dated December, 1950.)

The Train will carry **TWO TAIL LAMPS**. (Important.—**See paragraph 2 of R.E. Circular O RR, dated December, 1950.)

The Head Lamps and Tail Lamps must be lighted before leaving Paddington.

The Train will run over the Up Main Line from Paddington Arrival Signal Box to Subway Junction and thence on the Down Main Line to Slough (Middle Box).

THE PERMANENT AND TEMPORARY SPEED RESTRICTIONS MUST BE STRICTLY OBSERVED.

Distances from Paddington Mls. Chs.		PRINCIPAL STATIONS AND INTERMEDIATE SIGNAL BOXES.		Times.	REMARKS.
—		**PADDINGTON** ..	dep.	p.m. 12.35	The Royal Train must start from No. 8 Arrival Platform at Paddington, to be worked from Paddington Arrival Signal Box to Subway Junction under the Instructions shown on page 52 of the Appendix to No. 1 Section of the Service Time Table.
—	75	Subway Junction ..	pass	12.41	The 12.30 p.m. Paddington to Weymouth to start at 12.40 p.m. and run at revised times, see London District Operating Superintendent's Notice No. 9i.
2	65	Old Oak Common East ..	,,	12.43½	
8	0	Hanwell West Signals ..	,,	—	Intermediate Block Signals.
9	6	Southall Station ..	,,	12.53	The 10.45 a.m. Kensington to Swindon Milk Empties to run via the Relief Line from West Ealing to Reading East Main or Scowers Lane Junction according to circumstances.
18	36	Slough (Middle Box) ..	,,	1. 3½	
21	20	**WINDSOR & ETON (CENTRAL)** ..	arr.	1.10	The Royal Train must arrive at No. 4 Platform at Windsor & Eton (Central). (See special instructions below.)

SPECIAL INSTRUCTIONS.—WINDSOR & ETON (CENTRAL).—The Royal Train will run to No. 4 Platform Line. A Handsignalman exhibiting a red hand signal must be stationed on the Driver's side and the Train must be brought to a stand with the centre of the cab of the Engine opposite the hand signal.

The Royal Funeral Saloon No. 46 will be taken out of the train after arrival at Windsor & Eton (Central) and put in a position where it will be out of sight. The Saloon to be worked to Old Oak Common by special trip at times to be arranged subsequently.

BRITISH RAILWAYS

TIME TABLE
OF

ROYAL TRAIN

FROM

PADDINGTON

TO

WINDSOR & ETON (CENTRAL)

ON

FRIDAY, 15th FEBRUARY, 1952

In connection with the Funeral of

HIS LATE MAJESTY

KING GEORGE VI

Paddington - - -	depart 12.35 p.m.
Windsor & Eton (Central)	arrive 1.10 p.m.

Timetable of Royal Train, 15th February, 1952.

PRIVATE AND NOT FOR PUBLICATION. NOTICE No. 9.

BRITISH RAILWAYS

(WESTERN OPERATING AREA.)

(For the use of the staff concerned only.)

Notice of Special Passenger Trains between

Paddington and Windsor & Eton Central

On Friday, February 15th, 1952,

for the Conveyance of Guests proceeding to the Funeral Service of His Late Majesty King George VI.

TIME TABLE OF DOWN TRAINS.

	Special "A"	Special "B"	Special "C"	Special "D"	No. 6 Special
Empty Coaches leave Old Oak Common at ☛	*9.45 a.m.*	*9.55 a.m.*	*10.25 a.m.*	*10.30 a.m.*	*10.45 a.m.*
Platform at Paddington ☛	Platform 4.	Platform 5.	Platform 4.	Platform 5.	Platform 9 (To be backed in.)
	a.m.	a.m.	a.m.	a.m. *	p.m.
PADDINGTON .. .. dep.	10 50	11 0	11 10	11 20	12 25
Subway Junction .. .. pass	—	—	—	—	12 30
Southall .. .. pass	11 3	11 13	11 23	11 33	12 41½
Slough .. .. pass	11 13¼	11 23¼	11 33¼	11 43¼	12 51½
WINDSOR & ETON CENTRAL .. .. arr.	11 20	11 30	11 40	11 50	12 58
					See Note ¶ below.

Mr. Geden, Paddington, to advise Windsor & Eton Central the actual departure time of each Special.

* The 12.25 p.m. Special Train is booked to leave Paddington 10 minutes in advance of the Royal Train (see Notice No. 10). It will start from No. 9 Platform and run over the Up Main Line to Subway Junction under the instructions shewn on page 52 of the Appendix to No. 1 Section of the Service Time Table in connection with "Two-Way" working, **with the exception that Clause 8 will not apply,** passing on to the Down Main Line at Subway Junction. No Train or Engine must be allowed on the Down Hammersmith or Suburban Line between Paddington Suburban Station Platform and Subway Junction, while the 12.25 p.m. Special Train (No. 6) is running between Paddington and Subway Junction Box. The speed between Paddington and Subway Junction must not exceed 15 miles per hour and when passing through the junction from Up Main Line to Down Main Line at Subway Junction, it must not exceed 10 miles per hour. This train must run into No. 1 Platform Line at Windsor & Eton Central.

A spare Train (Special "E") formed with Brake First, 6 Corridor Firsts, Brake First (corridors on North side) to leave Old Oak Common at 10.40 a.m. for Paddington and stand at No. 4 Platform after the departure of Special "C." To leave Paddington, *if necessary*, at 11.30 a.m. for Windsor & Eton Central.

Special Trains "A," "B," "C," "D" and "E," from Paddington to Windsor & Eton Central are the Trains set apart for the conveyance of the invited Guests proceeding to the Funeral Service at Windsor; and No. 6 Special, which will start from No. 9 Platform, is to be **exclusively retained** for members of the Royal Suites and other important personages riding in the Royal Procession.

THE FORMATION OF THE SPECIAL TRAINS WILL BE AS UNDER :—

Special "A" 10.50 a.m.	Special "B" 11. 0 a.m.	Special "C" 11.10 a.m.	Special "D" 11.20 a.m.	No. 6 Special. 12.25 p.m.
Engine Brake * 2 Coaches * Kitchen Car 9633 2 Coaches * Kitchen Car 9670 2 Coaches * Brake *	Engine Brake * 2 Coaches * Kitchen Car 9666 2 Corr. Firsts Kitchen Car 9668 2 Corr. Firsts Brake *	Engine L.M.R. Brake First L.M.R. First * W.R. Dining Car 9558 2 L.M.R. Firsts * W.R. Dining Car 9561 2 L.M.R. Firsts * W.R. Dining Car 9537 (Kitchen end leading) L.M.R. First * W.R. Brake First	Engine Brake First 70′ 2 Corr. Firsts Kitchen Car 9663 2 Corr. Firsts Kitchen Car 9669 2 Corr. Firsts Brake First 70′	Engine First 8125 labelled "A." Brake Saloon 9004 " "B" Special Saloon 9111 " "C" " " 9112 " "D" Kitchen Saloon 9117 " "E" Special Saloon 9113 " "F" " " 9114 " "G" Kitchen Saloon 9118 " "H" Special Saloon 9115 " "J" " " 9116 " "K" Brake Saloon 9005 " "L"
* Vestibule Stock 448 Seats 642′ excluding Engine **14 seats to be reserved for "Gentlemen of Arms"**	* Vestibule Stock 360 Seats 583′ excluding Engine See Note V	* Vestibule Stock 360 Seats 749′ excluding Engine	* Vestibule Stock 324 Seats 674′ excluding Engine See Note V	317 Seats 702′ excluding Engine *Two Guards to be provided on this train.*

NOTE V—Corridors must be on South side leaving Paddington.

RETURN SPECIAL TRAINS.

The Special Trains will return from Windsor & Eton Central after the Funeral as under :—

No. 6 Special.*—Will leave Windsor & Eton Central at 3.0 p.m., Slough pass 3.6, Southall 3.17½. Paddington arrive 3.30 p.m. (No. 9 Platform).*

"A," "B," "C," "D" and "E" (if run) Specials.*—Will leave Windsor & Eton Central as required between 3.0 p.m. and 4.0 p.m. and run to Nos. 8 or 9 Platforms at Paddington.*

The Staff at all Stations must be on the look-out for Telegraphic Advice of the starting of the Special Trains from Windsor & Eton Central and the Line must be kept clear for them.

GENERAL INSTRUCTIONS.

For General Instructions to be observed in connection with the running of the Special Trains shewn above, see the British Railways Rule Book dated 1st January, 1950, and the General Appendix dated July, 1936.

Receipt of this Notice to be acknowledged to District Operating Superintendent, Paddington, BY WIRE.

N. H. BRIANT,
District Operating Superintendent.
PADDINGTON, February, 1952.

GILBERT MATTHEWS,
Operating Superintendent.

Timetable for the Guest Specials to King George VI's Funeral.

taining the coffin at 11.50 and was entrained at 12 noon! The Processional train was got away 5½ minutes early at 12.19½ but it was necessary to hold the Royal Train to its booked departure time to ensure that the passengers on the Processional Train could be in their allotted places at Windsor before the arrival there of the Royal Train. The WR's Operating Superintendent, Gilbert Matthews, was strongly pressed by the GOC London District to start the Royal Train before its booked time (the Royal party had been seated since just after noon) but declined to do so.

The four guest trains were labelled A, B, C and D and some interesting details are:

'A' 10.50 am, locomotive 4091, 448 seats, 308 passengers
'B' 11.00 am, locomotive 4097, 360 seats, 201 passengers
'C' 11.10 am, locomotive 5039, 318 seats, 85 passengers
'D' 11.20 am, locomotive 5065, 287 seats, 62 passengers

A fifth (standby) train 'E', hauled by locomotive 5013, was not required and returned to Old Oak Common.

The Processional Train was hauled by locomotive 7004, and conveyed 409 guests, although having seats for only 354 – one wonders, did some stand? The Royal train was drawn by 'Castle' class locomotive No. 7013 *Bristol Castle* which had been renumbered and renamed No. 4082 *Windsor Castle* to maintain tradition, the latter engine being in Works at the time. This action attracted a lot of 'media attention' and some criticism and the official records, in noting this, declare that such a renaming should be avoided in future. The Royal train had been reduced to eight vehicles (nine in 1936) but seven of these were exactly the same vehicles that had been conveyed in the 1936 funeral train.

At Windsor the station was closed from 10 am (later agreed to have been too early) and the advertised service suspended after the arrival of the 9.25 am Relief from Paddington at 9.58 am until the 4.30 pm 'auto' from Slough to Windsor. The day had been grey but as the Processional Train arrived at 12.54 pm the sun broke through. The Royal duchesses on this train walked to the Royal waiting room, in use in this way for the first time since 1936, and now normally a police office. Here they were able to wait in private until the arrival of the Royal Train at 1.10 pm. The official report records that this facility was much appreciated and it, or an equivalent, 'would be required on future (such) occasions'.

Following the precedent set at Queen Victoria's funeral the coffin was loaded on to a gun carriage at Windsor:

> The Orb and Sceptre, and the Imperial Crown with its myriad jewels, resting on a purple velvet cushion on the Royal Standard covering the coffin, sparkled in the winter sun. Also on the coffin was the Queen Mother's wreath of orchids and lilies of the valley.
>
> Then came perhaps the most never-to-be-forgotten moment when many watching wept unashamedly. A Naval piping-party of HMS 'Vanguard' piped an Admiral's Salute, the shrill notes dying to a mournful wail in a final moment of emotion.

The procession left the station at 1.18 pm passing through 'crowded, but not packed' streets on its way to the service in St George's Chapel. The procession halted with the gun carriage outside the Great West Door of the

King George VI's coffin leaves Windsor station on 15th February, 1952.   *British Rail*

Viewing Stand 'A' at Paddington Station, built out over the track of platform 9; 15th February, 1952.   *British Rail*

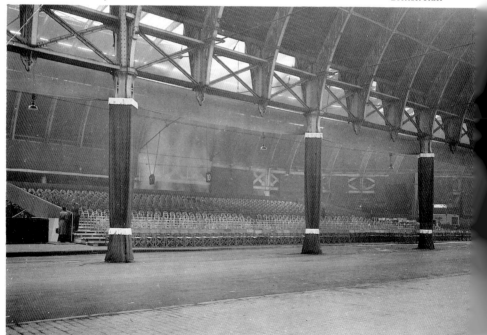

The Royal funeral train arrives at Windsor on 15th February, 1952 hauled by 'Castle' class 4–6–0 No. 4082 *Windsor Castle*.   *British Rail*

In the front row of those following the coffin from the station to the Castle may be seen Prince Philip (*left*) and the Duke of Windsor (*3rd from left*); 15th February, 1952.   *British Rail*

8701/36

THE RAILWAY EXECUTIVE

WESTERN REGION

GILBERT MATTHEWS
Operating Superintendent

C. W. POWELL
Assistant Operating Superintendent

OPERATING SUPERINTENDENT
PADDINGTON STATION
LONDON W.2

Telephone PADDINGTON 7000 (Ext.   )

Telegraphic Address
TRAFFIC PADDINGTON STATION LONDON 14th February, 1952.

Your reference :-   Please quote this reference

MEMORANDUM.

Funeral of His Late Majesty
King George VI, Friday,
15th February, 1952.

The bearer may be admitted
to all Platforms or Reserved Enclosures
at WINDSOR STATION.

for Operating Superintendent.

Chapel at exactly 2 o'clock, at which time the official Two Minutes silence began.

After the short service, conducted by the Archbishop of Canterbury and which ended at 2.43 pm, the Queen, Queen Mother and other members of the Royal Family decided to return by road to London. The Royal Train therefore was not required as such, but was run as an express passenger train conveying the railway officials concerned with the arrangements.

Departures from Windsor were as follows:

Processional Train 3.00 pm 447 passengers (platform 1)
'A'   3.07 pm 328 passengers (platform 2)
'D'   3.16 pm 180 passengers (platform 3)
'Royal'   3.23 pm   (platform 4)
'B'   3.32 pm 43 passengers (platform 1)
'C'   3.45 pm   8 passengers (platform 2)

For those not privileged to travel in the guest special trains, 'ordinary' Special trains also left Windsor at 4 pm for Paddington (138 passengers) and 4.30 pm for Reading (60 passengers). As in 1936, down express trains called additionally at Slough as follows: 3.50 pm (Penzance): 4.04 pm (Birmingham & North); 4.15 pm (Carmarthen); 5.05 pm (Worcester & Hereford); and 5.15 pm (Cheltenham). In these days of ever-changing timetables it is interesting to note that three of these departure times were exactly as they were in 1936!

Once again segregation of passengers had been less than successful, observe the already overcrowded Processional Train carried even more passengers on return, almost 100 more than there were seats. The official report identifies this 'lesson to be learned' for a second time and recommends proper tickets in future for all trains, indicating the specific train to be used on the forward and return journeys.

The comment has already been made about the cost of these occasions, and one wonders how much the railway was 'out-of-pocket' after an event such as this. The official records state that 'standby' locomotives (all 'Castle' class engines, specially overhauled) were located at Ranalagh Bridge (No. 5002), Old Oak Common (5081), Southall (5035), Slough (4085 and 5049) and Reading (7025). In addition the breakdown gangs at Old Oak Common, Southall, Slough and Reading (the latter actually at Taplow) were all on duty. As a small aside it was found that the purple draping material used for the funeral of King George V had been used for black-out purposes during World War II and none remained, so it was necessary to purchase no less than 1,500 yards of material, to enable proper solemnity and dignity to be given to the occasion.

Notices advertising the wonders of the electric telegraph on the GWR.   *British Rail*

Telegraph Cottage at Slough from which the message that caught John Tawell was sent.
British Rail

Chapter Nine
Traffic and Operations

The traffic for which the Windsor branch was most famous was that concerned with the Royal Family and Windsor Castle, and has been described already. Here we can consider the other, more ordinary, aspects of traffic and operations, although, inevitably, from time to time there will be a Royal involvement in the matter.

The first 'Bradshaw' showed 11 trains each way at Slough, increased by summer 1843 to 14, plus two goods trains which also conveyed 3rd class passengers. Until the fast Exeter expresses were started in 1845, all trains stopped at Slough.

The first Electric Magnetic Telegraph was installed by the GWR between Paddington and Hanwell in 1839 and was extended to Slough in 1843; it was the first long distance public electric telegraph in daily use and became a much-visited 'wonder'. On 6th August, 1844 it received nationwide publicity when it was used to summon Queen Victoria's ministers to Windsor Castle for the birth of her fourth child, Prince Alfred:

> At two minutes past six o'clock, a messenger, mounted upon one of the fleetest horses in the royal stables, was despatched from the Castle to Mr Howell, the superintendent at the Slough station, with instructions to communicate, by means of the electro-magnetic telegraph to the person in attendance at the Telegraph Office, at Paddington, to the effect that the letters, which had been waiting there for several days past, addressed to the Cabinet Ministers . . . were to be delivered at the residences of the respected parties without delay. The messenger reached the Slough station within 8 minutes of his departure from the Castle, then 10 minutes past 6 o'clock, and although Mr Russell . . . who was the superintendent of the Telegraph Office and Mr Howell had to be called from their beds . . . within three minutes of the instructions reaching Slough . . . the telegraph was not only at work, but the communication was despatched to Paddington . . . and all this was effected within eleven minutes of the special messenger's departure from the Castle!

Thus, dramatically, wrote the *Illustrated London News* in its next edition. Three special trains brought the VIP's to Windsor, the first leaving Paddington at 8.05 am and reaching Slough, 18¼ miles, in 18 minutes ('being at the extraordinary rate of more than 60 mph' *ILN*). The next special arrived at 8.40 am, having been somewhat delayed by the 8.00 down train ahead of it, and the third special conveying just the Duke of Wellington arrived soon afterwards having covered the distance from Paddington in 17½ minutes. His Grace continued to Windsor in a 'carriage and four' and reached the Castle in 11 minutes, or less than half an hour after leaving Paddington. All, however, arrived after the birth which occurred at 7.50 am. During the period from 13th July to 6th August an engine had been kept in steam at Paddington continuously in order to bring Cabinet Ministers and doctors to Windsor for the confinement.

The paper also recorded that a special passenger train between Slough and Paddington on the same day made the journey in only 15 minutes and 10 seconds, or more than 70 mph.

The following New Year's Day (1845) Slough and its telegraph apparatus became the centre of much greater attention when it lead to the capture of a murderer. A former Quaker, John Tawell (who some 30 years earlier had been transported to New South Wales for 21 years for forgery, but had been released after seven years) went to Slough to murder his former mistress. This lady, known as Sarah Hart (her true name being Sarah Lawrence) aged 39, had two children by him and was claiming support. John Tawell, after release from his sentence had set himself up as a chemist and become wealthy, eventually returning to this country six or seven years previously, and now living with his wife and daughter at Berkhampstead. He administered prussic acid in a glass of stout to the unfortunate Sarah Hart and then made his way to Slough station. However, the lady let out a piercing scream as she died and a doctor was soon on the scene. Hearing that a person dressed like a Quaker, with a brown great coat almost reaching his feet, had been seen leaving the house, the doctor went to Slough station and saw Tawell in the last compartment of the second 1st class carriage.

This information was immediately telegraphed to Paddington and the train was met by Sergeant Williams, a detective in the GWR police who followed Tawell to his lodgings. The next day Tawell was arrested and he eventually stood trial at Aylesbury for murder, of which he was found guilty and hanged. He was the first murderer in the world to be arrested through a telegraphic message. Sadly, despite this extensive publicity, the telegraph apparatus did not 'pay' and it was removed in June 1849. In the autumn of 1850, however, the GWR reached agreement with the Electric Telegraph Co. for installation of a line between Oxford and Banbury, and in the following year this agreement was extended to cover general installation.

Mention has been made earlier of the introduction of fast expresses to Exeter, which omitted a stop at Slough. On 17th June, 1845 the 9.45 am Paddington to Exeter was travelling at almost 70 mph approaching Langley, 2½ miles on the London side of Slough. The train was a short one, consisting of a four-wheeled luggage van, two first class and two second class carriages; it was well loaded, containing some 60 1st class and 130 or more 2nd class passengers. At a point called Dog Kennel bridge where the railway crossed the road from Langley to Iver, the 4-wheeled luggage van, which had been running derailed on the longitudinal timbers for ½ mile, struck the girders of the bridge, deflecting the van into the ballast and dragging the rest of the train off the rails. The luggage van remained connected to the engine, but the two first class carriages and the leading second class coach tumbled down a 10 ft embankment, one of the first class coaches ending up upside down. According to the *Windsor Express* (but not the *Illustrated London News*) the driver immediately uncoupled the engine and raced on to Slough to raise the alarm; in any case information reached Slough within 15 minutes of the accident and a convoy of road vehicles conveying doctors etc., was despatched to the site. The Royal Hotel at Slough station was made ready to receive the injured, and Mr Howell, the station superintendent, made up and despatched a train to Langley so that the uninjured passengers could continue their journey.

Miraculously although several passengers were injured, a few seriously, the strongly constructed broad gauge carriages 'though very much damaged and shattered, stood the shock so as to enable the passengers to move freely in them', and no one was killed. Some important GWR officials were on the train, including I.K. Brunel, and Seymour Clarke, London Division traffic superintendent and his wife. Forty persons were conveyed to the Royal

Hotel where they received medical attention and were looked after. Others continued their journey on the relief train or returned to London by the 10.15 am ex-Paddington which had subsequently arrived at Langley and could not continue westwards.

The up line was reopened within 3 hours, and the down line, despite the need for extensive relaying, was open by 5 pm. 'By the extraordinary exertions of upwards of 100 men and a large number of horses', the derailed carriages were dragged up the embankment and placed upon the rails by 1 am on Wednesday 18th June. The telegraph had been knocked down in the accident, and this was back in operation by 9 am on the 18th.

Just three days later on 20th June, 1845, the noon express from Exeter experienced a similar calamity at Hay Mill, just west of Slough. However this time the 4-wheeled luggage van which became derailed was at the rear of the train and so it did not derail the other carriages, but it crossed over and damaged the down line. The first intimation of trouble came with the arrival at Slough station of the express engine on its own, just after 4 pm. According to the *Windsor Express*, the driver was the same man who had charge of the derailed train the previous Tuesday! On informing the overworked Mr Howell that the luggage van was derailed at a point midway between Maidenhead and Slough, the latter obtained 20 or 30 men and the necessary jacks etc., and returned with the engine to the derailment. On this occasion no one was injured and after a delay of 40 minutes, the train restarted, leaving Slough at 5.05 pm and reaching Paddington 45 minutes behind schedule. One hopes, after this repeat performance, that the GWR 'learned the lesson' and discontinued the attaching of these lightweight vans to the fast express trains.

Just a fortnight later the *Windsor Express* described a malicious act as 'a most wicked and abominable attempt to injure the passengers' travelling in the noon train from Paddington. When the train passed Langley, close by the spot of the earlier derailment, a labourer working on the line threw a white earthen pint pot at the door window of a first class carriage. Mr John Secker, town clerk of Windsor, received a violent blow on the temple and another gentleman and two ladies were severely struck on the head and face. Once again Mr Howell at Slough was called upon to take action and, doubtless, the person responsible lost his employment with the GWR that same day, as well as being liable to prosecution by the police.

Apparatus for picking up and setting down mail bags was installed at Slough in September 1858, but, until 1866, the important Bristol up and down mail trains called at Slough. From 1st March, 1866 onwards they used the mail apparatus and omitted the Slough stop.

The first GWR slip coaches were introduced on 29th November, 1858 and Slough and Banbury became the first Great Western towns to enjoy this new facility, each having a carriage detached from the 9.30 am Paddington to Birmingham. MacDermot in his *History of the GWR* records that the guard pulled a rope to uncouple the slip carriage!

On 1st October, 1863 a through service from Farringdon Street (Metropolitan Railway) to Windsor was introduced. During the 1860s and 1870s, until the amalgamation of the Bristol & Exeter Railway with the GWR, it was not unusual, according to the *GWR Magazine*, to see a Bristol & Exeter Railway guard working a through train from the Metropolitan line to Windsor, presumably a fill-in job to make up his day.

There is another reference in some correspondence between the GWR and the Court in 1863 to keeping an engine in steam all night in case of problems at Windsor Castle. On 31st March, 1863 Charles Saunders, GWR Secretary, wrote to Earl Grey confirming arrangements had been made to keep an engine available at Paddington in case of a need to bring the Queen's medical attendant to Windsor (she was unwell). 'In order that no time may be lost here I would ask you to send a man on horseback to Slough station, if at night, in order to telegraph to this station that the train will be required at once' [Windsor telegraph office being closed at night].

On 13th May, 1864 the unthinkable happened during one of Queen Victoria's journeys from Windsor to Balmoral. The tubes of engine No. 158 were leaking badly; the train left Windsor 14 minutes late and Oxford was reached 23 minutes late and left 25 minutes late. However, some remedial work may have been done there because Bushbury Jn (Wolverhampton) was reached only 19 minutes late, despite a loss of 3 minutes at Birmingham (Snow Hill) following examination of reported hot wheels on the coaches.

The General Manager of the GWR made a fortnightly report to the Board of matters relating to traffic, revenue and incidents and accidents. The report dated 2nd December, 1868 contained details of an incident at the home signal at Windsor (probably the 'drum' signal) passed at danger by a passenger train, which then collided with some empty carriages which were being shunted. The driver concerned was subsequently fined one pound.

Mention was made earlier of the first slip coach, at Slough in 1858. Between 1866 and 1868 there was even a slip at Paddington. A through board gauge branch train from Windsor to the Metropolitan Railway slipped a coach as the train passed Westbourne Bridge signal box. The slip coach was then diverted into the arrival platform at Paddington, while the rest of the train stopped at Bishop's Road platforms (the present suburban station). The only apparent gain by this operation was to give the passengers an arrival close to the taxi rank!

A report by the General Manager on suburban passenger traffic dated 4th February, 1869 revealed that the two places with the largest increases in suburban traffic between 1861 and 1867 were Ealing and Windsor. So far as the latter was concerned, traffic between Windsor and Paddington and vice versa had grown from 60,000 passengers in 1861, to 136,000 in 1867. The report noted that it was difficult to run extra trains at certain times of the day to cope with the general increase in suburban traffic 'in consequence of the number, and occasionally unpunctuality, of the main line trains'. However, the report concluded, previous experience indicated that with better facilities the suburban traffic could be considerably increased.

The broad gauge Windsor branch line was converted to mixed gauge in March 1862, including the west curve at Slough. A note in the Working Timetables in the 1870s said: 'The gauge on the Windsor Branch is uncertain'. What this actually meant was that, by use of a 'buffer-truck', or conversion vehicle, trains of mixed vehicles (i.e. different gauges) were run. There is little written evidence of this practice, unfortunately, but see Chap-

GWR poster advertising Ascot Races 1897.   *British Rail*

ter Five for reference to it. The broad gauge rails were lifted on the Windsor branch after June 1883.

On Sunday 12th March, 1876 a sudden snowstorm brought down telegraph poles and wires across the railway and prevented the Empress of Austria from returning from Windsor Castle to London. Marooned at Slough station for some hours, she was 'entertained' by Mr Hart, the station master, who provided some food from his home nearby and lent the Empress the 'Ingoldsby Legends' to read. Afterwards Mr Hart received a handsome present from the Empress.

In 1874 the Board of Directors agreed to appoint another shunter at Slough because of delays to traffic and complaints from traders. The present sole shunter could not cope with the level of traffic and in addition, the shunting engine was not being fully utilised.

Ascot Races, in June each year, brought a significant amount of extra traffic to the Windsor branch. From a circular dated 1879 in the Royal Archives the following details are extracted for Gold Cup day Thursday 12th June, 1879:

Special Trains for Carriages and Horses will leave Paddington for Windsor between 5.0 am and 8.0 am as required, returning empty at once, until Paddington telegraphs Slough to stop them.

A Special Train, consisting of 3 Firsts, 4 Seconds, and 7 Third Class coaches and 2 Vans (Narrow Gauge) will leave Paddington for Windsor, following the 9.0 am Express from Paddington, and stopping at Westbourne Park, Ealing, Southall, West Drayton, and Slough.

Special Passenger Trains will leave Paddington for Windsor at 9.20, 9.40, 10.5, 10.25, 10.35, 10.55, 11.50 am and 12.15 pm. Other Trains will be run if required; each Train to consist of about 12 Coaches and 2 Breaks (Narrow Gauge).

Special Trains leaving Paddington at 10.35 and 10.55 am to stop at Westbourne Park and Southall; the other Special Trains will call at Slough only.

Special Trains will leave Windsor for Paddington after the races, as required, until 10.30 pm, calling at Slough and Westbourne Park only. Special trains of Carriages and Horses will also leave Windsor for Paddington, as required, after the Passenger Specials in the evening, and it is of the utmost importance that they should not be delayed on the road.

Mr Hill to arrange for two extra coaches to run on the Victoria trains.

Paddington to telegraph all specials to West London Junction, Acton, Castle Hill, Southall, West Drayton, Langley, Slough and Windsor immediately each train leaves.

Windsor to telegraph Slough who will advise Langley, West Drayton, Southall, Castle Hill, Acton and Paddington immediately each Special leaves.

Inspector Noble and Sub Inspector Turner to be at Windsor during the day.

A Lamp foreman and a staff of two men to be sent from Paddington to Windsor by the 6.38 pm train. They must be provided with a supply of lamps for the up trains and they must see to the lighting and trimming during the evening and if necessary to be sent to Slough to light up any spare trains that may be standing there.

Tickets of Down Specials to be collected at Slough and of the Up Specials at Westbourne Park.

Six extra ticket collectors to be at Slough by 9.0 am, and remain there until 2.0 pm and then return to Westbourne Park.

A narrow gauge pilot engine to stand at Slough and Windsor.

MONDAY JUNE 9TH TO FRIDAY, 13TH JUNE, 1879
The signal for Down trains at the Thames Bridge outside Windsor Station will be brought into use on the above named dates and drivers must be prepared to pull up at it if at danger. A signalman with hand signals will be stationed outside the Up Windsor Distant signal at Slough to repeat the signal. The Iver signal box between West Drayton and Langley and the Dolphin signal box between Langley and Slough will be opened on Tuesday, Wednesday and Thursday, June 10th, 11th and 12th, from 10 am until 10 pm. Special attention of engine drivers and guards is directed to this.

Traffic levels at Windsor had increased again since the figure of 136,000 passengers in 1867. In the early 1880s, the following statistics were recorded:

1880	149,203	passengers	£17,318	30,540	tons goods		£8,553
1881	154,429	"	£18,049	35,313	"	"	£10,473
1882	156,966	"	£19,084	33,521	"	"	£9,858

Windsor had had the benefit of through trains to the City via the Metropolitan line since 1863. In 1883 this was supplemented by a service provided by the Metropolitan District Railway Company (the 'District') from Mansion House to Windsor via a new connection at Ealing Broadway. Initially eleven trains each way were provided (nine on Sundays). The District company provided the locomotives (Beyer, Peacock 4−4−0s) and drivers, each company supplying the coaching stock and guards. Two additional head guards and two junior guards were necessary at Windsor, at a wage of 27s. and 25s. per week respectively, and an extra porter (at 18s.) because the signalman no longer had spare time to assist on the platform. The service started on 1st March, 1883 and included one fast train in each direction on weekdays. From October 1884 the service was reduced to four each way and it was withdrawn completely in September 1885, the track connection at Ealing being removed in 1898.

Despite the short life of this particular train service, one of these trains was involved in a collision, fortunately without injury to staff or passengers or much damage to rolling stock. The accident was a classic case of a signalman forgetting a train.

On 13th October, 1883, a dense fog prevailed in the London District, a factor present in several other accidents recorded in these pages. Signalman John Ormond at West Drayton West cabin had signalled the 2.40 am Paddington Goods to Langley (the next box to the west) via the Down Relief line at 6.52 am, but doubtless there was congestion at Slough and he did not receive 'Line Clear' (i.e. the section to Langley was clear) until 8.38 am. Meanwhile the 7.44 am Hammersmith (Met. District) to Windsor arrived in the station (at 8.29 am); this train had run via Ealing Junction on to the GWR. At 8.32 am he allowed it down to his advanced starting signal − as it passed the box it ran over two detonators, placed by a fogman, indicating the advanced starting signal was at danger. On receipt of 'Line Clear' for the arrival of the goods train at Langley at 8.38 am, Signalman Ormond sent 'Train on Line' to that box for the District train but, unfortunately, omitted to pull off the advanced starter.

The following 7.55 am ex-Paddington had been checked by the District train all the way from Castle Hill (West Ealing). This train was quite short comprising a tender engine, four coaches and a brake van. The District train was of nine coaches hauled by a tank engine. The Paddington train arrived at West Drayton at 8.38 am and at about 8.41 the station starting signal was lowered for the train to 'drop down' to the advanced starter, about 500 yards away. The train passed the West cabin at about 6–10 mph, exploding the detonators again placed by the fogman to warn the driver that the advanced starter was at danger. As he ran over the detonators the driver of the Great Western train caught sight of the District train irregularly ahead of him; despite reversing his engine and applying his hand brake (this train was not continuously braked) a slow speed collison occurred, derailing the last coach of the District train and causing minor damage to the GWR engine.

Colonel Rich of the Railway Department, Board of Trade recommended that in future if a train was detained at an advanced starting signal, one of the traincrew should remain in the signal box as a human reminder to the signalman. A similar accident on the LNWR had occurred some years back and that company had accepted this recommendation at the time.

On Boxing Day, 1886, the telegraph wires in the London Division were 'enlarged almost to the size of a man's arm' by the sheer weight of accumulated and frozen snow; eventually the weight caused the wires to snap, wrecking the system for miles around. A detachment of Royal Engineers was sent to Slough to assist with the placing of fresh poles and reconnecting or replacing the wires, but it is reported that the block system had to be suspended for a period of many weeks until communication could be restored.

Traffic levels at Slough in 1890, excluding the Windsor branch line trains, were 66 passenger and 47 goods trains 'down', and 60 passenger and 47 goods trains 'up'. On average, excluding branch line trains, a train passed

through Slough every 5 minutes throughout the 24 hours. In 1892, including the locomotive department, over 300 staff were employed there. (Nowadays it is probably little more than a tenth of that figure.)

One of the Eton boys, Cyril Armstrong, wrote a poem to commemorate the final demise of the broad gauge on 20th May, 1892. This boy was a brilliant scholar but rather eccentric. His room contained a door which was plastered over with very accurate drawings of locomotives and there were several carved on the inside of the cupboard which held his folding bed. When he left, his father bought the door so as to preserve the drawings. In his latter years at Eton he used to pretend to be a steam engine and could be seen, puffing across from the College to the Library. His top hat became his smoke-stack but 'finding it difficult to keep tidy he gummed it, but it cracked in the sun and became an indescribable object'. This information comes from Guy Kendell, later headmaster of University College School, Hampstead who was at Eton with Armstrong. The latter's poem was as follows:

IN LOVING AND REGRETFUL MEMORY
OF BROAD GAUGE
DIED MAY 20, 1892

On May the 20th a train
Was speeding o'er sweet Thames' plain
  Upon the Broadgauge line
And from her whistle moans arise
That rend our hearts; and loud she cries
  'O' woful fate is mine,
Next morn to Swindon Shops I go
Where hammers clank and forges glow,
Where I was born scarce four years past,
And yet this trip shall be my last;
  '"Great Western" is my name;
'I thought to run for many a year
Upon the line whose name I bear
  'And win for swiftness fame;
'But now my trav'ling days are o'er
This track shall know me now no more,
She spake; and as her plight I spied,
In wrath 'Ye fools and blind,' I cried
  'O brutal, bungling, board!
'That dare Brunel's great work undo,
A greater man than all of you
  and hope thereby your board
To heap on high with L.S.D.
May ruin ruthless rout your glee;
Brunel's sad shade, I see it stand,
With Gooch from Clewer, hand in hand
  And scan the iron Way
Not bright and polished, as of yore,
By thund'ring trains with rush and roar
  But rusting in decay.'

    ☆ ☆ ☆ ☆ ☆

Next morn in sorrow rose the Sun
He saw with shame the deed was done
  Broadgauge had passed away.

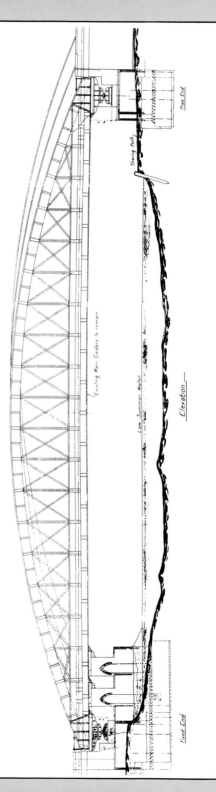

G. W. R. Windsor Branch.

New Floor, Bearings & Abutments for Bridge at 20ᴹ 56ᶜᴴ.

over the River Thames.

Fixed End

Existing Main Girders to remain

Low Summer Water

Elevation

Towing Path

Free End

Part of one of a series of engineering drawings prepared in connection with the repairs to Windsor River Bridge in 1907.

Following the building of the new station at Windsor in 1897 (see Chapter Six) it was necessary to employ additional staff there. Revenue had increased from £37,000 in 1893 to £46,000 in 1899 and the following additional men were needed:

1 Yard Foreman
5 Porters, in place of 1 summer Porter
1 Weighbridge lad
1 Policeman, in place of Summer Policemen
1 Lavatory Attendant, in place of lad
1 Lad clerk

These staff would, in total, cost an extra £361 per annum (which is a reflection of the low level of railway wages at that time).

Although it would compete with the railway, the GWR opened a motor bus service between Slough and Windsor on 18th July, 1904, which enabled it to serve Eton for the first time. Needless to say there were protests from the College about the resulting noise, fumes and dust, but the company pressed on. An hourly service was operated at a through fare of 3d. The service ran for the last time on 26th July, 1913; it was withdrawn following agreement with the London General Omnibus Co. which already operated to Windsor, the latter giving an undertaking not to run a service to Farnham Common (to which place the GWR ran buses) in return.

The GWR were called upon to provide 11 troop trains from Windsor to Aylesbury and 10 from Twyford to Thame on the night of 1st September, 1907 in connection with military manoeuvres. These trains left between 10 pm and 8 am and, in total, conveyed 10,000 officers and men, and a large number of horses, guns, wagons and carts, etc. The soldiers were conveyed in vacuum fitted open goods wagons, at the military's request, and the GWR Magazine reported that the men appeared to enjoy the experience! The arrangements were carried out without a hitch.

In 1907 it was necessary to repair Windsor bridge. The main girders, though nearly 60 years old, were still quite serviceable, but it was necessary to replace the cross girders under the bridge flooring, and also the flooring which carried the permanent way. At the same time the 12 cast iron cylinders filled with concrete which supported the ends of the main girders (two at each end of each of the three main girders) were replaced by substantial brick abutments. (The original main girders are still in use today.)

While this work was in progress it was only possible to use one line over the bridge and a temporary 10 lever signal box (Windsor Bridge) with 8 working levers and 2 spares, was provided at the site (20¾ mp). Ordinary block working existed between Windsor Bridge and Eton box in one direction and with the Windsor Station box in the other, and no two trains were allowed to approach the Thames Bridge from opposite directions at the same time.

Royal garden parties at Windsor were a source of heavy additional traffic and if they coincided with a race meeting much ingenuity was needed in dealing with the number involved in the limited Windsor layout. The following report from the 1908 GWR Magazine gives a slight indication of what was involved:

GREAT WESTERN RAILWAY

ALL NIGHT TRAIN SERVICES

On *Wednesday night, June 21st and Thursday morning, June 22nd, 1911.*

CORONATION

OF

Their Most Gracious Majesties

The KING and QUEEN

Special Train Arrangements

JUNE 19th, 20th, 21st, 22nd, 23rd & 24th.

LONDON AND SUBURBAN DISTRICT,

READING, OXFORD, Etc.

Any further information may be obtained at the Company's Stations, Offices, of **Mr. J. DUNSTER,** Divisional Superintendent, Paddington Station, W., or of **Mr. C. ALDINGTON,** Superintendent of the Line, Paddington Station, W.

JAMES C. INGLIS,

PADDINGTON, June. 1911. General Manager.

WYMAN & SONS, Ltd. Printers, Fetter Lane, London, E.C., and Reading.—12596.

The attractively designed cover of the special timetable for the Coronation in 1911.

Royal Garden Party Windsor

Saturday June 20th, 1908 will be remembered at Paddington as one of the heaviest days on record. Eleven special trains, with first class accommodation only, conveyed some 4,000 of His Majesty's guests to Windsor and back. These specials were despatched with clockwork regularity, and covered the distance to Windsor in from 27 to 29 minutes. At the latter place special arrangements had been made to keep the incoming guests apart from the general passengers and those returning from the Windsor Races which latter were held on the same day. To this end, the organisers of the races (Messrs Frail Bros) were asked to make the last event half-an-hour earlier. This they agreed to do, with the result that the bulk of the race traffic was despatched by the time the King's guests began to arrive at the station for the return journey.

For the races four specials were run each way and contained some 2,000 passengers. In addition to those from London, special trains from Wolverhampton and the Berks & Hants line were run, and a large horse box traffic had to be dealt with. The circumstances at Windsor were somewhat exceptional, as every empty train had to be stabled at Slough and worked as required, whilst at Paddington a similar state of things prevailed.

The tremendous amount of work devolving on the company at Windsor when the monarch died is recorded elsewhere. The coronation of the succeeding King or Queen did not affect Windsor so much as the ceremony took place in London, although extra passenger trains and an all night suburban service were needed to convey sightseers etc. to town.

A special service ran for the crowning of King George V on Thursday 22nd June, 1911. As far as Windsor was concerned there were through trains to Paddington at 12.00 (mdt), 1.00, 2.00, 2.45, 3.00, 3.15, 4.00, 4.15, 5.00, 5.15, 5.45, 6.00, 6.15, 6.30, 7.00, 7.28, 8.15, 8.53 am and then roughly two trains per hour (not all were through) until 10.55 pm. Late night return trains from Paddington were provided at 12.05 am Friday (Windsor 12.41 am), 1.10 am (1.44), 1.20 am (2.15) and 1.35 am (also 2.15). The 1.20 am special service from Paddington also ran on Tuesday, Wednesday, Thursday and Sunday mornings of that week. On the early morning of Coronation Day itself, the Thursday, as well as the 1.20 am from Paddington there was a 2.30 am from Paddington due at Windsor at 3.25 am.

There were some extra through services from Windsor to Paddington early on the day following the Coronation, the Friday, at 4.15, 4.45, 5.15, 5.45 and 7.00 am and extra return late night services at 1.10 am from Paddington, Saturday (Windsor 1.44) and 1.25 am (2.20).

The King and Queen returned to Windsor Castle on 1st July. Slough station, where they detrained was tastefully decorated and the Royal party viewed the station and the cheering crowds before departing through beautifully decorated streets via Eton to Windsor. On the following Monday and Tuesday, 3rd and 4th July, first 17,000 members of the Officers' Training Corps and then (on the Tuesday) 35,000 members of the Boy Scouts were reviewed by the King in Windsor Great Park. It is not recorded how many trains brought the OTC contingent but no less than 25 were provided for the Boy Scouts, so far as the GWR was concerned, all coming to Windsor station! It is recorded that the arrangements worked without the slightest hitch.

No doubt the needs of the First World War brought an increased use of the Windsor branch by troop trains but such things tended to go unrecorded

LONDON DIVISION.—WEEK-DAYS.

SLOUGH—(Cont.)

No. of Turn	Train	From	To	Time Due	Remarks
180	5.30 p.m.	Thame	P. Risboro (Mixed)	5.53 p.m.	TO W'rk'd by Relief Guard
181	7.22 a.m.	Slough	Reading	7.58 a.m.	
	9.33	Reading	Slough	10.10	
182	12.49 p.m.	Slough	Windsor	12.55 p.m.	SO
	1.48	Windsor	Slough	1.54	SO Head
	2.1	Slough	Bourne End	2.28	SO
	2.35	Bourne End	Slough	3.14	SO
	3.53	Slough	Windsor	4.0	
	4.12	Windsor	Slough	4.19	
	4.42	Slough	Windsor	4.48	
	5.10	Windsor	Slough	5.17	
	5.59	Slough	Windsor	6.3	SO
	6.30	Slough	Windsor	6.36	SX
	7.2	Windsor	Slough	7.9	Assisting.
183	6.35 a.m.	Slough	Maidenhead	6.45 a.m.	Empty.
	7.0	Maidenhead	Slough	7.16	
	8.55	Slough	Windsor	9.20	Goods.
	10.15	Windsor	Slough	10.22	
184	7.55 a.m.	Slough	Maidenhead	8.9 a.m.	
	8.30	Maidenhead	Slough	8.45	
	9.18	Slough	Reading	9.53	
	10.20	Reading	Slough	11.4	Asstg.
184A	12.20 p.m.	Slough	Paddington	1.13 p.m.	SO Asstg.
	2.33	Paddington	Windsor	3.17	SO
	3.27	Windsor	Slough	3.34	SO

WINDSOR

No. of Turn	Train	From	To	Time Due	Remarks
185	8.12 a.m.	Windsor	Paddington	8.49 a.m.	Head to Slough.
	9.32	Paddington	Slough	10.23	Head to West Drayton.
	11.58	Slough	H. Wycombe	12.46 p.m.	
	1.5 p.m.	H. Wycombe	Slough	2.10	Head from Maidenhead SO
	2.38	Slough	Windsor	2.45	SX
	2.49	Slough	Windsor	2.55	SO
186	1.5 p.m.	Windsor	Slough	1.12 p.m.	Head on Sats.
	1.32	Slough	Windsor	1.38	SX
	1.37	Slough	Windsor	1.43	SO
	2.2	Windsor	Slough	2.9	
	2.15	Slough	Paddington	3.9	Head to W. Ealing on Sats.
	4.33	Paddington	Windsor	5.3	
	5.43	Windsor	Paddington	6.25	Head from Slough.
	7.35	Paddington	Windsor	8.16	
187	11.7 a.m.	Windsor	Paddington	11.55 a.m.	Head West Ealing to Southall.
	12.35 p.m.	Paddington	Wycombe	2.16 p.m.	SX
	2.52	Wycombe	Paddington	4.15	SX Head from Maidenhead.
	12.47	Paddington	Windsor	1.43	SO
	3.27	Windsor	Paddington	4.10	SO Junior from Slough
	5.40	Paddington	Windsor	6.15	SX
	5.18	Paddington	Slough	5.51	SO
	6.30	Slough	Windsor	6.36	SO

WINDSOR (Cont.)

No. of Turn	Train	From	To	Time Due	Remarks
188	4.45 p.m.	Windsor	Slough	4.52 p.m.	Assisting.
	5.0	Slough	Maidenhead	5.17	
	5.28	Maidenhead	Slough	5.42	Assisting.
	5.59	Slough	Paddington	6.52	Assisting
	7.30	Paddington	Henley	8.35	
	9.25	Henley	Paddington	10.40	
	11.30	Paddington	Windsor	12.15 a.m.	
189	6.22 a.m.	Windsor	Paddington	7.25 a.m.	Head to Slough.
	8.30	Paddington	Maidenhead	9.16	
	10.23	Maidenhead	Reading	10.42	SX Head to Twyford
	11.48	Reading	Slough	12.26	SX Assisting
	12.48 p.m	Slough	Windsor	12.55	SX
	1.40	Windsor	Slough	1.47	SX
	10.23	Maidenhead	Twyford	10.33 a.m.	SO Asstg.
	10.37	Twyford	Henley	10.50	SO
	11.10	Henley	Paddington	12.15 p.m.	SO
	1.25 p.m.	Paddington	Slough	1.55	SO
	2.2	Slough	Windsor	2.8	SO
190	3.30 p.m.	Windsor	Slough	3.38 p.m.	SX
	3.45	Slough	Paddington	4.10	SX Asstg.
	5.18	Paddington	Maidenhead	5.55	SX Asstg.
	6.11	Maidenhead	Slough	6.25	SX Asstg.
	3.57	Windsor	Slough	4.4	SO
	4.17	Slough	Windsor	4.24	SO Asstg.
	6.12	Windsor	Slough	6.19	SO
	6.45	Slough	Windsor	6.51	
	7.2	Windsor	Slough	7.9	
	7.33	Slough	Windsor	7.40	SO Assisting.
	7.45	Slough	Windsor	7.52	SX
	7.58	Windsor	Slough	8.5	SO
	8.10	Slough	Windsor	8.16	SO Asstg.
	8.50	Windsor	Slough	9.0	Goods.
	9.43	Slough	Windsor	9.50	
	Assist as required until 11.0 p.m.				
190A	8.12 a.m.	Windsor	Slough	8.18 a.m.	Asstg.
	8.30	Slough	Windsor	8.36	
	8.47	Windsor	Slough	8.53	
	9.5	Slough	Windsor	9.12	
	9.27	Windsor	Slough	9.35	SO
	9.59	Slough	Windsor	10.5	SO Asstg.
190B	6.22 a.m.	Windsor	Slough	6.29 a.m.	Assisting.
	6.42	Slough	Windsor	6.49	
	7.5	Windsor	Slough	7.12	
	8.28	Slough	Maidenhead	8.42	
	9.12	Maidenhead	Slough	9.27	
	9.59	Slough	Windsor	10.5	Head on Sats.
	10.37	Windsor	Slough	10.44	
	11.45	Slough	Windsor	11.51	
	12.15 p.m.	Windsor	Slough	12.21	SO
	12.32	Slough	Windsor	12.38	SX
	1.9	Slough	Windsor	12.41	SO
	Station duty until finish.				
190C	3.57 p.m.	Windsor	Slough	4.4	SX
	4.9	Slough	Windsor	4.15	SX Assistng
	4.43	Windsor	Slough	4.50	SX Asstg.
	5.12	Slough	Windsor	5.19	SX
	6.12	Windsor	Slough	6.19	Assisting.
	6.29	Slough	Windsor	6.35	
	10.45	Windsor	Slough	10.52	
	11.27	Slough	Windsor	11.33	

§ Works late train to and from Maidenhead.

Duties for the passenger guards based at Windsor (from 14th July, 1924 and until further notice).

Saturday 15th September, 1923 and an animated scene outside Slough station as workers hurry home at 1.30 pm doubtless with thoughts of football or other leisure pursuits in mind. Note the vintage motor cycle and sidecar (*left*) and the GWR bus (*centre*). *British Rail*

An undated 1920s scene and I have no information as to the line-up of vehicles in front of Slough station, but possibly a special party is expected. The station master (and child?) is standing in front of the right hand vehicle. *British Rail*

The west end of Slough looking east at an unknown date, but before 1916 when catch points were installed in the bay lines. Windsor bay platform *extreme right*. There is a wonderful bracket signal consisting of five backing signals (for wrong direction movements), *extreme left*. *LGRP*

Relaying the Windsor (east) junction at Slough on 29th March, 1936. Slough engine shed can be seen, *left*. *British Rail*

Slough goods yard, looking west about 1909.   *British Rail*

The west end of Slough after multiple aspect signalling was in place (1963). The single junction from the down main line to Windsor can be seen (*centre*), the line to its left leads from the south bay platform at Slough.   *S.J. Dickson*

In this 1919 view can be seen the (1905) West signal box and the expanded area for sidings west of the goods shed (*left*). An engine is signalled from the down sidings along the down goods loop, possibly to pick up the three wagons standing on the West Curve. The down relief line home signal carries a bracket which probably is new, for its arm is marked with an 'X', meaning signal not in use.

LGRP

A fine view of the Slough station and junction to Windsor, with Slough Middle box at left (1919). Slough engine shed (*centre left*) and carriage shed just to its right can be seen; the signals are worthy of inspection under a magnifying glass.   *LGRP*

A May 1953 photograph of Windsor looking towards the buffer stops. *British Rail*

This May 1953 picture includes a portion of the little-photographed lower goods yard. *British Rail*

'Castle' class 4–6–0 No. 5022 *Wigmore Castle* rests in platform 1 at Windsor on 17th
May, 1959.   *Michael Hale*

The scissors crossover between platforms 3 and 4 can be seen in this view looking
out from the buffer stops.   *Lens of Sutton*

The station frontage at Windsor in 1990, the building no longer, alas, in railway use, but at least still standing. *Author*

All that remains at Windsor today is a single line leading to platform 1, and even some of that is fenced off to form a public walkway to the coach park in the former goods yard below. Behind the high fence on the right is the Royalty and Empire exhibition of which the previous Royal waiting room forms a part. *Author*

because of the heavy demand for war transport throughout the nation.

After World War I, when the railways were still under government control, attempts were made to standardize the mens' wages, and separate the 'war wage' element from the overall rate of pay with a view to reducing the 'war wage' as inflation fell. A satisfactory arrangement was arrived at for drivers, firemen and engine cleaners but the NUR was dissatisfied with the proposals for other conciliation staff, even though an assurance was given that no reduction in pay would take place before 31st December, 1919 and the whole matter would be reviewed then. On Tuesday 23rd September, 1919 the NUR sent an ultimatum to the government that unless revised proposals for higher payment were submitted by noon on Thursday 25th September all railwaymen would strike. A meeting between the parties was held on 25th September, but agreement could not be reached and the NUR called out all its members from midnight on Friday 26th September. ASLEF, the footplatemen's union, decided to join the strike during that Friday.

Despite the very short notice given of the strike, a volunteers' organisation was set up, just as occurred during the General Strike in 1926. The number of trains run steadily increased; so far as the whole of the GWR was concerned, on the first strike day 54 passenger and 1 freight trains ran and by Saturday 4th October the numbers run had reached 568 (passenger) and 79 (freight). The Windsor branch re-opened on 3rd October with a shuttle service of nine down and eight up trains. The strike was called off on Sunday 5th October after the Government promised to maintain wages at their present level up to 30th September, 1920.

When the General Strike was called in 1926 this ran from 3rd to 14th May. Again volunteers supplemented non-striking staff and the Windsor branch re-opened on 6th May, the first train to run leaving Slough at 3.49 pm. As recorded earlier the Windsor station master worked the signal box and the former (retired) station master Mr Maun took up his old duties for the duration of the strike. On 5th May 41 trucks were unloaded at Slough and their contents delivered by the Eton College boys. On 10th May a freight service was operated over the Windsor branch, also additional passenger services. Trains run throughout the GWR improved from 194 (passenger) on 5th May to 1,245 on the 14th; and from 8 (freight) on 5th May to 157 on the 14th.

Staff employed at Windsor as at 31st March, 1925 were a station master (graded Special Class, the same grade as Slough) and 46 others including 7 passenger guards. The signal box was graded class 2, a high grade for a branch line terminus. Four years later there were only two less staff, but by March 1933 the total complement was down to 40 and the following October it would appear that the station master's job was downgraded to Class 1.

A halt was opened at Chalvey (19 m. 12 ch.) costing £823 on 6th May, 1929, intended to service a district 'developing as a residential area', but this had a very short life and closed just over a year later, for lack of traffic, on 6th July, 1930. The platform was re-used at Cashes Green between Stroud and Stonehouse. The GWR had to apologise to Eton College for opening the halt without permission!

In the period just before World War II started, the GWR, in common with the other railways, drew up plans for the evacuation of children from

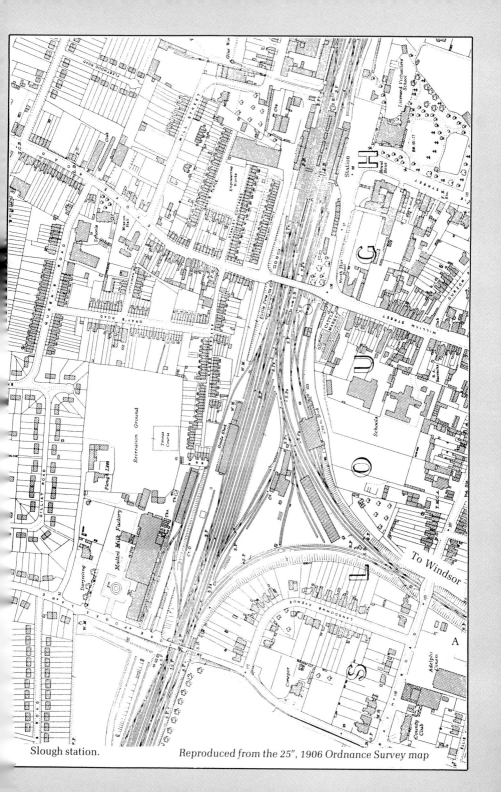

Slough station.

Reproduced from the 25", 1906 Ordnance Survey map

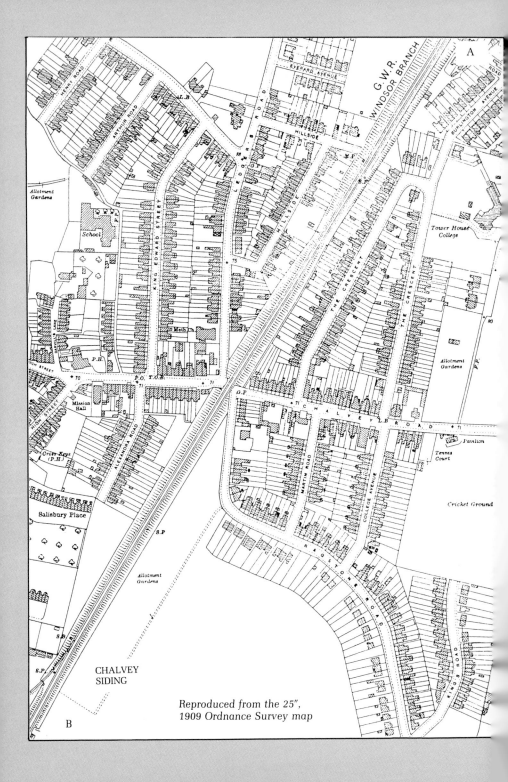

Reproduced from the 25″,
1909 Ordnance Survey map

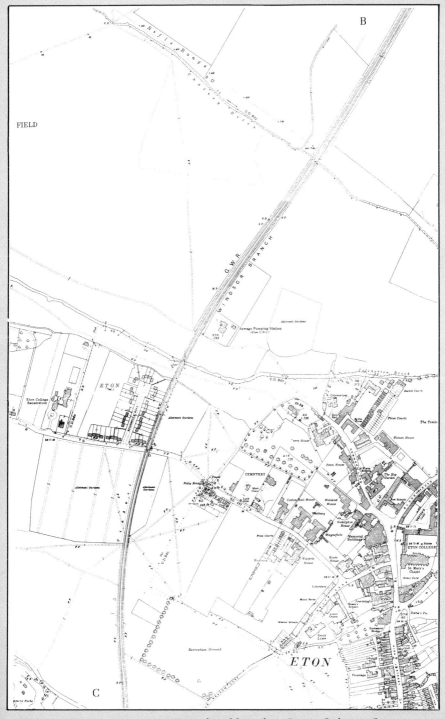

Eton.   *Reproduced from the 25″, 1909 Ordnance Survey map*

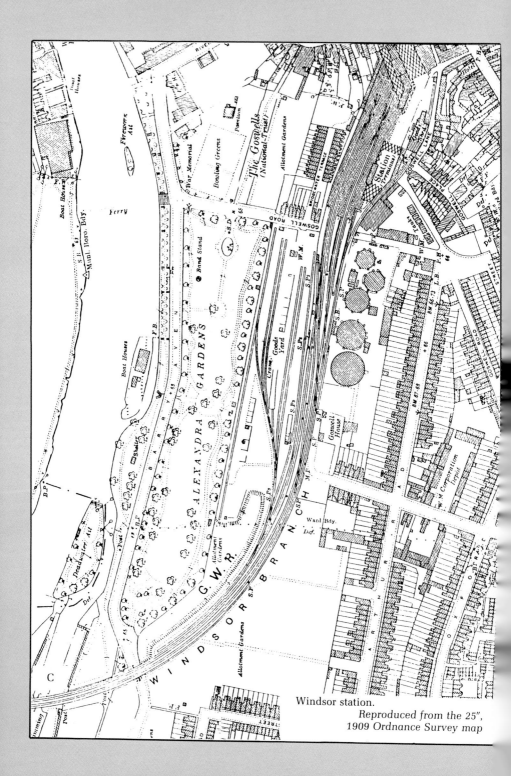

Windsor station.
Reproduced from the 25",
1909 Ordnance Survey map

London. Special timetables were prepared ('The arrangements shown in this Notice must not be circulated to more members of the staff then is necessary . . . and information, other than details of the ordinary train services, must not be circulated to the general public'). The plan for the Windsor branch during this evacuation period legislated for through trains from/to Paddington only, at roughly hourly intervals. All other trains would be withdrawn, although 'Additional branch trips may be run to and from the Bay line at Slough if found necessary and practicable, otherwise local trips to be suspended'.

During World War II the blackout conditions led to a spate of personal accidents arising from people walking off the edge of platforms. There were at least two cases of this at Windsor in 1941, with, in each case, a lady passenger walking off the edge of platform 2. A rather different accident occurred at Slough on 4th August, 1941 when the 8.25 pm Paddington to High Wycombe arrived composed of five coaches for High Wycombe and five for Windsor (rear). As the train was too long for the platform, after passengers had detrained from the front coaches, and the train had been at a stand for 3 or 4 minutes, the train was drawn up to allow passengers to detrain from the rear coaches. After it again came to a stand a passenger for Windsor travelling in one of the leading coaches, now off the platform, got out of the train and fell onto the ballast, fracturing his ankle.

On 4th December, 1940, at 7.40 pm, a high explosive bomb landed in Windsor mileage yard, causing a crater about 40 ft by 20 ft. Much damage was done to the weighbridge office and trackwork in Nos. 3, 4 and 5 sidings; in addition three wagons were completely destroyed, the wheels from one going through the roof of a house in Bridgwater Terrace. Seven other wagons were damaged as were Corridor Thirds Nos. 4471 and 4707. A great quantity of debris and coal was thrown up on the passenger station, breaking a large amount of glass.

The above details happen to have come to hand but are doubtless but a very small part of the wartime mishaps which occurred locally during six long years of conflict.

After the war came Nationalisation. At one minute past midnight on 1st January, 1948, the Windsor branch, and the rest of the GWR became 'British Railways (Western Region)'. But no noticeable change, apart, eventually, from livery alterations, took place for some time to come.

For the Queen's Coronation on Tuesday 2nd June, 1953 the Windsor branch was kept open continuously with a special service during the early hours to enable sightseers to get up to London in time to acquire a good position to watch the processions. Trains left Windsor at 12.10, 12.42, 2.48, 3.52, 4.25, 5.15 and 5.45 am before the normal first up departure at 6.32 am. Returning sightseers could connect with special late trains from Slough at 12.42, 1.25 and 2.38 am on the morning of 3rd June. These return trains also ran on the three remaining weekday nights of that week (the 2.38 am only on the Saturday morning).

The steam suburban service in the London Division (Paddington–Reading) was replaced by diesel multiple units in 1960 (the branches were dieselised in 1959) and it was necessary to create a new up bay line at Slough to allow for turn-back workings. Between 12th and 14th October,

1958, the middle siding between the relief lines was removed and the up relief slewed into the siding's former position. A temporary timber platform 420 ft long was erected alongside the slewed line and the wall for the extended permanent up relief platform was subsequently built underneath the temporary one.

Since its rationalisation in the 1960s the Windsor branch has continued as a very basic branch line with no goods traffic or Royal trains but at least residents can be thankful to have a passenger service of two trains each way every hour. These are well supported by local people and, of course, the tourists.

The *New Statesman* of 5th August, 1983 reported that BR had been approached by a firm called Rail Ltd with a proposal to buy the line, and the report indicated that BR was giving the proposal 'serious consideration'. The approach was regarded as an early example of attempted privatisation, but of the railway itself, rather than a subsidiary such as the hotels. However the *Sunday Times* of 6th January, 1985 carried an article stating that despite nearly two years examination of the proposal by a Working Party, BR had rejected the plan. It stated that Rail Ltd had offered BR £560,000 for the line; the firm proposed using a new railbus on the service, with the prospect of steam operation on summer weekends. However BR declared that the workload involved in effecting the privatisation would be too high, diverting senior managers 'from the main task of keeping the (whole) railway running'.

A recent development, in March 1988, was the introduction of Driver Only operation (and the withdrawal of the guards). Because slam door stock was used on the branch it was necessary to install Emergency Stop Signals which were operated if the driver had to be stopped after leaving the platform with a clear signal and the 'RA' (Right Away) indication from the station staff. These Emergency Stop signals were usually unlit, but if an Emergency Stop plunger was depressed by staff at either Slough or Windsor the Emergency Stop signals displayed a red aspect and also caused the starting signal onto the single line to go back to red. This arrangement (and the D.O. operation) came into effect on 17th March, 1988.

SIGNALLING

Slough

Between 1859 and 1870, as far as can be established,* the signalling at Slough comprised only the Centre signal cabin with a tall post alongside, at first equipped with lamps only, later, not before 1865, with disc and crossbar signals for both directions, all the points being worked by hand. Ground signalmen were also located at the east and west ends of the station working station and auxiliary signals to instructions received from the Centre signalman. Further details are in Chapter Twelve.

In 1879 the GWR extended its gradual quadrupling of the track westwards from London and gave notice to the Board of Trade that it intended to open new standard gauge relief lines from West Drayton to the east end of Slough

---

*These dates are obtained from accident reports – see Chapter 12. It is likely that the Centre cabin was there before 1859 but how long before is unknown. Some interlocking was installed at Slough in 1870. Comprehensive changes were made in 1879, but what happened in between is also unclear.

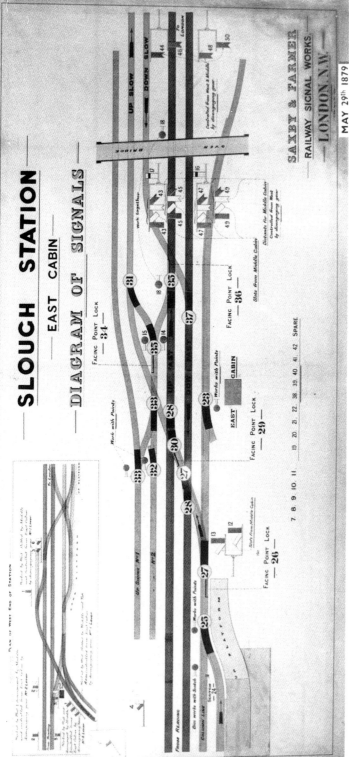

The layout at the east end of Slough (1879) to which Col Yolland took strong exception. The up platform is shown at bottom left, served by the platform line, the other lines, from bottom to top, being the 'column line' (presumably water column), down fast and up fast. The two new slow lines commence just to the right of the East box and are the two lines immediately above the (darker) fast lines at the overbridge. Note how a train from up platform to up slow has to cross both fast lines and a siding. Middle box is just off the left hand end of the diagram. The inset (top left) shows the Slough west end layout, the West box is in the 'V' of the double junction to Windsor. The down platform is on the left hand continuation of the up platform line (bottom line in the inset). Col Yolland also expressed surprise at the provision of a facing point lock (No. 36) on a pair of trailing points to a siding (No. 35), provided because the points were in constant use for shunting. The full size plan, in colour, is exhibited in the GWS Museum at Didcot and is worthy of detailed study there.

Great Western Trust, Courtesy Laurence Waters

on 1st June, 1879. As usual it sought permission to bring the works into use before actually complete and would give further notice when they were ready for BOT inspection. Col Yolland, for the BOT, inspected the works on 15th October, 1879 and although quite satisfied with the arrangements between West Drayton and Langley was shocked with what he found at Slough.

First of all he gave a description of the new signalling. Because the four lines ended east of the station a new East box had been opened (?29th May, 1879) with a frame of 50 levers of which 9 were spare. In the plan of Slough station dated 3rd October, 1879 which is in Chapter Twelve, the *new* East has been drawn on in pencil at the extreme right hand end on the downside of the line (*bottom*) under the figure '1' of '18 miles'. The other boxes shown, the former Centre cabin and that at the west end became 'Middle' and 'West' respectively (certainly they are so described in the 1881 accident detailed in Chapter Twelve). A siding needed to be lengthened, a facing point lock did not work properly and the locking bars (18 ft) were not sufficiently long for the coaching stock now in use. But he reserved his main criticism for the arrangements whereby the traffic of four lines fed into one (for trains calling at Slough) because the old antiquated layout was still in place. Slough was a one sided station with separate up and down stations south of a loop line, the loop itself south of the main (through lines). The up station was at the London end, some 6 chains east of the down station.

> Slough station is a peculiarly constructed station and it may possibly be said that I have no right to comment on its construction, in as much as the two additional narrow gauge lines which I have had to look at on this occasion, terminate on the eastern side of the station. These additional lines have been very well constructed, and are in very good order, but they do not comply with the requirements of the Board of Trade, which stipulates that platforms for the passenger traffic, shall be provided for each line, whereas at Slough station, the passenger traffic for four lines of railway are brought onto one line of railway, and railway level crossings have been introduced, which have not been sanctioned by legislature. To give an instance, I may state that the new additional narrow gauge up slow line, starts from the platform line at the south side of the main lines by means of a pair of facing points, then crosses the down and up main fast lines on the level, as well as a siding line also on the level and then becomes the proper up slow line to Langley in an unobjectionable manner. It is quite impossible that I should recommend the Board of Trade to sanction the existing arrangements. Slough station requires to be completely remodelled and the additional lines carried at all events, right through the station and a proper amount of platform accommodation provided for the main lines, branch to Windsor lines and these additional lines. I can recommend the Board of Trade to sanction the use of the additional lines through West Drayton and up to Langley Station where the requisite platform accommodation has been provided but the portion between Langley and Slough stations, cannot by reason of the incompleteness of the works be opened for traffic without danger to the public using the same.

Taken aback by this outright rejection, the GWR's General Manager asked for an interview with the BOT officials, following which the company wrote on 21st November that it would apply to Parliament for permission to construct two additional lines between Slough and Taplow and gave an undertaking to rebuild Slough completely within 3 years of the passing of the relevant Act. The BOT consulted Colonel Yolland on this, and the latter made the following comments:

a) the GWR must have known that the proposed junctions at the east end of Slough would not pass the inspector

b) it was possible the GWR would seek to perpetuate the objectionable layout by obtaining legislation to sanction it

c) the Windsor branch was made unnecessarily dangerous by the nature of the junctions which now exist *involving danger to all up and down Royal trains* and . . . the unnecessary railway level crossings and facing points should be got rid of with the least possible delay.

Following this the BOT wrote on 20th December, 1879 that the GWR could use the lines between Langley and Slough (they already were) providing the company gave an undertaking to alter Slough and provide additional platforms within 3 years *of the present date*. In the meantime the greatest care needed to be taken to serve the public safety in working this layout.

The GWR pointed out that, as they had missed the opportunity of presenting a Bill to the next session of Parliament, the target date for completion must be 3 years *from the passing of the Act* and the BOT agreed to substitute as completion date, '(3 years from) 1st September, 1880'. Finally the GWR sent the required sealed undertaking on 17th February, 1880 – with an accompanying note stating that obviously its fulfilment did rest upon Parliament sanctioning the necessary Bill.

There is then a gap in the correspondence (but not in the accidents) until 30th July, 1883 when the GWR wrote to the effect that although works were being proceeded with rapidly it would be impossible to finish by 1st September, 1883, but would complete them as soon as possible!

The four line section from Slough to Taplow was ready first and in a report dated 20th August, 1884 Colonel Rich had this to say:

Slough Station is now provided with two platforms for the up lines and two for the down lines. The station has been very much enlarged and improved but will not be completed until the traffic has been turned on to the new lines. This has been done with the sanction of the BOT and junction works are being completed as quickly as possible.

There are signal cabins at the east and west ends of Slough. The latter, together with a ground frame which is worked in connection with it are only to be used temporarily until the new West cabin is built. The new cabin could not be constructed until the site was cleared of the old roads and connections. There are also new cabins at the Slough West Curve, at Hay Mill which is a block station only, at Taplow East and West and at the new junction at the east end of Maidenhead (the end of the 4-track section).

Unfortunately the plan of Slough station to accompany this work is missing from the set of plans at the Public Record Office (as it was on 19th August, 1884, Col Rich notes on the papers!) so it is impossible to verify the position of the Slough signal boxes. (But by 27th February, 1885 when Col Rich next inspected the Slough layout, as follows, the East box was a new one at the east end of the up main line platform, whereas the *1879* East box was on the downside of the down main line. I think it more than likely that this new East box was actually opened in 1885 when the new platforms were brought into use.) Approval was given, subject to certain requirements of

Bath Road Junction signal box, seen in 1919, with the Slough West Curve to the left and the line to Slough station to the right; Slough Middle home signals can be seen to the right of the Carriage Shed behind the box. Note that the West Curve is being used, at least temporarily, for wagon storage. One wonders if the locomotive in the siding neck (*right*) is a long term 'cripple'. *Courtesy J.P. Morris*

The 'Emergency Stop' signal ES1 at Windsor in 1990; normally blank, it only illuminates at red when operated by station staff in emergency. Above the signal is the Right Away (RA) indicator, the driver's indication to proceed, also operated by station staff. Madame Tussauds is behind the fence (*left*) on what remains of platform 2. The walkway behind the high wire fence on the remaining platform leads to the coach park in the former goods yard. *Author*

The junction to Windsor, two days before the relaying seen in the photograph on page 144, 27th March, 1936. Slough Middle signal box is prominent, left.   *British Rail*

A photograph taken to record the new Stoke Road overbridge, but also illustrating the mechanical signalling, a few months before the opening of the new Panel box. On 15th March, 1963, a 2-car dmu from Windsor is running into the south bay, while on the up relief line a 3 car dmu for Paddington approaches Slough station. Note Middle box beyond the new overbridge.   *British Rail*

The interior of Slough West signal box, photographed at an early date.

GWR, Courtesy of J.P. Morris

Although a poor photograph this view of the Slough end of Windsor (from platform 1) is included because it is the only picture I have managed to obtain which shows Windsor signal box (1948). *Mowat Collection*

A single power car and drive end trailer leave Slough for Windsor; 3 car dmu L415, in the short-lived white livery, is stabled in the adjacent siding.　　　　*T. Wright*

Windsor new signal box under construction at Reading signal works in 1963. After closure in 1968 it was reused at Viaduct Jn (near Kensington Olympia).　　*British Rail*

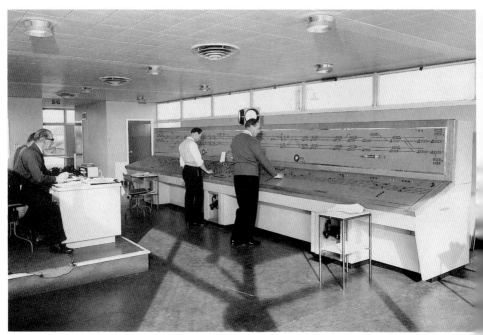

The interior of Slough Panel box photographed on opening day, on 14th October, 1963. The double junctions at Dolphin can be seen on the track circuit diagram in front of the right hand signalman. *British Rail*

A 3-car dmu awaits its next run to Windsor in Slough down bay platform, 1990.
Author

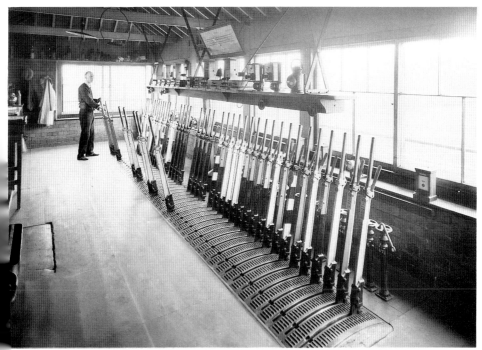

Slough, Dolphin Jn signal box at an unknown date, but post-1904.   *British Rail*

detail, and to the new West cabin at Slough being inspected when completed.

At last the works at Slough were ready, and the GWR wrote to tell the BOT this on 10th February, 1885. Colonel Rich came back to inspect, his report being dated 27th February, 1885. He noted that there were four lines of rails through the station, all connected with the Windsor branch, plus two dock platform lines, one at the west end of the centre platform and one at the east end of the down main line platform, south side. There were four signal boxes, all with points interlocked with signals, described in the report as follows:

> East cabin (London side of station) – 43 working levers, 1 spare lever
> West cabin (at the junction of the Windsor branch) – 89 working, 1 spare lever [this box also known as 'Middle']
> Bath Road cabin (in fork of Windsor branch where line goes left to Reading and right to Slough station) – 15 working, 7 spare levers
> West Curve cabin (junction of Windsor branch west curve with GW main lines) – 29 working and 7 spare levers [this box also known as 'West']

Doubtless breathing a sigh of relief, having investigated several accidents at this location, including two between the date of the sealed undertaking and the inspection, the BOT sanctioned the use of the new layout. The telegraph apparatus, used for signalling trains, was superseded by disc block instruments in 1896.

Following the serious collision at Slough between the 1.15 pm from Paddington to Falmouth and the 1.05 pm Paddington to Windsor on 16th June, 1900 (see Chapter 12), a new west-facing double junction between the main and relief lines was authorised at Dolphin, a mile to the east of Slough. This box had opened sometime before June 1879 but was merely a 'break section' box (it did not even control the relief lines until 1896) until the installation of these junctions which were inspected and passed on 19th September, 1901. A new signal box of 27 levers was included in the scheme which cost £2,482. Further east-facing junctions were provided at this site and inspected on 26th March, 1904. This addition cost £1,732, the frame in the box being extended to 38 working and 9 spare levers. A new Slough West box of 95 levers was authorised in 1900 in connection with new running line junctions; it was built by 1905. Just to complete the picture, although not part of the Windsor story, a new signal box at Farnham Road, a mile west of Slough, was passed in September 1904 and cost £1,523; at the end of World War I a new junction leading to a Slough Estates station on a large industrial site being developed there necessitated a much larger 74 lever signal box (60 working), opened on 9th March, 1919.

An innovation for the GWR was a new signal box at Bath Road Junction, described as the first installation 'of electro-pneumatic plant' on the system. (It was intended to be a trial run for a similar system at Paddington, but this was cancelled because of World War I). The power for actuating the signals and points was compressed air at a pressure of 70 lb p.s.i. and the air compressor was steam driven from Slough engine shed. The brick-built signal box contained a locking frame of 17 miniature levers and six spaces. The GWR Magazine for December 1913 contains a comprehensive, illus-

GREAT WESTERN RAILWAY

IMPORTANT NOTICE.

OPENING OF INTERMEDIATE SIGNAL BOXES.

LONDON DIVISION.

ETON REGATTA, TUESDAY, JUNE 4TH.

The "Iver" and "Dolphin" intermediate Signal Boxes, situated between West Drayton and Langley and Langley and Slough, with their Distant and Home Signals controlling Trains running on the Main Lines, will be brought into use from 10.0 a.m. to 11.0 p.m.

The "Eton" intermediate Signal Box, situated between Slough and Windsor with its Distant and Home Signals, will also be brought into use for the first time between 10.0 a.m. and 11.0 p.m. on this date.

The special attention of all concerned is directed to this.

ALFRED HIGGINS,

PADDINGTON, 30th May, 1889.   Divisional Superintendent

l.)·   JUDD & Co., Limited, Printers, Farringdon Road and Doctors' Commons.   [674A

The opening notice for Eton signal box (between Slough and Windsor). It is thought that it may only have opened on special occasions such as this (it does not appear, for example, in the 1901 Working Timetable), nor are there any staff allocated to it in the GWR's establishment records for 1925–1934.   *Royal Borough Collection*

trated article describing, in detail, the technical aspects of the installation. The box was opened towards the end of 1913 and cost £1,882; however it continued to switch out outside the periods when the West Curve was in use and an unusual arrangement applied so far as its up home signal (to Slough station) was concerned. When the box was closed this signal (No. 23) was treated as an additional home signal to Slough Middle box. When Bath Road switched out, the pulling of the switch lever released lever 24 in Middle box. When the latter lever was operated it locked the switch lever in Bath Road box and allowed Middle box to work the Bath Road home signal. The box reverted back to a conventional type of locking frame in 1931.

Windsor

All we know about Eton signal box is that it was situated on the up side of the line at 19 m. 71 ch. from Paddington (about 1¼ miles from Windsor) and that it opened on 4th June, 1889 (see opening day circular). It is thought unlikely, however, that this box was in *regular* use until sometime early in the 20th century (c.1909). Even in the 1920s, no resident staff were allocated to the box, so it may have always been an 'open as required (by relief signalmen)' job. Any other information which readers have would be most welcome!

Reports into accidents are often the only documents giving details of signalling before the introduction of properly interlocked signal boxes. In Chapter Twelve such details are to be found in the various accidents occurring at Windsor. For example the accident at Windsor on 13th June, 1885 describes the signalling then applicable. All the points were worked by hand, as had been the case until recently at Slough. The first signal, sighted about ½ mile before reaching Windsor, was a Stop signal which was only used at times of exceptionally heavy traffic, such as Ascot Races. Then some 660 yds beyond, came the famous Windsor 'drum' signal (which the report tells us had been operated by a particular individual for 30 years, so there is a good chance it was built when the branch opened). MacDermot describes the signal thus:

> The Windsor 'Drum' or 'Tambourine' signal remains to be noticed. Owing to the right-angle curve of the railway approaching Windsor station an ordinary Disc-and-Crossbar was found to be useless, as the *Danger* signal would appear when first sighted to be an *All Right* one, and vice versa. So Brunel designed a modification which when at *Danger* would show a crossbar in all directions. In the *All Right* position it showed the driver first an upright bar and then, as he came round the bend, the usual disc. This signal seems to have been unique; so far as can be discovered there was no other of the kind on the system. It remained in use till the end of the 'eighties.

The signal, unlike most other disc and crossbar signals, moved vertically from danger to 'all right' rather than horizontally. This signal was worked in conjunction with the Station signal, some 200 yards beyond; the drum-signal operator watched the Station signal and repeated that signal's positions.

Considering the GWR had been running Royal trains over the branch for 40 years, it is perhaps a little surprising that it took until May 1889 for a

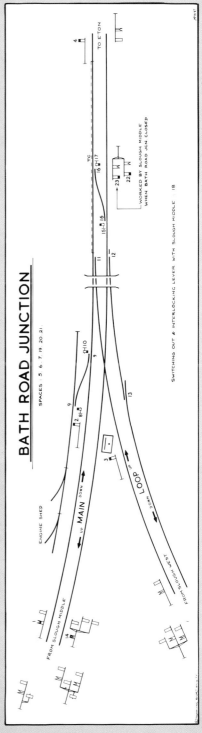

Bath Road Jn signalling plan.

Slough West signalling plan.

Signalling Record Society

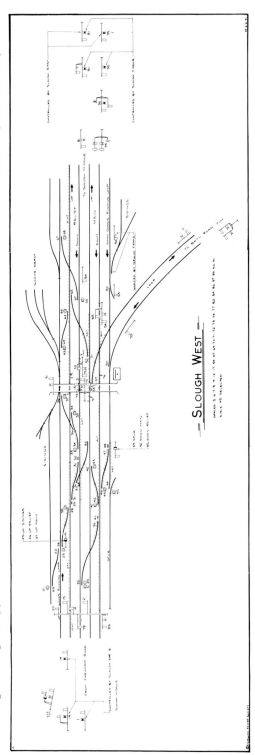

SLOUGH WEST

The new Panel signal box at Slough, photographed on 12th September, 1963.

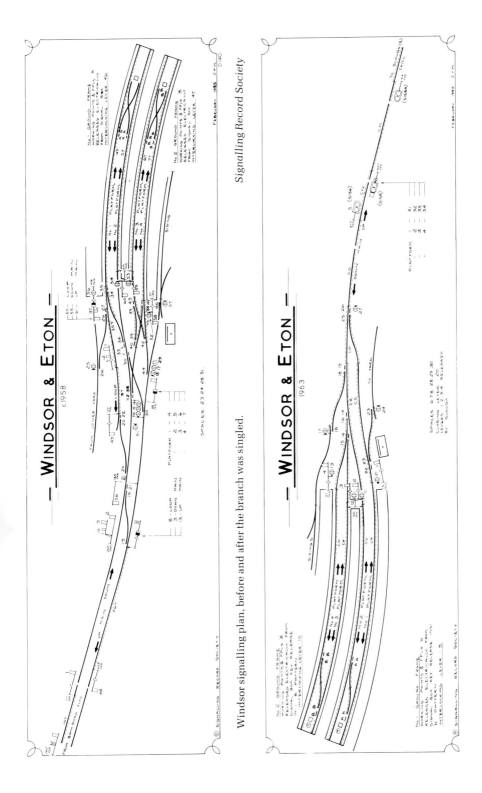

Signalling Record Society

Windsor signalling plan, before and after the branch was singled.

BRITISH RAILWAYS
(WESTERN REGION)

Notice to Enginemen, Guards, etc.

SIGNAL ALTERATIONS—

WINDSOR BRANCH

MONDAY, 9th SEPTEMBER, 1963

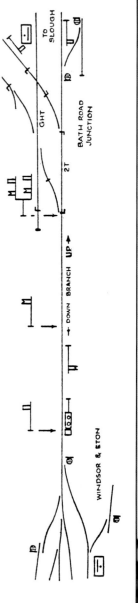

Between the hours of 7.30 a.m. and 5.0 p.m. the Chief Signal and Telecommunications Engineer will be engaged in singling the Windsor Branch between the limits of the crossover at Bath Road Junction and the trailing connection in the Down Main at Windsor & Eton as shewn on the attached diagram.

Permanent Way Alterations

The existing Up Line between Windsor & Eton and Bath Road Junction will be taken out of use and the existing Down Line will become a single line. The connection to the existing Up Main at Windsor & Eton will be clipped, spiked and padlocked out of use, pending recovery.

Signalling Alterations

At Bath Road Junction, the Down Main Starting signal will be taken out of use and the Up Main Home signals will in future apply to the single line. The disc reading from the Down Main to the West Loop or Up Main will be removed.

At Windsor & Eton, signals and discs at present reading to the Up Main will in future read to the single line.

A.W.S. ramps on the Branch will be recovered.

Method of Working

The Double Line Absolute Block working between Bath Road Junction and Windsor & Eton will be discontinued and Electric Token Block working instituted in accordance with pages 23–27 of the General Appendix.

The switching-out facility at Bath Road Junction will be taken out of use.

Track Circuit Alteration

The existing track-circuit (2T) to the rear of the Down·Main Starting for Bath Road Junction will be shortened to a position opposite the Up Home signals and will lock the existing crossover which becomes the new single to double line junction, in the reverse position. An emergency release plunger will be provided.

Occupation of the locking frames at Bath Road Junction and Windsor & Eton will be required for alterations and testing purposes. Occupation of the locking frame at Slough Middle will be required for the purpose of securing levers.

During the occupation the Down Main Distant for Bath Road Junction will be disconnected and maintained at Caution.

All arrangements for the safe working of the line (including the appointment of Handsignalmen) must be made by the District Inspector in accordance with Rule 77.

G. A. V. PHILLIPS,
Divisional Manager,
　PADDINGTON STATION.
August, 1963.

　　　　　　　　　　　　　H. M. LATTIMER,
　　　　　　　　　　　　　Movements Manager,
　　　　　　　　　　　　　PADDINGTON STATION.

Singling the line between Slough and Windsor: September 1963.

Schematic diagram of multiple-aspect colour-light signalling in the Slough Area. Windsor & Eton signalbox is retained for local operating requirements; when Windsor box is closed, a shuttle service can be operated between Windsor and Slough controlled from Slough signalbox

Courtesy Railway Gazette

The new signalling in the Slough/Windsor area.

properly interlocked signal box to be provided at Windsor. However on 23rd May, 1889, Col Rich of the BOT inspected and passed a signal box with 50 working and 3 spare levers and block telegraph. The alterations had also entailed the provision of a short bay departure platform, No. 3, in addition to the two main platforms which were bi-directional. (In addition to 'splitting' home signals leading to either main platform there were splitting distants also.)

The station was completely re-arranged in 1897 to celebrate the Queen's Diamond Jubilee and became a spacious terminal of four platform lines, all bi-directional. The existing box (and probably lever frame) was used and the new frame consisted of 52 working levers and 1 spare. Ground frames and scissors crossovers were provided at the buffer stop ends of platform lines 1/2 and 3/4 to enable train engines to be released from incoming arrivals without shunting the coaches out of the platform. The completed work was inspected and passed by Colonel Yorke on 27th February, 1902.

This exceptionally well designed layout continued in use, practically unscathed by change, until 1963 and the coming of Multiple Aspect Signalling, controlled by Slough Panel.

Multiple Aspect Signalling

As part of the signalling modernisation of the London Division, a new power signal box ('Panel' in Western Region parlance) was to be built at Slough covering an area from Dawley (between Hayes and West Drayton) to a point between Maidenhead and Twyford. It was intended that the Windsor branch remain double track, but as a result of increasing costs, largely arising from the 1960 Guillebaud Pay award (the authorised scheme in 1959 cost £2,076,000 and in 1961 had increased to £2,335,900), the Western Region was forced to go back to the British Transport Commission with a reduced scheme. This now cost £1,581,100, and as well as reducing the Windsor branch to single line, the modified plan dropped the following facilities from the project:

Connection Windsor branch to relief lines
down goods loop at Slough
relief to main double junction at West Drayton
main to relief double junctions at W. Drayton and Maidenhead to be 25 mph (not
    40 mph)
various connections at W. Drayton, Langley and Taplow
up goods loop Dolphin Junction–Langley
relief to main double junction at Maidenhead
down and up goods loops at Maidenhead to be refuge sidings
track realignment at W. Drayton and Taplow not done

The up line between Windsor and Slough, Bath Road Junction, was taken out of use on Monday 9th September, 1963. (Previously a new all-timber signal box had opened at Windsor, on the opposite side of the line, on 5th May, 1963.) Electric Token Block Working between the two points replaced the former double line Absolute Block Working. Just over a month later all four signal boxes at Slough closed and Slough Panel box opened (14th October, 1963).* For the present Windsor signal box remained, as did all

*The complete scheme involved closure of 14 boxes and saved 74 signalmen, train recorders etc.

four platform lines at Windsor but the short-lived Electric Token working was replaced by Track Circuit Block working from Slough. Windsor box was normally closed, only being opened if more than a single platform (No. 2) was needed or if a locomotive-hauled train used the station.

From 25th November, 1963, Windsor dealt only with coal traffic so far as goods was concerned and all freight facilities were withdrawn on 6th January, 1964, and the lower yard was removed the following April.

Windsor signal box was closed on 17th November, 1968 and platforms 3 and 4 were taken out of use on the same date; platform 2 only lasted a few more months being taken out of use on 5th September, 1969, leaving just platform 1 in use, the position which still obtains today. Whether both platforms 2 and 1 were in use together between November 1968 and September 1969 is not clear. There is no record of a ground frame being installed to give access to the second platform and it may be that until September 1969 platform 2 was in use on its own, the track thereafter being slewed to serve Platform 1. The West Loop at Slough was taken out of use on 26th July, 1970.

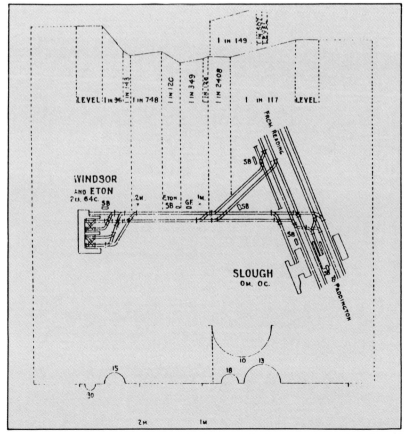

The gradient diagram for the branch. The figures at the bottom indicate the radius of the curves.

SLOUGH.

INSTRUCTIONS FOR SWITCHING OUT BATH ROAD SIGNAL BOX, AND SUPPLEMENTARY BLOCK INSTRUCTIONS FOR WORKING BETWEEN SLOUGH AND WINDSOR WHEN BATH ROAD SIGNAL BOX IS SWITCHED OUT.

The Block Telegraph Switch at the Slough Bath Road Signal Box is coupled up to lever No. 19 in the Locking Frame, and the following is the regulation for the opening and closing of the Signal Box, which regulation supersedes Regulation No. 24 of the Standard Double Line Block Regulations.

When lever No. 19 is back in the frame, that is, in the position corresponding to the Danger position of the Signal levers, the Block Instruments are switched in. When the lever is pulled over, that is, in the position corresponding to the " All Right " position of the Signal levers, the Block Instruments are switched out. The rule for switching out is as follows :—

At the time specified for switching out, the Signalman must give 17 beats on the bell, thus :—(7 pause 5 pause 5) to the Slough Middle and Windsor Signal Boxes, provided that there is no Up Train in either section and that all the Block Instruments for the Up Line are in the " Normal " or " Line Blocked " position. The Signalmen at Slough Middle and Windsor must return the signal, and when this has been done, the Signalman at Bath Road must pull off his Signals for the Down Line and also his Up Home to Slough Middle Signal, and lever No. 19 must then be pulled over. The pulling over of lever No. 19 will complete the switching out of the Bath Road Signal Box so far as the Signalman there is concerned. The pulling over of lever No. 19 in the Bath Road Signal Box will also release a mechanical lock on lever No. 24 in the Slough Middle Box, and the Signalman there, on seeing the electric indicator in connection with that lever showing " Unlocked " must pull over that lever. This will mechanically bolt lever No. 19 in the Bath Road Signal Box and cause the electric indicator in connection with that lever in the Bath Road Signal Box to show " Locked." When these operations have been completed the Slough Middle Box must exchange the test signal, 16 beats on the bell, with Windsor. The Signalman at Bath Road Signal Box must, before leaving the Box, see that the electric indicator in connection with lever No. 19 shows " Locked," and ascertain from the Middle Box that the Switching out operations at that Signal Box have been correctly carried out.

When Bath Road Signal Box is switched out, the Up Windsor Branch Signal for the Bath Road Signal Box is controlled by Slough Middle Signal Box.

The rules for switching in the Bath Road Signal Box are as follows :—

When the Bath Road Signal Box is ready to switch in, the Signalman there must obtain permission from Windsor and the Slough Middle Box, by means of the telephone, to switch in, and this permission must only be given, provided that there is no Up Train in the section, and that the Block Instruments for the Up Line are in the " Normal " or " Line Blocked " position. The Slough Middle Box, after giving permission to the Bath Road Signal Box to switch in, must put lever No. 24 back in the frame. This lever will be electrically locked in the " Off " position, and to release the lock, the Signalman must operate the plunger provided for the purpose. The putting back of lever No. 24 in the Middle Box will withdraw the bolt bolting lever No. 19 in the Bath Road Signal Box, and when the Bath Road Signalman sees the electric indicator in connection with that lever showing " Unlocked," he must put the lever back in the frame. The putting back of lever No. 19 in the Bath Road Box will bolt lever No. 24 in the Slough Middle Box. The Bath Road Signalman must then send the " Opening of Signal Box " signal, 15 beats (5 pause 5 pause 5) to Windsor and Slough Middle Boxes, and when that Signal has been repeated to him from both of those Signal Boxes, he must advise Slough Middle and Windsor by telephone that he has properly switched in.

SHUNTING ON TO UP WINDSOR BRANCH.

Middle Box.—If any Engine, with or without vehicles attached, is sent on to the Up Windsor Branch for Shunting purposes the last vehicle must in all cases go beyond the Inner Home Signal before being brought to a stand, and must remain there until the road is set and the proper Signal lowered for the Up Main, Up Relief Lines and South Bay, as the case may be.

When vehicles are shunted on the Up Windsor Branch, as described in the preceding paragraph, the " Blocking Back Outside Home " Signal (3—3) must be sent to the Box in circuit in the rear.

SIGNALLING OF UP EXCURSION TRAINS FOR WINDSOR.

Up Excursion Trains for Windsor to be signalled from Reading East Main Signal Box under the Special Bell Code (2—5—1).

BELL COMMUNICATION BETWEEN SOUTH BAY AND MIDDLE BOX.

Engine over, reverse Points in South Bay for Middle Road .. 1 Ring.
Engine clear in Middle Road .. .. 2 pause 1.

WORKING OF CHALVEY SIDING, WINDSOR BRANCH.

The Chalvey Siding is situated on the Up Side of the Line on the Windsor Branch at 19 miles 35 chains adjoining the Metropolitan Electric Supply Co.'s works.

There is a Ground Frame at the Siding and the following points and signals are worked from the Ground Frame :—

Up Home Signal for Chalvey Siding.
Up Distant ,, ,, ,, (Lower Arm on Eton Up Home).
Points from Up Line to Chalvey Siding.
Independent Discs from Up Line to Siding and from Siding to Up Line.

There are no Block Instruments at the Ground Frame, but there is a telephone connected with Slough—Windsor Circuit. The Up Distant Signal is electrically repeated in the Ground Frame.

There is no connection with the Down Line, and only Up Freight Trains can do work at the Siding. The key of the Ground Frame must be kept in the Windsor Signal Box when not in use. Before leaving Windsor the Guard of a Freight Train having work to do at the Siding, must go to the Windsor Signal Box and inform the Signalman that the train has to call at the Siding, and obtain the key of the Ground Frame. The Signalman at Windsor must then telephone to the Signalman at Eton Box (when open) and Bath Road Box (when open) or Slough Middle Box, stating that the train has to call at the Siding, and the Signalman at Bath Road must not ask " Is Line Clear ? " ahead for the train until he has been advised by the Guard on the telephone that the train is about to leave the Siding.

The Up Line at the Siding is on a gradient of 1 in 127 falling towards Windsor.

When the train having to do work arrives at the Siding, the Guard must immediately unlock the Ground Frame, and telephone to Bath Road Box (when open) or Slough Middle Box informing the Signalman there that the train has reached the Siding and the Guard must also place the Home and Distant Signals at " Danger." The Signal must be kept at " Danger " until the work at the Siding is done and the train is about to leave for Slough.

Before uncoupling the engine or engine and wagons to go into the Siding, the Guard must put the hand brake hard down on his van, and he must also put down sufficient brakes on the wagons to prevent them running back.

Extracts from Appendix to No. 1 Section (London District) to the Service Timetables, June 1938.

Slough—continued.

Working of Chalvey Siding, Windsor Branch—continued.

The Guard must see that the Signals are placed in the " All right " position before he leaves the Siding. and he will be responsible for seeing that the wagons in the Siding are properly secured and clear inside the catch points before leaving the Siding.

The Guard must telephone to the Signalman at Bath Road or Slough Middle Box when the train is ready to leave the Siding, informing him that the train is about to leave and that the points and signals are right for passing trains.

If the Guard of the train is not returning to Windsor, he must, on arrival at Slough, take the key of the Ground Frame to the Inspector on duty, who will be responsible for seeing that it is booked to Windsor by the next train, addressed to the Windsor Station Master. If the Guard returns to Windsor he must take the key back with him and hand it over to the Signalman there.

No train must be allowed to do work at the Siding during fog or falling snow.

WINDSOR.

SHUNTING IN GOODS YARD.

Whenever shunting operations are being carried on in the Goods Shed Road, and it becomes necessary to open the catch points which protect the No. 5 Line, the Signalman on duty must in every case, before opening those points, stop the Shunting Engine and satisfy himself that the Driver and Shunter understand what is about to be done.

Whenever the catch points are open, the shunting must be carried on with the greatest care so that no risk may be run of the engine or wagons passing through them.

The Starting Signal for No. 5 Line must never be passed when at " Danger," either for shunting purposes or otherwise.

WORKING TRAINS AND ENGINES BETWEEN THE PASSENGER STATION AND THE LOW YARD LEVEL.

The line leading from the Passenger Station to the Low Level Goods Yard is on a falling gradient of 1 in 45.

The Speed of Trains and Engines passing over this Line must not exceed 5 Miles an Hour.

No train must be allowed to be propelled down the incline into the Low Level Yard or pulled up the incline except upon the authority of the Station Master. In all cases the train must be fully vacuum brake fitted and coupled throughout in order that the enginemen can have complete control over the train working Up or Down the incline.

Every train or engine working from the Passenger Station into the Low Level Yard must be piloted down the incline by the foreman or man in charge of the operations, and he must, in cases where an engine is already in the Low Level Yard, satisfy himself that the points leading to the Siding into which the vehicles are to run are not fouled.

The Signalman must never allow a train or engine to leave the Station for the Low Level Yard until he has satisfied himself that there is a man in charge acting as Pilotman.

The number of wagons working down from the Passenger Station to the Low Level Goods Yard must not exceed 20.

A good supply of Sprags must always be kept at the foot of the incline, near the Distant Signal, and at the top of the Incline.

The instructions for working Inclines shown in the Appendix to the Rule Book must be strictly adhered to, special attention being given to the necessity of putting down sufficient brakes on the wagons to prevent the engine being overpowered.

INSTRUCTIONS TO BE OBSERVED BY THE SIGNALMEN AND SHUNTERS WHEN THE GROUND FRAMES AT PLATFORM DEAD ENDS AT WINDSOR STATION HAVE TO BE WORKED, AND IN LETTING TRAINS INTO THE PLATFORMS WHEN VEHICLES ARE STANDING AT THE DEAD ENDS.

When it is necessary to work either of the Ground Frames to enable an engine, or engine and vehicles to run round a train standing on the Platform Lines the following code of Bell Signals from the Ground Frames to the Signal Box must be made use of :—

	Beats on Bell	How to be given
Release Lock for Ground Frame Levers Nos. 1 and 2.	3	1 pause 2
Release Lock for Ground Frame Levers Nos. 3 and 4.	7	3 pause 4

When the Lock has been released the points must be set for the engines to pass over the Scissors Crossing.

If from any cause the engine is detained on the Platform Line, when running round, the Shunter must proceed on foot to the Signal Box and advise the Signalman accordingly, and the Shunter must not leave the box until the engine has passed from the Platform Line and been disposed of by the Signalman.

TRAFFIC DEALT WITH AT STATIONS

Station	Year	Staff			Passenger Train Traffic					
		Supervisory and Wages (all grades)	Paybill Expenses	Total Receipts	Tickets issued	Season Tickets	Passengers (including Season Tickets, etc.)	Parcels	Miscellaneous	Total
		No.	£	£	No.	No.	£	£	£	£
Slough	1903	89	5,662	23,164	252,908	*	18,795	2,800	1,569	23,16
Passenger	1913	89	6,332	32,847	462,962	2,418	27,567	3,036	1,744	32,34
	1923	101	18,909	65,693	486,395	4,768	56,231	5,665	3,797	65,69
	1929	113	20,063	89,749	536,093	10,451	64,825	18,848	6,081	89,74
	1930	111	20,099	81,739	431,192	9,657	54,137	23,356	4,246	81,73
	1931	111	21,253	73,976	369,369	8,471	45,916	23,830	4,230	73,97
	1932	106	20,377	72,132	358,828	7,820	44,411	23,578	4,143	72,13
	1933	107	21,175	70,182	341,600	7,432	44,951	22,047	3,184	70,18
	1934	108	20,997	77,856	388,999	8,451	51,439	23,218	3,199	77,8
Windsor and	1903	51	2,906	48,448	228,766	*	24,054	4,346	4,738	33,1
Eton	1913	51	2,507	46,586	186,247	1,402	23,774	3,327	4,018	31,1
	1923	46	6,974	61,591	311,933	3,291	42,060	2,136	2,076	46,2
	1929	46	6,529	60,486	249,275	5,421	37,700	2,723	1,489	41,9
	1930	46	6,735	45,415	168,695	4,464	26,555	2,785	1,636	30,9
	1931	46	7,061	36,934	114,795	3,650	20,564	2,702	1,806	25,0
	1932	45	6,184	33,829	102,660	3,533	19,402	2,602	1,809	23,8
	1933	45	6,031	33,649	97,751	2,804	19,050	2,448	1,460	22,9
	1934	40	6,497	35,384	105,851	3,061	19,206	2,452	1,864	23,5

*Figures not available.

Goods Train Traffic

Station	Year	Staff Supervisory and Wages (all Grades) No.	Paybill Expenses £	Total Receipts £	Forwarded Coal and Coke 'Charged' Tons	Forwarded Other Minerals Tons	Forwarded General Merchandise Tons	Received Coal and Coke 'Charged' Tons	Received Other Minerals Tons	Received General Merchandise Tons	Coal and Coke 'Not Charged' (Forwarded and Received) Tons	Total Goods Tonnage Tons	Total Receipts (excluding Coal and Coke 'Not Charged') £	Livestock (Forwarded and Received) Wagons	Total Carted Tonnage (incl. in Total Goods Tonnage) Tons
Slough Goods	1903	*	*	20,924	832	12,161	5,475	4,499	11,766	19,825	23,766	77,324	20,924	1,091	10,265
	1913	20	1,390	23,684	26	4,667	7,521	3,018	10,464	20,087	32,782	78,565	23,684	1,041	13,375
	1923	34	5,116	83,281	106	2,473	22,229	6,371	13,781	30,843	46,160	121,963	83,281	379	19,276
	1929	38	7,742	156,054	837	9,786	40,818	8,422	51,699	46,597	70,811	228,465	156,054	244	38,601
	1930	55	9,321	156,896	1,019	9,898	36,514	9,729	62,927	47,099	68,389	235,575	156,896	221	39,844
	1931	57	9,108	140,331	961	10,660	33,888	8,398	44,218	40,636	70,891	209,647	140,331	183	40,533
	1932	57	9,355	114,297	716	7,003	23,505	5,397	36,798	36,682	70,175	180,276	114,297	111	32,216
	1933	59	10,238	126,873	676	7,265	26,000	6,490	31,025	41,263	71,477	184,196	126,373	70	38,873
	1934	63	11,425	144,070	168	7,172	32,373	7,860	26,760	48,666	81,353	204,352	144,070	59	48,507

*Figures not available

BRANCH LINES—LONDON DIVISION—continued.

CLASS OF ENGINE.

From	To	40XX	29XX 43XX 31XX	"County" 22XX 102-3-104	"Bull Dog" 44XX & 45XX, B 0-4-0 T., B & C Groups (New Boilers) 4-4-0 Cam. (Belpaire).	"City," "Atbara," "Duke," 36XX 2 & 39XX, 0-4-2 T., C Groups—Old Boilers 0-6-0 M.&S.W. (G.W. Boilers).	3521 Type 0-6-0 & 0-6-0 T. (Stand. Gds.) 0-4-2 T. A & B Groups (Sml Boilers) 0-6-0 Cam. (Belpaire) 0-6-0 M.&S.W. (Old Boilers).	3201 to 3205 3501 to 3520 3206 to 3225 3526 Type (Small Boiler) 2-4-2 T. (Convertible) 4-4-0 M.&S.W. (New Boilers).	998 to 1082 Cam. 4-4-0 M.&S.W. (Old Boilers).	3232 to 3251 2-4-0 T. Metro 4-4-4 T. M.&S.W. 1112, 1118 1, 26-9 Cam.	0-4-2 T. (517 Type) 0-4-4 T. Metro 4-4-4 T. (M.&S.W.) 2-4-0 (M.&S.W.).
		Tons	Tons	Tons	Tons	Tons	Tons	Tons	Tons	Tons	Tons
Princes Risboro	Aylesbury	—	—	—	—	—	—	—	—	—	168
Aylesbury	Princes Risboro	—	—	—	—	—	—	—	—	—	112
Princes Risboro	Oxford	336	308	280	252	224	196	182	—	168	140
Oxford	Princes Risboro	364	336	308	280	252	224	210	—	224	196
Radley	Abingdon	—	—	—	—	—	—	—	—	224	196
Abingdon	Radley	—	—	—	—	—	—	—	—	224	196
Reading	Basingstoke	392	364	336	208	280	252	238	—	224	196
Basingstoke	Reading	392	364	336	208	280	252	238	—	224	196
Slough	Windsor	392	364	336	208	280	252	238	—	224	196
Windsor	Slough	392	364	336	208	280	252	238	—	224	196
Southall	Brentford	—	—	—	—	—	—	—	—	196	—
Brentford	Southall	—	—	—	—	—	—	—	—	196	—
Twyford	Henley	392	364	336	308	280	252	238	—	224	196
Henley	Twyford	336	308	280	252	224	196	182	—	168	140
West Drayton	Staines	392	364	336	308	280	252	238	—	224	196
Staines	W. Drayton	392	364	336	308	280	252	238	—	224	196
W. Drayton	Uxbridge	392	364	336	308	280	252	238	—	224	196
Uxbridge	W. Drayton	392	364	336	308	280	252	238	—	224	196

Standard Loads of Passenger, Parcels and Fish Trains Notice: January 1927.

Chapter Ten
Locomotive Matters

As recorded in Chapter Three the first locomotive to visit Windsor just before the line opened was a new saddle tank, but no more positive identification is given, nor is the name of the locomotive used on opening day mentioned in the reports. The earliest information about motive power on the Windsor branch comes from Daniel Gooch's engine book 1850–1853 and is recorded in Appendix One. As will be seen the engines employed at this time were already about 10 years old or more and were probably those least suited to main line work, the four engines privately built particularly so. Having said that, Windsor driver Samuel Guest invariably drove *Snake* during this period, if it was available, so maybe it was quite up to this branch work. The engine book shows that the trains worked by the Slough-based engines were of 3 or 4 carriages only. The book shows the branch engines (in total) working about 2,500–3,000 miles per fortnight. Some further detail comes from the memories of Mr R. Neville Grenville, who was a schoolboy at Eton from 1858 to 1864. Some brief extracts from these memories appeared in the *Western Region Magazine* in 1953 (see also Appendix Two).

> The two Windsor drivers were Butler and Guest. The latter, I think, used to drive Mr Gooch's steam-boat when it went on a cruise. He had a son who was in one of the railway offices, and who drew me a picture of *Sebastpool* [sic] which I have to this day: one of the famous 4–2–2 8 ft wheel engines.
>
> When the boiler of *Perseus* burst at Paddington shed, Butler got me a photograph of it which I have now. I also got her name-plate when she was broken up and that of *Hirondelle*.
>
> Guest's engine was *Rocket*, and that driven by Butler was *Assegais* [sic], both built in 1841 by Stothert at Bristol. They were of the 'Sun' class, but altered to saddle tank 2–2–2, and had 6 ft driving wheels.
>
> A driver named Roscoe – brother to Roscoe the patentee of the lubricator – used to come sometimes to Windsor. He was reputed to be rather a ferocious gentleman, but I made friends with him and had pleasant chats. His engine was *Seneca*, built by Hawthorn at Newcastle in 1854 – bogie saddle tank.
>
> On Sundays a big engine used to spend some hours waiting on a siding. I crawled underneath her (it was *Prometheus*), having made friends with the fireman, and got the link motion clear in my head – it being somewhat of a mystery before. Some more water being wanted in the boiler, we went a trip down the line about as far as the river bridge and back. I DROVE! and I shall never forget the thrill and feel of the regulator when the great engine obeyed a small boy.

The two engines of the 'Sun' class mentioned were built as 2–2–2 tender engines but later altered to saddle tanks, broad gauge of course, the 21 members of the class being so treated in 1849 and 1850. It is possible that it was one of this class that was the first engine seen at Windsor. *Seneca* was a 4–4–0 saddle tank of the 'Bogie' class, while *Prometheus* was an 'Iron Duke' class 4–2–2 or '8 ft single' the driving wheel being of 8 ft diameter.

For the opening of the Metropolitan Railway in 1863, Gooch designed the 'Metropolitan' class of 22 broad gauge locomotives of 2–4–0T wheel arrangement, with condensing tanks to enable them to work through the tunnels of the Metropolitan Railway. After withdrawal of broad gauge trains from the Metropolitan Railway in 1869, the class was displaced and the condensing apparatus was removed. Seven of the class were altered to tender locomotives. For a few years the 'Metropolitans' were employed on

'3031' class 4–2–2 *Hurricane* speeds through Slough with a down express in 1902.
Ivor Smart Collection

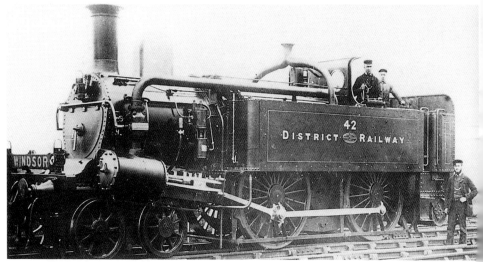

District Railway 4–4–0T locomotive No. 42 of the class that was used to haul the through trains from Mansion House to Windsor during their brief existence. Note that the engine is fitted with condensing apparatus and has a destination board 'Windsor'. *Lens of Sutton*

The mainstay of the through services to/from Windsor from the 1930s until the end of steam – a '61XX' class 2–6–2T heads an up train in Windsor platform 1.
Lens of Sutton

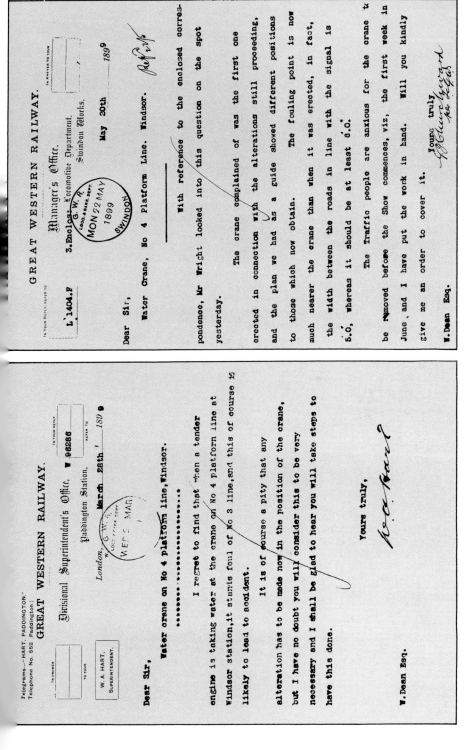

GREAT WESTERN RAILWAY.

Manager's Office,
3.Enclos. Locomotive Department.
Swindon Works,
May 20th 1899

L 1404.F

LOCO. & BANK DEPT.
MON 22 MAY 1899
SWINDON

Dear Sir,

Water Crane, No 4 Platform Line. Windsor.

With reference to the enclosed correspondence, Mr Wright looked into this question on the spot yesterday.

The crane complained of was the first one erected in connection with the alterations still proceeding, and the plan we had as a guide showed different positions to those which now obtain. The fouling point is now much nearer the crane than when it was erected, in fact, the width between the roads in line with the signal is 5.0, whereas it should be at least 6.0.

The Traffic people are anxious for the crane it be Removed before the Show commences, viz, the first week in June, and I have put the work in hand. Will you kindly give me an order to cover it.

Yours truly,

V.Deen Esq.

Telegrams—HART, PADDINGTON.
Telephone No. 552 (Paddington.)

GREAT WESTERN RAILWAY.

Divisional Superintendent's Office,
Paddington Station,
London, March 28th 1899

96286

W. A. HART,
SUPERINTENDENT.

Dear Sir,

Water crane on No 4 platform line, Windsor.

I regret to find that when a tender engine is taking water at the crane on No 4 platform line at Windsor station, it stands foul of No 3 line, and this of course is likely to lead to accident.

It is of course a pity that any alteration has to be made now in the position of the crane, but I have no doubt you will consider this to be very necessary and I shall be glad to hear you will take steps to have this done.

Yours truly,

V.Deen Esq.

When the Great Western got it wrong! This water crane was wrongly sited during the rebuilding which started in 1897 and had to be moved.

Windsor and other London area services but they had an early demise, most of the class being withdrawn by 1874.

Details of broad gauge locomotives coming to Windsor are sparse but in 1862 the line was converted to mixed gauge which would have expanded considerably the stock of locomotives able to work over the branch. The '517' class of 0–4–2T introduced in 1868 was a regular user of the branch. Numerically large, the class continued to be built until 1885 and the last engine to be withdrawn almost survived into BR days; No. 1159 (built 1876) was condemned in August 1947. One such locomotive which features in these pages, mentioned in Chapter Twelve, was No. 569 (built 1870, withdrawn 1933).

Once the broad gauge was removed from the Metropolitan Railway a new class of locomotive was required to work the GWR trains and a narrow gauge 'Metropolitan' tank (2–4–0T) fitted with condensing apparatus, was produced in 1869. Like the '517' class, the 'Metro' tanks were built in some numbers, between 1869 and 1899, and in this case 10 locomotives did pass into BR ownership, being condemned by the end of 1949. Examples working trains on the Windsor branch recorded in Chapter Twelve were Nos. 463 (built 1869, withdrawn 1929), 469 (built 1869, withdrawn 1932), and 5 (built 1869, withdrawn 1932). 'Metro' tank No. 3585 (built 1894, withdrawn 1948) worked the 10.54 am Bishops Road to Windsor on 12th August, 1932.

These 'Metro' tanks were capable of hauling heavy loads at a fair turn of speed and an interesting article in the GWR Magazine (November 1907) headed 'Some Wonderful Little Engines' praises them strongly, as the following extract shows:

> Great Western locomotive practice for several years has been responsible for many notable classes of express and goods locomotives, but until the advent of the present standard 2–4–2 ['3600' class] tank engines, practically all the work suitable for such locomotives and not requiring six-coupled engines, was done by the well-known 2–4–0 tank engines designed more than thirty years ago by Mr Armstrong, though many of them are of much more recent build.
>
> The 2–4–0 tank engines now under notice are of small dimensions, the coupled wheels being 5 feet in diameter and the cylinders 16 in. by 24 in. other dimensions being in proportion, so that nowadays they present a very diminutive appearance when attached to a train of clerestoried bogie coaches; yet it is very common for them to work short distance express trains with fair loads. A few years ago, besides the ordinary underground and suburban services round London they were almost universally employed for the Windsor and High Wycombe trains, working through to Reading, Henley, and Aylesbury in many cases, and although much of this work has been given to the 2–4–2 tank engines, the old class still take a share.
>
> Formerly they were employed for the services from Victoria and from Aldgate over the Metropolitan Railway, necessarily in the latter case, as condensing apparatus was required in the tunnels. On the Victoria trains, which as a rule are very light, the journeys do not often go beyond Southall or Uxbridge, and except for one or two stations, the only fast work required is on the Sunday Henley Express. From Aldgate, however, several trains require some rather fast work, and several of these trains go as far as Windsor, and one through to Reading. For example, the 8.44 am train from Taplow to Aldgate stops only at Langley and West Drayton, and is booked to and from the latter station to Bishops Road, which requires a transfer from the main to the relief lines in approaching Westbourne Park, in eighteen minutes. This journey is a notable performance. A Sunday

An estimate for cleaning and painting the water tank at Windsor, 1904. Then, as now, labour was the most expensive element.

Henley express from Victoria was booked to run between Uxbridge Road and Taplow, twenty miles, in thirty-one minutes down and thirty-seven minutes up. The best work, however, is done on the main line services from and to Paddington. The Windsor expresses, apart from those which are provided by 'slips' at Slough, are booked to run eighteen and a half miles in twenty-four, twenty-five, twenty-six or twenty-seven minutes start to stop. Yet this is done many times daily by these little engines, sometimes with eight or nine bogie coaches.

Another class of locomotive which probably saw regular use on the Windsor branch was the 'Standard Goods' a large class of 0–6–0 tender locomotive, standard gauge, built between 1866 and 1876, and withdrawn by 1930. One such makes an appearance in Chapter Twelve, No. 782 built in 1873 and withdrawn in 1921. Despite their name, they were, until the introduction of mixed traffic 2–6–0s in the second decade of the 20th century, used frequently on passenger trains.

Another known locomotive was No. 238 (built in 1867) which on 18th July, 1898 was working the 4.15 pm express from Windsor to Paddington (non-stop from Slough). At Acton, the 11-coach train was running at about 50 mph when the locomotive's right hand inside connecting rod broke and pierced the firebox and the boiler, flooding the footplate with boiling water and steam. The driver and fireman were badly burned and later died of their injuries. Giving evidence at the BOT Inquiry, locomotive superintendent John Armstrong said that the locomotive was quite suitable for this type of work, for which it was often used. On the day in question it was deputising for '3232' class 2–4–0 No. 3250 which had broken down at Trowbridge. No. 238 was condemned in 1922.

In 1902 a more powerful 2–4–2T type of tank engine, the '3600' class was introduced, following the building of a prototype in 1900. These engines were specifically designed for fast suburban work, which certainly would have included the Windsor services. However their lives were much shorter than those of the 'Metro' tanks, all being withdrawn by 1935. No. 3601 is recorded at Windsor on the 7 pm Paddington–Windsor on 7th January, 1931, two months before withdrawal. Their work was taken up by the 'County' 4–4–2 tanks (built between 1905 and 1912) or the '3100' (built 1903–1906), or '5101' and '6100' class 2–6–2 tanks (built from 1929 and 1931 onwards respectively), all of which featured on the Windsor services. The 'County' tanks themselves were superseded by the more powerful 'Prairies' and were all scrapped by 1936.

It is known that steam railmotors worked on the Windsor branch, but the length of their stay is unclear. First introduced in 1903, ninety-nine coaches were built in the ensuing five years. The Working Timetable for 1911 shows no such trains on the Windsor branch, but that for May 1913 shows a number of entries marked 'Mtr' and the time allowed for the 2¾ miles journey is nine minutes, whereas 'normal' trains are allowed six or seven minutes. However this could have been the petrol-electric railcar (see below).

The steam railmotors were underpowered, even having difficulty in hauling a trailer, and from 1905 onwards the GWR fitted auto-gear to the '517' class of 0–4–2T, 'Metro' class 2–4–0 and others, to enable them to haul or propel a trailer or pair of trailers (known as auto-working) the driver

The petrol-electric railcar used on the Windsor branch in 1912. It cost £1,437 and was sold to Messrs Lever Bros for the same amount in 1919. *British Rail*

A GWR streamlined railcar approaches Windsor station having just crossed the River Thames bridge. *British Rail*

Drive End Trailer L283 leads single power car L130 (class 121) approaching the relief road connection near Slough on 28th May, 1986. *T. Wright*

L406, a hybrid 3-car multiple unit, near Eton Wick on 8th October, 1988. *T. Wright*

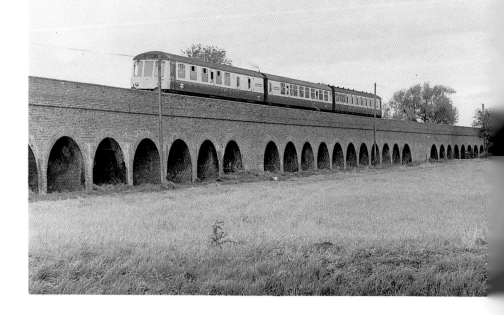

controlling the train from a compartment in the trailer when propelling. The first steam railmotors were withdrawn in 1914 and all were gone by the end of 1935. There is no reference in the 1920s and 1930s WTTs to which I have access to auto-working on the Windsor branch, but certainly in the 1950s auto-trains powered by '57XX' class 0–6–0PTs were in evidence.

The GWR made a short-lived experiment between 1912 and 1919 with a Petrol-Electric Railcar, powered by a 40 hp Maudsley petrol engine driving a dynamo which supplied current to electric motors on the axles. Top speed was only 35 mph and enough fuel could be carried for a range of 250 miles; seats were provided for 44 passengers. It was built by British Thomson-Houston and made a trial run from Leamington to Slough on 28th January, 1912. It was in use on the Windsor branch in 1912 (and possibly thereafter), but was sold to Messrs Lever Bros for use on their line at Port Sunlight in October 1919 for £1437 (plus cost of transit from Swindon) – the same price as the GWR paid when the company acquired it on 1st January, 1913. The RTCS in Part 11 of The Locomotives of the GWR note that the car was used by Lever Bros until about 1923, when it was withdrawn and dismantled. About four years later, however, it was purchased by a member of staff who converted it into an attractive summer bungalow at Prestatyn, where it still existed in 1956!

As noted in Chapter Eleven, the GWR's fleet of diesel railcars, first introduced in December 1933, were also seen on the Windsor branch, particularly parcels cars No. 17 and 34 which were used for London area parcels traffic and were based at Southall for most of their lives.

Following problems with corrosion in the boilers of '61XX' class locomotives working the Windsor branch in the 1930s, the water supply at Windsor was analysed and found to be very hard, capable of depositing nearly 5 lb. of scale-forming matter per 1,000 gallons evaporated. The GWR's chemist recommended either boiler disincrustant in the engines' tanks, as was already done at Slough, or alternatively, softening the water supply at source by chemical means.

The branch was dieselised in 1959 and since then has settled down to a fairly humdrum existence with 2 or 3 car dmus shuttling backwards and forwards. After the closure of Windsor signal box (in 1968) and the subsequent removal of all except one platform line (in 1969) it is no longer possible to run locomotive-hauled trains to Windsor, hence the need for a dmu to provide the service. The 30 year old class 117 dmus were superseded by the new class 165 'Networker Turbos' in 1993. Very soon after their introduction, on Sunday 21st February, 1993 (at 16.56 hrs) unit No. 165138 became derailed, on plain line, about 100 yds outside Windsor station. The reason for the derailment was connected with the condition of the track, which the author had considered very 'rough' in 1992. Extensive track repairs were necessary and the line did not re-open until 11.45 on Friday 26th February, buses covering the train service in the interim.

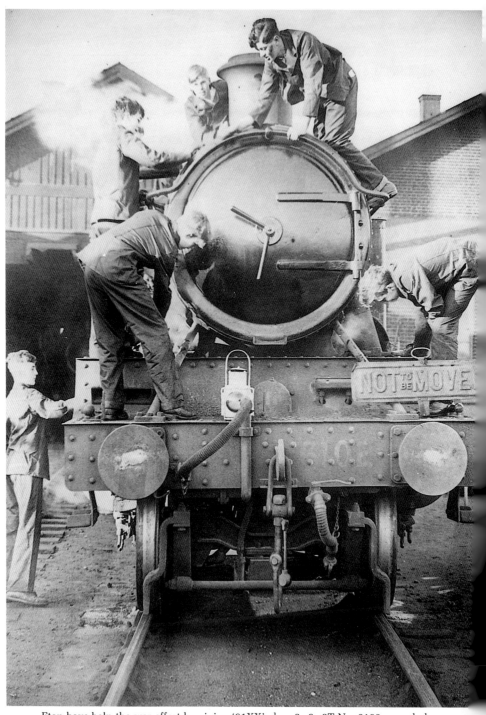

Eton boys help the war effort by giving '61XX' class 2–6–2T No. 6102 a good clean at Slough shed on a day in 1943.

British Rail, Courtesy Ian Coulson

SLOUGH SHED

Slough shed was opened a few months after Slough station, in November 1840. The shed consisted of a long narrow structure, 135 ft by 18 ft, containing a single stabling road. It was situated west of the station on the down side. There were the normal facilities for refuelling locomotives and a small 25 ft turntable stood outside the eastern entrance to the shed, over which all locomotives had to pass.

Engine allocations during the early 1850s are shown in Appendix One and were solely the engines required to work the Windsor branch, normally two. By reason of its authorising Act, there was never a shed at the Windsor terminus, quite unusual for a branch line on the GWR.

Slough shed closed in 1868 and was replaced by a much larger facility capable of housing engines used on the main line as well as the branch. The new shed was situated alongside the curve of the Windsor branch line, on the downside, and was 135 ft long and 65 ft wide, with three through roads and one dead end. The usual servicing facilities, including a turntable, were provided; the 40 ft coal stage dated from 1881.

It will be observed from Appendix One and Two that driver Samuel Guest was a regular driver on the Windsor branch from 1851 onwards. He was still there in the period described by Mr Neville (i.e. up to 1864). The *Windsor & Eton Express* of 21st August, 1888 carried a report of a Samuel Guest, the foreman at Slough shed, having been knocked down and killed by a passing train, and from the content of the report it would seem that this was the same man. Mr Guest had been on his way to examine a defective wagon. He waited until a down train had passed but then, sadly, stepped onto the line without realising an up train from Oxford was approaching. He was 58 years old and left a widow.

Slough shed in 1921 supported an allocation of 29 locomotives as follows:

'Metro' 2−4−0T:	8
'3232' class 2−4−0:	1
'3600' class 2−4−2T:	5
'1076' class 0−6−0T:	1
'2021' class 0−6−0T:	3
'Standard Goods' 0−6−0:	2
'2221' class 4−4−2T:	8
'3100' class 2−6−2T:	1

The last allocation under the GWR in 1947 was 44 locomotives as follows:

0−4−2T:	1
0−6−0PT:	15
2−6−2T:	28

The shed closed shortly before the end of Western Region steam in June 1964.

A chronology of Minor Locomotive Department matters 1882−1927

Authority Date

23rd May, 1882	Authority for coal stage at Slough
29th May, 1882	Provision of new water tank at Slough

Two views of Slough engine shed and coaling stage, looking west, c.1964.

(Both) S.J. Dickson

'61XX' class 2−6−2T No. 6167 heads a line of locomotives at Slough shed on 12th
May, 1962.   *T. Wright*

'16XX' class 0−6−0PT No. 1654 stands at the head of a line of locomotives at Slough
shed; one of the usurping dmus stands alongside.   *Roger Carpenter Collection*

0–6–0PT No. 2069 of the '2021' class at Slough on 17th May, 1930. Built in 1899 as a saddle tank this locomotive was fitted with panniers in 1920 and survived until 1959 before being condemned. *H.C. Casserley*

'14XX' class 0–4–2T No. 1421, acting as shed pilot, sits quietly outside Slough Middle signal box on 12th May, 1962. *T. Wright*

3rd June, 1882	New turntable pit at Slough
18th March, 1884	Lay in new water pipes, fix two 8 in. water columns at Slough
24th July, 1884	Order to sink well, provide and erect tank 20 ft × 12 ft × 8 ft and supplying and fixing engine pumps, water columns and mains at Windsor
3rd May, 1889	Remove and refix 8 in. water crane at Windsor
19th January, 1897	Remove and re-erect water tank at Windsor
23rd July, 1898	Remove and re-erect water cranes and alter mains at Windsor
22nd July, 1899	Fit extension rails to turntable at Slough
18th September, 1899	Improve lighting in Slough loco. yard
12th August, 1903	Repairs to turntable and engine shed at Slough ('Repairs that are absolutely necessary') £236 6s. 9d. Repair water tank and coal stage.
20th November, 1903	Erect water tank and crane, lay necessary main and remove existing 1000 gallon pillar tank at Slough £325 11s. 4d.
20th September, 1904	Put in pit alongside engine shed, Slough £97 3s. 8d.
16th June, 1906	Repair smoke trough etc. Slough £34 13s. 6d.
7th November, 1906	Alter engine pit and lengthen 40 ft, Slough (? not done)
22nd January, 1907	Renew coal tip to our standard (Slough) £94 6s. 3d.
18th October, 1910	Between Slough station and West box the spring hanger of the L.H. middle driving wheel on engine 4001 broke while hauling 8.45 pm ex-Paddington (-Fishguard), 88 minutes delay
11th August, 1913	Do necessary work i/c/w supply of steam to electro-pneumatic signalling Bath Road Junction
28th January, 1914	Between Slough and Farnham Road. Engine No. 2939 failed in consequence of R.H. connecting rod breaking while working the 11.35 pm goods Paddington–Exeter. Another engine sent from OOC, 75 mins delay.
30th November, 1916	Repairs to 45 ft turntable Slough, estimated cost £375
15th March, 1917	Renew water mains in Slough shed, £170
4th December, 1919	Replace water crane in Slough Loco Yard with standard 8 in. water crane, £230
24th February, 1927	Windsor. Remove existing vertical boiler and engine and install electric motor, automatic control apparatus and necessary gearing to operate existing pumps £450

Great Western Railway.

Cheap Excursion by the

ROYAL ROUTE TO WINDSOR,

On Monday, July 30th, 1883,

A Special FAST TRAIN

Will leave	A.M.	Will leave	A.M.
Wolverhampton,		Handsworth	7.40
Low Level,	7.10	Soho	7.45
Priestfields	7.15	Hockley	7.50
Bilston	7.20	Birmingham,	
Wednesbury	7.25	Snow Hill	8.0
Swan Village	7.30	Bordesley	8.5
West Bromwich	7.35		

FOR

WINDSOR CASTLE

Fare there & back 5/6 · Third Class

First Class double the above fare, Children under 12 half price.

This Train after leaving Bordesley will run EXPRESS to WINDSOR, annd return same day at 7-0 p.m.—All Tickets are available for the day of issue only.

Excursionists will also be admitted to

THE STATE APARTMENTS.

The Queen's Audience Chamber,
The Queen's Presence Chamber, The Grand Chamber,
St. George's Hall, The Grand Reception Room,
The Waterloo Chamber, Grand Vestibule,
The State Ante Room. Zuccarelli Room, Vandyk Room, &c.,
The St. George's Chapel, North Terrace, Round Tower,
The Royal Stables, The Great Park,
Long Walk; Virginia Water, &c.

Tickets and further particulars see small bills, to be had at all Stations,

Excursion by a Special FAST TRAIN to Windsor, 30th July, 1883.

David Castle Collection

Chapter Eleven
Timetables and Excursions

In GWR days, but regrettably not under BR since the 1960s, the Windsor branch enjoyed a remarkably comprehensive service of through trains to and from London. Initially these were all to and from Paddington, but from October 1863 this service was supplemented by a limited service to and from Victoria (consisting of through carriages attached to the Paddington trains), which station was leased out by the owner (The Victoria Station & Pimlico Railway Company) to the various users. Mixed gauge track was laid and access to it was gained by the spur to the West London line (the 'Victoria Branch' – as it was still called by BR right up to 1991) via Old Oak Common, North Pole Jn and Kensington. The use of broad gauge coaches to Victoria ceased in October 1866.

Also in October 1863 there began a service of through trains between Farringdon Street and Windsor over the Metropolitan Railway, via Bishop's Road station. At first, like the Victoria trains, the service comprised through coaches attached to already-scheduled trains to and from Paddington, so did not give additional trains on the Windsor branch, but later separate trains were run. The trains were broad gauge until 15th March, 1869 and narrow (standard) gauge from 1st June, 1869, no through services running in the interval. As outlined in Thomas Peacock's book *Great Western London Suburban Services* (The Oakwood Press), these through trains enjoyed a variety of destination terminals in the City over the years:

Farringdon Street	until April 1866
Aldersgate Street	May and June 1866
Moorgate Street	from July 1866
Bishopsgate	from July 1875
Moorgate Street	from 1st January, 1877
Aldgate	from 1st July, 1894
Liverpool Street	from 1st July, 1910

For a brief spell from 1st March, 1883 there was a through service of District line trains from Mansion House to and from Windsor via Ealing Broadway, but this was not well patronised and ceased on 30th September, 1885.

The initial branch timetable in 1849 has been described in Chapter Three. In June 1865 there were 29 down arrivals at Windsor on weekdays between 7.53 am and 12.50 am (next day), of which three were from Farringdon Street (two with portions attached from Victoria). Out of the 29, there were 19 through trains from Paddington (seven of which had portions from Victoria and two of which had portions from Farringdon Street). Two of these down through trains from Paddington were actually slip coaches. Interestingly, there were also slip coaches off two up trains which were taken on to Windsor, arriving there at 10.15 pm (from Reading) and 10.55 pm (from Plymouth).

In the up direction on weekdays there were 21 departures from Windsor between 7.20 am and 10.50 pm, including 2 for Farringdon Street, 7 for Paddington, 7 for Paddington with a portion for Victoria, 1 for Paddington with a portion for Farringdon Street and 1 for Paddington with a portion for both Victoria and Farringdon Street. The shunters certainly had to earn their pay in those days!

The Sunday service consisted of 13 down trains between 8.42 am and 10.45 pm, of which nine were through from Paddington (four had a portion from Victoria). In the up direction there were 15 departures from Windsor between 8.20 am and 10.33 pm, of which nine were through to Paddington (again four with a portion to Victoria).

In February 1868 the timetable offered, on weekdays, 23 down trains between 7.47 am and 12.47 am the following morning. In the up direction there were 21 trains between 7.15 am and 10.50 pm. The timetable concerned is the Working edition for the branch (only) and does not show through trains to/from Paddington. Goods traffic was catered for by two down and two up trains (one each way designated as 'narrow gauge trucks'). On Sundays there were 16 down trains between 8.32 am and 12.47 am (Monday) and 15 up trains between 8.20 am and 10.35 pm, plus one down working which the timetable described as 'Trks' (trucks).

In March 1884 (the branch now narrow gauge), the inauguration of the through trains from the District Railway made the timetable somewhat more complicated as follows:–

WEEKDAYS
Down Trains
29 down trains leaving Slough between 6.33 am and 11.29 pm
13 through District trains leaving Slough at 7.18*, 8.28*, 8.37, 9.38, 10.48,
    11.40 am, 12.38, 4.38, 5.24, 6.39, 7.38, 8.35 pm, 12.38 am
9 trains described as 'Through Pass.' (i.e. from London†) ex Slough at 12.48, 2.18,
    4.08, 4.48, 6.33, 8.22, 10.24 pm, 12.10, 12.58 am

———
51

2 goods trains at 6.00 and 9.20 am
(Between 6 am and 1 am a total of 53 movements or an average of nearly 3 per
    hour.)
*Empty train from Slough; †'London' could be Farringdon Street (Met Ry), Victoria or
    Paddington

Up Trains
20 up trains leaving Windsor between 6.50 am and 10.33 pm
13 through District trains leaving Windsor at 7.45, 8.56, 9.38, 10.50, 11.48 am,
    12.40, 1.45, 5.40, 6.43, 7.20, 8.25, 9.20 pm*, 1.00 am*
8 'Through Pass.' (to London) at 7.30, 7.50, 9.05, 10.30 am, 1.00, 2.30, 3.40,
    6.25 pm (3.40 pm also conveyed gas tanks)

———
41

1 goods train at 7.35 pm
The imbalance between down and up movements is explained by a note 'Engines
    will work between Windsor and Slough as required'.
*Empty train to Slough

SUNDAYS
Down Trains
9 down trains (incl. 1 empty) leaving Slough between 8.23 am and 10.18 pm
9 through District trains leaving Slough at 10.33, 11.26 am, 2.20, 3.35, 4.34, 5.36,
    6.34, 8.35, 10.38 pm (plus 2 empty movements Slough–Windsor)
6 'Through Pass.' leaving Slough at 8.43, 10.03 am, 3.03, 4.28, 6.58, 11.23 pm

———
24

Up Trains
10 up trains leaving Windsor between 8.10 am and 10.00 pm
  9 through District trains leaving Windsor at 8.30, 9.40 am, 1.40, 2.40, 3.39, 4.39,
    5.39, 6.39, 7.39 pm (plus 2 empty movements Windsor–Slough)
  6 'Through Pass.' ex Windsor at 9.15 am, 2.00, 4.10, 7.10, 8.20, 10.45 pm

25

The Working Timetable is unfortunately not clear on the matter, but it is likely that some of those trains not described as 'Through Pass.' were actually through, to or from London.

The July 1884 timetable was very similar except that 5 of the 28 weekday ordinary down trains (i.e. not 'District' or 'Through') were described as 'Slip Pass.', being slip coaches detached from down trains at Slough, giving even more opportunities for through journeys to Windsor.

In October 1884, as mentioned in Chapter Nine, the District's through trains were reduced to four each way, weekdays and Sundays and the branch service was now as follows:

WEEKDAYS
Down Trains
27 down trains or slip coaches leaving Slough between 7.13 am and 11.29 pm
  4 District leaving Slough at 5.24, 6.39, 7.38 and 8.35 pm (plus two empty move-
    ments in the morning)
  9 'Through Pass.' leaving Slough at same times as in March except last train
    12.53 am

40

  2 goods trains at 6.00 and 9.20 am

Up trains
19 up trains leaving Windsor between 8.30 am and 10.33 pm
  4 District leaving Windsor at 8.53, 9.38 am, 6.43, 7.20 pm (plus two empty move-
    ments to Slough in the evening)
  7 'Through Pass.' leaving Windsor at 7.35 (first up train), 7.50, 9.05, 10.30 am,
    12.50, 2.25, 3.40 pm

30

  2 goods trains at 2.45, 7.35 pm

SUNDAYS
Down Trains
10 down trains leaving Slough between 9.28 am and 10.18 pm
  4 through District trains leaving Slough at 5.36, 6.34, 8.35, 10.38 pm (plus two
    empty movements Slough–Windsor)
  5 'Through Pass.' leaving Slough at 10.08 am, 2.43, 4.28, 6.58, 11.23 pm

19

Up Trains
11 up trains leaving Windsor between 8.50 am and 10.45 pm
  4 through District trains leaving Windsor at 1.40, 2.40, 6.39, 7.39 pm (plus two
    empty movements Windsor–Slough)
  4 'Through Pass.' leaving Windsor at 2.00, 4.25, 7.10, 8.20 pm

19

WINDSOR BRANCH.

WEEK DAYS.

DOWN TRAINS.

	1 Gds G.T	2 Eng	3 Pas	4 Eng	5 Eng	6 Pas	7 Pas	8 Pas	9 Gds	10	11 Pas	12 Thr Pas	13 Thro' Pas	14 Pas	15 Thr' Pas	16 Pas	17 Pas	18 Pas	19 Pas	20 Eng	21 Eng	22 Slip Pas	23 Pas	24 Pas	25 Sat. Pas	26 Pas	27 Eng	28 Pas	29 Pas	30 Thro' Pas
Slough ......dep.	A.M. 6 0	A.M. 6 10	A.M. 6 7	A.M. 7 10	A.M. 7 40	A.M. 7 58	A.M. 8 44	A.M. 9 8	A.M. 9 20		A.M. 9 49	A.M. 9 55	A.M. 10 23	A.M. 10 28	A.M. 11	A.M. 11 6	A.M. 11 49	P.M. 12 28	P.M. 1 6	P.M. 1 8	P.M. 1 39	P.M. 1 45	P.M. 3 8	P.M. 3 15	P.M. 3 35	P.M. 4 15		P.M. 4 30	P.M. 4 48
Windsor ......arr.	6 10	6 15	7 15	7 17	7 47	8 5	8 50	9 15	9 20		9 55	10 30	10 35		5 11	5 11	13 11	13 11		1 15	1 45	9 25	3 10		3 42			4 37	4 55

DOWN TRAINS.

	35 Thro' Pas	36 Thr' Pas	37 Thro' Pas	38 Slip Ely. Con.	39 Slip Ely. Con.	40 Pas	41 Pas	42 Pas	43	44 Thr' Pas	45 Pas	46	47 Pas	48 Thro' Pas	49	50 Thro' Pas	51 Night Pas	52	53	54	55 Thro' Pas
Slough ......dep.	P.M. 5 33	P.M. 6 23	P.M. 6 30			P.M. 7 3	P.M. 8 11	P.M. 8 18		P.M. 8 38	P.M. 8 58		P.M. 9 5	P.M. 9 88		P.M. 9 98	Night 19 56				
Windsor ......arr.	5 40	6 30	6 35			7 10	7 11			8 45	9 5			9 45		11 35	13 97				1 5

SUNDAYS.

DOWN TRAINS.

	1 Eng	2 Thro' Pas	3 Pas	4 Thro' Pas	5 Pas	6 Thro' Pas	7 Pas	8 Thro' Pas	9	10 Pas	11 Pas	12 Pas	13 Pas	14 Pas	15 Thro' Pas	16 Thro' Pas	17 Pas	18 Thro' Pas	19 Thro' Pas	20 Eng	21 Eng	22 Pas	23 Pas	24 Pas	25 Pas	26 Pas	27 Pas	28 Thr' Pas	29 Pas	30 Thro' Pas	31 Pas	32
Slough ......dep.	A.M. 8 30	A.M. 9 13	A.M. 9 43	A.M. 10 3			A.M. 11 13	A.M. 11 58			A.M. 4 98	A.M. 5 45	A.M. 5 68	P.M. 6 38	P.M. 7 30	P.M. 7 68	P.M. 8 10	P.M. 8 25	P.M. 8 50	P.M. 9 0		9 13	10 20	10 38	11 23	11 30						
Windsor ......arr.	8 27	9 20	9 50	10 30			2 6	2 55			4 35	5 52	6 45	7 40	8 5	8 10	8 35	9 0	9 25										10 45	11 30		

WEEK DAYS—Continued.

UP TRAINS.

	1 Eng	2 Thro' Pas	3 Pas	4 Thro' Pas	5 Pas	6 Pas	7 Thro' Pas	8 Pas	9 Thro' Pas	10 Pas	11 Thr Pas	12 Pas	13 Thr' Pas	14 Sat. Pas	15 Pas	16 Thr' Pas	17 Thr' Pas	18 P.M.	19 P.M.	20 Pas	21 Gds	22 Thro' Pas	23 Pas	24 Eng	25 Pas	26 Eng	27 Thr' Pas	28 Thr' Pas	29 Eng
Windsor ......dep.	A.M. 6 30	A.M. 6 45	A.M. 7 35	A.M. 7 48	A.M. 8 5	A.M. 8 35	A.M. 9 5	A.M. 9 20	A.M. 9 35	A.M. 9 55	A.M. 10 25	A.M. 10 40	A.M. 11 5	A.M. 11 30	P.M. 10 30	P.M. 5 65	P.M. 5 68	P.M. 1 6	P.M. 1 15	P.M. 1 30	P.M. 2 10	P.M. 2 25	P.M. 3 40	P.M. 3 50	P.M. 4 15	P.M. 4 45	P.M. 4 59	
Slough ......arr.	6 52	6 52	7 43	8 42	8 11	8 42	9 11	9 27	9 49	10 2	10 39	11 2	12 19	10 37				1 20	1 30	1 37	2 20	2 33	3 47				4 52	5 2

UP TRAINS.

	34 Pas	35 Pas	36 Pas	37 Gds	38 Pas	39 Eng	40 Pas	41 Pas	42 Pas	43 Thro' Pas	44 Sat. Pas	45 Pas	46 Thro' Pas	47 Pas	48 Pas	49 Eng	50 Eng	51 Eng	52 Gda	53 Thro' Pas	54 Pas	55 Eng	56 Eng	57 Eng	58 Thr' Pas	59 Pas
Windsor ......dep.		P.M. 7 5	P.M. 7 12		P.M. 7 30		P.M. 8 0	P.M. 8 30	P.M. 9 0	P.M. 9 45	P.M. 9 52		P.M. 10 5	P.M. 10 12		P.M. 11 50	P.M. 12 57		A.M. 1 30	1 37						
Slough ......arr. "		7 12			7 40		8 37		9 7	9 52			10 12			11 57										

SUNDAYS—Continued.

UP TRAINS.

	1 Pas	2 Pas	3 Pas	4 Eng	5 Pas	6 Gds	7 Pas	8 Pas	9 Pas	10 Thro' Pas	11 Pas	12 Thro' Pas	13 Pas	14 Sat. Pas	15 Thro' Pas	16 Thro' Pas	17 Thro' Pas	18 Thro' Pas	19 Pas	20 Eng	21 Eng Pas	22 Eng Pas	23 Pas	24 Pas	25 Pas	26 Eng	27 Thro' Pas	28 Eng	29 Eng	30	31	32
Windsor ......dep.	A.M. 8 15	A.M. 8 50	A.M. 8 57	A.M. 9 20	A.M. 10 25	A.M. 10 32			A.M. 2 45	A.M. 2 52		A.M. 4 25	A.M. 5 30	A.M. 5 37	A.M. 6 30	A.M. 6 37	A.M. 7 10	A.M. 7 17	A.M. 7 50	A.M. 7 57	A.M. 8 25	A.M. 8 35	A.M. 8 42	A.M. 9 25	A.M. 9 27	P.M. 10 15	P.M. 10 22	ngt. 12 0				
Slough ......dep.					10 32				2 52			4 39	5 37		6 37		7 17		7 57		8 39			9 27		10 16	10 17	13 7				

By June 1888 the timetable was as follows (the District trains were discontinued in 1885):

WEEKDAYS
Down Trains
27 down trains or slips between 7.10 am and 11.20 pm
10 'Through Pass.' between 12.48 pm and 12.58 am

———

37

2 goods trains at 6.00 am and 9.20 am

Up Trains
22 up trains between 7.35 am and 10.20 pm (plus a Saturday extra at 10.15 pm)
8 'Through Pass.' between 7.35 am and 6.25 pm

———

30

2 goods trains at 2.00 and 7.10 pm

SUNDAYS
Down Trains
15 down trains between 9.23 am and 10.18 pm
5 'Through Pass.' between 10.08 am and 11.23 pm

———

20

Up Trains
14 up trains between 8.50 am and 10.45 pm
5 'Through Pass.' between 2.00 pm and 9.25 pm

———

19

The Working Timetable included notes to the effect that 'Mixed Trains on this Branch must not convey more than 6 goods trucks' and 'The load of goods trains are limited to 25 wagons and the van.'

The July 1894 timetable was to a similar pattern to those of the 1880s just described. As the Working Timetable was rather more compact than before and printed on one page it can be included in the book, and the reader can see for himself the full complexities of traffic working on the branch. (Note the footnote which now states that 'There are no Mixed Trains on this Branch.') From the arrival back at Slough at 1.37 am of the light engine off the last 'Through Pass.' to Windsor, to the early morning goods departure at 6.00 am, this busy traffic byway was only shut for a little more than four hours each weekday. Remember that this comprehensive service was run into and out of a three platform dead-end terminus!

Between 1897, the Queen's Diamond Jubilee Year, and 1902, Windsor station was rebuilt and greatly enlarged, its handling capacity more than doubled. The Winter 1902 service showed an increase over the July 1894 timetable and there were now 34 down and 29 up trains on the branch on weekdays. The public timetable is not as clear as the Working Timetable about 'Through Coaches' but at least 18 down and 14 up trains are through from or to Paddington respectively. Additionally two down trains from Aldgate and one from Victoria reached Windsor; in the up direction the pattern was reversed with one train to Aldgate and two to Victoria. There

were two through trains to Basingstoke (via Slough West Curve) at 12.55 and
4.35 pm and one from Basingstoke at 4.35 pm due in Windsor at 5.55 pm.
Following the 1900 smash at Slough (see Chapter Twelve), the 1.05 pm
Paddington to Windsor omitted the Slough stop and ran non-stop, arriving
at 1.33 pm. Any passenger who just missed this train at Paddington would
have cursed his luck; although the train was followed at 1.15 pm by another
through service to Windsor, this called at all stations from Westbourne Park
and was not due at Windsor until 2.17 pm!

On Sundays the branch enjoyed a comprehensive service of 19 down and
21 up trains, at least 8 down and 7 up being through from or to Paddington.
What a pity that BR does not see any scope for a through service to Windsor
these days, when it is such a haven for tourists.*

By October 1909, the already intensive service had increased again. There
were now no less than 39 down trains on weekdays, plus two goods trains
(at the traditional times of 5.45 and 9.03 am), a Mondays-only cattle train (at
3.15 pm), a train from Basingstoke (a second on Saturdays) and two Satur-
days-only extras. In the opposite direction the 35-train service was enhanced by two trains to Basingstoke and two goods trains at 8.35 and
10.28 pm. The last movement at night was a light engine from Windsor to
Slough at 12.45 am, and the branch shut for five hours until the 5.45 am
goods from Slough. On Sundays there were 21 down and 23 up trains, the
branch opening from 8.10 am (the first train from Windsor) to 12.07 am
(Monday) when the light engine off the last train arrived back at Slough.

1911 was Coronation Year and for two nights in June the branch was open
all night (details are in Chapter Nine). The timetable for July 1911 was fairly
similar to those of 1909. In 1911 there was a shunting engine at Windsor
from 5.35 am to 10.35 pm daily, working out with the 10.35 pm goods from
Windsor to Slough. On Sundays the shunting engine worked from 9 am to
8 pm.

The year after World War I ended is the next timetable available to the
author. In December 1919 there were still 33 down trains (35 Sats-only) and
32 up trains on weekdays, and 19 trains each way on Sundays. In broad
terms, about one train every hour in each direction was through to or from
London on weekdays. In September 1926, less than 4 months from the end
of the disastrous General Strike, there was no apparent adverse affect on the
Windsor branch service. No less than 38 down trains (40 Sats-only) and 36
up trains traversed the branch on weekdays, and 22 down and 20 up trains
ran on Sundays. In August 1928, 43 down (44 Sats-only) and 38 up weekday
trains ran, with 24 (down) and 20 (up) on Sundays.

The year 1935 was the GWR's Centenary Year and it is pleasing to be able
to include the Working Timetable for July of that year. Among the interesting features, note that the 3.55 pm from Slough and 4.10 pm from Windsor
were worked by 'oil-engined railcar', and that, on weekdays, the branch was
only shut between 1.22 am and 5.35 am.

For the remaining peacetime years of the 1930s, Windsor continued to
enjoy this high level of service. Even after the outbreak of war, when many
branches saw their train services drastically reduced, Windsor saw little
cut-back and in the Emergency Timetable introduced on 25th September,
1939, there were still 32 trains in each direction on weekdays (and one more

---

*As this book went to press, it was announced that a through train, 10.18 am Paddington
–Windsor, would commence running from June 1993!

No. 1.

WINDSOR BRANCH.

DOUBLE LINE.

Distance M	Distance C	Mile Post Mileage M	Mile Post Mileage C	DOWN TRAINS	Ruling Gradient 1 in	Time allowances for Ordinary Freight Trains—See page 2. Point to point times	Allow for stop	Allow for start	WEEK DAYS. Eng.	Gds	Pas.	5.45 a.m. Ptn	Ety. C'h's	Pas.	SX Eng.	Pas.	Eng.	Pas.	Eng.	Pas.		8.5 a.m. Ptn.	Y Gds	8.33 a.m. Ptn.		Pas.	10.3 a.m. Ptn.		Y RR Gds.	Pas.		Thro Pas.	11 40 P'd SX Pas.	11 40 P'd SO Pas.
						Mins.	Mins.	Mins.	A.M.	A.M.	A.M.	A.M.	A.M.	A.M.	A.M.	A.M.	A.M.	A.M.	A.M.	A.M.		A.M.	A.M.	A.M.		A.M.	A.M.		A.M.	A.M.		A.M.	P.M.	P.M.
—	—	18	36	Slough .... dep	—	—	—	1	5‖35	5 45	6 21	6 43	6†52	7 5	7‖30	7 35	7‖50	8 2	8‖11	8 30	...	8 46	8V55	9‡ 6	...	10 6	10 40	...	10 55	11 17	...	11 54	12 32	12 34
2	64	21	20	Windsor & Eton arr.	96 R	8	1	—	5‖42	5 55	6 27	6 49	7‡ 0	7 11	7‖36	7 41	7‖57	8 8	8‖18	8 36	...	8 52	9 20	9‡ 12	...	10 12	10 46	...	11 5	11 23	...	12 0	12 38	12 40

DOWN TRAINS.	Pas.	12 35 Pad. SO		1.5 Pad. SO	SX Pas.	12.50 Pad. SO	Pas.	1.22 p.m. Ptn.	SX Pas.	SO 2.18 Ptn.	2 35 p.m. Ptn.	RR Mon Ctl.		Pas. ¶	Pas.	4.13 Pad Pas.	4.33 Pad. Pas.	Pas.	S'all Pass. SX	5.18 p.m. Ptn.		5.18 Pad SO	Q 5.40 Pad.	Thr' Pass SX	Pas. SO	6.13 Pad. SX	6 38 p.m. Ptn.	7.0 p.m. Ptn.	Pas.	7.32 Pad. Pas.	Pas.	Eng. SX	8.35 Pad Pas.	8.40 Pad. Pas.	Pas.	Pas.
	P.M.	P.M.		P.M.	P.M.	P.M.	P.M.	P.M.	P.M.	P.M.	S O	P.M.		P.M.	P.M.	P.M.	P.M.	P.M.	P.M.	SX		P.M.	P.M.	P.M.	P.M.	P.M.	P.M.	P.M.	P.M.	P.M.	P.M.	P.M.	P.M.	P.M.	P.M.	P.M.
Slough .... dep.	12 49	1 12	...	1 37	1 40	1 46	2 6	2 17	2 42	2 49	3 14	3 15	...	3 55	4 9	4 43	4 57	5 15	5 31	5 47	...	5 55	6 8	6 33	6 36	6 41	7 7	7§33	7 47	8 3	8 38	8§45	9 10	9 34	9 56	10 42
Windsor & Eton ...... arr.	12 55	1 18	...	1 43	1 46	1 52	2 12	2 23	2 48	2 55	3 20	3 23	...	4 1	4 15	4 49	5 3	5 21	5 37	5 53	...	6 1	6 14	6 39 W	6 42	6 47	7 13	7§39	7 53	8 9	8 44	8§52	9 16	9 40	10 2	10 48

DOWN TRAINS.	WEEK DAYS. Pas.		11.30 p.m. Pad.	Pas.		SUNDAYS. Pas.	Pas.	8.5 a.m. Pad.	Pas.	Pas.	9 32 a.m. Pad.	10 15 a.m. Pad.		Pas.		Pas.	11.35 a.m. Ptn.	Pas.	1 45 p.m. Pad.	Pas.	Pas.	3.35 Pad. Pas.		Pas.	Pas.	5.10 P.M. Ptn.		6.5 p.m. Ptn.	Pas.		Pas.	Pas.	Pas.	Pas.	9.35 p.m. Ptn.	10.15 p.m. Ptn.	11.20 p.m. Ptn.
	P.M.		A.M.	A.M.		A.M.	A.M.	A.M.	A.M.	A.M.	A.M.	A.M.		A.M.		P.M.	P.M.	P.M.	P.M.	P.M.	P.M.	P.M.		P.M.	P.M.	P.M.		P.M.	P.M.		P.M.	P.M.	P.M.	P.M.	P.M.	P.M.	MID
Slough............dep.	11 32	...	12 16	12 53	...	7 22	8 35	8 48	9 12	9 39	10 18	10 40	...	11 34	...	12 14	12 23	1 44	2 28	3 14	4 10	4 24	...	5 30	5 50	6 0	...	7 8	7 35	...	8 34	9 0	9 24	10 9	10 23	11 4	12 9
Windsor & Eton arr.	11 38	...	12 22	12 59	...	7 28	8 41	8 54	9 18	9 45	10 24	10 46	...	11 40	...	12 20	12 29	1 50	2 34	3 20	4 16	4 30	...	5 36	5 56	6 6	......	7 14	7 41	...	8 40	9 6	9 30	10 15	10 29	11 10	12 15

UP TRAINS.	Ruling Gradient 1 in	Time allowances for Ordinary Freight Trains—See page 2. Point to point times	Allow for stop	Allow for start	WEEK DAYS. Thr' Pas.	Thr' Pas		Pas	Thr' Pas.	Pas.		Pass.	Thr' Pas.		Thr' Pas.	Thr' Pas.	Pas.	Thro Pas.		Pas.	Thr Pas.	Pas.		Pas.	Pas.	Pas.	Thr' Pas.		Thr' Pas.		Pas.	Pas.
		Mins.	Mins.	Mins.	A.M.	A.M.		A.M.	A.M.	A.M.		A.M.	A.M.		A.M.	A.M.	A.M.	A.M.		A.M.	A.M.	A.M.		A.M.	A.M.	P.M.	P.M.		P.M.		P.M.	P.M.
Windsor & Eton ... dep.	—	—	—	1	6 20	6 45	...	7 8	¶7 28	7 45	...	8 2	8 11	...	8 37	8 47	9 8	9 35	...	10 20	10 40	10 58	...	11 35	11 55	12 15	12 32	...	1 2	...	1 48	2 3
Slough .... arr.	117 R	3	1	—	6 27	6 52	...	7 14	¶7 34	7 51	...	8 8	8 17	...	8 43	8 53	9 14	9 42	...	10 26	10 46	11 4	...	11 41	12 1	12 21	12 38	...	1 8	...	1 54	2 9
					RL	RL	...	SB	ML	SB	..	SB	ML	...	ML	ML	SB	RL	...	SB	RL	SB	...	SB	SB	SB	RL	...	ML	...	SB	SB

UP TRAINS.		Thr' Pas.	Thr' Pas.		Pas.		Pas. ¶		Thr' Pas.	Pas.		SX Eng.	Thr' Pas.		SX Thr' Pas.	Pas.	SX C'h's.	Pas.	SX Eng.	Pas.			Pas.	Pas.			Gds.	Pas.		Pas.	Pas.		Pas.	Pas.		Eng or C'h's
		P.M.	P.M.		P.M.		P.M.		P.M.	P.M.		P.M.	P.M.		P.M.	P.M.	P.M.	P.M.	P.M.	P.M.			P.M.	P.M.			P.M.	P.M.		P.M.	P.M.		P.M.	P.M.		ngt.
Windsor & Eton dep.	...	2 47	3 32	...	3 57	..	4 10	...	4 47	5 14	...	5‖30	5 45	...	6 3	6 12	6†50	7 3	7‖10	7 32	...	...	8 20	8 35	...	...	9 5	9 20	...	9 48	10 20	...	10 55	11 18	...	1 15
Slough ....arr.	...	2 53	3 38	...	4 3	..	4 16	...	4 53	5 20	...	5‖36	5 51	...	6 9	6 18	6†57	7 9	7‖17	7 38	...	...	8 26	8 42	...	...	9 15	9 26	...	9 54	10 26	...	11 1	11 24	...	1 22
	...	RL	RL	...	SB	...	SB	...	ML	SB	...	SB	RL	...	RL	SB	SB	RL	SB	SB	...	...	SB	RL	...	...	RL	SB	...	RL	SB	...	SB	SB	..	SB

UP TRAINS.		SUNDAYS. Pas.	Thr' Pas.	Pas.	Pas.	Pas.	Thr' Pas.	Pas.		Pas.	Thr' Pas.	Pas.	Pas.	Pas.	Thr' Pas.		Pas.		Thr Pas.		Thr' Pas.		Pas.		Thr' Pas.		Thr' Pas		Thr' Pas.		Pas.		Pas.	Pas.	Pas.	Eng.
		A.M.	A.M.	A.M.	A.M.	A.M.	A.M.	A.M.		P.M.	P.M.	P.M.	P.M.	P.M.	P.M.		P.M.		P.M.		P.M.		P.M.		P.M.		P.M.		P.M.		P.M.		P.M.	P.M.	P.M.	ngt
Windsor & Eton dep.	...	8 10	9 0	9 20	9 38	10 5	11 12	11 55	...	12 55	2 0	2 42	3 12	3 58	5 0	...	5 20	...	6 15	...	6 35	...	6 55	...	7 15	...	8 10	...	9 0	...	9 45	...	10 44	10 55	11 30	12‖30
Slough .... arr.	...	8 16	9 6	9 26	9 44	10 11	11 18	12 1	...	1 1	2 6	2 48	3 18	4 4	5 6	...	5 26	...	6 21	...	6 41	...	7 1	...	7 21	...	8 16	...	9 6	...	9 51	...	10 50	11 1	11 36	12‖37
		SB	RL	SB	SB	SB	ML	SB	...	SB	RL	SB	SB	SB	RL	...	SB	...	RL	...	RL	...	SB	...	RL	...	ML	...	RL	...	SB	...	SB	SB	SB	SB

SB To South Bay, Slough. **ML** To Main Line (No. 2) Platform, Slough. **RL** To Relief Line (No 4) Platform, Slough. Engines will work between Windsor and Slough, and vice versa as required.
Q 5.40 p.m. Paddington **SX**, Branch Train **SO**. **V** Bath Rd. arr. 9.0, dep. 9.14 a.m. **W**—5.15 p.m. ex Liverpool Street, **SX**. **Y** Via Slough West Curve. ¶ Worked by oil-engined rail car.
‡ 2 m'ns. later on Saturdays. § 3 mins. later on Saturdays. There are no Mixed Trains on this Branch.

The Working Timetable for July 1935.

WINDSOR BRANCH.

DOUBLE LINE.

Down Trains.
Week Days.

Distance.	Mile Post Mileage.	STATIONS.	Ruling Gradient 1 in.	News Van.	Coaches ex Hayes.	Pass. enger.	Pass enger.	Pass. enger.	1.24 p.m. Paddington Pass. enger. SO	8.30 a.m. Paddington Pass. enger.	Engine	Pass. enger.	Pass. enger. SX	Pass. enger. 5.40 p.m. Paddington Pass. enger. ¶	Pass. enger.	Pass. enger.	Pass. enger.	Pass. enger.	11.35 SX 11.38 SO Paddington Pass.	12.38 Paddington Pass. enger. SO	12.50 p.m. Paddington Pass. enger. SO
M C / 2	M C 18 36 / 21 20	Slough .... dep.	— 96 R.	a.m. 5 8 5 14	a.m. 5 46 5T52	a.m. 6T22 6 28	a.m. 6T42 6 48		p.m. 2 20 2 26	a.m. 9 8 9 14	a.m. 8 34 8 40	a.m. 8I11 8I17	p.m. 7 58 8 4	a.m. 7 40 7 46	a.m. 7 5 7 11	a.m. 11 14 11 20	a.m. 11 54 12 0	a.m. 9 6 9 12	p.m. 12 45 12 51	p.m. 1 40 1 46	p.m. 1 43 1 49
64		Windsor & Eton .... arr.																			

Down Trains.

STATIONS.	Pass. enger. SO	Pass. enger. SX	Pass. enger.	Pass. enger.	4.55 p.m. Paddington Pass. SX	Pass. enger.	Pass. enger.	Pass. enger.	Pass. enger.	Pass. enger.	Pass. enger.	Pass. enger.	8.40 9.15 Paddington Pass. enger.	Pass. enger.	Pass. enger.
Slough .... dep.	2 42 2 49	2 45 2 51	4 28 4 34	3 56 4 2	5 27 5 33	5 9 5 15	5 5 5 11	5 35 5 42	5 52 5 58	6 12 6 18	6 44 6 50	6 58 7 4	7 14 7 20	8 22 8 28	9 40 9 46
Windsor & Eton .... arr.															

Up Trains.
Week Days.

STATIONS.	Ruling Gradient 1 in.	Engine	Thro' Pass.	Thro' Pass.	Pass. enger.	Pass. enger.	Pass. enger.	Pass. enger.	Thro' Pass.	Thro' Pass.	Pass.	Pass.	11.35 a.m. Paddington Pass.	Pass. enger.	4.50 p.m. Paddington Pass.	6.2 Paddington Pass.	6.35 Paddington Pass.	Pass.	Pass. enger.	Pass. enger.	10.15 Paddington Pass.	11.20 Paddington Pass.
Windsor & Eton .... dep.	117 R.	a.m. 6 25 6I31	a.m. 6 20 6 27	a.m. 6 45 6 63	a.m. 7 5 7 11	a.m. 7 26 7 32	a.m. 7 45 7 51	a.m. 8 0 8 6	a.m. 8 10 8 16	a.m. 8 45 8 52	p.m. 1 50 1 56	p.m. 12 35 12 41		p.m. 2 24 2 30	p.m. 3 15 3 21	p.m. 4 12 4 18	p.m. 5 44 5 50	p.m. 6 6 6 12	p.m. 7 8 7 14	p.m. 7 29 7 35	p.m. 8 6 8 12	p.m. 1 50 1 56
Slough .... arr.																						

Up Trains.

STATIONS.	Thro' Pass.	Pass. enger.	Pass. enger.	Pass. enger.	Thro' Pass.	Pass. enger.	Pass. enger.	Pass. enger.	Pass.	Pass. enger.	Pass. enger.	Thro' Pass.	Pass. enger.
Windsor & Eton .... dep.	a.m. 3 35 3 41	a.m. 4 12 4 18	a.m. 4 45 4 51	p.m. 5 42 5 48	p.m. 6 35 6 41	p.m. 6 10 6 16	p.m. 7 22 7 28	p.m. 8 0 8 6	p.m. 8 26 8 32	p.m. 8 52 8 58	p.m. 9 20 9 26	p.m. 10 28 10 34	p.m. 11 20 11 26
Slough .... arr.													

Sundays.

Down Trains (Sundays)

STATIONS.	Work- men's Pass. enger.	Pass. enger.	Pass. enger.	Thro' Pass.	Pass. enger.	Pass. enger.	Thro' Pass.	Pass. enger.	Pass. enger.	Thro' Pass.	Pass. enger.	Eng. or C'chs.
Windsor & Eton .... dep.	a.m. 6 40 6 46	a.m. 8 10 8 16	a.m. 10 8 10 14	p.m. 1 35 1 41	p.m. 3 0 3 56	p.m. 4 50 4 56	p.m. 5 20 5 26	p.m. 6 30 6 36	p.m. 7 42 7 48	p.m. 8 15 8 21	p.m. 8 42 8 48	night 12I46 12I51
Slough .... arr.												

SB—To South Bay, Slough. ML—To Main Line (No. 2) Platform, Slough. RL—To Relief Line (No. 4) Platform, Slough. Engines will work between Windsor and Slough, and vice versa as required. ‡—To RL on Saturdays. ¶—Through Train SX. Branch Train SO. Distance between Buth Road Junction and Slough Station 31 chains.

The Working Timetable for May 1942.

A single power car crosses the Thames backwater between the river bridge and Windsor station in August 1990. *T. Wright*

L406 (or is it L412?) seen at Windsor on 8th October, 1988. Former platform 2 (right) is fenced off and forms part of the ground occupied by the Royalty and Empire Exhibition. *T. Wright*

down train on Saturdays); 21 down and 20 up on Sundays. The Working Timetable introduced in May 1942 is illustrated; looking at its scope one would hardly guess that there was a war on! Note that on Sundays the first departure from Windsor was 6.40 am (described as 'Workmen's' – somewhat surprising for Windsor). This latter train last appeared in the May– September 1944 timetable.

The three wartime Working Timetables to which I have access make no mention of goods trains, but the May 1946 W.T.T. shows a freight train from Slough at 5.55 am (the third train on the branch, preceded by the 5.08 am News Van and a passenger service at 5.45 am). There was another goods at 8.55 am and a third ('run as required') at 10.55 am. In the reverse direction, goods trains left Windsor at 9.45 pm and 11.50 pm; this latter called at Chalvey siding as required. If it did call, it was 'shut in' for the last up train, the 12.00 midnight empty coaches Windsor–Slough, to pass.[1]

The May 1946 timetable also showed a path for the diesel parcels car to visit Windsor, leaving Slough at 1.02 pm each weekday and returning from Windsor at 1.25 pm. In other respects it was little different to the May 1942 timetable.

Such was the stability of the railway in those days that the last timetable ever issued by the GWR, from 6th October, 1947, was very little altered from those applicable in wartime, so far as the Windsor branch was concerned.

The summer 1954 Working Timetable for the Windsor branch was a mixture of auto-trains ('57XX engine and trailer'), diesel railcars, and through locomotive-hauled trains to Paddington, of which there were, roundly, six or so each way. The first passenger trains in each direction on weekdays were at 6.20 am, the last up train being 12.10 am and the last down, 12.30 am (12.35 am SO) the next day. In the afternoon, up until 7 pm, those trains worked by auto-trains conveyed two trailers. Goods trains ran at 8.55 am (down) and 9.40 pm (up). There were two workings of the diesel parcels railcar from Paddington, returning from Windsor at 2.15 pm and 10.20 pm (the latter empty). The weekday service comprised about 40 passenger trains each way, with 26 on Sundays.

The summer 1960 timetable gave an even more generous 42 trains each way on weekdays and 35 on Sundays. By now the off-peak timetable was at set times each hour (as it is today). On Sundays this gave a rather lopsided arrangement with departures from Slough at . . .30 and . . .47 minutes past each hour and from Windsor at . . .10 and . . .25 past each hour. There were five down and seven up trains (from/to Paddington) on weekdays, but 14 down and 15 up on Sundays, giving an hourly service. Unfortunately the Sunday through trains called at all stations to Paddington so London passengers probably caught the other departure from Windsor in each hour and changed at Slough.

The Sunday through trains were withdrawn in the Winter 1963 Timetable and the weekday through trains were now only four up and three down. From 6th May, 1968 the through service was reduced again to just two up trains, and a year later on 5th May, 1969 one solitary up through train remained (8.02 am from Windsor). This continued to run until 30th April, 1976 after which the Windsor branch operated on a shuttle basis to and from Slough only.

The quadrangle, Windsor Castle. *British Rail*

Messrs Salter Bros steamship *Mapledurham* (1927–1984) is seen near Windsor in
this GWR publicity photograph. *British Rail*

Great Western Railway.

EDUCATIONAL EXCURSION to
Windsor Castle & Runnymede

LIMITED EXCURSION to

WINDSOR

Including CONDUCTED TOUR of the STATE APARTMENTS in WINDSOR CASTLE (see note below); ST. GEORGE'S CHAPEL and ALBERT MEMORIAL CHAPEL; RIVER TRIP from WINDSOR TO RUNNYMEDE and MAGNA CHARTA ISLAND, with TEA ON BOARD THE STEAMER. (See overleaf.)

EACH WEDNESDAY,
MAY 27th to SEPTEMBER 23rd, 1931.

FROM	AT		INCLUSIVE CHARGE.			
	May 27th to July 15th and Sept. 16th and 23rd.	July 22nd to Sept. 9th.	(First Class Rail).		(Third Class Rail).	
			Adults.	Children under 14.	Adults.	Children under 14.
	a.m.	a.m.	s. d.	s. d.	s. d.	s. d.
PADDINGTON ..	10A45	10 40	7 6	5 9	6 0	5 0
ACTON	10B38	10C38	6 6	4 9	5 6	4 6
EALING BROADWAY	10A55	10 50	6 6	4 9	5 6	4 6
WINDSOR arr.	11 23	11 14				

A—*Change at Slough.*   B—*Change at Ealing Broadway and Slough.*
C—*Change at Ealing Broadway.*

NOTE.—On dates when the State Apartments are closed (usually during three weeks of June) an extended tour of the many other points of interest will be arranged in lieu.

The fares shewn cover all charges, viz. :—Rail, Boat, Tea, Admission Fees and the Services of Guides.

This Excursion is limited, and to save disappointment, intending passengers **should obtain their tickets in advance at**

PADDINGTON, ACTON AND EALING BROADWAY STATIONS
or at the Great Western Railway Booking Offices shewn below :

Great Western Railway Office	Telephone No.	Great Western Railway Office	Telephone No.
W. 407, Oxford Street	Mayfair 2561	E. 118, Minories	Royal 8201
(West End Travel Bureau		(Bank Offices, 87 & 88, King William St.	Royal 6498
S.W. (7 & 8, Charing Cross	Whitehall 1728	E.C. (5, Holborn Viaduct	City 6172
((Trafalgar Square)		(22, Long Lane, Smithfield	National 8011
W.C. (170b, Strand	Temple Bar 4641	S.E. 141, High Street, Borough	Hop 0962
(142, High Holborn	Holborn 8032	N.W. 285, Kentish Town Road	Gulliver 5240

Also at SELFRIDGE & CO., LTD., Travel Bureau, Third Floor, Oxford Street, W.1.

SEE OTHER SIDE.

Handbill detailing arrangements for the popular tour of Windsor Castle, combined with a river trip (1931).
David Castle Collection

The Windsor branch has continued to operate a shuttle service throughout the 1970s and 1980s with a generous two trains per hour each way on weekdays and Sundays. At the time of writing (winter 1991/2) there are 42 down and 41 up trains Saturdays Excepted (one less in each direction on Fridays); 35 in each direction on Saturdays; and 29 each way on Sundays. On weekdays the first train leaves Slough at 5.46 am and the last at 11.18 pm (10.46 pm on Friday and Saturdays); the first train from Windsor is 5.57 am and the last 11.29 pm (10.57 pm on Fridays and Saturdays). (The earlier finish on Fridays and Saturdays is a precaution against the incidence of 'hooliganism' on these late night trains, worked without a guard.) On Sundays trains leave Slough between 9.22 am and 11.22 pm and from Windsor between 9.33 am and 11.33 pm.

EXCURSIONS

Much less well documented is the story of the Windsor excursion traffic. Excluding the race traffic which just passed through Windsor on its way to Windsor or Ascot race courses, there were two principal attractions in Windsor; Windsor Castle and a trip on the river to Maidenhead or Marlow. Over the years many thousands of schoolchildren must have been conveyed to Windsor by the GWR to be shown the glories of Windsor Castle, the State Apartments and St George's Chapel. Parties of adults and children galore were brought to Windsor for a trip on the river, Windsor being one of the most important centres on the Thames for such excursion traffic.

Many GWR excursions embraced both aspects of Windsor, as witness the handbill included. On Tuesday 8th August, 1939 an excursion left Ross on Wye at 9.45 am and made several intermediate calls including Gloucester to Purton, after which it ran non stop to Windsor (via the West Curve at Slough of course), arriving at Windsor at 2.05 pm. The tourists were first taken on a conducted tour of Windsor Castle, St George's Chapel and the State Apartments; then at 4.00 pm they embarked upon a special steamer provided by Messrs Salter Bros for a river cruise to Marlow. During the journey, passing Maidenhead, Cookham, Bourne End, they enjoyed 'tea (ad lib.) without additional charge' and the cruise ended at Marlow at about 7 pm. There was just time for a quick look round that charming town before the excursionists' return train left at 7.50 pm. The residents of Ross on Wye finally reached their home town at 12.25 am, having enjoyed a wonderful day's entertainment (weather permitting) for the total sum of 11s. 6d. (7s. 2d. child)!

Another similar excursion took place on 11th August, 1949. Described as a half-day excursion the train left Kidderminster at 10.32 am, ran via Worcester and the Cotswold line to Oxford, and then non-stop to Slough West where a pilotman was picked up. Going forward via the West Curve, Windsor was reached at 1.20 pm. The return train left Marlow at 8.05 pm and after reversal at Bourne End, the main line was gained at Maidenhead; the return journey followed the same route via Oxford, finally reaching Kidderminster at 11.24 pm – some half day!

A week earlier, on 4th August, 1949 a half-day excursion left Bristol, Parson Street at 11.17 am, called at various stations to Swindon where it

G.W.R.

WINDSOR STEEPLECHASES

First Race 1.0 p.m. Last Race 3.30 p.m.

Wednesday and Thursday, December 10th and 11th.

TRAINS FROM LONDON, WEDNESDAY AND THURSDAY, DECEMBER 10th & 11th.

		a.m.	a.m.	a.m.	a.m.	a.m.	a.m.	Special 1 & 3 a m	p.m.	p.m.	p.m.	p.m.
PADDINGTON	dep.	9 15	9 B 21	10 10	10 B 19	10 53	11 15	11 33	12 5	12 30		2 0
WESTBOURNE PARK	,,	A	A	A	9 53	10 57	—	A	11 39	A	A	A
Ealing (Broadway)	,,	9 26	9 34	9 57	10 26	11 7	11 20	—	11 49	12 41	1 22	—
Slough	arr.	9 50	10 12	10 37	11 0	11 32	11 44	p.m.	12 34	12 59	1 51	2 29
WINDSOR & ETON	,,	10 0	10 29	10 47	11 6	11 39	12 22	12 3	12 43	1 23	2 3	2 42

A Passengers from Kensington and Hammersmith Lines change at Bishop's Road.   B Starts from Bishop's Road Station.

RETURN ARRANGEMENTS.

SPECIAL FAST TRAINS (First and Third Class) will start from Windsor & Eton for LONDON immediately the Races are over.
Special Trains will leave Windsor at 4.15 p.m. for Reading, Didcot and Stations to Swindon ; Oxford, connecting at Oxford with the 6.10 p.m. Express thence to Birmingham, Wolverhampton &c. ; at 4.55 p.m. for Reading, Didcot and Stations to Swindon, connecting at Reading with Trains to Southampton, the Berks and Hants Line, Bath and Bristol District. See below.

ORDINARY TRAINS TO LONDON, WEDNESDAY & THURSDAY, DECEMBER 10th & 11th.

		p.m.	p.m.	p.m.	p.m.	p.m.	p m.	p.m.	p.m.	p.m.	p.m.	p.m.	p.m.
WINDSOR & ETON	dep.	4 35	4 50	5 47	6 55	6 10	6 55	7 32	8 32	8 55	9 55	10 50	11 15
Slough	,,	4 43	5 5	5 57	6 3	6 28	7 2	7 44	8 48	9 14	10 10	11 0	—
Ealing (Broadway)	arr.	—	5 40	6 31	—	7 6	7 45	8 21	9 13	9 52	10 35	11 33	—
WESTBOURNE PARK	,,	—	5 52	6 44	—	7 19	7 30	8 33	9 26	10 5	10 46	11 45	11 44
PADDINGTON	,,	5 7	5 55	6 48	6 33	7 22	7 34	8 37	9 30	10 9	10 49	11 48	11 58

Train Service between Windsor & Eton, Hungerford and Reading Districts, December 10th and 11th, 1913.

TO WINDSOR & ETON.

		Special. a.m.			Special. a.m.	Ord'y a.m.
Oxford	dep.	8 45	..	..	11 6	
Swindon	,,	8 15	..	..	—	9 20
Shrivenham	,,	8 28	..	..	—	9 32
Uffington	,,	8 42	..	..	—	9 45
Challow	,,	8 52	..	..	—	9 53
Wantage Road	,,	9 23	..	..	—	10 4
Steventon	,,	9 33	..	..	—	10 13
Devizes	,,	8 55	..	..	—	—
Marlboro'	,,	9 7	..	..	—	—
Savernake	,,	9 31	..	..	—	—
Hungerford	,,	9 43	..	..	—	—
Newbury	,,	9 57	..	..	—	10 37
Compton	,,	8 D 52	..	..	9 D 29	9 D 29
Basingstoke	,,	9 0	..	..	10 5	10 5
Didcot	,,	9 45	..	..	—	10 29
Cholsey	,,	9 55	..	..	—	10 43
Goring	,,	10 5	..	..	—	10 51
READING & WINDSOR & ETON	arr.	10 30 / 11 0	..	..	11 48 / 12 15	11 25 / 12 22

FROM WINDSOR & ETON.

		Special. p.m.	Ord'y. p.m.	Special. p.m.	Ord'y. p.m.	Ord'y. p.m.
WINDSOR & ETON	dep.	4 A 15	4 25	4 B 55	5 20	6 27
Maidenhead	,,	—	4 48	—	6 0	7 11
READING	arr.	4 44	5 8	5 27	6 20	7 31
Goring	,,	—	—	5 42	7 32	..
Cholsey	,,	—	—	5 55	7 41	..
Didcot	,,	5 6	—	6 10	7 52	..
Basingstoke	,,	—	5 55	—	7 30	9 0
Newbury	,,	—	5 T 54	6 S 11	6 57	..
Compton	,,	—	—	—	7 N 43	..
Hungerford	,,	—	—	6 S 35	7 34	..
Savernake	,,	—	—	6 S 35	7 48	..
Marlboro'	,,	—	—	—	7 2	8 23
Devizes	,,	—	—	—	7 18	8 26
Steventon	,,	5 51	—	—	8 1	8 28
Wantage Road	,,	6 3	—	—	6 34	8 49
Challow	,,	6 13	—	—	6 53	8 56
Uffington	,,	6 23	—	—	7 10	9 7
Shrivenham	,,	6 33	—	—	7 20	9 19
Swindon	,,	6 43	—	—	7 30	9 30
Oxford	,,	5 A 28	—	—	7 32	9 30

A Will connect at Oxford with the 4.55 p.m. Express from Paddington for Banbury, Leamington, Birmingham, etc.   B The 4.55 p.m. Return Special from Windsor & Eton will call at Pangbourne, if required, upon notice being given to the Guard at Reading.   D Via Didcot.   N Via Newbury.   S Slip Coach.   T Thursday only.

NOTE.—If the Races are postponed or abandoned these special arrangements will be cancelled.

A good supply of Cabs, &c., meets all Trains.

Any further information may be obtained at the Company's Stations, Offices, or Agencies ; of **Mr. J. DUNSTER,** Divisional Superintendent, Paddington Station, W. ; or of **Mr. C. ALDINGTON,** Superintendent of the Line, Paddington Station.

THE ENQUIRY OFFICE AT PADDINGTON STATION WILL BE OPEN FROM 8.30 A.M. TO 7.0 P.M. (SATURDAYS FROM 8.30 A.M. TO 6.0 P.M.) Telephone Number: 7000, Paddington. Extensions 319 and 320.

PADDINGTON, November, 1913.   **FRANK POTTER,** General Manager.

WYMAN & SONS LTD., Printers, Fetter Lane, London, E.C., and Reading.—214s.

Handbill advertising Windsor Steeplechases 1913.

G.W.R.

WINDSOR STEEPLECHASES

First Race 1.0 p.m.   Last Race 3.30 p.m.

Wednesday & Thursday, December 10th & 11th, 1913.

Paddington to Windsor & Eton in 30 minutes.

SPECIAL FAST TRAIN

(Not Stopping between Paddington and Windsor).

		(1st & 3rd) A.M.
PADDINGTON - - - - dep.		**11.33**
		P.M.
WINDSOR & ETON - - - arr.		**12.3**

Special Fast Trains (First and Third Class) will start from Windsor & Eton (G.W.R.) for London immediately the Races are over.

FARES BETWEEN PADDINGTON AND WINDSOR & ETON.

SINGLE JOURNEY.		RETURN JOURNEY.	
1st Class.	3rd Class.	1st Class.	3rd Class.
S. D.	S. D.	S. D.	S. D.
3 6	**1 9**	**5 6**	**3 0**

Passengers booked at Ordinary Fares to **WINDSOR & ETON** from **VICTORIA**, Pimlico (S.E. & C. Rly.), Battersea, Chelsea, West Brompton, Kensington (Addison Road), Uxbridge Road and St. Quintin Park Stations, by the Train leaving Victoria Station at 10.40 a.m., may return to **PADDINGTON** by any Train during the day.

Through Tickets to **WINDSOR & ETON** are issued at Stations on the **METROPOLITAN RAILWAY** between Aldgate and Hammersmith, and at Stations on the **WEST LONDON LINE** between Victoria and Uxbridge Road, including Kensington (Addison Road), via **PADDINGTON OR WESTBOURNE PARK.**

☞ NOTE.—If the Races are postponed or abandoned these special arrangements will be cancelled. A good supply of Cabs, &c., meets all Trains.

For full times of Trains between Paddington and Windsor & Eton, see over.

PADDINGTON, November, 1913.   **FRANK POTTER,** General Manager.

(L.D. 432).   T'S   WYMAN & SONS LTD., Printers, Fetter Lane, London, E.C., and Reading.—214L   [P.T.O.

Ref.T.33,750.G/12.

THE RAILWAY EXECUTIVE (WESTERN REGION).

Tele.Extn :
2339.

Operating Superintendent,
Paddington Station, W.2.
23rd July, 1949.

Dear Sir,

EXCURSION THROUGH TRAIN ARRANGEMENTS.
THURSDAY, AUGUST 4th,1949.
HALF DAY EXCURSION - PARSON STREET TO WINDSOR & ETON & RETURN.

With further reference to the above, the following train times,
which have beenagreed with the Superintendents concerned, will apply
on the date stated :-

FORWARD
"A" HEADLAMPS.

	Arr.	Dep.	RETURN "A" HEADLAMPS	Arr.	Dep.
	am	am		pm	pm
Clifton Bridge	-	11/ 5	Windsor & Eton	-	8.15
Parson Sta.Jcn.	11/10 RL.	11.17	Slough West	8.21 P.	8.22ML
Bedminster	11.19	11.21	Maidenhead		8/30
Bristol T.M.	11.25	11.30	Reading		8/44
Oldfield Park	-	11.48	Didcot		9/ 4
Bath	11.51	11.53	Steventon		8/ 8
	pm	pm	Swindon Jcn.	9.34 C.	9.42
Corsham	-	12. 7	Chippenham	10. 6	10. 8
Chippenham	12.14	12.17	Corsham	10.15	10.16
Swindon Jcn.	12.49 A.	12.54	Bath	10.32	10.34
Steventon	1/20		Oldfield Park	--	10.39
Didcot	M1/25L		Bristol T.M.	11. 0	11. 4
Reading	1/46		Bedminster	11. 8	11.10
Maidenhead	2/ 0		Parson St.	11.12	11/15
Slough West	2. 8 P.	2.10	Clifton Bridge	11/25	-
Windsor & E.	2.16	-			

CHELTENHAM PORTIONS.

	am	am		pm	pm
Cheltenham (St.James)	-	11.20	Swindon Jcn.	-	9.39
Lansdown Jcn.	11/25		Loco Yard	9/41	
Gloucester	11.37 N.	11.45	Kemble	9.57	10. 0
Stroud	12.3pm	12.5pm	Stroud	10.20	10.22
Kemble	12.26	12.29	Gloucester	10.42 N.	10.50
Loco Yard	12/44		Lansdown Jcn.	11/ 2	
Swindon Jcn.	12.46		Cheltenham (St.James)	11.5	

A. - Attach portion ex Cheltenham rear.
C. - Detach portion for Cheltenham front.
N. - Reverse.

FORMATION :-   Brake Third X, 5 Thirds X, Brake Third X. from Parson
(each direction) 3 Thirds X, Brake Third X. from Cheltenham.   (St.
                  (Approx. 330 Tons, 608 Seats from Swindon Jcn.)

The above details will also be included in my Through Train
Arrangements Notice. Kindly arrange accordingly, so far as you are
concerned and acknowledge receipt.

Yours truly,
for Gilbert Matthews,

_____ Esq.,

....

THURSDAY, AUGUST 4th, 1949.   T.33,750.G/12.
HALF DAY EXCN - PARSON ST. TO WINDSOR & E. AND RETURN.
Received copy of Mr. Matthews' circular letter dated 23rd July,
1949, and will arrange accordingly.

Operating Superintendent,
PADDINGTON STATION, W.2.

Internal notice of a half-day excursion from Bristol Parson Street, 1949.

OXFORD & KINGSTON STEAMERS

DAILY SERVICE DURING SUMMER THROUGH 91 MILES OF THE MOST BEAUTIFUL RIVER SCENERY IN ENGLAND

TIME TABLE THREEPENCE *post free*

CAMPING HOLIDAYS

A RIVER TOUR
WITHOUT HOTEL BILLS

MOTOR CRUISERS

TWO AND FOUR BERTHS
fully equipped for
RIVER OR CANAL TOURS

CAMPING PUNTS & SKIFFS

WATERPROOF
TENT COVERS
and all
Camping Requisites.

*FULL PARTICULARS
ON APPLICATION*

SALTER BROS. LTD.
22, FOLLY BRIDGE, OXFORD.

BUILDERS OF STEAM AND MOTOR LAUNCHES
RACING & PLEASURE BOATS OF ALL CLASSES

LISTS ON APPLICATION   TELEPHONE 3421

Courtesy Ian Coulson

attached a 4-coach portion from Cheltenham, going forward with 11 coaches. After the usual stop for a pilotman at Slough West, Windsor was reached at 2.16 pm, some 3 hours after leaving Bristol. With this trip, the Marlow cruise would seem not to have been included because the return train left Windsor at 8.15 pm and arrived back at Bristol, Parson St at 11.12 pm and Cheltenham at 11.05 pm.

These few examples are included as being typical of their kind but how fascinating it would be to examine a list of the excursions which went to Windsor over the years, in the same way as it has been possible to record the Royal Trains. Sadly no such list exists, so far as the author has been able to discover.

The GWR and later Western Region had a business relationship with Messrs Salters of Oxford for many years. This Oxford-based firm had started their river service between Kingston and Oxford as far back as 1888. It was posible to do the whole journey in 3 days. Stage 1A was between Kingston and Windsor Bridge (4½ hours); Stage 1B, between Windsor Bridge and Marlow (3 hours), Day 2 (and Stage 2) was between Marlow and Reading (3½ hours) and Day 3, Reading to Oxford (9 hours). Days 1 and 2 could be split up differently with an overnight stay in Windsor if preferred, and a journey from Windsor to Reading taking 8¼ hours on the second day. Combined rail and river day tickets were available, passengers coming to Windsor (GWR) by rail, travelling up river to Marlow, and then rejoining the railway there.

Sadly, the great increase in private traffic on the river in the 1960s and 1970s lead to delays to the service boats at locks, such that people missed their trains and the rail/river arrangement fell into disrepute. By 1977 the through river service had shrunk to services between Oxford and Abingdon, Reading and Henley, and Marlow to Windsor and Staines to Windsor. In the 1980s Salters stopped working to Marlow.

Former Oxford-based fireman Richard Tolley has described an unusual trip with a return schools' special from Windsor to Fairford in August 1952. He and his driver travelled 'passenger' to Slough where they picked up 0−6−0 No. 2202 and a pilotman and took the engine light to Windsor. Leaving Windsor with the excursion they stopped briefly at Slough West to drop off the pilotman and then 'right away' to Yarnton Junction, non-stop. Water was picked up at Goring troughs; at Didcot East the train was routed via the Avoiding line, and on down to Oxford. Here the train was signalled on the down through line, a rare event for a passenger train, and Mr Tolley records that the signalmen were hanging out of their windows, waving encouragement. Five minutes later the train stopped at Yarnton, five minutes early, its 'express' run finished, and the remainder of the journey down the branch must have been a bit of an anti-climax!

Since the withdrawal of run-round facilities at Windsor it is no longer possible to run locomotive-hauled excursion trains on the branch, but the off-peak traffic on the line is bolstered for much of the year by the tourists who use the dmu service to reach Windsor.

NOTE

1. The Slough & Datchet Electric Supply Co. Ltd had a generating station at Chalvey, served by this siding. The Co. was acquired by the Metropolitan Electric Supply Co. in 1928. The siding was taken out of use 27th January, 1952. (Thanks to John Gillham for company information.)

Thames Valley Circular Tours.

Combined Rail and River

Thames Valley = =
Circular Tour Tickets,

In connection with Messrs. Salter Bros.' Oxford and Kingston Steamers, are issued daily (Sundays excepted), from

ABINGDON	GORING & STREATLEY	PANGBOURNE
AYLESBURY	HENLEY-ON-THAMES	READING
BANBURY	HIGH WYCOMBE	STAINES
BASINGSTOKE	LEAMINGTON	SWINDON
BATH	LIVERPOOL	WALLINGFORD
BIRKENHEAD	MAIDENHEAD	WESTBOURNE PARK
BIRMINGHAM	MANCHESTER	WINDSOR
BRISTOL	MARLOW	WITNEY
CHELTENHAM	NEWBURY	and
CHESTER	OXFORD	WORCESTER.
EALING	PADDINGTON	

Enabling passengers to make a tour of the River Thames Valley between Oxford, Kingston, and intervening towns upon the banks of the river. The through river journey from Oxford to Kingston, and *vice versa*, occupies two days, but passengers not desirous of making the complete tour can join or leave the steamers at any of the locks or regular stopping places. Approximate times of the steamer journey are given below. Light refreshments are provided on board, and the steamers stop each day at Wallingford, Henley-on-Thames, Windsor and Kingston, where arrangements are made for luncheon at 2/6 per head. The through steamers starting from Oxford and Kingston in the morning stop at Henley-on-Thames for the night, and during Sunday. Passengers holding through tickets complete the journey on the following day, or in the case of Saturday, on Monday. A moderate quantity of luggage may be taken free. No dogs allowed on board. The fares do not cover the cost of conveyance between the railway stations and the steamers.

Distances.	Time Table of Steamers between Kingston and Oxford.			Distances.	Time Table of Steamers between Oxford and Kingston		
Miles.		a.m.	p.m.	Miles.		a.m.	p.m.
—	Kingston, Sun Hotel ... dep.	9 0	2 30	—	Oxford, Folly Bridge ... dep.	9 30	2 15
2½	Molesey Lock ... ,,	9 30	3 0	1½	Iffley Lock ... ,,	9 50	2 35
5	Sunbury Lock ... ,,	10 10	3 40	3	Sandford Lock ,,	10 10	2 55
9	Shepperton Lock ... ,,	10 55	4 30	7½	Abingdon Lock ... ,,	10 55	3 50
11	Chertsey Lock ,,	11 20	5 0	10	Culham Lock ,,	11 30	4 30
13	Penton Hook Lock ,,	11 45	5 25			p.m	
		p.m.		13	Clifton Lock ,,	12 5	5 10
15	Staines Bridge ,,	12 5	5 45	16	Day's Lock... ,,	12 35	5 40
16	Bell Weir Lock ,,	12 20	6 0	20	Benson Lock ,,	1 20	6 30
19	Old Windsor Lock ,,	1 0	6 40		{ arr.	1 40	7 0
21½	Romney Lock ,,	1 35	7 10	21	Wallingford Bridge		
	{ arr.	1 40	7 15		{ dep.	2A40	a.m.
22	Windsor Bridge ... { dep.		a.m.	26½	Cleeve Lock ... ,,	3 25	9 45
		2A40	9 15	27	Goring Lock ,,	3 40	10 0
24	Boveney Lock ... ,,	3 5	9 40	31	Whitchurch Lock... ,,	4 15	10 35
27¾	Bray Lock ,,	3 45	10 20	33½	Mapledurham Lock ,,	4 40	11 0
29	Maidenhead Bridge ,,	4 0	10 35	38	Reading (Caversham Lock) ,,	5 25	11 45
29½	Boulter's Lock ,,	4 20	10 55				
31½	Cookham Lock ... ,,	4 45	11 20	40½	Sonning Lock ,,	5 55	12 15
			p.m.	43½	Shiplake Lock ,,	6 25	12 45
36	Marlow Lock ,,	5 40	12 10	46	Marsh Lock ,,	6 50	1 15
37½	Temple Lock ,,	6 0	12 35		Henley-on-Thames { arr.	7 0	1 30
38	Hurley Lock ,,	6 10	12 45	47	Bridge .. { dep.	a.m.	p.m.
41½	Hambledon Lock ,,	6 45	1 20			9 50	2 40
	Henley-on-Thames { arr.	7 15	1 40	49½	Hambledon Lock ,,	10 15	3 5
44	Bridge { dep.	a.m.		53	Hurley Lock ,,	10 45	3 40
		9 0	2 40	53½	Temple Lock ,,	10 55	3 50
45	Marsh Lock ,,	9 15	2 55	55	Marlow Lock ,,	11 20	4 10
47½	Shiplake Lock ,,	9 45	3 25			noon	
50½	Sonning Lock ,,	10 20	4 0	59½	Cookham Lock ,,	12 0	4 55
53	Reading (Caversham Lock) ,,	10 50	4 25			p.m.	
57½	Mapledurham Lock ,,	11 35	5 15	61½	Boulter's Lock ,,	12 30	5 25
		p.m.		62	Maidenhead Bridge ,,	12 40	5 35
60	Whitchurch Lock ,,	12 5	5 45	63½	Bray Lock ... ,,	12 55	6 5
64	Goring Lock ,,	12 45	6 25	67	Boveney Lock ,,	1 25	6 40
64½	Cleeve Lock ,,	12 55	6 35		{ arr.	1 45	7 15
	{ arr.	1 40	7 15	69	Windsor Bridge ...		a.m.
70	Wallingford Bridge ... { dep.	a.m.	9 0		{ dep	2B40	9 15
		2A40		69½	Romney Lock ,,	2 50	9 25
71	Benson Lock ... ,,	3 0	9 20	72	Old Windsor Lock ,,	3 30	10 5
75	Day's Lock ,,	3 45	10 0	75	Bell Weir Lock ,,	4 0	10 20
78	Clifton Lock ,,	4 15	10 30	76	Staines Bridge ,,	4 15	10 50
81	Culham Lock ,,	4 50	11 5	78	Penton Hook Lock ,,	4 35	11 5
83½	Abingdon Lock ,,	5 30	11 45	80	Chertsey Lock ,,	5 0	11 25
88	Sandford Lock ,,	6 25	12 35	82	Shepperton Lock ... ,,	5 25	11 50
89½	Iffley Lock ,,	6 50	1 0				p.m.
91	Oxford, Folly Bridge ...arr.	7 10	1 15	86	Sunbury Lock ,,	6 10	12 35
				88½	Molesey Lock ,,	6 40	1 5
				91	Kingston ...arr.	7 10	1 30

A One hour allowed for Luncheon.   **B** 55 minutes allowed for Luncheon.

For fares and full particulars see Pamphlets, which can be obtained at the Company's Stations.

On Henley Regatta days, July 7th, 8th, 9th, the morning Steamer from Windsor will start at 8.30, returning from Regatta Island, Henley, at 5.0 p.m., and the morning Steamer from Wallingford will start at 8.0 a.m., returning from Marsh Lock at 4.30 p.m. (*For intermediate times and particulars see special bills*).

Advertisement (July 1903) for combined rail and river tickets, using Messrs Salter's steamers.
David Castle Collection

On Sunday 21st April, 1963 the Great Western Preservation Society ran a Thames-side Railtour from Paddington to Brentford, Windsor, Marlow and High Wycombe, returning to London via Greenford and West Ealing. Intending passengers crowd round '57XX' 0–6–0PT No. 9661 at Paddington before departure; they had been promised a '61XX' class 2–6–2T! *The Late Alec Field, Courtesy K. Williams*

Here the Thamesside Railtour has arrived at Windsor and No. 9661 is being detached and replaced by '61XX' No. 6128 (at the other end of the train). *The Late Alec Field, Courtesy K. Williams*

Chapter Twelve
Sundry Mishaps

Slough, until its rebuilding, was one of those curious single-sided stations of which Reading is a better known example. Both up and down platforms were on a loop line, south of the main lines, the up platform being the one nearer London. Over the years several accidents occurred because of this layout, but despite the Inspecting Officers' comments, the GWR did not rebuild the station in conventional form until 1884.

The first accident to be considered in this chapter occurred in 1859. Signalling arrangements at this time were primitive in the extreme and from the information given in Colonel Yolland's accident report the following can be gleaned.

There was a signalman's box in the centre of Slough Yard equipped with telegraphic instruments; all down trains approaching Slough were tele-graphed by West Drayton and all up trains by Taplow passenger station. There was a signal adjacent to the box. As the accident concerned two up trains, the report only gives information on signalling on the west, or coun-try, side of Slough. Some 330 yds west of the Centre signal was a West End or Station signal for the up line, and some 940 yards further west an auxiliary, or distant, signal. A ground signalman was located at the West End signal and worked both that and the auxiliary signal. This ground signalman was in communication with the Centre signalman only by bell; it was his duty to keep his signals at Danger if the Centre signal was at Danger, and to seek permission to lower them each time (by bell).

Some ⅜ of a mile east (Slough side) of Taplow passenger station previous-ly mentioned, was Taplow goods station. At the goods station there was a signal, by observation of which the signal at Taplow passenger station was 'regulated' but no communication existed between the two places. If a goods train stopped at Taplow goods station, the porter on duty at the passenger station effectively had to guess when that train left the goods station when sending his 'train approaching' telegraph message to Slough.

On 14th September, 1859 the 4.00 pm 'Up Gloucester goods' (of 13th September) had left Reading at 1 am (some 100 minutes late). After working at Twyford it next called at Taplow goods, at which it arrived at about 1.55 am and left at about 2.08 am. The train comprised a tender engine, 52 wagons and rear brake van, and was accompanied by two guards. On leaving Taplow the under guard travelled in the van, while the head guard mounted a cattle truck some 12 vehicles from the engine for the short journey forward to Slough.

Shortly before the time the goods train was arriving at Taplow, a special empty coaching stock (ECS) train left Reading. Formed of a tender engine and 22 empty carriages weighing 254 tons, it was supposed to leave Reading at 1.50 am, but the driver being impatient to get away took advantage of the foreman porter's absence to leave 3 minutes early, without permission. Despite being told at Reading that there was a goods train ahead of him, the driver ran faster than he needed to keep time, passing the station signal at Taplow passenger station at danger (and ignoring a red handsignal from the night porter) at 2.14 am. A minute later the same circumstances occurred at Taplow goods, although the driver and fireman later stated that they got white (all clear) lights from both the signals and saw no hand signals.

At Slough, at 2.20 am, the goods train had arrived at the Centre signal and the signalman was explaining to the driver that he needed to draw ahead to clear the line for the following train when the collision occurred. The driver of the ECS train had been travelling at an estimated 40–50 mph and only shut off steam when he passed the Slough auxiliary signal. The driver claimed the auxiliary was at 'all right' (the West End signalman said it had been at 'all right' for the preceding goods train for no more than ¼ minute). Almost immediately afterwards, the driver saw the tail lights of the goods train; the inspector considered this sighting *could* have been made at a distance of about 1000 yds from the spot where the collision occurred, rather than the 870 yds or so which the driver claimed.

As was usual, braking power was restricted to three handbrakes, or a brakeforce of 34 tons out of a total weight of 254 tons. The collision with the goods train occurred 74 yards on the approach side of the West End signal and the ECS engine travelled forward those 74 yards until it fell on its side nearly opposite the signal. The brakevan and rear five trucks of the goods train were piled up in a heap, blocking both lines and in this debris the under-guard was regrettably killed. The head guard, travelling on the ledge of a cattle truck (!) was knocked off by the force of the collision, but not killed.

The inspecting officer, quite rightly, had a field day in his comments. Firstly the Great Western trains were sent on their journeys 'with a lamentable insufficiency of brake power', on which previous representations had been made. It was quite against the company's rules for the ECS train to start without permission and the driver had not kept a good look out. The driver *may* have been confused by the powerful back light of a down line signal at Taplow goods station, which pattern of signal lamp should be discontinued. There was no up distant signal for Taplow passenger station and there should be a means of communication between the two Taplow stations. But it was the lack of brake power that most annoyed the Colonel, for which he held the company entirely responsible, particularly bearing in mind the unpunctuality of the trains and the mixing in of specials and excursions with the timetabled trains. (All in all the service was being run with insufficient consideration for the passengers' safety.)

The next incident in our chronology of mistakes happened five years later on 22nd December, 1864 and was the first of several which really stemmed from the antiquated layout of Slough station. The signalling arrangements do not appear to have altered since 1859, the Centre signal box being the only one mentioned, and ground signalman at west and east ends working station signals governed by the aspect displayed at the Centre signal. In addition to his telegraph duties the Centre signalman was also responsible for altering, as required, the position of 18 sets of points, worked by individual hand levers, for which duty, of course, he had to leave his cabin.

The manoeuverings at Slough station that night were rather complicated, and understanding of them will be assisted by study of the plan of the layout included.

1. At 12.51 am an up broad gauge goods train ran into Slough up station, after detaching five trucks and the engine taking water, it left at 1.08 am.

G . W . R

WIDENING OF LINE FROM WEST DRAYTON TO SLOUGH

PLAN OF LINE BEFORE ALTERATIONS

SLOUGH STATION

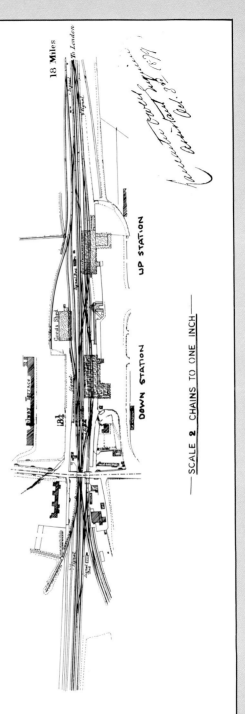

18 Miles

To London

Signal

Signal

UP STATION

DOWN STATION

Goods Shed

Elvey Terrace

18¾

SCALE 2 CHAINS TO ONE INCH

Slough station as it was in 1879.

2. An up narrow gauge goods train arrived on the up main line at 1.05 am to detach one truck and take water. The signalman then went to the broad gauge facing points in the up main line behind it and turned them towards the up station line.

3. Another up broad gauge train arrived and was sent towards the up station, and then reversed back into the down station.

4. The signalman then returned to the narrow gauge goods train (2) and backed it from the up main line to the down main line so as to clear the up main line for another up train. In this position the narrow gauge train straddled the crossover from the up main to the up station.

5. He then returned to his cabin, and when the up line was clear, put his signal lamp to 'all right' for a broad gauge up parcels train to run through non-stop. It was now about 1.30 am. Unfortunately he had forgotten to restore the up main/up station facing points to the normal (up main) position after movement (3).

At about 1.32 am he received the 'train approaching' advice from Taplow by telegraph and some eight minutes later the parcels train appeared travelling at 30–40 mph under clear signals. At the facing points leading to the up station the train suddenly veered to the right, crashing into the narrow gauge goods train standing on the down main line. The engine was derailed, and together with its tender which had become uncoupled from the train, ran in this state parallel to the goods train for some 128 yds before stopping. Despite the severity of the collision, no one was hurt. Some trucks were destroyed or damaged, the engine 'was a good deal damaged', and 'the down line was slightly broken up'.

Colonel Yolland, again, was critical of the working at Slough, particularly the arrangements for working the facing points. On narrow gauge railways, he pointed out, the switches were self-acting; weighted to stand open for a particular direction, and the lever handle held for a train to pass in the other direction. Once the lever handle was released, the switch would return to its normal position. This arrangement was preferable, he felt, to the GWR situation where the points had to be moved for either direction, the points pinned over and the pins locked. The Centre signal, also, only consisted of lamps for night signalling, all daytime signals being given by hand, and here a double semaphore signal was needed. Lastly, and not unnaturally, he was unhappy with the layout, and that at Reading, where 'a mere mistake or act of forgetfulness on the part of the switchman' could jeopardise the safety of the public. If the layout could not revert to the more conventional type, he said that for about £100 the facing points could be interlocked with the signals.

By 1870, the date of the next mishap at Slough, locking apparatus between points and signals had just been installed at the 'east signal box' (opposite the up station) but unfortunately the signalman concerned was not accustomed to working it, as will be seen! Looking at the plan of Slough which is dated 1879, and assuming that the up station had not been moved between these dates, this would seem to be what has previously been called the Centre signal box but, frustratingly, the report does not give full details of the signalling in place other than describing the items actively involved.

On 22nd September, 1870, the 7.25 pm express from Birmingham to Paddington attached at Reading, as usual, three coaches for Windsor, to be

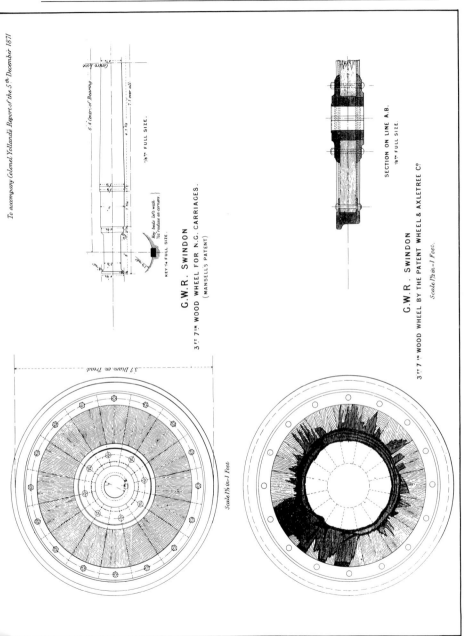

To accompany Colonel Yolland's Report of the 5th December 1871

G.W.R. SWINDON
3 ft 7 in WOOD WHEEL FOR N.G. CARRIAGES.
(MANSELL'S PATENT)

KEY 1/4 FULL SIZE.

1/8th FULL SIZE.

3 ft 1 Diam. on Tread.

Scale 1/8 in-1 Foot.

G.W.R. SWINDON
3 ft 7 in WOOD WHEEL BY THE PATENT WHEEL & AXLETREE Cº

SECTION ON LINE A.B.
1/8th FULL SIZE.

Scale 1 1/2 in-1 Foot.

Diagram of Mansell's patent wooden wheels, involved in the 1871 accident at Windsor. *Public Record Office, Kew*

slipped at Taplow. The coaches were slipped east of Taplow, some 1,900 yds from Slough but the slip guard allowed the slip portion to run too close to the rear of the main train. Now that interlocking had been installed at Slough, the signalman had to restore three signals to danger and then move three point levers to turn the slip coaches into the up station. On the night in question he had moved the three signal levers and two of the point levers but was unable to move the third before the slip portion ran past the points, still on the up main line, and stopped opposite the up platform some 75 yds east of the signalman's 'hut'.

It was decided to push (by hand) the slip carriages eastwards along the up main line so as to clear a set of points leading to the goods yard, where stood the pilot engine that was to take the coaches forward to Windsor. First of all however the pilot engine driver decided he needed to move along the siding to take water at the tower. Unfortunately at this stage and, without being asked, the signalman decided to set the points from the siding to the up main, and the pilot engine ran into the side of the rear slip coach! This coach was derailed and the locomotive's buffer plank damaged.

After criticizing all the staff involved for their lack of alertness, Col Rich of the Board of Trade recommended that a signal be provided to control movements from the goods siding, worked by the signalman and interlocked with the other signals and points. He also considered that it would be safer if the slip coaches were in future stopped on the up main line and then hauled to the up station, before proceeding to Windsor.

The next accident is the first one at Windsor for which a Board of Trade report has been found, and has already been previewed in Chapter Five by station master Simmons's account. On 9th November, 1871 Mr Simmons was dealing with a train recently arrived in the down platform when the 5.40 pm Windsor to Paddington narrow gauge train left the up platform. This train comprised a tank engine, eight carriages and a guard's van at the rear. As the train left Mr Simmons heard a peculiar lumping sound (the same word is used in the official report as Simmons used in his own account). He ran to the London end of the down platform but could not attract the driver's attention and could only resort to sending a telegraph message to Slough for the train to be stopped and the wheels examined.

The driver, however, realised the train was pulling heavily and, on looking back, as the train was crossing the River Thames bridge, observed flames coming from the left hand side of the carriages. He stopped the train some ¼ mile beyond the bridge and found that the leading wheels of the fourth carriage were derailed and the body of the vehicle was leaning against the wall of the viaduct. The vehicle concerned was a four-wheeled composite carriage with Mansell's Patent wooden wheels. The tyre of these wheels was attached to the outer circumference of 16 wooden discs by means of circular iron rings and bolted by nuts and bolts. The inner ends of the wood discs were secured to the boss of the wheel by further nuts and bolts. It would appear that the bolts had gradually loosened allowing the wooden discs to slip out of the left hand wheel and the wheel 'had apparently got out of its socket and left the left rail'.

Interestingly, Colonel Yolland notes that 'it appears to be very generally admitted that this is the best carriage wheel used in this country. It is therefore of importance that this novel kind of failure . . . should be generally made known'. The size of the bolts passing through the wheel boss would be increased by the GWR and instructions had been given to carriage examiners to check these bolts for slackness.

In Chapter Five station master Simmons describes the immense amount of work connected with the visit of the Shah of Persia in 1873. What he does not say is that the visit nearly did not take place at all. Despite the importance of their Royal passenger, a member of the staff at Slough made a most elementary mistake which, but for the alertness of a fireman, would have led to a collision. That fireman wrote to the *GWR Magazine* in 1912 and his letter can speak for itself:

June 1912
Dear Sir – I have good reason for remembering the day the photograph of *Lord of the Isles* was taken – June 24th 1873. We left Paddington with the Shah of Persia, the late King Edward with Queen Alexandra, and the late Czar of Russia and his Consort on the train, attended by many distinguished persons. In honour of the Shah's visit a great review was being held at Windsor, and many excursion trains were being run. All went well with the train until we were passing through Slough Station. At that time, there was no 'Locking gear' there, and trains had to pass from the down main line and go through the down platform road to reach Windsor. At the western end of the platform there was a pair of points turned by hand, which led either to Windsor, or across the Windsor Branch to the main line.

On passing through Slough Station I noticed that these points were wrong, being set for the main line instead of Windsor. I shouted to my driver, 'Whoa, mate, the points are wrong', and we stopped the train just in time to avert a collision with an empty train coming from Windsor. We put the train back over the points, and I jumped down and turned the points myself, the man whose duty it was to attend to them being so overcome that he was unable to do any more work. Mr Tyrell (then Superintendent of the Line) was on the platform, and witnessed the whole affair. He got onto the engine and rode with us to Windsor.

After we started from Slough he enquired from my driver who had first noticed that the points were wrongly set, and the engineman, who was Jos. Groves, replied: 'My fireman, sir'. Mr Tyrell turned to me and expressed his pleasure at my having observed the position of the points. Subsequently I was sent to Swindon to see Mr Joseph Armstrong (late Locomotive Superintendent), who promised that I should receive recognition for the occurrence.

Shortly afterwards I was promoted to be a driver, and before long made a driver on the broad gauge expresses, being the youngest man ever promoted to that position. Many people wondered at the time at my early promotion, but it was the prevention of the collision that led to it. It may be imagined that the occasion on which the photograph was taken stands out as a red letter day in my life.

I must say that during my service with the Company I had the good fortune to be the means of preventing five other collisions with passenger trains.

Yours faithfully,
JAMES HENDERSON

Incidentally, records in the Royal Archives show that a Review held in Windsor Park this day started one hour late 'in consequence of delay with train'. Could this have been the Shah's train?

DIAGRAM No. 2.

GREAT WESTERN RAILWAY.

SWINDON.

Goods Engine, No. 25.

Scale $\frac{3}{8}$ in. 1 Foot.

To accompany Captain Tyler's Report.
Dated June 7th, 1876.

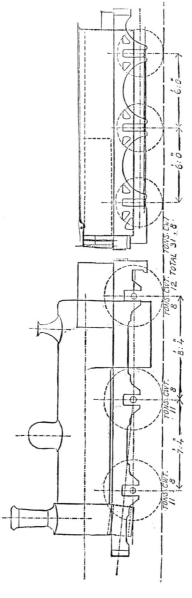

DESCRIPTION.

CYLINDERS	..	..	..	17 in. diam. 24 in. stroke.
BOILER	..	..	..	11·0 in. long × 4·1⅜ in. diam. (Inside).
FIRE BOX	..	..	..	5·4 in. long × 4·1¼ in. wide. Inside do. 4·0 in. long × 3·6¼ in. wide × 5·8½ in. high.
TUBES	..	..	..	248 Tubes, 1⅞ in. diam. outside.
WHEELS	..	..	..	L^ns D^ve and T^ve 5·0 diam.
HEATING SURFACE	..		..	Fire Box, 98·0 sq. ft.—Tubes, 1187·3 sq. ft.—Total, 1285·3 sq. ft.
AREA OF FIRE GRATE	..			16·6 ft. (super).

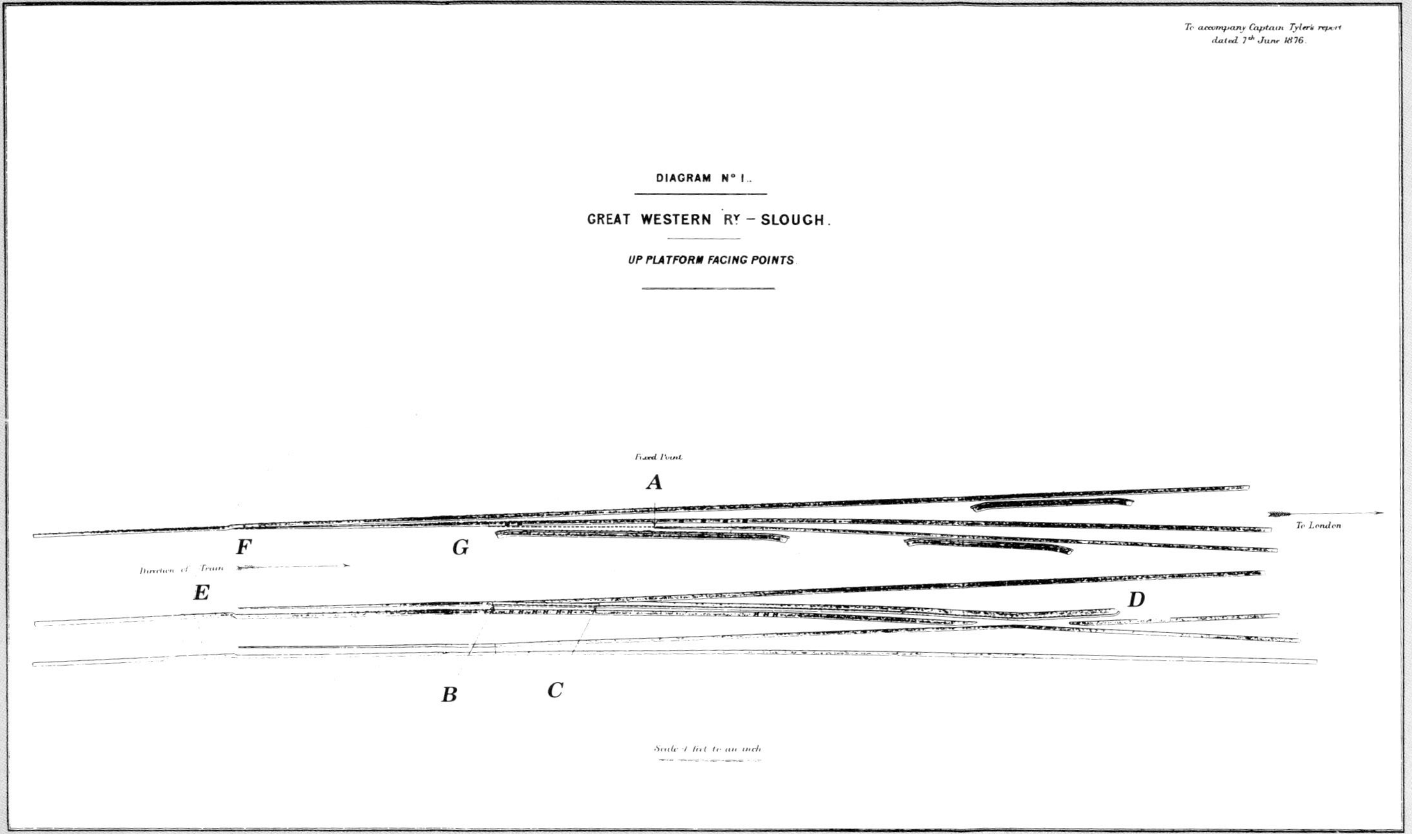

DIAGRAM Nº 1.

GREAT WESTERN RY – SLOUGH.

UP PLATFORM FACING POINTS

To accompany Captain Tyler's report
dated 7ᵗʰ June 1876.

To London

To Station of Town

Fixed Point.

A

B

C

D

E

F

G

Scale 4 feet to an inch

Diagram of the up platform facing points at Slough (1876).

Public Record Office, Kew

The permanent way at Slough caused the next accident, and indirectly again, the lop-sided layout was responsible which Captain Tyler did not hesitate to point out. On 3rd June, 1876 the 8.10 am narrow gauge passenger train from Swindon, comprising 'Standard Goods' 0–6–0 No. 25 (built January 1876), brake van, 9 carriages and brake van, due at Slough at 11.05 am, was passing over the connection from the up main to the up station at about 8 mph when the engine and two leading vehicles became derailed. The facing points were worked from the East box, some 130 yds away, (the old Centre cabin) and were properly provided with a locking bolt and bar, and the lever working this was properly interlocked with the levers of the signals. These points were constructed, as was usual with mixed gauge, with a *fixed* point ('A' in the diagram), some 9 feet from 'G', the heel of the tongue of the moveable points.

Captain Tyler put the mishap down to 'defects of principle and construction in the permanent way'. Quoting from his report (reference should be made to the accompanying diagram):

> The leading wheels of the engine passed properly through the moveable tongues of the points from F to G on the nearside, and from E to B on the offside. From B forward, the off-leading wheel, instead of running along its proper rail HHHH, commenced to mount with its flange at the point B, and followed the dotted line in the diagram, running forward along the guard rail from C to D. The near-leading wheel, at the same time, instead of running along on its flange, as it ought to have done, gradually leaving the rail MMM and passing to the offside of the fixed point A, followed the dotted line on that side to the near or wrong side of the fixed point. The engine having thus been thrown off . . . it dragged the tender and two leading vehicles . . . after it.
>
> The connecting rail BC, between the tongue EB and the guard rail CD, forms an obtuse angle with the tongue EB. This portion of rail BC, and the guard rail beyond it, form the only check to the off-leading wheel of an engine, to guide it in turning off somewhat sharply from the straight line, leading towards London, to the line leading to the [station] shed at the south side of the main lines; and the near-leading wheel loses its support at the same time, just when it most requires it, in passing from G, as it ought to do, to the offside of the fixed point A.

There was an indentation produced by blows at 'B' showing the tendency of flanges of narrow gauge trains to mount this rail when being turned off towards the up station. Although the points had been in place for 2 years without any previous accident, Captain Tyler commented that a potential for offside wheels to mount the rails at B or C undoubtedly existed, with no support for the nearside wheel to counteract that tendency. He closed by firing another salvo at the GWR concerning the one-sided station: undoubtedly the cost of conversion would be high, but 'having regard to the magnitude and importance of the traffic in connection with the Windsor branch, as well as with the main line of the GWR', he would not be doing his duty if he failed to recommend that such work take place quickly.

The GWR did not introduce block working on the Windsor branch, despite its heavy usage by Royalty, until 1889. Until then trains were worked 'by timetable', and reliance on drivers keeping a sharp lookout. Of course, special precautions were taken for Royal Trains, and no train was allowed to follow a 'Royal' until it had cleared the branch.

On 12th December, 1878, Samuel Panter was in charge of standard gauge '517' class 0–4–2T No. 569 (built 1870) hauling a train of 28 trucks (mostly empty) and brake van. The train, the 7.35 pm goods Windsor to Slough left on time, the weather being foggy. After passing the Chalvey Road under-bridge the train exploded two detonators placed by a fogman who was displaying a red light by a packers' hut about 100 yards on the Windsor side of the Slough distant signal (which the driver could not see in the fog until past the detonators). The distant was passed at about 5 mph and the driver stopped his train with the engine just beyond the Bath Road bridge (44 yds past the distant signal), and then drew up slowly to the home signal, arriving there at 7.44 pm. He was still there at 8 pm, the tail of the train only 132 yds in front of the distant signal.

After the goods train had passed the packers' hut (known locally as 'Gammon's Hut') the fogman walked back a further 200 yards and replaced the detonators (i.e. 300 yds on the approach side of the distant signal), anticipating correctly that the goods train would be held outside Slough.

In Windsor station 'Standard Goods' No. 782 a standard gauge 0–6–0 tender locomotive built in 1873, running tender first, headed the 11-vehicle 7.50 pm Windsor to Slough passenger train. Its driver was Bristol-based John Tucker who was not very familiar with the branch, having driven over it on only six or seven previous occasions. He was also unaware that the branch was not worked on the Block system, assuming, not unreasonably, that no train would leave Windsor until the previous one had arrived at Slough. His train was not fitted with the vacuum brake, but a guard travelled in the front and rear vehicles to apply that vehicle's hand brake as required.

Leaving Windsor on time (according to the guard, 4 minutes late accord-ing to the driver) the powerful goods locomotive soon had its train up to a good speed ('I think the speed of the train was a little higher than usual all the way from Windsor' said the under-guard later). George Hatton, chief goods porter at Windsor, and acting as guard to the 7.35 pm goods train heard it in the distance as he stood besides the van of his train (the Rules did not require him to protect it by placing detonators). Then, hearing two detonators exploded, he started to run in the direction of Windsor, display-ing a red light. He had only covered about 150 yards, and had managed to place no detonators, when in Hatton's words,

> . . . an engine and passenger train passed me running so fast that I feared it would run into my train . . . I shouted out to the driver, 'Can't you see my tail lamp? Are you mad?' After the train had passed I heard the sound of a collision.

The Rule Book in those days required a driver to be prepared to stop at a *Distant* signal at danger, 'but if he sees the way in front of him is clear, he must proceed slowly and cautiously within the Distant signal, having such control of his train as to be able to stop it short of any obstruction that may exist between the Distant signal post and the Home signal . . .' Driver Tucker later admitted passing the signal at between 15 and 20 mph, ('the fog was so thick at the time that I did not see the distant signal until I had got nearly under it'), but that by reversing the engine and blowing for the guards' brakes he had reduced speed to 5 mph when the collision occurred.

The accident had happened at about 8.01 or 8.02 pm, just as the 6.22 pm

No. 569 working the 7.35 pm goods involved in the mishap at Slough on 12th December, 1878 was a sister engine to No. 517 (of the '517' class), seen here at Bristol, c.1904.   *Ivor Smart Collection*

The 5.30 am Paddington express on 31st December, 1881 was hauled by No. 209, a sister engine of No. 211 seen here. These engines were built by Beyer, Peacock in 1861.   *Locomotive Publishing Co.*

from Moorgate Street, hauled by 'Metro' 2–4–0T No. 463 (built 1869) was leaving Slough station. The force of the smash was such that a truck from the goods train was knocked foul of the down line. Observing this, Samuel Panter, the driver of the goods ran towards Slough station waving a red light but was unable to stop the down (Moorgate Street) train, although that driver did see his red light and shut off steam. In the latter's words,

> I saw nothing unusual until I had passed the [Slough] coke stage, and had nearly reached the engine shed when I saw a red light being waved in front . . . I think we might be running 12 or 13 miles [sic] when I first saw the red light. The break-van was a good deal damaged. I think I was running eight or nine miles an hour when we struck the break-van.

The Moorgate Street train, of eight carriages, was another passenger train only equipped with handbrakes – as Col Yolland of the Board of Trade pointed out in his report, it is unlikely that either collision would have occurred had the trains been fitted with the vacuum brakes. Fortunately no injuries occurred in either train.

To emphasise further the very risky form of 'signalling' then employed on the Windsor branch, the report reveals that after the first collision occurred, the under-guard of the 7.50 pm from Windsor had gone back and protected his train and stopped yet another train from Windsor which left that place at 8.15 pm. So although driver Tucker was blamed for the accident, having run 'at too high a rate of speed', the Colonel reserved strong criticism for the lack of proper block signalling, which comment however the GWR was not to follow up for over 10 years! Col Yolland also recommended that the distant signal should be moved further back from its home signal, and be repeated in the signal box.

The next two accidents both took place at Slough within weeks of each other at the end of 1881. In both cases signalmen were at fault but the primitive signalling arrangements then prevailing, and the bottleneck of a layout at Slough, were much to blame.

In 1879 the GWR had constructed two additional lines, relief lines, from West Drayton to Slough station, so for those trains calling at Slough the traffic of four lines fed into one. As Col Yolland said in his report on the collision which is about to be related, 'the greatest care is necessary to avoid collisions taking place.' Plans had been agreed for the rebuilding of Slough and the extension of the relief lines westwards, but for the present this very unsatisfactory layout had to be worked. There were three signal boxes, East, 105 yards east of the London end of the up platform, Middle about 283 yards west of the former box and almost at the west end of the up platform, (the old Centre cabin), and West box, 360 yards west of Middle and located in the fork between the down main line and the branch to Windsor.

Access to the down platform could be either from the main to loop facing points, or, alternatively by proceeding along the down main line to West box and then setting back into the loop line at that end. Another curious method of working was that goods trains having traffic to detach at Slough proceeded along the main line past West box and detached their traffic on the west facing curve (i.e. from Windsor facing towards Reading) between the Windsor branch and the main line. These points were 426 yards west of the

West signal box and were unlocked by a train staff obtained from West box. Once this staff had been handed over, no trains were allowed over the down main line past West box until the staff was returned.

On 29th November, 1881, the 3.30 pm down goods train from Paddington arrived at Slough at 4.50 pm; in its formation it included a meat van for Windsor so, after picking up the staff and keys at West box, the train continued to the West loop curve where the train was stabled and the wagon for Windsor detached. The engine and meat van then returned to the down main line prior to propelling the van back to the station sidings.

At Slough things had become somewhat congested. The 4 pm passenger from Paddington arrived at the down relief line home signal about 4.55 pm, from where it was signalled to the main line and stopped at the Middle box. The up platform was occupied by the 2.30 pm from Oxford and the down platform by the 4.50 pm from Windsor so the only place for the 4 pm from Paddington was to proceed to West box and shunt to the down platform 'on top' of the train from Windsor (a regular occurrence according to its driver). Signalman Wardell in Middle box asked the West signalman, Green, whether the train might proceed to him and this was agreed, the 4 pm drawing down to the 'starting signal' worked by West box, on the authority of a white light displayed by Wardell.

Signalman Green at West box, aware that two fast express trains were due to pass, one 'up' at 5.03 pm and one 'down' at 5.07 pm now broke the instructions which were intended to prevent a train passing his box whilst a train was shunting the West Curve, and in possession of the staff. He admitted at the subsequent inquiry that this instruction had been disregarded for at least the last 12 months. He called the driver of the 4 pm Paddington forward with a green light, authorising him to pass the starting signal at danger, so as to clear the trailing points leading from the passenger loop, prior to setting back over them. Unfortunately the shunter at the West curve waiting with his engine and single van saw the light and took it as his authority to set back towards the station. As no tail lamp had been placed on the meat van, it was not until the two movements collided, on the trailing points, that the driver of the Paddington train even realised that the shunt movement was coming towards him. The wheels of the meat van were knocked out from under the vehicle and off the rails; two passengers and two staff were injured in the collision.

Naturally Col Yolland blamed Signalman Green for his infringement of the signalling regulations but it seems clear that staff were having to work an impractical and inadequate layout. The station master was also criticised for having failed to report the flagrant disobedience of the Rules but it may well be that he knew that it was impossible to work to the timetable without some 'rule-bending', and, until the station could be rebuilt, had become resigned to that fact. Doubtless his public rebuke from the Colonel will have led to his removal from the post.

Less than a month after the collision just described, came the next in a series of serious accidents which occurred at Slough station in the space of a few years. Nowadays with domestic dependence on 'central heating' and few coal fires, and with no steam locomotives to fill the atmosphere with sulphur, fogs are a comparatively rare event. It comes as a surprise, there-

fore, to realise how often 'fog' played a part in an accident in the period of
railway development presently being considered.

So it was, when on Christmas Eve 1881 (a Saturday), during 'a very dense
fog' (to quote from the BoT Accident Report), the 5.30 am down passenger
train from Paddington came into collision with an empty coal train at
Slough at about 6.40 am. Col Yolland, who had not yet concluded his
investigation into the 29th November collision, returned to Slough to enquire into the causes of this fresh mishap.

Because of the short distances between the three signal boxes at Slough,
special regulations applied between them. Signalling was by bell and single
needle telegraph and, briefly, arrangements for down trains were as follows:

Fast Train approaching
A train not stopping at Langley was bell-signalled by Langley when passing
W. Drayton (7 beats) – 'Train signalled from station in the rear'. Slough East
immediately sent the 7 beats on to Middle box, the latter did likewise to West box.

If the line was obstructed at Middle or West boxes: this box or boxes would return
5 beats ('Line obstructed') and keep its signals at danger. As Middle had a 'slot' on
the East home signal that would also be kept at danger.

If the line was clear to West box starting signal only: West box would return 5
pause 5 beats ('Line clear to starting signal') to Middle and release that signalman's
home signal by taking off his 'slot', but the latter (Middle) would maintain the
signal at danger. Middle would similarly send 5-5 to East and release the 'slot' on
the latter's home signal. East box would keep that signal at danger until the train
had almost stopped at it, when it would be lowered and the driver cautioned past
it, Middle box acting in the same way in his turn.

If the line was clear to box beyond Slough West (Hay Mill)
West box would return 3 beats ('Line Clear') to Middle and release his and
Middle's signals, Middle would act in the same way to East box, so the train could
have a clear run through.

In the event of fog or falling snow there was a further precaution at Slough:
a ground signalman was appointed to each box, whose duty it was to walk
through the section and advise the signalman when the section was clear,
'and the signalmen in the box must not admit a train into the station, or give
"Line Clear" back to the station in rear, until he has been assured by the
ground signalman that the station is clear.' At Slough East on this day the
night signalman assumed this ground duty at 6.03 am, and at the Middle box
the night signalman there became ground signalman at 6.20 am. There were
also fogsignalmen out at Slough East's home and distant signals on both the
main and relief lines.

The 2.30 am empty coal train from Paddington to Aberdare hauled by a
six-coupled tank engine arrived at the East down relief line home signal at
5.58 am where it was held for 12 minutes (18 mins according to the guard).
The driver was then called past the signal by the ground fogman, proceeding
on to the main line where he drew down to the water tank at Middle Box.
Before he had finished taking water, however, he was asked to shunt to the
up main line to allow the 5.30 am ex-Paddington to pass, and proceeded to
propel his 43 wagon train through the crossover on to the up line.

The early turn signalman at Slough East was William Guttridge who, before coming to the Slough area, had been a signalman at Doncaster on the Great Northern Railway. His first box locally had been Hay Mill in December 1872, followed by promotion to Slough East, on the opening of the relief lines, in September 1879. Coming on duty at 6.03 am he had given a 'Line Clear' to Langley on the down main at 6.05 am but had been unaware then that the 5.30 am ex-Paddington had only just left the terminus, 34 minutes late. At 6.20 am he therefore sent 'Line Obstructed' to Langley (for the down main line) to allow the coal train to come off the relief line, which it did at 6.24 am. At 6.25 am he received 7 beats from Langley, advising the approach of the 5.30 am Paddington.

Considering his many years of experience, Guttridge then acted quite inexplicably. He sent 'Line Clear' to Langley at 6.26 am despite:

a) having received 'Line Obstructed' from Middle Box on receipt of his (East's) 7 beats bell signal for the 5.30 am Paddington

b) not having consulted his fogman and obtained an assurance that the line was clear

His only explanation after the event was, 'I knew that there were fog signalmen both at the home and distant signals, and I thought this would be sufficient protection'.

Unfortunately as is so often the case in these mishaps, a second person then acted incorrectly, removing the only remaining line of defence. The fogsignalman at the East down main line distant signal, hearing the approach of the 5.30 am Paddington, looked at the signal and thought he saw a white (proceed) light displayed, even though he could not see the signal arm. He normally looked at the arm weights (which were much lower down the post) for confirmation but on this occasion failed to do so. He was wrong, however, the signal was still at danger, but he removed the detonators and allowed the Paddington passenger train to pass at a speed the driver estimated at 35–40 mph.

At Slough the Middle signalman, George Pope, was getting worried by the delay in clearing the goods train and despite having 'Obstructed the Line' with his 5 beat bell signal sent a further telegraph message to the East box, 'Do not clear line'. This, he said, he sent at 6.26 am, but Gutteridge at East said he received it at 6.31 am. (However Gutteridge's times were at variance with both Middle and Langley boxes.) Possibly one of the groundmen had told Pope what Gutteridge had done in clearing the line for the Paddington train? Gutteridge telegraphed back, 'I have cleared line', but nothing more could then be done, the train had by now passed Langley.

The 5.30 am was a heavy train conveying mails and newspapers as well as passengers. Formed of 6 vans, 9 passenger carriages and 1 brake van, and hauled by No. 209* an old West Midland Railway 2–4–0 (built by Beyer-Peacock in 1861 as a 2–2–2), the 16 vehicle train was unbraked apart from the locomotive brakes and hand brakes controlled by guards riding in the front and rear vehicles only. Only when driver Harry Bathe heard the explosion of detonators at East's down home signal, some 486 yds to the rear of the tail of the goods train, was he able to place his whereabouts exactly. A

---

*In the accident report, the driver describes No. 209 as four-coupled but the RCTS in *Locomotives of the GWR, Part Three*, page C33, show this altered wheel arrangement as applying from 1883(?).

vacuum braked train would have stopped in that distance, but despite reversing the engine and whistling for the guards' brakes, a collision was inevitable and this occurred at an estimated 10 mph.

No passengers were injured but four members of staff received slight injuries. Apart from three empty coal trucks derailed and smashed, a fourth truck destroyed and some minor damage to the two engines and a couple of vehicles in the passenger train, very little damage was done – indeed the 5.30 am passenger continued its journey after No. 209 and the damaged vehicles were removed.

Signalman Guttridge, who until then had a clear record as a signalman was blamed for the accident, and his distant signal fogsignalman was criticised for removing his warning detonators. Col Yolland also bemoaned the absence of automatic braking on such a heavy passenger train, a lament that was repeated many more times until the Regulation of Railways Act, 1889 made their provision mandatory.

Our next accident is at Windsor and was quite minor but is worthy of inclusion for the detail it reveals of train-working at this period.

When reviewing and passing some minor trackwork alterations made at Windsor at the end of 1880, Major Marindin made a particular point of emphasising that approval of the alterations should not be taken 'as a general approval of the arrangements at this station which are far from satisfactory inasmuch as the points and signals are not interlocked, the facing points are not provided with locking bars and facing point bolts . . .' In 1885, his colleague Colonel Rich had cause to say very much the same thing following his investigations into this accident, but it took until 1889 for the GWR to act upon these criticisms and provide a properly signalled layout at Windsor.

At this time Windsor passenger station comprised only two platform lines and a middle siding between the two. The three lines continued in parallel to the station throat but it was the practice to use the main down line as a stabling siding for a distance of about 120 yards between the outermost pair of points and points about 120 yards closer to the platform, necessitating trains for the downside platform being turned into the middle siding for that distance.

Points were worked by hand levers and signalling was primitive in the extreme. At the platform end on the downside (nominally 'arrival' platform) was a home signal, used for all trains irrespective of which platform they ran into. About 200 yards north and acting as a repeater to the home signal was the unique Windsor 'drum-signal'.* These signals were worked independently, but the man at the drum-signal watched the home signal and repeated that signal's positions. The drum-signal was also used irrespective of the line to which the train was running. Some 660 yards to the rear (Slough side) of the drum-signal was a further stop signal but this as only used at busy times, such as Ascot Races, and was not in use at the time of this accident.

On 13th June, 1885 the 1.59 pm Slough to Windsor left Slough 11 minutes late at 2.10 pm. Comprising a tank engine, horse box, carriage truck, another horse box and two carriages it ran into the upside (nominally 'departure')

---

*See Chapter Nine for description, and *History of the GWR* (revised edition) volume 1, page 319 for picture.

platform at about 2.16 pm. Aware that the 1.20 pm through train from Paddington was not far behind, as soon as the passengers had alighted the shunter hand signalled the train back via the middle siding to the portion of the down line used for stabling vehicles, which was already occupied by three empty coaches and a horse box.

Whilst this move was taking place, the 1.20 pm from Paddington, a vacuum braked train of eight coaches hauled by 'Metro' 2–4–0T No. 468 (built 1869), had left Slough at 2.18 pm and was approaching the down signal, which was at danger. The empty train by now was in the down siding but its engine was foul of the points; the shunter had intended to uncouple the engine and take it to the middle siding but signalman Lawford in the platform box told him to push 'inside clear' so that the 1.20 pm Paddington could run to the up platform. As the engine moved clear of the points so Lawford pulled off the home signal, which was observed by the drum-signalman (Edwin Witteridge who had been carrying out this duty for 30 years); the latter gave an 'all right' signal with his arm to the driver of the Paddington train to prevent it stopping, and then pulled off the signal, which the train passed at walking pace.

As the empty train in the down siding was pushed slowly back it hit the four empty vehicles standing there and set them in motion. The leading vehicle, a horsebox, jumped over the chock block which formed a wheel stop at the Slough end of the siding and came into sidelong collision with the middle of the passenger train. Some minor damage was done to the coaches and the horsebox was derailed, but no one was injured. The signalman and shunter were punished by being 'sharply censured' by Mr Tyrell, the superintendent of the line.

Col Rich blamed the Windsor platform signalman for lowering the home signal before the empty train had been inside the siding at a stand (in fact it was too long for the siding) but said,

> This man could not have committed this mistake, if the signals and points had been interlocked and I would strongly urge the GWR Company to re-arrange the station at Windsor, to signal it properly, to interlock the points with the signals, and to work the whole from a properly constructed cabin. The points are now worked by levers, which are close to the points and are distributed about the yard.

There was a gap of three years before the next mishap, also at Windsor, and this was an accident of the type repeated on many other dead-end branch lines, a train approaching the terminus and unable to stop!

Driver Thomas Keys, (actually graded 'Engine Turner', a lower grade then Third Class Engineman) was looking forward to the end of his shift as he backed his 2–4–0 'Metro' tank No. 5 on to the through coaches of the 11.20 pm Paddington to Windsor at Slough, a minute or two after midnight on 6th November, 1888. Since booking on at Slough at 3 pm he had already made 10 return trips over the Windsor branch, with one more loaded journey to do after this one. His train comprised seven carriages all fitted with the vacuum brake, and at the rear of the train, unbraked, a gas-tank truck (used for charging the gas cylinders of coaches at Windsor).

Driver Keys pulled away from Slough at 12.11 am, one minute late, and soon had the train up to 30 mph. He had a cleaner acting as fireman that day,

'Metro' tank No. 6, seen here outside Paddington, was a sister to No. 5, involved in the collision at Windsor on 6th November, 1888. *Ivor Smart Collection*

Driver Marment of Newton Abbot drove No. 3076 *Princess Beatrice* on 23rd November, 1899 when it collided with another train at Slough. Here is sister engine No. 3075 *Princess Louise* (built July 1898) at an unknown location. They were members of a handsome class of locomotive. *Ivor Smart Collection*

John Greening, also from Slough; approaching the Thames river bridge Keys shut off steam and, doubtless as he had done on the other trips, Greening screwed on the engine hand brake. Approaching the drum signal, some 335 yards from the buffer stops, and at a speed of about 25 mph, the driver applied the vacuum brake but the needle on the brake gauge did not move at all. Shouting to his fireman to apply sand to the wheels, Keys put his engine in reverse and applied steam, at the same time blowing the brake whistle as a signal to the guard to apply his brake. However the rails were greasy after a shower of rain and despite all these efforts, the train continued on into the platform at about 7 mph and collided with a horse box and carriage truck stabled at the buffer stops, driving the carriage truck through the outer wall of the station. There were only five passengers on the train, none of whom was injured. Station Master F.H. Frazer was summoned and later testified to driver Keys' sobriety.

Subsequent investigation revealed that two nuts on the locomotive's vacuum brake lever handle had become partially unscrewed, causing the handle to slip back on its spindle and fail to come into contact with the rack that operated the brake. However Col Rich in a brief report blamed the driver for the accident:

> . . . the result of improper driving (on his part). This man approached Windsor, which is a terminal station, at such speed that he could not stop his train with the screw and steam brake on his engine.

One wonders whether his instructions called upon him to be able to stop the train in this way – if so what was the point of equipping the train with vacuum brakes? It seems unfair to expect the driver to anticipate that they would not work! However Keys was suspended for 8 days without pay and severely reprimanded by the Directors.

On 10th October, 1890, the 10.25 pm goods train from Paddington had been running in foggy conditions from West London Junction to beyond Langley. All the way down the driver had run over fog detonators and was expecting the same indication approaching Slough but for some reason Slough distant signal was not 'fogged' and the driver ran past it (at danger) without seeing it. Observing the home signal at danger he whistled for the guard to apply his handbrake – the guard later intimated he had already applied this as he considered the train was going too fast.

Standing in Slough station were the Windsor slip coaches off the 10.30 pm ex Paddington. Fortunately Inspector Welch at Slough heard the goods train coming and managed to get all the passengers out before the collision occurred, also stopping the Windsor engine from backing on to the coaches. Driver Ridge and fireman Coggins were later fined £3 and £1 respectively, while Inspector Welch and three others shared a £5 award for their vigilance.

The last day of 1891 saw an unusual accident in the bay line at Slough. An unidentified tank engine was standing on Slough shed manned only by the fireman, the driver having left to obtain some oil. The fireman left the engine to turn some points but before doing so opened the regulator, thinking he would be able to regain his post before the engine had proceeded far. This he was unable to do, and the engine, running a distance of about 400 yds at a speed of from 15 to 20 mph, came into collision with the stop block (in one of the bay lines) and caused considerable damage to the District Engineer's office. The New Year did not prove to be happy for the fireman who received a month's notice of dismissal.

The buffer stops in the South bay line at Slough were again hit on 29th October, 1896, when the 10.55 pm ex Windsor collided with them. The driver *and fireman* were both suspended for six days for not having their train under proper control. On 19th July, 1898 the train due at Windsor at 1.20 pm collided with four vehicles standing at the platform; the driver and an accompanying pilotman were found to be at fault, the former being suspended for four days, the latter being severely reprimanded.

We return to Slough for nearly all of the remaining accidents in this chapter; in the first mishap, fog again was a principal ingredient in the event.

On 23rd December, 1899 the 10.40 am Plymouth to Paddington express loaded heavily and was booked an assistant engine from Newton Abbot to Paddington. This was No. 3076 *Princess Beatrice*, a 4−2−2 of the '3031' or 'Achilles' class 7 ft 8 in. Singles, built only that February. Driver Charles Marment left Newton Abbot with No. 3076 leading the train at 12.02 pm, seven minutes late and at Bristol the train engine (inside engine) was changed for No. 3071 *Emlyn* another 7 ft 8 in. Single built in February 1898, leaving that place with 13 vehicles in tow at 3.29 pm, 29 minutes late. The train was booked to call at Bath, Swindon, Didcot and Slough. Time continued to be lost and the express was 36 minutes late by the time it left Didcot at 5.25 pm.

Meanwhile up at Slough a thick fog had descended at 4.30 pm and the fogman had been sent for at 4.40 pm by the Slough West and Middle box signalmen. Fogmen are required to place detonators when the signals they are repeating are at danger and display a hand danger signal to the driver, or a proceed signal (with no detonator) when the signals are cleared. Unfortunately as this was a Saturday afternoon all the permanent way staff who carried out these duties were at home and the caller-up could not be contacted until 5.30 pm. He then had to walk several miles to the various fogmen and the first man was not in position for another hour.

The 10.40 am Plymouth ran through Reading without stopping, then, entering the thick blanket of fog, was stopped by signals at Ruscombe (east of Twyford) and checked at Maidenhead. Neither driver saw the signals at Burnham but driver Marment on the leading engine saw the fogsignamen's proceed handsignals through the enveloping mist. Although only 2½ miles from Slough, the next stop, Marment kept the regulator open and speed was maintained at about 40 mph.

There were three signal boxes at Slough, East at the London end of the platforms, Middle at the west end of the station and controlling the junction to Windsor and West box about ¼ mile in the direction of Burnham. (The station had been rebuilt in 1884 and these boxes are not the ones described in the 1881 accidents.) Because these boxes were only a short distance apart, during fog or falling snow, and in the absence of fogsignalmen, the signalling regulations demanded that two sections should be clear for the passage of each train, i.e.:

- 'Line clear' could not be given to Burnham by Slough West unless he had received 'Train out of Section' (TOS) from Slough Middle.
- Middle box could not give 'Line clear' or 'Line clear to clearing point only'* to West box unless he had received 'Line Clear' or 'Line clear to clearing point only' from East box
- East box could not give 'Line clear' to Middle unless he had received 'TOS' from Dolphin but he could give 'Line clear to clearing point only' if the previous train had passed his clearing point and was proceeding towards Dolphin.

At 6.09 pm William Draper, a time-served signalman who had worked Slough Middle box for 16 years out of his 26½ years in the grade, was asked 'Is Line Clear' by West box for the Plymouth train. As he had received 'Train out of Section' from East box for the previous train, the 2.45 pm from Worcester, he asked 'Is Line clear' of East box but received no acknowledgement so he kept his up main line signals at danger. At almost the same time however, Draper was asked 'Is Line Clear' by Bath Road signal box (on the Windsor branch) for the 5.40 pm Windsor to Paddington, which had left Windsor 30 minutes late at 6.10 pm, and after gaining acceptance from East box for this train over the up *relief* line he returned 'Line Clear' to Bath Road for the Windsor train, set his junction from Windsor to the up relief line and pulled off the appropriate signals.

At 6.15 pm as the Plymouth express passed Burnham, the signalman there sent 'Train Entering Section' to Slough West; the latter signalman had still not received permission to send the train forward, and with his signals at danger, and no fogsignalman present, the rules required him to place two detonators on the line, which he did 20 yards west of the signal box. Having done this, and on his way back to the box, he was somewhat taken aback when the express passed him, without slackening speed, despite his showing the driver a red light and shouting at him.

On the footplate of No. 3076, Driver Marment had lost his whereabouts after passing Burnham and missed both Slough West distant and home signals, not really surprising as both were exceedingly tall signals, the distant being 46 ft high and the home 49 ft 6 in. He heard the West signalman's detonators and saw his red light, however, and then saw the box and realised where he was. In his statement he said that he had shut off steam about ½ minute before this but was still travelling at about 40 mph, and now made a full brake application.

From the detonators at West box to the home signal of Middle box was only 358 yards and with a greasy rail Marment was unable to pull up and passed the Middle home at danger also, at a speed he estimated at 10 mph. Only 28 yards beyond that the 5.40 pm from Windsor was crossing the main line on its way to the up relief platform and at a speed of about 8 mph the Plymouth express collided with the middle of this 10 coach train, hauled by a four-coupled tank locomotive. The time was 6.19 pm.

The two engines and tenders and the leading vehicle of the Plymouth train, and the rear five coaches of the Windsor train were derailed, but the leading engine of the Plymouth train mounted the rails of the route to the up relief line and travelled along it for a few yards before stopping. The rear of

---

*Because of the short sections, insufficient braking distance obtained, and on receipt of this bell signal, the signalman in *rear* kept his distant signal at danger.

the Windsor train became jammed up against the side of the rear engine on the Plymouth train. Fortunately as it was a relatively low speed collision only 28 passengers were slightly injured, and driver Marment's fireman was thrown off the footplate. Later £386 was paid in compensation to the injured passengers.

After some delay the first five coaches of the Windsor train, which had escaped unscathed, continued their journey to London, leaving Slough at approximately 7 pm. Ironically, the first of the fogmen, whose post was the up main distant for Slough West box arrived at that box at 6.30 pm – one assumes he did not have too much 'fogging' to do that night!

Col Yorke of the Board of Trade published his report the following February; having made due allowance for the thickness of the fog and the absence of fogmen he held the drivers of the Plymouth train responsible for the collision, and driver Marment 'more at fault' than the other driver, Butcher. Their speed, he considered, 'dangerously high . . . shown by the fact that after passing over the detonators they were unable to bring the train to a stand within a distance of 378 yards'. He had no criticism of the time taken to call the fogmen except to say that the men should have proceeded to their posts without waiting to be called. The company had informed him that, in future, in such conditions before the fogmen arrived, trains would not be allowed to leave Burnham unless three sections were clear, i.e. to Slough East box, thus obviating any possible confliction at the junction. Finally he suggested that the very tall signals at Slough West should be provided with repeater arms lower down their posts at drivers' eye level. Driver Marment received 14 days' suspension for his mistake, the other three footplatemen, seven days each.

On 21st February, 1900 after the arrival of the 8.20 pm passenger train from Paddington at Slough, the Windsor coaches were detached and left at the West end of the down main platform. It was necessary to move the coaches off the 7.52 pm ex Paddington from a siding on the upside to a siding alongside the down main, involving a movement along the latter line. Unfortunately the signalman forgot to tell the driver that the line was occupied and the shunt movement ran into the rearmost Windsor carriage. The shunter in charge of the movement did see the coaches and applied the brake but not quite quickly enough to prevent the accident, which caused slight damage and minor injuries to eight passengers. The signalman on duty received four days' suspension, while those slightly less involved received two days' suspension (driver) and one day's suspension (fireman). A very similar accident occurred on 30th March, 1901 when an empty coach and a loaded horsebox were attached to the rear of the 10.07 am Paddington – Windsor at Slough. The shunt movement was made sharply, derailing the horse box. In this case the shunter received three days suspension, the driver and fireman one day each.

The next accident to be described was by far the most serious of all. This time there was no fog but despite this an engine driver managed to 'lose his way' with disastrous (and costly) results for the company.

Saturday 16th June, 1900 was a Race Day at Ascot. These were always popular events, being fairly close to London, and a Race special left Paddington for Windsor at 12.05 pm. Cheap tickets on ordinary services were withdrawn until 1 pm, to avoid overcrowding, but on this day the Races were somewhat later than usual and so the 1.05 pm Paddington to Windsor scheduled service quickly began to fill up. Anticipating this the divisional superintendent had instructed that the train be strengthened but unfortunately this order had not been properly carried out. So at the last moment the train had to be strengthened by an extra carriage, making a total of eight bogie vehicles conveying approximately 450 passengers, and entailing a 7 minute later start at 1.12 pm. The train was hauled by a four-coupled tender engine and weighed 235 tons inclusive of locomotive and was fitted with the vacuum brake throughout.

While this last minute activity was taking place the engine for the 1.15 pm Paddington to Falmouth express was backing on to its train in platform 3. This was No. 3015 *Kennet* a 7 ft 8 in. Single of the 'Achilles' or '3031' class, built in 1892 as a 2−2−2 but altered to a 4−2 2 in 1894. Originally built for the West of England route (via Bristol of course), these handsome locomotives were gradually superseded on these trains by 4−4−0s from 1900 onwards as the trains became too heavy for them.

Driver Henry George Woodman, a driver for 29 years, had come on duty at 5.30 am at Bristol and worked the 6.30 am thence, reaching Paddington at 10.32. He arrived with his engine at Westbourne Park shed about an hour later, turned it on the turntable and examined it, and, at about 11.45, left it in charge of his fireman Henry Cann, while he went to a coffee house just outside the shed gates for some refreshments (but no alcohol). This was a practice to which the GWR did not object.

A very conscientious man, driver Woodman was not away long and was back on the engine by about 12.10 pm. After carrying out necessary preparation work for the return journey, Woodman took the engine up to the shed exit signal, controlled by Green Lane signal box, at 12.45, and some seven or eight minutes later was signalled out for Paddington, arriving there just after 1 pm.

The 1.15 pm to Falmouth consisted of nine 8-wheeled coaches and one 6-wheeler in the middle of the train; the train weighed 291 tons inclusive of locomotive and was fitted with the vacuum brake throughout. The first booked stop was Reading and the train pulled out at the start of its 9¾ hr journey westwards at 1.16 pm, one minute late.

Meanwhile the 1.05 pm ex Paddington, which was first-stop Slough and worked by driver Henry Napper of Paddington was making good progress with its heavy load, passing Langley at 1.33 pm, Dolphin (an 'intermediate' box some 1,828 yds east of Slough East box) at 1.35 pm and arriving at Slough down main line platform at 1.37 pm, eight minutes late, having dropped a further minute on its schedule. Here extra ticket collectors had been provided to take the tickets from the race-goers as Windsor was an 'open station'. Despite this, the station time of two minutes was extended by another two minutes before the Windsor train was ready to leave.

Not far behind the 1.15 pm Falmouth express was also making good progress (its driver later estimated its speed at 52 mph). Dolphin box was asked 'Line Clear' for this train by Langley at 1.35 pm as soon as Dolphin

A view of the havoc caused when the 1.15 pm Paddington to Falmouth ran into the 1.05 pm Paddington to Windsor at Slough on 16th June, 1900: the scene from the up platform.

Ivor Smart Collection

A second view of the collision at Slough on 16th June, 1900, this time seen from the down platform. *LGRP*

Kennet, the locomotive hauling the 1.15 pm from Paddington, seen here *c*.1904.
Roger Carpenter Collection

cleared the section for the 1.05 pm Paddington and Dolphin in turn asked 'Line clear' of Slough East at 1.37 pm, but this was refused by Slough. On receipt of 'Train Entering Section' from Langley at 1.38 pm, Dolphin again asked 'Line Clear' and this time received from East the 'Warning' signal: 'Section Clear but Station or Junction blocked', at 1.40 pm (Slough East recorded '1.39 pm' for both these bell signals).

On receipt of the 'Warning' signal, a signalman had to stop and verbally caution a driver that the section ahead was clear but that the junction was blocked (i.e. in this case be prepared to stop at Slough East's home signal). As he was booking the 'Warning' bell signal in his train register, however, Signalman Colbourn at Dolphin was amazed to see the Falmouth express pass his signals at danger at full speed. Unable to attract the driver's attention, Colbourn attempted to speak to Slough East on the phone but could obtain no reply.

On the footplate of *Kennet* fireman Cann was heaving coal into the 6 ft 4 in. – long firebox with its 20.8 sq. feet of grate with a view to keeping boiler pressure at its maximum 160 lb. for this demanding duty. Pausing momentarily he noticed that all Langley's signals were off for the train, but, returning to his arduous firing duties, he did not observe Dolphin's signals. Next looking up as the train *passed* Slough East's distant he was sure it was 'on', but looking across at his driver standing motionless gazing straight ahead and taking no action to stop the train, Cann became unsure and stared ahead for a first glimpse of the home signal.

As the train sped under an overbridge only 367 yards from the home signal Cann could see the signal was firmly at danger and, shouting 'whoa' to his mate, Cann simultaneously shut the regulator and applied the vacuum brake. This brought driver Woodman out of his reverie and as the driver brought the screw reversing handle to the full reverse gear position, fireman Cann re-opened the regulator in a desperate bid to reduce further the speed of the train, by now passing the home signal.

Only 227 yards ahead stood the tail of the Windsor train. In Slough East box signalman William Wardell (also involved in the 1881 incident) saw the train burst through the overbridge at full speed and took commendably prompt action. Seizing a red flag he thrust it through the open window, at the same time shouting to the platform staff to clear the Windsor train. As if this was not enough he called out to a shunter, engaged in putting race specials away in Slough Yard, and the latter immediately ran towards the oncoming express waving his arms. The driver of the Slough pilot, stationary in the middle siding between the Relief lines, seeing the red flag waved from the box, opened his brake whistle in a further effort to attract the express driver's attention.

Sadly all this good work could not avoid the inevitable collision – the distance between the spot where the brake was applied and the standing train was insufficient, only some 594 yds. At a speed variously estimated at between 15 and 35 mph, *Kennet* piled into the rear coach of the Windsor train completely destroying it and the one in front and lifting the penultimate vehicle up level with the station roof, from which it fell back on top of *Kennet* and caught fire. The Windsor train had fortunately been standing with the brakes off, causing it to be propelled forward about 15 yds, followed by a rebound and then a further forward movement. Five people were killed in this disastrous mishap which blocked the main lines for several hours, 35 were seriously injured and a further 90 complained of shock or minor injuries, according to the Board of Trade report. None of the train crew involved received injuries worse than severe bruising, but guard Pedrick of Plymouth suffered a nervous breakdown and was unable to work again. He received a pension of 12s. a week (and £150 under the Workmen's Compensation Act).

The Queen, who was at Balmoral but about to return to Windsor, was shocked by the accident and caused the following letter to be written to the Board of Trade:

> Dear Richie,
> The Queen is grieved and shocked at the terrible railway accident at Slough on Saturday last. Perhaps it all comes especially home to Her Majesty as the scene of the disaster was almost at her own door and the ill fated train is that by which all coming to Windsor for luncheon travel. The Queen feels that with block systems and other modern inventions it is almost incredible that such an accident should occur in open day unless through some grievous negligence. Her Majesty trusts that you will place the matter most seriously before the railway company and do all in your power to prevent what the Queen fears are the *too frequent* fatal railway accidents.
> Yours very truly,
> Arthur Bigge
>
> H.M. gets to Windsor Thursday morning.

In a somewhat lengthy report published the following September, Col H.A. Yorke endeavoured to examine 'every possible scrap of information . . . likely to throw any light on this lamentable disaster'. There was no doubt that the accident had been caused by driver Woodman's failure to observe the danger signals exhibited at Dolphin and Slough East boxes. In his own evidence, Woodman had said:

> I cannot say in what position the Dolphin signals were. I did not see them. I am at a loss to say how it was that I failed to do so. . . I do not remember seeing the distant for Slough East box. I saw the home signal for Slough and that was at danger. . . I think I saw it just before I reached the overbridge nearest to Slough. My mate first drew my attention to the signal being at danger. I can give no explanation . . . other than that I seem to lose myself.

Col Yorke concluded that Woodman (whose eyesight had since been found quite satisfactory) had allowed his mind to wander. He was critical of fireman Cann's reactions 'for it was his duty, almost in the same degree as the driver's, to keep a good lookout . . . when not necessarily otherwise engaged. . . It is to be regretted that an exaggerated amount of public credit has been bestowed upon this man, for at the best he was only doing his duty, and as a fact was doing it indifferently'. Yorke considered that Cann should have paused in his firing between Langley and Dolphin to observe the signals, which seems a perfectly ridiculous thing to say – after all Dolphin was only a simple intermediate box – except with the benefit of hindsight.

Col Yorke also criticised the guard who had been dealing with luggage and mails at the time for not keeping a good lookout, quoting Rule 170 which said: 'Guards of passenger trains must, *after* the safe working of the train, give their *next* attention to the luggage (etc) . . .' He considered, quite unrealistically as the GWR later pointed out, that either of the two guards should have been looking out for the Dolphin signals.

Other features drawn attention to by the Colonel were that the GWR did not medically examine drivers until they were 60 (Woodman was in his sixtieth year but had 'all the appearance of a man ten years older than this' – he wanted regular examinations after age 55; some comment regarding the need to block the main line at Slough whilst tickets were examined on the Windsor train; and the fact that the GWR should again be reminded of the need to reduce the occasions on which the 'Warning' bell signal was used to the absolute minimum. Finally he had considered some mechanical contrivance which would render it impossible for a driver to pass a signal at danger without becoming aware of the fact, but conceded that nothing suitable was yet available. [93 years later we are still waiting for this, but will perhaps soon get it in the shape of Automatic Train Protection!]

In a subsequent report to the GWR Board of Directors almost as lengthy as Yorke's report, the General Manager dealt with these points as well as mentioning some other features which the Board of Trade had not uncovered.

As a principle, the company did not agree with the Colonel's strictures regarding compulsory medical examinations after age 55, supported by statistics that out of 177 examinations of drivers over 60 in the last 10 years, only 28 had been found unfit (15½%). It was in any case already the practice to examine anyone under 60 who showed signs of being unfit and out of 205 such examinations in the last five years, only 40 drivers or fireman had been rejected (19½%). Mr Dean, the locomotive & carriage superintendent, had expressed a definite opinion that Woodman would have passed such examination if introduced at 55 and annually thereafter. As for Mr Woodman's present appearance, all who knew him best considered the premature aging had occurred after the accident.

Having said all that the General Manager did make two admissions not known to the Inspector:

> . . . it is unsatisfactory as far as the company is concerned, to find that he had not been subjected to the eyesight test ordered by the Directors on the 22nd March, 1893 [to be taken every 5 years – although in the event the subsequent independent examination had proved his eyesight practically normal] and although the fact was not made prominent, it is unfortunately true that he had been guilty of absent mindedness in failing to stop at appointed stations on at least two occasions within the immediately preceding three months, and in respect of these latter two instances alone it is a question whether Woodman should have been allowed to continue as a driver.

Dealing with fireman Cann, whom the General Manager considered 'did no more than his duty in acting as he did when he became aware of the danger', the report does not follow Yorke's line in considering him an indifferent worker and does, grudgingly, concede that it is questionable 'whether the ordinary duties of a Fireman on an express train leave him much, if any, time in which effectually to supplement the Driver's observations of signals . . .' Quite! Perhaps not surprisingly in view of the Colonel's remarks, the General Manager's report reveals that Cann had since left the service.

The company did not accept the Inspector's interpretation of Rule 170 so far as the guard was concerned and pointed out that 'safe working of the train' included matters of couplings, brakes, communication and continuous attention to the running of the train. In addition the guard is responsible for luggage and mails etc. and,

> . . . it is impossible . . . to attend to these duties and at the same time keep a continuous watch on the signals and it was not intended that the Rule should be capable of any such constructions . . . even where 'look-out' wings are provided the guards cannot possibly . . . see the whole of the signals . . .

The General Manager considered it might be necessary to rewrite this rule to make it clearer.

The company were examining the use of the 'Warning' arrangement and would limit its use to those places where 'traffic cannot properly be conducted without it'.

Some idea of the high esteem in which the Directors held the Windsor traffic can be gained from two further actions. To avoid lightning striking in the same place twice the 1.05 pm Paddington now ran non-stop to Windsor (tickets were collected at Paddington), although the reason given was that,

> . . . this alteration had been influenced by the fact that this is a train chiefly used by members of the Court and by her Majesty's guests proceeding to Windsor Castle to lunch, and also by parents visiting Eton.

Consideration had been given to collecting tickets at Windsor, not just in this case but for other trains which stopped at Slough but,

> . . . the general arrangements at the new station at Windsor do not lend themselves to the collection of tickets . . . and would affect the comfort and convenience generally of an important section of the public using that station if we were to attempt it.

The GM was somewhat terse regarding the delay in despatching the 1.05 pm to Windsor from Paddington after attaching the extra coach, for if it had been on time the train would have been clear of the main line when the Falmouth express passed through Slough. He considered that the 1.05 pm should not have been held at all and the overflow passengers re-directed to the 1.10 pm local train to Windsor:

> This phase of the matter does not reflect credit on the part of those responsible . . . it is not creditable to those in charge that the use of this [1.10 pm] train did not suggest itself; and such notice . . . has been taken as will prove salutary in its effects.

[What does this diplomatic language mean – was the assistant station master removed from his post?]

Subsequently, to enable the main line to be cleared promptly in the event of late running, the Directors had authorised a double junction between the Main and Relief lines at Dolphin (installed mid-1901) and in his long report the GM discussed some further alternative schemes to expand the accommodation at Slough, favouring a scheme entailing separate Windsor lines from Dolphin Jn running south of the Main lines (in the event not done).

Other minor matters attended to were the expansion of the description of the emergency bell signals for 'vehicles running away in (either) right or wrong directions', which if used by the Dolphin signalman would have given earlier warning of the runaway, to include the word 'trains' in its description in case there was confusion in signalmen's minds as to its applicability, and the authorisation of a steam locomotive crane following experience of clearing up the debris.

Finally it is worth noting that driver Woodman's unfortunate aberration had cost the company dear. As at July 1901, a report to Traffic Committee reported that 5 people had been killed, 289 injured and that 317 claims had been received of which 295 had been settled at a total cost of £74,239 13s. 6d. (or an average cost of £251 13s. 2d. each), a tremendous sum of money in those days. Fourteen claims had been declined and eight were still outstanding. The Directors awarded a 5 guinea gratuity to signalman William Wardell of Slough East and porter Oliver Penn (who had managed to get a number of passengers to leave the 1.05 pm train) as a mark of their appreciation of these men's conduct. Poor Woodman was put on trial for manslaughter but in November 1900 a verdict of 'Not Guilty' was delivered, which was greeted with loud applause in Court.

There is no doubt that Slough was an accident black spot in the 19th century but in the 20th century there was only one major mishap at Slough, and that was caused by a broken rail, rather than the direct failing of the key staff involved as was the case in most of the 19th century accidents. There were, however, a number of collisions, etc. of a more minor nature caused by human failings, only a small proportion of which will have come to light, mainly from the War years. I have excluded the serious accident in 1941 at Dolphin Jn, which is a mile from Slough and did not involve a Windsor train.

On 10th June, 1904 the driver of the 9.03 am goods train from Slough to Windsor passed a signal at danger and stopped just foul of the up Windsor branch, just as the 9.30 am passenger train from Windsor to Paddington was passing. The wing of the rear brake third coach was scraped by the coal bunker of the goods engine.

Severe retribution was handed out to the goods driver; he was reduced to a shunting engineman and received 10 days suspension. The fireman received 10 days suspension (hardly his fault) and the signalman involved, who had failed to caution the goods' driver that he was being signalled under the 'Warning' arrangement ('section clear but junction blocked') was suspended for six days.

Owing to a mistake by the signalman at Slough Middle box, a light engine from Slough shed to the station was turned onto the down branch line instead of the up branch. This happened on 30th June, 1914; the driver noticed that a train was signalled on the down branch line (the 3.30 pm Paddington–Windsor) and immediately opened his brake whistle which alerted the signalman to his mistake. The latter stopped the approaching

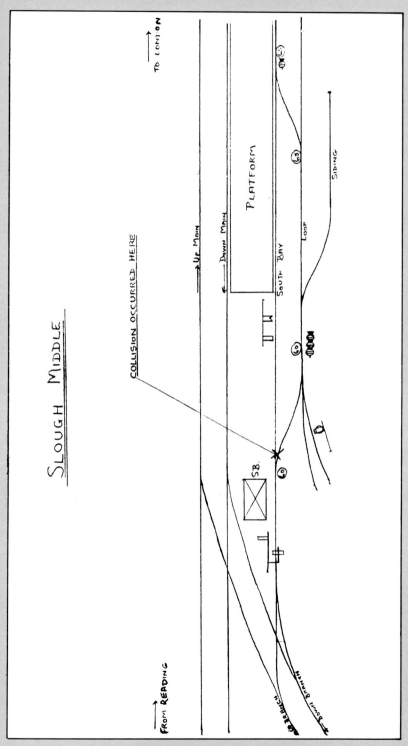

The location of the minor collision on 1st January, 1944. This diagram also shows the position of No. 65 points, involved in the 30th October, 1944 mishap.

passenger train outside his box. The driver and fireman of the light engine were each awarded one guinea for their vigilance.

In 1941 the engine pit alongside the coal stage at Slough shed was being rebuilt, but, to allow the coal stage to remain in use, half the pit was relayed at a time. On 30th January, 1941 at 11 pm, engine No. 6143 was taken for coaling but after this was finished the fireman in charge of the movement forgot to reverse the engine, with the result that No. 6143 knocked down the temporary sleeper 'stop block' and fell into the hole where the pit was being rebuilt!

On 10th October, 1941, as the 5.40 pm Paddington–Windsor, hauled by '61XX' class 2–6–2T No. 6120 approached the outer home signal at Windsor, the left-hand eye glass of the locomotive was struck by a missile, shattering the glass and causing a foreign body to bruise the fireman's eye. In their reports, both driver and fireman stated the missile was actually a bullet, from a shot fired at the train.

At 3.30 pm on 18th April, 1942, extensive damage was caused at Slough carriage shed following a supremely clumsy act of shunting. After the 3.05 pm train from Windsor had unloaded its passengers, it was backed from the south bay to the middle siding of the carriage shed, prior to working the 4.00 pm Slough to Paddington. On this line was standing the London Division Inspection Coach No. 80974 and this was struck by the empty train, badly damaging it such that it had to be sent to Swindon for repair. The collision also smashed the buffer stops and succeeded in completely demolishing the west end of the carriage shed (one wonders if availability of materials allowed it to be replaced in wartime). Furthermore GWR coaches 4453, 2393, 6665, 6664 and 2392 were all damaged; a heartily bad day's work.

Just six months later on 17th October, 1942, the driver of pilot engine No. 2785 working in the down main line sidings at Slough West passed a signal at danger, not once, but twice, and succeeded in becoming derailed at the second attempt! At about 11.20 am an engine for Slough station was standing at the (West box) down Windsor branch home signal No. 93 (see signal plan, page 170). The West signalman placed signal No. 55 on the down loop to danger in order to cross the light engine for the station to the up main line, when No. 2785 with four wagons came out of the sidings, and passed the loop signal at danger; the pilot then went back into the sidings whereupon the signalman reversed points 50 and pulled off signal 93. Unfortunately the pilot again came out of the sidings, passed signal 55 at danger for the second time and became derailed on points 50! However the breakdown vans were quickly on the spot and all was cleared up by 1.30 pm.

A minor collision occurred on the bay line just outside Slough Middle signal box on 1st January, 1944. After the 8 am Windsor to Slough arrived in the south bay line, locomotive No. 6157 uncoupled and was crossed to the loop line (see diagram), through points 65 to run to the down branch line through points 60. On points 60 it came into collision with locomotive No. 6113 which should have gone forward onto the coaches in the bay line which No. 6157 had just left. The impact caused No. 6113 to be pushed forward, damaging points No. 60. The Signalman in Slough Middle and the

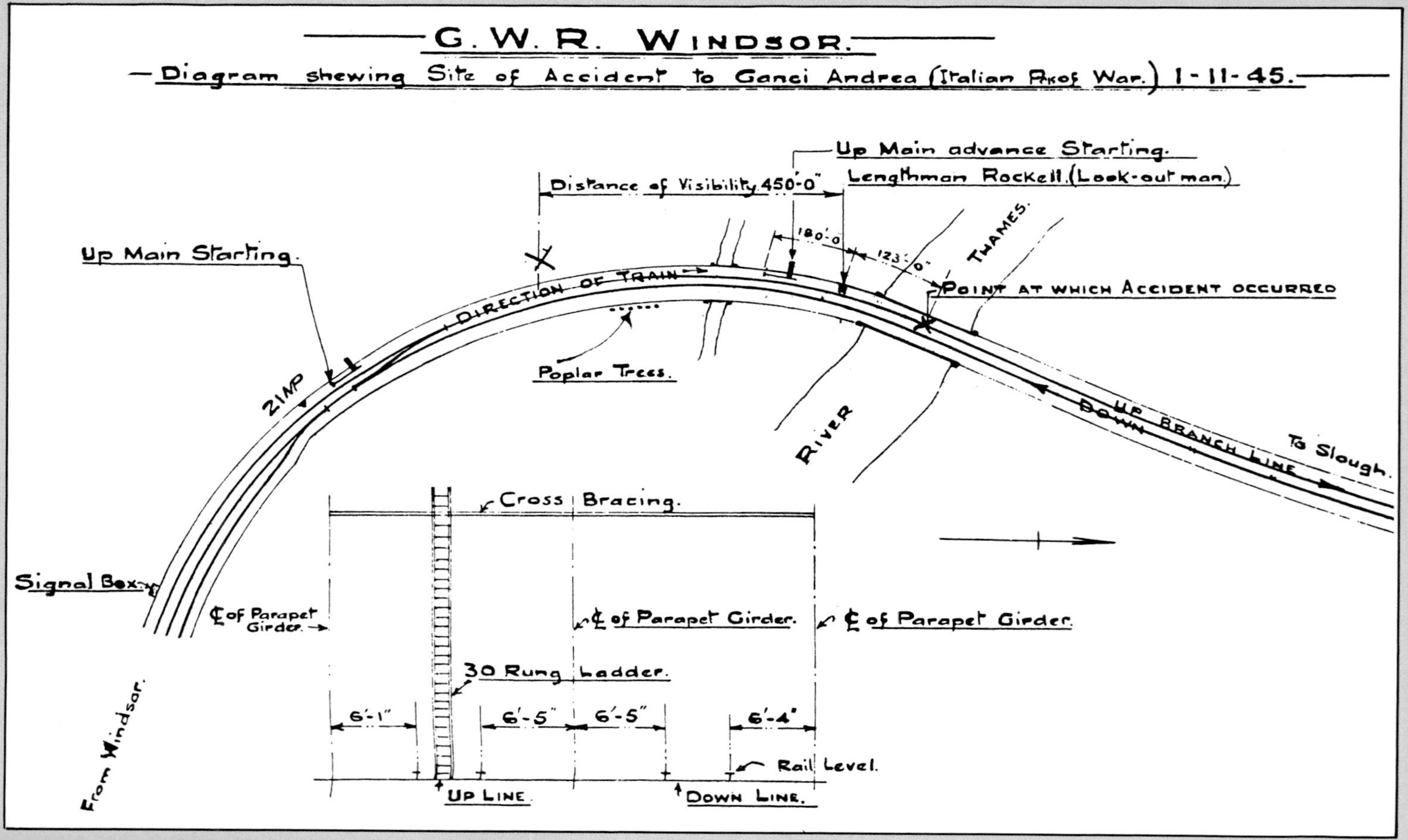

— G.W.R. WINDSOR. —

— Diagram shewing Site of Accident to Ganci Andrea (Italian Prof. War.) 1-11-45. —

Up Main advance Starting.

Lengthman Rockett (Look-out man)

Point at which Accident Occurred

To Slough.

Up Branch Line.

Down Line.

THAMES

RIVER

Distance of Visibility 450'-0"

123'-0"

180'-0"

Direction of Train →

Poplar Trees.

Up Main Starting.

Signal Box →

From Windsor

Cross Bracing.

€ of Parapet Girder.

€ of Parapet Girder.

€ of Parapet Girder.

€ of Parapet Girder.

Rail Level.

Down Line.

Up Line.

30 Rung Ladder.

6'-4"

6'-5"

6'-5"

6'-1"

The ... of the mishap on 1st November 1945

driver of No. 6113 were found jointly responsible. It was decided that in future when a train arrived in the south bay and would be worked away by a different engine, the replacement engine would proceed onto the train and make any movements necessary to release the incoming engine.

A driver and signalman acting without thinking conspired to create a totally unnecessary accident on 30th October, 1944. After the arrival at Slough south bay of the 9.38 am ex-Windsor, engine No. 6101 was detached and was destined for shed after the departure of its coaches with the 10.08 am Slough to Windsor. After the latter had left, the driver of 6101 asked a soldier standing nearby(!) to press the plunger of the shunting bell which was an indication to the Middle box signalman to reverse 65 points (see diagram). Despite the latter knowing that some coaches were standing on the middle line, the signalman reversed the points with the inevitable conclusion – a collision, which damaged Compo. No. 6702 and Third No. 7029.

After the war finished, gangs of Prisoners of War (POW) remaining in this country continued to be employed on railway repairs and maintenance. Such a gang of Italian POWs had been employed painting the steelwork of the River Thames bridge near Windsor station for some five weeks prior to the next accident on 1st November, 1945. Two Italians were working in a position requiring a lookout, with a 30-rung ladder placed in the 'four foot' way of the up line, one man holding the ladder, the other painting the bracing of the bridge from the latter, with his back to up trains. The lookout man (a regular lengthman from the P. Way gang) placed himself 41 yards on the Windsor side of the ladder. In that position he was 60 yards from the up advanced starting signal (101 yds Windsor side of the ladder) and he could see for a further 90 yds only beyond the signal, after which the line curved sharply to the south-east. He relied on the lowering of the signal as an indication that an up train was approaching.

At 11.45 am the signal lowered and almost immediately a light engine came into sight, travelling fast. The lookout, named Rockell, blew his whistle, shouted an alarm and then ran towards the engine waving a red flag. The painter/acting chargeman, (another Englishman) shouted to the Italians and also ran towards the engine waving his arms. The light engine, No. 6113, passed both men, the driver oblivious of the warnings. The Italian at the foot of the ladder left his post, while the one on the ladder, Ganci Andrea, managed to scramble onto the bridge. No. 6113 ran into and smashed the ladder, stopping no more than 6 yds beyond it. Fortunately no-one was injured in the mishap.

The subsequent Inquiry by the Divisional Engineer found lengthman Rockell responsible for not keeping a good lookout, but the Chief Engineer felt that the painter/acting chargeman was partly at fault for not appointing a second lookout (at 'x' on the diagram), as 150 yds visibility was insufficient.

On 1st May, 1959 the 1.05 pm Pembroke Dock to Paddington 'Pembroke Coast Express' was running about 6 minutes late as it passed through Maidenhead. Hauled by 'Castle' class 4–6–0 No. 5016 Montgomery Castle, which the driver described as being in perfect condition, the 9 coach train was travelling at 71 mph as it approached Slough.

Signalman P. Davies in Slough West box was watching the express approach when he heard a terrific bang as the engine passed over the trailing crossover from the down main. He observed sparks from the 3rd or 4th coach and so sent 'Stop and Examine Train' (7 beats) to Slough Middle box, which the latter immediately transmitted to Slough East, because of the short sections involved. As the train passed West box, however, signalman Davies could see that a coach was derailed and so sent 'Obstruction Danger' (6 beats) to Middle box and placed his down line signals to danger. The train passed at an estimated speed of 65–70 mph, creating such a cloud of dust that he could not see that the train had, in fact, become divided.

At Slough Middle signalman T. Nowicki and rlf signalman S. Eldridge were working the box; the 7.00 pm ex-Paddington had been accepted on the down main line but on receipt of the '7 bells' all signals were replaced to danger. As the train passed the box 'in a cloud of smoke and steam' the signalmen could see the train was divided and the rear portion was derailed. 'Obstruction Danger' was therefore sent for all four running lines.

At Slough East signalman W. Bastin had charge of the box; he had placed his signals at danger on receipt of the 7 beats from Middle box and the front part of the 'Pembroke Coast Express' stopped by his starting signal. As the train passed the box at almost 45 mph he observed that the last coach of the front portion was derailed and sent 'Obstruction Danger' for the down main and down relief lines to Dolphin Jn, the next box towards London.

At Dolphin Jn, signalman A. Cheney, a young man of 23 years and a signalman for 3 years, was on duty. When he received the 'Obstruction Danger' signal the 7.00 pm ex Paddington was just passing his down main home signal (20 yds from the box) at about 60 mph. Reacting very promptly he pulled over his detonator placer and exhibited a red hand signal to the driver who applied the brake and stopped the train at Uxbridge Road bridge, on the London side of Slough station, thus averting a collision with the derailed train. In his report on the accident, Brigadier Langley congratulated all the signalmen involved for their rapid response to the events unfolding before their eyes.

The rear six coaches came to rest approaching the east junction from Windsor, completely derailed and with the fourth, fifth and sixth vehicles tilting sideways, the seventh on its side and the rear two tilting sideways. (The engine and leading three vehicles travelled almost another ½ mile before coming to a stand with the trailing bogie of the third coach derailed.) There were 310 passengers in the train, but of these only four people, plus two of the train staff, were taken to hospital with minor injuries.

The track was severely damaged, the worst line affected being the up main of which no less than 825 yds of plain line had to be relaid, together with six single connections and three diamond crossings. Signalling equipment also was badly affected; including the demolition of a signal. The coaching stock comprised steel-bodied BR Mark 1 vehicles which stood up well to the derailment; although the undergear was much damaged, internal damage was very slight.

The cause of the derailment was a broken rail in the right hand rail of the up main line, in the plain line between the diamond in the down main to down relief crossover and the trailing crossover from down main to up main at Slough West. The fracture resulted in an 8 inch gap, just in advance of a rail joint. The track was due for relaying that autumn. The inspecting officer commented that this was the first recorded derailment caused by a broken rail on the Western Region or GWR.

This was the last serious accident at Slough but on 6th February, 1970, an accident occurred here which could have been very serious. After the 7.25 am Swansea to Paddington, which called at Slough, left the up main platform at 10.46 am, two postmen crossed the barrow crossing pushing a BRUTE trolley containing mail without checking the warning lights (which were extinguished if a train was approaching). As a result the trolley was run into by the down 'Cornish Riviera Express', 10.30 am Paddington–Penzance double-headed by 'Warship' class diesels Nos. D803 and D823. The train, which was travelling at about 80 mph pulled up ¾ mile west of the station with No. D803 badly damaged. The train was propelled back to Slough station where the two 'Warships' were detached and replaced by the engine off the 10.30 Acton to Slough freight, 'Hymek' No. D7034. The 'Cornish Riviera' train eventually proceeded 62 minutes late; fortunately no one was injured in the mishap.

To this posed picture of a driver at the controls of a dmu (obviously stationary because the brake handle is not in place!) has been added the attractive backcloth of the River Thames and Windsor Castle. However the picture is of interest and is worthy of inclusion because these dmus will soon be extinct.   *British Rail*

Appendix One

Engines used on the Windsor Branch
1850–1853

Fortnight ending	Engines employed	Drivers names
27. 7.1850	Snake, Viper	Josh.Todd
10. 8.1850	Snake, Viper	Todd
24. 8.1850	Snake	Todd
7. 9.1850	Viper	Todd
21. 9.1850	Snake, Viper	Todd
3.10.1850 to 25. 1.1851	Eagle, Viper	Todd
8. 2.1851	Viper	Todd
22. 2.1851	Eagle, Viper	Todd
8. 3.1851	Eagle	Todd
22. 3.1851	Eagle, Viper	Todd
5. 4.1851	Eagle, Viper	Todd
19. 4.1851	Eagle, Viper	Todd, Samuel Guest
3. 5.1851	Eagle, Snake, Viper	Josh.Lintern, Guest
17. 5.1851 to 30. 6.1851	Eagle, Snake, Viper	Lintern, Guest, Thos. Davison
12. 7.1851	Eagle, Harpy, Snake, Viper	Lintern, Guest, Davison
26. 7.1851	Eagle, Snake, Viper	Lintern, Guest, Davison
9. 8.1851	Eagle, Minos, Snake, Viper	Lintern, Guest, Davison
23. 8.1851	Eagle, Minos, Snake, Viper	Lintern, Guest, Davison, White
6. 9.1851	Eagle, Snake, Viper	Lintern, Guest, Davison, White
20. 9.1851	Eagle, Snake, Viper	Lintern, Guest, Davison
4.10.1851	Eagle, Proserpine, Snake, Viper	Lintern, Davison, Guest, J. Davidson
18.10.1851 to 15.11.1851	Eagle, Proserpine, Snake	Lintern, Davison, Guest
29.11.1851	Proserpine, Snake	Davison, Guest
13.12.1851	Eagle, Proserpine, Snake	Davison, Guest
31.12.1851	Proserpine, Snake	Davison, Guest
10. 1.1852	Proserpine, Snake	Davison, Guest
24. 1.1852	Firefly, Proserpine, Snake	Davison, Guest
7. 2.1852	Firefly, Proserpine	Davison, Guest
21. 2.1852	Firefly, Proserpine, Snake	Davison, Guest
6. 3.1852	Firefly, Proserpine, Snake	Davison, Guest
20. 3.1852	Eagle, Proserpine, Snake	Davison, Guest
3. 4.1852	Eagle, Snake, Wild Fire	Davison, Guest, J. Davidson
17. 4.1852	Snake, Wild Fire	Guest, Davidson
1. 5.1852	Snake, Viper, Wild Fire	Guest, Davidson
15. 5.1852	Snake, Viper	Guest, T. Davison
29. 5.1852	Eagle, Snake, Viper	Guest, Davison, Davidson
12. 6.1852	Eagle, Viper, Wild Fire	Guest, Davison
30. 6.1852	Eagle, Viper, Wild Fire	Guest, Davison
10. 7.1852	Eagle, North Star, Viper, Wild Fire	Guest, Davison, Davidson

Fortnight ending	Engines employed	Drivers names
24. 7.1852 to 4. 9.1852	Eagle, North Star, Viper	Guest, Davison, Davidson
18. 9.1852	Eagle, North Star, Wild Fire	Guest, Davison, Davidson
2.10.1852	Atlas, Eagle, North Star, Wild Fire	Guest, Davison
16.10.1852	Atlas, Eagle, North Star, Snake	Guest, Davison
30.10.1852	Atlas, North Star, Snake	Guest, Davison
13.11.1852 to 19. 3.1853	Atlas, North Star, Snake	T. Clarke, Guest
2. 4.1853	North Star, Snake	Clarke, Guest
16. 4.1853	Alas, Etna, North Star, Snake	Clarke, Guest
30. 4.1853	Etna, Snake, Viper	Clarke, Guest, Read
14. 5.1853	Snake, Viper	Guest, Clarke
28. 5.1853	Snake, Viper	Guest, Clarke
11. 6.1853	Javelin, Snake, Viper	Guest, Clarke
30. 6.1853	Javelin, Viper	Guest, Clarke
9. 7.1853	Javelin, Snake, Viper	Guest, Clarke
23. 7.1853	Javelin, Snake, Viper	Guest, Clarke
6. 8.1853	Snake, Viper	Guest, Clarke
20. 8.1853 to 1.10.1853	Snake, Viper, Western Star	Guest, Clarke
15.10.1853	No details	
29.10.1853	Snake, Viper	Guest, Clarke

The Locomotives

Snake	built Haigh Foundry	2–2–2 tank engine built 1838, withdrawn 1870
Viper	built Haigh Foundry	2–2–2 tank engine built 1838, withdrawn 1870
Eagle	built Sharp, Roberts	2–2–2 tender engine built 1838, rebuilt as tank 1860, withdrawn 1871
Harpy	'Fire Fly' class	2–2–2 tender engine built 1841, sold to Steam Coal Co. Abercarn 1873.
Minos	'Fire Fly' class	2–2–2 tender engine built 1841, withdrawn 1870
Proserpine	'Fire Fly' class	2–2–2 tender engine built 1842, sold to Fielding & Platt 1873
Fire Fly	'Fire Fly' class	2–2–2 tender engine built 1840, withdrawn 1870
Wild Fire	'Fire Fly' class	2–2–2 tender engine built 1840, withdrawn 1870
North Star	'Star' class	2–2–2 tender engine built 1837, withdrawn 1871
Atlas	built Sharp, Roberts	2–2–2 tender engine built 1838, rebuilt as tank 1866, sold 1872
Etna	'Leo' class	2–4–0 tender engine built 1841, rebuilt as tank by 1849, withdrawn 1870
Javelin	'Sun' class	2–2–2 tender engine built 1841, rebuilt as tank by 1850, withdrawn 1870
Western Star	'Star' class	2–2–2 tender engine built 1841, withdrawn 1870

Source: Daniel Gooch's Engine Book 1850–1853

Appendix Two
Engines used on the Windsor Branch 1861–1862

4 weeks ending	Engines employed	Drivers names
13. 4.1861	Assagais, Eclipse, Rocket	W. Chivers, C. Butler, S. Guest
11. 5.1861	Assagais, Eclipse, Rocket	ditto
8. 6.1861	Assagais, Eclipse, Rocket, Comet	ditto
30. 6.1861	Assagais, Comet, Eclipse	ditto
20. 7.1861	Assagais, Comet, Eclipse, Rocket	ditto
17. 8.1861	Assagais, Eclipse, Rocket	ditto
14. 9.1861	Djerid, Assagais, Eclipse, Rocket	ditto
12.10.1861	Djerid, Assagais, Eclipse, Rocket, Zebra	ditto plus J. Geary, A. Woodham
9.11.1861	Djerid, Assagais, Rocket, Zebra	Chivers, Butler, Guest, Woodham
7.12.1861	Djerid, Assagais, Rocket, Zebra	ditto plus Swinney
31.12.1861	Assagais, Djerid, Eclipse, Gazelle, Rocket, Zebra	Chivers, Butler, Guest, Woodham [plus illegible name D. . .]
18. 1.1862	Djerid, Eclipse, Rocket, Sun, Zebra	Chivers, Butler, Guest, Woodham, Turner
15. 2.1862	Djerid, Eclipse, Rocket, Sun, Zebra	ditto, minus Turner
15. 3.1862	Assagais, Djerid, Eclipse, Rocket, Sun	Chivers, Butler, Guest, Woodham
12. 4.1862	Assagais, Djerid, Eclipse, Rocket, Sun, Lance	ditto plus Powell, Cantrell
10. 5.1862	Antelope, Assagais, Djerid, Eclipse	Guest, Chivers, Reading,* Woodham
	Meridian, Rocket	Henley,* Butler, Barefoot
7. 6.1862	Meridian, Rocket	S. Woodham, Chivers, Butler, A. Woodham, Powell, Guest
30. 6.1862	Antelope, Assagais, Eclipse, Rocket, Shah	Chivers, Woodham, Butler, Guest, Powell
19. 7.1862	Assagais, Djerid, Eclipse, Rocket, Shah	Chivers, Woodham, Butler, Guest, Gray
16. 8.1862	Assagais, Bey, Djerid, Hornet, Rocket, Sunbeam, Sun	Chivers, Woodham, Butler, Guest, Batten, Powell
13. 9.1862	Antelope, Assagais, Djerid, Khan, Kaiser, Rocket, Sunbeam	Guest, Powell, Chivers, Woodham, Gray, Batten, E. Cantrell, Butler
11.10.1862	Antelope, Assagais, Djerid, Khan, Kaiser, Locust, Sunbeam, Wasp	Guest, Chivers, Woodham, Butler
8.11.1862	Antelope, Assagais, Djerid, Sunbeam, Wasp	Guest, Chivers, Woodham, Butler
6.12.1862	Antelope, Assagais, Djerid, Sunbeam	ditto
31.12.1862	Antelope, Assagais, Djerid, Sunbeam	ditto plus J. Knibb

*I assume this means Reading driver, Henley driver.

The Locomotives

Assagais	'Sun' class	2−2−2 tender engine built 1841, rebuilt as tank by 1850, withdrawn 1875
Eclipse	'Sun' class	2−2−2 tender engine built 1840, rebuilt as tank by 1850, withdrawn 1870 (actually ceased work 1864)
Rocket	'Sun' class	2−2−2 tender engine built 1841, rebuilt as tank by 1850, withdrawn 1870
Comet	'Sun' class	2−2−2 tender engine built 1840, rebuilt as tank by 1850, withdrawn 1871
Djerid	'Sun' class	2−2−2 tender engine built 1841, rebuilt as tank by 1850, withdrawn 1870
Zebra	'Sun' class	2−2−2 tender engine built 1841, rebuilt as tank by 1850, withdrawn 1871
Gazelle	'Sun' class	2−2−2 tender engine built 1841, rebuilt as tank by 1850, withdrawn 1879 (the last of the class to go)
Sun	'Sun' class	2−2−2 tender engine built 1840, rebuilt as tank by 1850, withdrawn 1873
Lance	'Sun' class	2−2−2 tender engine built 1841, rebuilt as tank by 1850, withdrawn 1870
Antelope	'Sun' class	2−2−2 tender engine built 1841, rebuilt as tank by 1850, withdrawn 1870
Meridian	'Sun' class	2−2−2 tender engine built 1840, rebuilt as tank by 1850, withdrawn 1870
Shah	'Metropolitan' class	2−4−0 tank engine built June 1862 (so brand new), fitted with condensing apparatus, withdrawn 1872
Bey	'Metropolitan' class	2−4−0 tank engine built July 1862, as above, withdrawn 1872
Hornet	'Metropolitan' class	2−4−0 tank engine built June 1862, as above, altered to tender engine, withdrawn 1873
Sunbeam	'Sun' class	2−2−2 tender engine built 1840, rebuilt as tank by 1850, withdrawn 1870
Khan	'Metropolitan' class	2−4−0 tank engine built Sept. 1862 (so brand new) fitted with condensing apparatus, withdrawn 1872
Kaiser	'Metropolitan' class	2−4−0 tank engine built Sept. 1862, as above, withdrawn 1872
Locust	'Metropolitan' class	2−4−0 tank engine built Aug. 1862, as above, withdrawn 1876
Wasp	'Metropolitan' class	2−4−0 tank engine built Aug. 1862, as above, withdrawn 1877

Source: Daniel Gooch's Engine Book 1861−1862

Appendix Three
Royal Trains – Windsor Branch

Date		Train	Remarks
23.11.1849		Windsor – Basingstoke	QV for Osborne
12.1849		Basingstoke – Windsor	QV
12.02.1850		Windsor –?	
14.10.1852		Bordesley – Windsor	QV from Balmoral
11.1852		Windsor – Basingstoke	QV for Osborne
06.10.1853		Leamington – Windsor	QV from Balmoral
10.1854		Paddington – Windsor	QV
02.05.1859	6.00am	Windsor – Saltash	Prince Albert, Saltash Bge
02.05.1859	6.50pm	Cornwall Jn – Windsor	Pr. Albert arr. W.12.05am
30.04.1862	6.50pm	Windsor – Bushbury	QV for Aboyne
15.05.1863	6.50pm	Windsor – Aboyne	QV
05.06.1863	2.30pm	Aboyne – Windsor	QV arr.Windsor 9am 06.06
27.10.1863	2.30pm	Aboyne – Windsor	QV arr.Windsor 9am 28.10
13.05.1864	6.50pm	Windsor – Aboyne	QV
07.06.1864		Aboyne – Windsor	QV arr.Windsor 9am 08.06
29.08.1864	6.50pm	Windsor – Aboyne	QV
28.10.1864	2.30pm	Aboyne – Windsor	QV
19.05.1865		Windsor Aboyne	QV
15.06.1865	2.30pm	Aboyne – Windsor	QV arr.Windsor 9am 16.06
30.06.1865	1.00pm	Paddington – Windsor	Queen of the Netherlands
	3.30pm	Windsor – Paddington	
04.07.1865	10.00am	Windsor – Paddington	QV
	xx.xx	Paddington – Windsor	
10.07.1865	4.00pm	Windsor – Basingstoke	QV for Osborne
11.09.1865	6.50pm	Windsor – Aboyne	QV
28.10.1865	2.30pm	Aboyne – Windsor	QV arr.Windsor 8.45am 29.10
16.11.1865	10.50am	Windsor – Paddington	QV
	xx.xx	Paddington – Windsor	
28.11.1865	11.00am	Windsor – Paddington	QV
	xx.xx	Paddington – Windsor	
18.12.1865	10.25am	Windsor – Basingstoke	QV for Osborne
05.02.1866		Basingstoke – Windsor	QV
06.02.1866	10.35am	Windsor – Paddington	QV to open Parliament
	4.50pm	Paddington – Windsor	
07.02.1866	2.15pm	Windsor – Basingstoke	QV for Osborne
21.02.1866		Basingstoke – Windsor	QV
09.03.1866	11.00am	Windsor – Paddington	QV
10.03.1866	1.00pm	Paddington – Windsor	QV
15.03.1866	12.00nn	Windsor – Paddington	QV
	xx.xx	Paddington – Windsor	
22.03.1866	1.00pm	Windsor – Paddington	QV
24.03.1866	1.00pm	Paddington – Windsor	QV
10.04.1866	3.00pm	Windsor – Basingstoke	QV for Osborne
03.05.1866		Basingstoke – Windsor	QV arr.Windsor 5.30pm
05.05.1866	11.00am	Windsor – Paddington	QV
	5.55pm	Paddington – Windsor	
14.05.1866	11.00am	Windsor – Paddington	QV
	4.55pm	Paddington – Windsor	
06.06.1866	12.15pm	Windsor – Paddington	QV
	6.25pm	Paddington – Windsor	QV
13.06.1866	7.00pm	Windsor – Aboyne	QV
25.06.1866		Aboyne – Windsor	QV
07.07.1866	3.45pm	Windsor – Basingstoke	QV for Osborne
22.08.1866		Basingstoke – Windsor	QV arr.Windsor 6.30pm
23.08.1866	6.50pm	Windsor – Aboyne	QV
01.11.1866	2.10pm	Ballater – Windsor	QV arr.Windsor 8.45am 02.11
14.11.1866	11.00am	Windsor – Paddington	QV
	xx.xx	Paddington – Windsor	
30.11.1866		Windsor – Wolverhampton	QV to unveil statue P.Albert

For Notes see page 276.

Date		Train	Remarks
15.12.1866	11.00am	Windsor–Basingstoke	QV for Osborne
04.02.1867		Basingstoke–Windsor	QV arr.Windsor 5.45pm
05.02.1867	10.00am	Windsor–Paddington	QV
	4.55pm	Paddington–Windsor	
06.02.1867	10.35am	Windsor–Basingstoke	QV for Osborne
22.02.1867		Basingstoke–Windsor	QV arr.Windsor 6.00pm
27.02.1867	10.35am	Windsor–Paddington	QV
	xx.xx	Paddington–Windsor	
06.03.1867	3.45pm	Windsor–Paddington	QV
09.03.1867	5.30pm	Paddington–Windsor	QV
12.03.1867	3.30pm	Windsor–Paddington	QV
	xx.xx	Paddington–Windsor	
19.03.1867	11.15am	Windsor–Paddington	QV
	xx.xx	Paddington–Windsor	
22.03.1867	3.45pm	Windsor–Paddington	QV
23.03.1867		Paddington–Windsor	QV
28.03.1867	11.30am	Windsor–Paddington	QV
	xx.xx	Paddington–Windsor	
10.04.1867	2.20pm	Windsor–Paddington	King of Denmark
13.04.1867	3.30pm	Windsor–Paddington	QV
	5.35pm	Paddington–Windsor	
22.04.1867	3.30pm	Windsor–Paddington	QV
	xx.xx	Paddington–Windsor	
30.04.1867	3.30pm	Windsor–Paddington	QV
	xx.xx	Paddington–Windsor	
02.05.1867	3.15pm	Windsor–Basingstoke	QV for Osborne
18.05.1867		Basingstoke–Windsor	QV arr.Windsor 2.15pm
20.05.1867	10.35am	Windsor–Paddington	QV
	xx.xx	Paddington–Windsor	
22.05.1867	6.50pm	Windsor–Ballater	QV
18.06.1867	2.00pm	Ballater–Windsor	QV arr.Windsor 8.45am 19.06
21.06.1867	11.35am	Windsor–Paddington	QV
	xx.xx	Paddington–Windsor	
02.07.1867	11.30am	Windsor–Paddington	QV
	xx.xx	Paddington–Windsor	
06.07.1867	10.20am	Windsor–Paddington	Queen of Prussia
	6.15pm	Paddington–Windsor	
08.07.1867	11.10am	Windsor–Paddington	QV
	xx.xx	Paddington–Windsor	
13.07.1867	4.30pm	Windsor–Basingstoke	QV for Osborne
19.08.1867		Basingstoke–Windsor	QV arr.Windsor 6.00pm
20.08.1867	10.00pm	Windsor–Kelso	QV
01.11.1867	9.00pm	Ballater–Windsor	QV arr.Windsor 4.55pm 02.11
16.11.1867	11.00am	Windsor–Sevenoaks	QV
	xx.xx	Sevenoaks–Windsor	
03.12.1867	11.45am	Windsor–Paddington	QV
	xx.xx	Paddington–Windsor	
17.12.1867	10.45am	Windsor–Basingstoke	QV
03.03.1868		Basingstoke–Windsor	QV arr.Windsor 6.02pm
06.03.1868	11.35am	Windsor–Paddington	QV
	xx.xx	Paddington–Windsor	
12.03.1868	11.35am	Windsor–Paddington	QV
	5.30pm	Paddington–Windsor	
30.03.1868	4.00pm	Windsor–Paddington	QV
04.04.1868	1.10pm	Paddington–Windsor	QV
17.04.1868	3.00pm	Windsor–Basingstoke	QV for Gosport
08.05.1868		Basingstoke–Windsor	QV arr.Windsor 6.10pm
12.05.1868	10.35am	Windsor–Paddington	QV
13.05.1868	5.xxpm	Paddington–Windsor	QV
19.05.1868	6.45pm	Windsor–Ballater	QV
16.06.1868	2.00pm	Ballater–Windsor	QV arr.Windsor 8.50am 17.06

Date	Train		Remarks
22.06.1868	11.35am	Windsor–Paddington	QV
23.06.1868	10.30am	Paddington–Windsor	QV
03.07.1868	3.20pm	Windsor–Aldershot C.	QV
06.07.1868	10.45am	Windsor–Paddington	QV
	xx.xx	Paddington–Windsor	
08.07.1868	4.45pm	Windsor–Basingstoke	QV for Gosport
08.09.1868		Basingstoke–Windsor	QV arr.W.5.40pm, from Lucerne
14.09.1868	6.50pm	Windsor–Ballater	QV
04.11.1868	2.00pm	Ballater–Windsor	QV arr.Windsor 8.50am 5.11
17.12.1868	10.45am	Windsor–Basingstoke	QV for Osborne
26.02.1869		Basingstoke–Windsor	QV arr.Windsor 1.50pm
03.03.1869	11.15am	Windsor–Paddington	QV
05.03.1869	6.00pm	Paddington–Windsor	QV
09.03.1869	11.35am	Windsor–Paddington	QV
12.03.1869	1.10pm	Paddington–Windsor	QV
06.04.1869	11.25am	Windsor–Paddington	QV
10.04.1869	12.45pm	Paddington–Windsor	QV
20.04.1869	3.15pm	Windsor–Basingstoke	QV for Osborne
08.05.1869		Basingstoke–Windsor	QV arr.Windsor 6.00pm
11.05.1869	10.30am	Windsor–Paddington	QV
12.05.1869	xx.xx	Paddington–Windsor	QV
14.05.1869	7.00pm	Windsor–Ballater	QV
15.06.1869	2.00pm	Ballater–Windsor	QV arr.Windsor 8.50am 16.06
24.06.1869	6.30pm	Paddington–Windsor	Viceroy of Eygpt/P&Pr of Wales
28.06.1869	10.35am	Windsor–Paddington	QV
29.06.1869	10.15am	Paddington–Windsor	QV
08.07.1869	3.20pm	Windsor–Paddington	QV
	xx.xx	Paddington–Windsor	
20.07.1869	9.05am	Windsor–Basingstoke	QV for Gosport
18.08.1869		Basingstoke–Windsor	QV arr.Windsor 6.30pm appx.
19.08.1869	7.55pm	Windsor–Ballater	QV
03.11.1869	2.00pm	Ballater–Windsor	QV arr.Windsor 8.50am 04.11
06.11.1869	10.50am	Windsor–Paddington	QV to open Blackfriars Bridge
12.11.1869	3.00pm	Windsor–Paddington	QV
	xx.xx	Paddington–Windsor	
22.11.1869	3.15pm	Windsor–Paddington	King of the Belgians
02.12.1869	3.10pm	Windsor–Paddington	QV
	xx.xx	Paddington–Windsor	
09.12.1869	3.15pm	Windsor–Paddington	QV
	xx.xx	Paddington–Windsor	
18.12.1869	10.35am	Windsor–Basingstoke	QV for Osborne
18.02.1870		Basingstoke–Windsor	QV arr.Windsor 5.25pm appx.
24.02.1870	3.40pm	Windsor–Paddington	QV
26.02.1870	4.30pm	Paddington–Windsor	QV
08.03.1870	3.50pm	Windsor–Paddington	QV
12.03.1870	5.20pm	Paddington–Windsor	QV
22.03.1870	11.00am	Windsor–Paddington	QV
13.04.1870	3.35pm	Windsor–Basingstoke	QV for Gosport
07.05.1870		Basingstoke–Windsor	QV arr.Windsor 6.15pm appx.
09.05.1870	5.05pm	Windsor–Paddington	QV (BG)
19.05.1870	7.55pm	Windsor–Ballater	QV
17.06.1870		Ballater–Windsor	QV arr.Windsor 8.50am 18.06
02.07.1870	9.30am	Windsor–Paddington	QV (BG)
	11.50am	Paddington–Windsor	
11.07.1870	9.35am	Windsor–Paddington	QV (BG)
	11.30am	Paddington–Windsor	
14.07.1870	9.45am	Windsor–Basingstoke	QV for Osborne
16.08.1870		Basingstoke–Windsor	QV arr.Windsor 6.40pm appx.
17.08.1870	7.45pm	Windsor–Ballater	QV
23.11.1870	2.00pm	Ballater–Windsor	QV arr.Windsor 8.50am 24.11

Date	Train		Remarks
03.12.1870	10.15am	Windsor–Paddington	QV (BG)
	12.55pm	Paddington–Windsor	
10.12.1870	10.20am	Windsor–Watford	QV via Kensington
		Watford–Windsor (1.20pm	
		ex Kensington)	
19.12.1870	10.35am	Windsor–Basingstoke	QV for Osborne
07.02.1871		Basingstoke–Windsor	QV arr.Windsor 5.40pm appx.
09.02.1871	10.05am	Windsor–Paddington	QV (BG) to open Parliament
	5.10pm	Paddington–Windsor	
20.02.1871	3.50pm	Windsor–Paddington	QV (BG)
24.02.1871	4.45pm	Paddington–Windsor	QV (BG)
28.03.1871	10.55am	Windsor–Paddington	QV (BG)
30.03.1871	5.05pm	Paddington–Windsor	QV (BG)
03.04.1871	10.50am	Windsor–Basingstoke	QV for Gosport
03.05.1871		Basingstoke–Windsor	QV
06.05.1871	9.45am	Windsor–Paddington	QV (BG) to R.Albert Exhb.
	1.00pm	Paddington–Windsor	
09.05.1871	10.30am	Windsor–Paddington	QV (NG)
11.05.1871	12.15pm	Paddington–Windsor	QV (NG)
17.05.1871	7.55pm	Windsor–Ballater	QV
19.06.1871	2.00pm	Ballater–Windsor	QV arr.Windsor 8.50am 20.06
21.06.1871	11.00am	Windsor–Paddington	QV to St Thomas's Hospital
	1.00pm	Paddington–Windsor	
23.06.1871	10.40am	Windsor–Paddington	QV Garden Party at B.P.
24.06.1871	12.00nn	Paddington–Windsor	QV (BG)
04.07.1871	2.xxpm	Paddington–Windsor	Emp and Empress of Brazil
05.07.1871	11.30am	Windsor–Paddington	QV (BG)
	1.30pm	Paddington–Windsor	
08.07.1871	11.25pm	Paddington–Windsor	QV (BG)
12.07.1871	10.30am	Windsor–Basingstoke	QV for Osborne
15.08.1871	xx.xxpm	Basingstoke–Windsor	QV arr.Windsor abt 8.00pm
16.08.1871	7.55pm	Windsor–Ballater	QV
24.11.1871	2.00pm	Ballater–Windsor	QV arr.Windsor 8.50am 25.11
09.01.1872	9.50am	Windsor–Basingstoke	QV for Osborne
22.02.1872		Basingstoke–Windsor	QV arr.Windsor abt 1.30pm
25.02.1872	3.30pm	Windsor–Paddington	QV (BG)
01.03.1872	4.15pm	Paddington–Windsor	QV (BG)
11.03.1872	4.10pm	Windsor–Paddington	QV (BG)
14.03.1872	6.00pm	Paddington–Windsor	QV (BG)
23.03.1872	3.xxpm	Windsor–Basingstoke	QV for Gosport
08.04.1872		Basingstoke–Windsor	QV arr.Windsor abt 12.30pm
23.04.1872	10.35am	Windsor–Paddington	QV (BG)
25.04.1872	4.30pm	Paddington–Windsor	QV (BG)
06.05.1872	10.35am	Windsor–Paddington	QV (BG)
08.05.1872	6.40pm	Paddington–Windsor	QV (BG)
09.05.1872	1.20pm	Paddington–Windsor	King of the Belgians (BG)
	10.30pm	Windsor–Paddington	
14.05.1872	7.55pm	Windsor–Ballater	QV
18.06.1872	2.00pm	Ballater–Windsor	QV arr.Windsor 8.50am 19.6
01.07.1872	9.50am	Windsor–Paddington	QV (BG)
	11.10am	Paddington–Windsor	
11.07.1872	9.xxam	Windsor–Basingstoke	QV for Osborne
22.11.1872	2.00pm	Ballater–Windsor	QV arr.Windsor 8.50am 23.11
18.02.1873		Basingstoke–Windsor	QV arr.Windsor abt 1.30pm
24.02.1873	10.15am	Windsor–Paddington	QV to Kensington Palace
	12.15pm	Paddington–Windsor	
27.02.1873	10.50am	Windsor–Paddington	QV (BG)
01.03.1873	4.40pm	Paddington–Windsor	QV (BG)
12.03.1873	10.50am	Windsor–Paddington	QV (BG)
15.03.1873	4.40pm	Paddington–Windsor	QV (BG)
01.04.1873	10.15am	Windsor–Paddington	QV (BG)

Date	Train		Remarks
03.04.1873	4.45pm	Paddington–Windsor	QV (BG)
09.04.1873	9.50am	Windsor–Basingstoke	QV for Osborne
30.04.1873	xx.xxpm	Basingstoke–Windsor	QV arr.Windsor abt 6.00pm
05.05.1873	2.55pm	Paddington–Windsor	King & Queen o.t.Belgians
06.05.1873	12.xxpm	Windsor–Paddington	King & Queen o.t.Belgians
07.05.1873	10.55am	Windsor–Paddington	QV (BG)
09.05.1873	5.20pm	Paddington–Windsor	QV (BG)
13.05.1873	11.20am	Windsor–Paddington	King & Queen o.t. Belgians
15.05.1873	7.55pm	Windsor–Ballater	QV
17.06.1873	2.00pm	Ballater–Windsor	QV arr.Windsor 8.50am 18.06
20.06.1873	1.00pm	Paddington–Windsor	Shah of Persia
	3.05pm	Windsor–Paddington	
21.06.1873	1.05pm	Paddington–Windsor	Czareivitch (BG)
	5.xxpm	Windsor–Paddington	
24.06.1873	HM HELD REVIEW IN WINDSOR PARK AT 5.00pm		
24.06.1873	2.45pm	Paddington–Windsor	Shah of Persia (BG)
	5.30pm	Windsor–Paddington	
01.07.1873	3.40pm	Paddington–Windsor	Czareivitch & PoWales (NG)
02.07.1873	1.10pm	Windsor–Paddington	Czareivitch & PoWales (BG)
02.07.1873	2.45pm	Paddington–Windsor	Shah of Persia (BG)
	6.xxpm	Windsor–Paddington	
11.07.1873	9.45am	Windsor–Basingstoke	QV for Osborne
28.11.1873	2.00pm	Ballater–Windsor	QV arr.Windsor 8.50am 29.11
19.12.1873	10.xxam	Windsor–Basingstoke	QV for Osborne
17.02.1874	12.20pm	Basingstoke–Windsor	QV arr.Windsor abt 1.20pm
25.02.1874	3.35pm	Windsor–Paddington	QV
27.02.1874	4.45pm	Paddington–Windsor	QV
12.03.1874	11.00am	Windsor–Paddington	QV
14.03.1874	4.45pm	Paddington–Windsor	QV (NG)
23.03.1874	4.35pm	Windsor–Paddington	QV (NG)
25.03.1874	4.45pm	Paddington–Windsor	QV (NG)
01.04.1874	10.30am	Windsor–Basingstoke	QV for Osborne
29.04.1874	5.05pm	Windsor–Paddington	QV (NG)
	6.45pm	Paddington–Windsor	
04.05.1874	11.00am	Windsor–Paddington	QV (NG)
06.05.1874	4.45pm	Paddington–Windsor	QV (NG)
15.05.1874	11.00am	Windsor–Paddington	The Tzar (BG)
17.05.1874	1.00pm	Paddington–Windsor	The Tzar (BG)
	3.15pm	Windsor–Paddington	
20.05.1874	7.55pm	Windsor–Ballater	QV
05.06.1874	1.30pm	Paddington–Windsor	Empress Eugenie
	xx.xxpm	Windsor–Paddington	
23.06.1874	2.00pm	Ballater–Windsor	QV arr.Windsor 8.50am 24.06
09.07.1874	6.20pm	Basingstoke–Windsor	Pr.& Princess of Germany
10.07.1874	4.50pm	Windsor–Paddington	P/Pr Germany Note (a)
14.07.1874	9.45am	Windsor–Basingstoke	QV for Osborne
20.11.1874	2.00pm	Ballater–Windsor	QV arr.Windsor 8.50am 21.11
23.11.1874	9.35am	Windsor–Paddington	QV
	5.30pm	Paddington–Windsor	
17.12.1874	1.xxpm	Windsor–Basingstoke	QV for Osborne
26.02.1875	4.xxpm	Basingstoke–Windsor	QV arr.Windsor abt 5.30pm
08.03.1875	11.05am	Windsor–Paddington	QV
11.03.1875	4.20pm	Paddington–Windsor	QV
18.03.1875	12.05pm	Windsor–Paddington	QV
20.03.1875	5.20pm	Paddington–Windsor	QV
02.04.1875	2.30pm	Windsor–Basingstoke	QV for Osborne
23.04.1875	4.xxpm	Basingstoke–Windsor	QV arr.Windsor abt 5.45 pm
28.04.1875	11.00am	Windsor–Paddington	QV
	xx.xx	Paddington–Windsor	
05.05.1875	10.50am	Windsor–Paddington	QV

Date	Train		Remarks
08.05.1875	12.30pm	Paddington–Windsor	QV
14.05.1875	7.55pm	Windsor–Ballater	QV
18.06.1875	2.00pm	Ballater–Windsor	QV arr.Windsor 8.50am 19.06
21.06.1875	2.05pm	Paddington–Windsor	Sultan of Zanzibar
	4.30pm	Windsor–Paddington	
24.06.1875	6.50pm	Paddington–Windsor	Queen of Netherlands
25.06.1875	3.35pm	Windsor–Paddington	" "
12.07.1875	3.15pm	Paddington–Windsor	Prince of Italy
	5.20pm	Windsor–Paddington	
13.07.1875	4.00pm	Windsor–Basingstoke	QV for Osborne
23.11.1875	2.00pm	Ballater–Windsor	QV
04.12.1875	2.20pm	Windsor–Paddington	QV
	5.35pm	Paddington–Windsor	
17.12.1875	10.30am	Windsor–Basingstoke	QV for Osborne
08.02.1876	5.30pm	Paddington–Windsor	QV
24.02.1876	10.35am	Windsor–Paddington	QV
26.02.1876	4.45pm	Paddington–Windsor	QV
06.03.1876	10.25am	Windsor–Paddington	QV
09.03.1876	4.40pm	Paddington–Windsor	QV
27.03.1876	3.45pm	Windsor–Portsmouth	QV via Kensington
22.04.1876		Portsmouth–Windsor	QV via Basingstoke
02.05.1876	11.00am	Windsor–Basingstoke	QV arr.Windsor 6.45pm
	5.45pm	Basingstoke–Windsor	
08.05.1876	10.55am	Windsor–Paddington	Empress of Germany
	5.05pm	Paddington–Windsor	
10.05.1876	10.40am	Windsor–Paddington	QV & Empress of Germany
13.05.1876	6.00pm	Paddington–Windsor	QV
19.05.1876	7.55pm	Windsor–Ballater	QV
21.06.1876	2.00pm	Ballater–Windsor	QV arr.Windsor 8.50am 22.06
30.06.1876	5.05pm	Windsor–Paddington	QV (RAO)
07.07.1876	5.00pm	Windsor–Paddington	QV to Exhibition at S.Kens.
	6.35pm	Paddington–Windsor	
14.07.1876	4.00pm	Windsor–Basingstoke	QV for Osborne
23.11.1876	2.00pm	Ballater–Windsor	QV arr.Windsor 8.50am 24.11
30.11.1876	3.30pm	Windsor–Paddington	QV
	5.00pm	Paddington–Windsor	
13.01.1877	3.35pm	Windsor–Paddington	QV to St James Palace
	5.00pm	Paddington–Windsor	
23.01.1877	10.xxam	Windsor–Basingstoke	QV for Osborne
03.03.1877	4.50pm	Paddington–Windsor	QV
12.03.1877	11.05am	Windsor–Paddington	QV
15.03.1877	4.50pm	Paddington–Windsor	QV
28.03.1877	10.xxam	Windsor–Basingstoke	QV for Osborne
21.04.1877		Basingstoke–Windsor	QV arr.Windsor abt 1.30pm
01.05.1877	10.35am	Windsor–Paddington	QV
04.05.1877	5.15pm	Paddington–Windsor	QV
09.05.1877	11.00am	Windsor–Farnborough	QV via Basingstoke
09.05.1877	5.20pm	Farnborough–Windsor	QV arr.Windsor 6.45pm
18.05.1877	7.55pm	Windsor–Ballater	QV
21.06.1877	2.00pm	Ballater–Windsor	QV arr.Windsor 8.50am 22.06
30.06.1877	4.45pm	Windsor–Paddington	QV to St James Palace
	7.10pm	Paddington–Windsor	
12.07.1877	4.35pm	Windsor–Paddington	QV Gdn Pty Marlborough Ho.
	6.55pm	Paddington–Windsor	
19.07.1877	9.50am	Windsor–Basingstoke	QV for Osborne
05.12.1877	2.00pm	Ballater–Windsor	QV arr.Windsor 8.50am 06.12
11.12.1877	4.30pm	Windsor–Paddington	QV
	6.45pm	Paddington–Windsor	
15.12.1877	12.40pm	Windsor–High Wycombe	QV Visit to Ld Beaconsfield
	3.45pm	High Wycombe–Windsor	
28.12.1877	10.15am	Windsor–Basingstoke	QV for Osborne

Date	Train		Remarks
19.02.1878	12.xxpm	Basingstoke–Windsor	QV arr.Windsor 1.50pm
27.02.1878	12.05pm	Windsor–Paddington	QV
01.03.1878	4.45pm	Paddington–Windsor	QV
19.03.1878	11.05am	Windsor–Paddington	QV
22.03.1878	4.45pm	Paddington–Windsor	QV
05.04.1878	10.20am	Windsor–Basingstoke	QV for Osborne
25.04.1878	4.55pm	Basingstoke–Windsor	QV arr.Windsor 5.55pm
07.05.1878	11.05am	Windsor–Paddington	QV
10.05.1878	5.05pm	Paddington–Windsor	QV
13.05.1878	11.05am	Windsor–Farnborough	Crn P'cess Germany Note (b)
	5.25pm	Farnborough–Windsor	
20.05.1878	7.45pm	Windsor–Ballater	QV
21.06.1878	2.00pm	Ballater–Windsor	QV arr.Windsor 8.50am 22.06
06.07.1878	5.10pm	Windsor–Paddington	QV
	7.10pm	Paddington–Windsor	
13.07.1878	4.20pm	Windsor–Paddington	QV
	7.10pm	Paddington–Windsor	
19.07.1878	9.50am	Windsor–Basingstoke	QV for Osborne
21.11.1878	2.00pm	Ballater–Windsor	QV arr.Windsor 8.50am 22.11
26.11.1878	4.35pm	Windsor–Paddington	QV
	6.10pm	Paddington–Windsor	
20.12.1878	10.20am	Windsor–Gosport	QV for Osborne
18.02.1879	4.30pm	Basingstoke–Windsor	QV arr.W.5.40pm (10L)
25.02.1879	3.35pm	Windsor–Paddington	QV
	6.35pm	Paddington–Windsor	
25.03.1879	9.40am	Windsor–Portsmouth	QV for Italy
26.04.1879		Portsmouth–Windsor	QV arr.Windsor abt 6.15pm
30.04.1879	9.35am	Windsor–Paddington	QV
	11.00am	Paddington–Windsor	
06.05.1879	10.30am	Windsor–Paddington	QV
09.05.1879	5.15pm	Paddington–Windsor	QV
21.05.1879	7.55pm	Windsor–Ballater	QV
20.06.1879	2.00pm	Ballater–Windsor	QV arr.Windsor 8.50am 21.06
03.07.1879	5.15pm	Windsor–Paddington	QV
	7.15pm	Paddington–Windsor	
05.07.1879	9.35am	Windsor–Queens Park	QV Visit to Royal Agr. Show
	11.30am	Queens Park–Windsor	
19.07.1879	10.05am	Windsor–Basingstoke	QV for Osborne
25.11.1879	2.00pm	Ballater–Windsor	QV arr.Windsor 8.50am 26.11
12.12.1879	4.35pm	Windsor–Paddington	QV
	6.30pm	Paddington–Windsor	
18.12.1879	10.05am	Windsor–Gosport	QV for Osborne
21.02.1880	5.10pm	Paddington–Windsor	QV
09.03.1880	1.00pm	Paddington–Windsor	Empress of Austria
	3.00pm	Windsor–Paddington	
10.03.1880	10.35am	Windsor–Paddington	QV
13.03.1880	5.18pm	Paddington–Windsor	QV
25.03.1889	10.05am	Windsor–Basingstoke	QV for Germany
17.04.1880	4.30pm	Queenborough–Windsor	QV (NG) GW saloon,arr.W.6.30pm
11.05.1880	11.05am	Windsor–Paddington	QV
14.05.1880	5.20pm	Paddington–Windsor	QV
21.05.1880	7.55pm	Windsor–Ballater	QV
22.06.1880	2.50pm	Ballater–Windsor	QV arr.Windsor 8.50am 23.06
06.07.1880	5.05pm	Windsor–Paddington	QV to Duchess of Cambridge
	6.50pm	Paddington–Windsor	
13.07.1880	4.50pm	Windsor–Paddington	QV Prince of Wales Gdn Pty
	7.25pm	Paddington–Windsor	
19.07.1880	10.xxam	Windsor–Basingstoke	QV for Osborne
23.11.1880	2.00pm	Ballater–Windsor	QV arr.Windsor 8.50am 24.11
07.12.1880	4.35pm	Windsor–Paddington	QV visit D. of Cambridge
	6.00pm	Paddington–Windsor	

Date	Train		Remarks
18.12.1880	10.30am	Windsor–Portsmouth D.	QV for Osborne
24.02.1881	11.05am	Windsor–Paddington	QV
26.02.1881	4.50pm	Paddington–Windsor	QV
28.03.1881	11.05am	Windsor–Paddington	QV
30.03.1881	4.50pm	Paddington–Windsor	QV
03.05.1881	11.00am	Windsor–Paddington	QV
06.05.1881	5.05pm	Paddington–Windsor	QV
21.06.1881	2.50pm	Ballater–Windsor	QV
14.07.1881	4.05pm	Windsor–Paddington	QV
22.11.1881	2.00pm	Ballater–Windsor	QV arr Windsor 8.50am 23.11
08.12.1881	3.50pm	Windsor–Paddington	QV
	6.20pm	Paddington–Windsor	
18.02.1882	4.50pm	Paddington–Windsor	QV
28.02.1882	11.05am	Windsor–Paddington	QV
02.03.1882	4.50pm	Paddington–Windsor	QV
14.04.1882		Basingstoke–Windsor	QV from south of France
28.04.1882	12.50pm	Windsor–Paddington	King & Queen Netherlands
09.05.1882	10.50am	Windsor–Paddington	QV
12.05.1882	5.25pm	Paddington–Windsor	QV
19.05.1882	7.55pm	Windsor–Ballater	QV
20.06.1882	2.50pm	Ballater–Windsor	QV arr.Windsor 8.50am 21.06
13.07.1882	4.40pm	Windsor–Paddington	QV
	7.35pm	Paddington–Windsor	
19.07.1882		Windsor–Basingstoke	QV
14.11.1882	2.00pm	Ballater–Windsor	QV arr.Windsor 8.50am 15.11
18.11.1882	10.18am	Windsor–Paddington	QV
	4.30pm	Paddington–Windsor	
21.11.1882	11.15am	Paddington–Windsor	?
	3.30pm	Windsor–Paddington	
04.12.1882	10.55am	Windsor–Paddington	QV
	1.15pm	Paddington–Windsor	
12.12.1882	4.20pm	Windsor–Paddington	QV
	6.30pm	Paddington–Windsor	
13.02.1883		Basingstoke–Windsor	QV
05.03.1883	11.25am	Windsor–Paddington	QV
07.03.1883	5.28pm	Paddington–Windsor	QV
12.03.1883	11.25am	Windsor–Paddington	QV
14.03.1883	5.28pm	Paddington–Windsor	QV
25.05.1883		Windsor–Ballater	QV
23.06.1883	3.20pm	Ballater–Windsor	QV arr.Windsor 9.15am 24.06
20.11.1883	2.00pm	Ballater–Windsor	QV
22.03.1884	4.40pm	Windsor–Paddington	QV
	6.20pm	Paddington–Windsor	
24.05.1884	8.35pm	Windsor–Ballater	QV
24.06.1884	2.50pm	Ballater–Windsor	QV arr.Windsor 8.50am 25.06
12.07.1884	4.40pm	Windsor–Paddington	QV
	6.40pm	Paddington–Windsor	
19.11.1884	2.00pm	Ballater–Windsor	QV
09.12.1884	4.40pm	Windsor–Paddington	QV
	6.10pm	Paddington–Windsor	
17.03.1885	3.35pm	Windsor–Paddington	QV
19.03.1885	4.05pm	Paddington–Windsor	QV
12.05.1885	4.00pm	Windsor–Paddington	QV
14.05.1885	5.35pm	Paddington–Windsor	QV
16.06.1885	2.50pm	Ballater–Windsor	QV arr.Windsor 8.50am 17.06
03.07.1885	5.05pm	Windsor–Paddington	QV
	7.00pm	Paddington–Windsor	
17.11.1885	2.50pm	Ballater–Windsor	QV
11.12.1885	4.35pm	Windsor–Paddington	QV
	6.20pm	Paddington–Windsor	

Date	Train		Remarks
26.02.1886	2.10pm	Windsor–Paddington	QV
	5.30pm	Paddington–Windsor	
03.03.1886	11.20am	Windsor–Paddington	QV
05.03.1886	5.03pm	Paddington–Windsor	QV
17.03.1886	1.15pm	Paddington–Windsor	QV
20.03.1886	10.40am	Windsor–Paddington	QV
	1.15pm	Paddington–Windsor	
22.03.1886	11.20am	Windsor–Paddington	QV
25.03.1886	1.15pm	Paddington–Windsor	QV
29.03.1886	3.25pm	Windsor–Paddington	QV
	6.40pm	Paddington–Windsor	
02.04.1886	10.05am	Windsor–Paddington	QV
	1.25pm	Paddington–Windsor	
05.04.1886	10.20am	Windsor–Paddington	QV
	1.15pm	Paddington–Windsor	
08.04.1886	4.00pm	Windsor–Paddington	QV
	6.40pm	Paddington–Windsor	
01.05.1886	11.10am	Windsor–Paddington	QV Colonial & Indian Exhibition R.Albert Hl
06.05.1886	5.30pm	Paddington–Windsor	QV
13.05.1886		Liverpool–Windsor	QV arr.Windsor 3.00pm (Exh. of Navigation)
21.05.1886	10.00am	Windsor–Paddington	QV
	12.25pm	Paddington–Windsor	
26.05.1886		Windsor–Ballater	QV
24.06.1886		Ballater–Windsor	QV
10.07.1886	4.30pm	Windsor–Paddington	QV
	7.20pm	Paddington–Windsor	
15.07.1886	10.00am	Windsor–Paddington	QV
	12.25pm	Paddington–Windsor	
03.11.1886		Edinburgh–Windsor	QV arr.Windsor 9.15am 04.11
11.11.1886	3.30pm	Windsor–Paddington	QV
	5.35pm	Paddington–Windsor	
19.11.1886	4.35pm	Windsor–Paddington	QV
	6.20pm	Paddington–Windsor	
02.03.1887	11.35am	Windsor–Paddington	QV
04.03.1887	5.05pm	Paddington–Windsor	QV
17.03.1887	11.35am	Windsor–Paddington	QV
19.03.1887	4.50pm	Paddington–Windsor	QV
09.05.1887	11.20am	Windsor–Paddington	QV
11.05.1887	6.40pm	Paddington–Windsor	QV
14.05.1887	3.20pm	Windsor–Paddington	QV
	7.05pm	Paddington–Windsor	
20.05.1887	8.10pm	Windsor–Ballater	QV
16.06.1887	2.50pm	Ballater–Windsor	QV
20.06.1887	11.20am	Windsor–Paddington	QV Golden Jubilee
29.06.1887	3.05pm	Windsor–Paddington	QV
	7.xxpm	Paddington–Windsor	
02.07.1887	12.55pm	Windsor–Paddington	QV
	7.50pm	Paddington–Windsor	
04.07.1887	11.10am	Windsor–Paddington	QV
	1.30pm	Paddington–Windsor	
13.07.1887	3.35pm	Windsor–Hatfield	QV arr.Windsor 8.20pm
	7.10pm	Hatfield–Windsor	
25.11.1887		Ballater–Windsor	
16.12.1887	12.35pm	Windsor–Paddington	QV
	4.05pm	Paddington–Windsor	
23.02.1888	11.05am	Windsor–Paddington	QV
25.02.1888	5.05pm	Paddington–Windsor	QV
08.03.1888	11.05am	Windsor–Paddington	QV
10.03.1888	11.05pm	Paddington–Windsor	QV

TIME TABLE.

FRIDAY, MAY 21st, 1897.

Miles distant from Windsor.	Station		A.M. / P.M.	Remarks
—	**Windsor**	...depart	A.M. 11 35	To precede the 11.35 a.m. Ordinary Train from Windsor.
$\frac{1}{8}$	Windsor Yard	„	11 40	
$2\frac{5}{8}$	Slough (through West Curve ...	pass	11 46	The Royal Train will travel on the Main Line between Slough (West Curve) and Didcot (East Junction).
$6\frac{1}{4}$	Taplow	„	11 51	
8	Maidenhead	„	11 54	
10	Waltham Siding	„	11 57	
$13\frac{3}{8}$	Ruscombe Siding	„	P.M. 12 1	
$14\frac{7}{8}$	Twyford	„	12 4	
18	Sonning Siding	„	12 8	
$19\frac{3}{4}$	Reading	„	12 11	Unless the 10.50 a.m. Train from Paddington can leave Reading exactly to time it must follow the Royal Train from Reading.
$20\frac{3}{4}$	Reading West Junction	„	12 13	The 10.55 a.m. Milk Train from Paddington must be kept back at Sonning until the Royal Train has passed Reading East Junction.
$21\frac{1}{2}$	Scours Lane Junction	„	12 14	
$22\frac{5}{8}$	Tilehurst	„	12 16	
$25\frac{1}{4}$	Pangbourne	„	12 20	
$28\frac{5}{8}$	Goring and Streatley	„	12 24	
$32\frac{1}{4}$	Cholsey and Moulsford	„	12 29	
$34\frac{5}{8}$	Moreton Cutting	„	12 32	
$36\frac{3}{4}$	Didcot (through Avoiding Line) ...	„	12 36	
$38\frac{1}{2}$	Appleford Crossing	„	12 39	
40	Culham	„	12 41	
42	Radley	„	12 44	
$44\frac{7}{8}$	Kennington Junction	„	12 48	
$47\frac{1}{8}$	Oxford	„	12 52	
$49\frac{1}{4}$	Wolvercot Siding...	„	12 55	
$49\frac{7}{8}$	Wolvercot Junction	„	12 56	
$52\frac{1}{2}$	Kidlington	„	1 0	
$54\frac{3}{4}$	Bletchington	„	1 3	
$58\frac{7}{8}$	Heyford	„	1 9	The 12.10 p.m. Train from Oxford must be worked punctually to Heyford, and shunt there for the Pilot and Royal Train to pass.
$61\frac{3}{4}$	Somerton	„	1 13	
$63\frac{7}{8}$	Aynho	„	1 16	
$66\frac{1}{8}$	King's Sutton	„	1 19	The running of the 12.20 p.m. Train from Birmingham must be so regulated as to ensure its arrival at Banbury after the Royal Train has left that Station. The Locomotive department to arrange.
$67\frac{3}{4}$	Astrop Siding	„	1 21	
$69\frac{3}{4}$	**Banbury**	arr.	1 25	Refreshments.
		dep.	1 35	
$73\frac{3}{8}$	Cropredy	pass	1 42	At Leamington, the Royal Train will be run to and brought to a stand at the Great Western Down Goods Loop Line Platform, where the Carriages will be examined and the Engine detached, and the Great Western Pilot Engine attached at the rear. The Pilot Engine will then draw the Train to the Up Great Western Main Line, clear of the points, when the L. & N.W. Engine (which must be standing on the Junction Loop) will be attached to the front of the Royal Train, and proceed with it on to the L. & N. W. Down Line for Derby.
$78\frac{1}{2}$	Fenny Compton	„	1 49	
$82\frac{3}{4}$	Greaves Siding	„	1 55	
$83\frac{5}{8}$	Southam Road and Harbury	„	1 56	
$86\frac{3}{4}$	Fosse Road	„	2 0	
$89\frac{5}{8}$	**Leamington**	... arrive	2 5	

For full details as to the working at Leamington Station, see Mr. MURPHY's Local Notice.

Part of the timetable for Queen Victoria's journey to Sheffield and Ballater 21st May, 1897. *Madame Tussaud's Collection*

TIME TABLE

SHOWING THE STATIONS AT WHICH

HER MAJESTY'S TRAIN

WILL STOP ON THE JOURNEY

From Windsor to Holyhead

(Admiralty Pier),

Via WOLVERHAMPTON (G. W. Ry., Low Level) and STAFFORD,

On Monday, the 2nd and Tuesday, the 3rd April, 1900.

Name of Railway.	Name of Station.	Distance from Windsor.	Time of Arrival.	Time of Departure
		Miles.	P.M.	P.M.
Great Western	Windsor	...	...	9 30
	Leamington	89⅝	11 56	A.M. 12 6
London & North Western	Wolverhampton (Low Level)	125¼	A.M. 1 6	1 13
	Llandudno Junc.	230¾	3 45	7 45
	Holyhead (Admiralty Pier)	271¼	9 0	

This elaborate timetable card would have been placed in the Queen's vehicle.

Date	Train		Remarks
08.05.1888	11.00am	Windsor–Paddington	QV
10.05.1888	5.25pm	Paddington–Windsor	QV
21.05.1888	8.20pm	Windsor–Ballater	QV
20.06.1888		Ballater–Windsor	QV
12.07.1888	4.30pm	Windsor–Paddington	QV
	6.45pm	Paddington–Windsor	
15.11.1888		Ballater–Windsor	QV arr.Windsor 8.50am 16.11
27.11.1888	10.50am	Windsor–Paddington	QV
	12.30pm	Paddington–Windsor	
06.06.1889	8.20pm	Windsor–Ballater	QV
25.06.1889		Ballater–Windsor	QV
22.08.1889		Windsor–Llanderfel	QV
20.11.1889		Ballater–Windsor	QV arr.Windsor 9.10am 21.11
22.05.1890	8.50pm	Windsor–Ballater	QV
20.06.1890	2.50pm	Ballater–Windsor	QV 'difficulty with locking' at Windsor
27.06.1890		Windsor–Paddington	QV 'after luncheon'
19.11.1890		Ballater–Windsor	QV arr.Windsor 9.10am 20.11
21.05.1891	1.35pm	Windsor–Ballater	QV (train ran via Derby)
19.06.1091		Ballater–Windsor	QV arr.Windsor 8.59am 20.06
20.11.1891	2.15pm	Ballater–Windsor	QV arr.Windsor 9.10am 21.11
20.05.1892		Windsor–Ballater	QV
21.06.1892	3.00pm	Ballater–Windsor	QV
17.11.1892	2.15pm	Ballater–Windsor	QV arr.Windsor 9.05am 18.11
19.05.1893	8.20pm	Windsor–Ballater	QV
20.06.1893		Ballater–Windsor	QV arr.Windsor 9.05am 21.06
17.11.1893		Ballater–Windsor	QV arr.Windsor 9.10am 18.11
21.05.1894	11.05am	Windsor–Ballater	QV train ran via Manchester
20.06.1894	3.00pm	Ballater–Windsor	QV arr.Windsor 9.00am 21.06
13.11.1894	2.15pm	Ballater–Windsor	QV arr.Windsor 9.20am 14.11
28.05.1895		Windsor–Ballater	QV
21.06.1895		Ballater–Windsor	QV
26.05.1895	8.25pm	Windsor–Ballater	QV
21.05.1897	11.35am	Windsor–Sheffield	QV
16.06.1897	3.00pm	Ballater–Windsor	QV arr.Windsor 9.00am 17.06
21.06.1897	11.50am	Windsor–Paddington	QV 60th Anniversary Dinner†
26.02.1898	5.20pm	Paddington–Windsor	QV
17.05.1899	5.20pm	Paddington–Windsor	QV
21.07.1899	4.10pm	Windsor–Gosport	QV
10.11.1899	3.30pm	Ballater–Windsor	QV arr.Windsor 8.45am 11.11
15.11.1899	11.30am	Windsor–Bristol	QV to open Royal Convalescent Home
15.11.1899	4.10pm	Bristol–Windsor	QV arr.Windsor 6.30pm
20.11.1899	11.00am	Portsmouth–Windsor	Emperor/Empress of Germany
24.11.1899		Windsor–Blenheim & bk	Emperor of Germany
25.11.1899		Windsor–Wolferton	Emperor/Empress of Germany
28.12.1899	10.30am	Windsor–Gosport	QV for Osborne
20.02.1900	11.45am	Gosport–Windsor	QV arr.Windsor 1.55pm
08.03.1900	11.50am	Windsor–Paddington	QV
10.03.1900	5.00pm	Paddington–Windsor	QV
02.04.1900	9.30pm	Windsor–Holyhead	QV en route to Ireland
27.04.1900		Holyhead–Windsor	QV arr.Windsor 5.25pm
10.05.1900	11.35am	Windsor–Paddington	QV
12.05.1900	5.37pm	Paddington–Windsor	QV
22.05.1900	9.10pm	Windsor–Ballater	QV
20.06.1900	4.05pm	Ballater–Windsor	QV arr.Windsor 8.45am 21.06
28.06.1900	2.55pm	Paddington–Windsor	The Khedive of Egypt & Suite
11.07.1900	3.00pm	Windsor–Paddington	QV
	7.00pm	Paddington–Windsor	
20.07.1900	10.30am	Windsor–Gosport	QV for Osborne
07.11.1900	3.30pm	Ballater–Windsor	QV arr.Windsor 8.45am 08.11

Date	Train		Remarks
18.12.1900	11.45am	Windsor–Gosport	QV Her Last Journey
02.02.1901	FUNERAL	OF QUEEN VICTORIA	See Chapter Eight
05.02.1901	1.00pm	Windsor–Paddington	The Kaiser and other guests
05.02.1901	7.30pm	Paddington–Windsor	The King
07.02.1901	3.15pm	Windsor–Paddington	The King & Queen
16.02.1901	1.00pm	Paddington–Windsor	'Special Passenger Train'
18.02.1901	3.15pm	Windsor–Paddington	'Special Passenger Train'
30.03.1901	4.30pm	Paddington–Windsor	?
09.04.1901	1.00pm	Windsor–Paddington	?
	7.00pm	Paddington–Windsor	
13.04.1901	10.30pm	Windsor–Paddington	28 minute timing, Note (c)
25.05.1901	4.45pm	Paddington–Windsor	?
29.01.1902	3.20pm	Windsor–Paddington	28 minute timing
17.05.1902	5.00pm	Paddington–Windsor	27 minute timing
22.05.1902	12.30pm	Windsor–Paddington	28 minute timing
23.06.1902	12.00nn	Windsor–Paddington	28 minute timing
23.08.1902	3.53pm	Paddington–Windsor	Shah of Persia
23.08.1902	5.55pm	Windsor–Crystal P.	Shah of Persia
17.11.1902	6.35pm	Paddington–Windsor	The King & Queen
17.11.1902	4.45pm	Dover–Windsor	King of Portugal arr.7.15pm
19.11.1902		Wolferton–Windsor	The Queen arr.W. 3.28pm
24.11.1902	10.25am	Windsor–Handborough	King of Portugal
24.11.1902	11.20am	Windsor–Paddington	The King & Queen
14.01.1903	12.40pm	Paddington–Windsor	The King
	4.30pm	Windsor–Paddington	
20.01.1903	5.00pm	Paddington–Windsor	The King & Queen
04.02.1903	1.30pm	Windsor–Rowsley	?
09.02.1903	12.45pm	Windsor–Paddington	?
30.05.1903	4.35pm	Paddington–Windsor	The King
06.06.1903	3.30pm	Windsor–Paddington	25 minute timing
15.06.1903	3.05pm	Paddington–Windsor	The King & Queen
22.06.1903	12.00nn	Windsor–Paddington	?
16.11.1903	5.25pm	Paddington–Windsor	The King & Queen (28 min)
17.11.1903	1.05pm	Portsmouth D.–Windsor	King & Queen of Italy
19.11.1903	10.30am	Windsor–Paddington	King & Queen of Italy
	3.45pm	Paddington–Windsor	
21.11.1903	9.30am	Windsor–Portsmouth D.	King & Queen of Italy
23.11.1903	11.05am	Windsor–Paddington	The King & Queen (28 min)
01.02.1904	12.00nn	Windsor–Paddington	The King & Queen
08.02.1904	12.45pm	Paddington–Windsor	The King & Queen
11.02.1904	11.50am	Windsor–Paddington	The King & Queen
21.05.1904	4.45pm	Paddington–Windsor	The King & Queen
26.05.1904	11.45am	Windsor–Paddington	The King & Queen
	6.00pm	Paddington–Windsor	
30.05.1904	10.25am	Windsor–Paddington	The King & Queen
14.11.1904	5.15pm	Paddington–Windsor	The King & Queen
15.11.1904	1.00pm	Portsmouth–Windsor	King & Queen of Portugal
17.11.1904	11.45am	Windsor–Paddington	King & Queen of Portugal
	3.10pm	Paddington–Windsor	
21.11.1904	11.30am	Windsor–Rowsley	King & Queen of Portugal
21.11.1904	11.40am	Windsor–Paddington	The King & Queen
21.01.1905	2.00pm	Wolferton–Windsor	Queen & P/Princess o.Wales
30.01.1905	11.20am	Windsor–Paddington	The King & Queen
09.06.1905	12.00nn	Paddington–Windsor	The King/King of Spain
16.06.1905	12.00nn	Windsor–Paddington	The King & Queen
13.11.1905	10.25am	Wolferton–Windsor	The King & Queen (a.1.30pm)
13.11.1905	1.50pm	Portsmouth–Windsor	The King of Greece (a.4pm)
15.11.1905	11.55am	Windsor–Paddington	The King of Greece
	3.30pm	Paddington–Windsor	
20.11.1905	10.45am	Windsor–Paddington	King/Queen & King of Greece
20.01.1906		Wolferton–Windsor	The Queen arr.W.6.30pm

'Star' class 4—6—0 No. 4021 *King Edward* suitably decorated for King Edward VII's funeral train.

The Railway & Travel Monthly

Date	Train		Remarks
30.01.1906	12.30pm	Windsor–Paddington	?
30.01.1906	4.00pm	Windsor–Wolferton	?
18.06.1906		Wolferton–Windsor	The King arr.W. 6.30pm
12.11.1906		Wolferton–Windsor	The King & Queen a.W. 1pm
12.11.1906	1.10pm	Portsmouth–Windsor	King/Queen Norway a.W. 3.20pm
14.11.1906	11.05am	Windsor–Paddington	?
	3.20pm	Paddington–Windsor	
19.11.1906	11.00am	Windsor–Paddington	?
15.12.1906	10.20am	Paddington–Windsor	?
	4.00pm	Windsor–Paddington	
21.01.1907		Wolferton–Windsor	The Queen arr.W. 5.12pm
29.01.1907	11.30am	Windsor–Paddington	The King & Queen
11.11.1907	9.55am	Wolferton–Windsor	King & Queen a.W. 1.05pm
11.11.1907	1.30pm	Portsmouth–Windsor	Emp./Empress Germany arr. Windsor 3.30pm
13.11.1907	11.20am	Windsor–Paddington	Emperor/Empress Germany
	3.00pm	Paddington–Windsor	
14.11.1907	9.35am	Windsor–Paddington	Empress of Germany
	12.10pm	Paddington–Windsor	
16.11.1907	9.45am	Windsor–Paddington	Empress of Germany
16.11.1907	11.00am	Windsor–Paddington	Emperor of Germany
16.11.1907	3.15pm	Paddington–Windsor	Emp./Empress of Germany
18.11.1907	11.00am	Windsor–Hinton Adm.	Emp./Empress of Germany
18.11.1907	11.10am	Windsor–Paddington	The King & Queen
21.01.1908	2.15pm	Wolferton–Windsor	The Queen & P/Pr of Wales
28.05.1908	2.50pm	Paddington–Windsor	President of France
	6.10pm	Windsor–Paddington	These trains hauled by loco. 'The President'
15.06.1908	4.15pm	Paddington–Windsor	The King & Queen
22.06.1908	12.00nn	Windsor–Paddington	The King & Queen
16.11.1908	10.20am	Wolferton–Windsor	King & Queen a.W. 1.30pm
16.11.1908	2.00pm	Portsmouth–Windsor	The King & Queen of Sweden
18.11.1908	11.50am	Windsor–Paddington	The King & Queen of Sweden
	3.30pm	Paddington–Windsor	
21.11.1908	11.45am	Windsor–Paddington	The King & Queen of Sweden
23.11.1908	1.00pm	Windsor–Wolferton	The King & Queen
15.11.1909	10.20am	Wolferton–Windsor	King & Queen & K/Q Norway
15.11.1909	1.40pm	Portsmouth–Windsor	The King of Portugal
17.11.1909	11.50am	Windsor–Paddington	The King of Portugal
	3.30pm	Paddington–Windsor	
22.11.1909	10.30am	Windsor–Paddington	The King & Queen, King of Portugal, Queen of Norway
21.01.1910	1.55pm	Wolferton–Windsor	The Queen & P/PR of Wales
21.01.1910	5.00pm	Paddington–Windsor	The King
20.05.1910	FUNERAL OF KING EDWARD VII		See Chapter Eight
24.06.1910	12.50pm	Paddington–Windsor	The King & Queen
26.10.1910	10.45am	Paddington–Windsor	The King & Queen Funeral of
	12.30pm	Windsor–Paddington	Prince Francis of Teck
19.11.1910	12.25pm	Wolferton–Windsor	King & Queen a.W. 3.35pm
28.11.1910	10.00am	Windsor–Paddington	The King
28.11.1910	1.00pm	Windsor–Wolferton	The Queen
21.01.1911	12.25pm	Wolferton–Windsor	The King & Queen
02.02.1911	12.00nn	Windsor–Paddington	The King & Queen
06.05.1911	11.45am	Paddington–Windsor	?
	xx.xxpm	Windsor–Paddington	
10.06.1911	10.25am	Paddington–Windsor	?
	xx.xxpm	Windsor–Paddington	
17.06.1911	10.30am	Windsor–Paddington	The King & Queen
05.07.1911	11.00am	Windsor–Paddington	The King & Queen
28.02.1912	10.45am	Paddington–Windsor	The King & Queen
	12.30pm	Windsor–Paddington	

Date	Train		Remarks
06.05.1912	11.15am	Paddington–Windsor	?
	xx.xxpm	Windsor–Paddington	
24.06.1912	10.00am	Windsor–Paddington	The King & Queen
18.11.1912	11.35am	Wolferton–Windsor	King & Queen a.W. 2.45pm
25.11.1912	12.45pm	Windsor–Worksop	The King & Queen
20.01.1913	11.35am	Wolferton–Windsor	King & Queen a.W. 2.45pm
02.04.1913	10.10am	Windsor–Paddington	The King & Queen
06.05.1913	11.15am	Paddington–Windsor	The King & Queen
	xx.xxpm	Windsor–Paddington	
26.06.1913	9.00am	Paddington–Windsor	President of France
	11.30am	Windsor–Paddington	
15.11.1913	11.35am	Wolferton–Windsor	King & Queen a.W. 2.45pm
17.11.1913	5.35pm	Paddington–Windsor	Archduke Ferdinand Austria
21.11.1913	11.20pm	Windsor–Paddington	Archduke Ferdinand Austria
24.11.1913	10.10am	Windsor–Fencehouses	The King & Queen
06.05.1914	11.15am	Paddington–Windsor	The King & Queen
	xx.xxpm	Windsor–Paddington	
06.05.1915	11.00am	Paddington–Windsor	The King
	12.45pm	Windsor–Paddington	
22.07.1915	9.00am	Windsor–Leamington	The King
23.07.1915	4.35pm	Adderley Pk–Windsor	The King a.Windsor 7.15pm
02.09.1915	8.30am	Windsor–Lyminge	The King
02.09.1915	1.45pm	Cheriton Halt–Windsor	The King a.Windsor 3.35pm
07.09.1915	9.45am	Wind.–Shirehampton etc	The King & Queen
10.09.1915	1.15pm	Torquay–Windsor	King & Queen arr.W. 4.55pm
25.04.1916	10.35am	Windsor–Paddington	The King & Queen
	12.25pm	Paddington–Windsor	
02.05.1916	1.35pm	Windsor–Paddington	The King & Queen
	5.30pm	Paddington–Windsor	
05.05.1916	9.25am	Windsor–Bulford	King arr.Windsor 3.25pm
	1.30pm	Bulford–Windsor	
09.05.1916	10.25am	Windsor–Paddington	The King & Queen
	4.15pm	Paddington–Windsor	
10.05.1916	9.55am	Windsor–Paddington	The King & Queen
	xx.xx	Paddington–Windsor	
27.09.1916	9.25am	Windsor–Bulford	King arr.Windsor 3.36pm
	1.30pm	Bulford–Windsor	
19.03.1917	10.30am	Paddington–Windsor	The King & Queen
	12.50pm	Windsor–Paddington	
·17.04.1917	9.40am	Windsor–Bulford	King arr.Windsor 3.36pm
	1.45pm	Bulford–Windsor	
20.04.1917	10.20am	Windsor–Paddington	The King & Queen
	4.15pm	Paddington–Windsor	
01.05.1917	9.40am	Windsor–Bulford	King arr.Windsor 2.50pm
	1.00pm	Bulford–Windsor	
16.09.1917	10.00pm	Windsor–Glasgow	The King
18.09.1917	9.00am	Windsor–Coventry	The Queen arr.W. 7.20pm
	5.00pm	Coventry–Windsor	
21.09.1917		Glasgow–Windsor	The King arr.W. 7.30am
01.11.1917	10.27am	Paddington–Windsor	The King & Queen, Prince
	12.30pm	Windsor–Paddington	Christian's Funeral
08.04.1918	5.30pm	Wind.–Skellingthorpe	The King & Queen
11.04.1918	1.30pm	Leadenham–Windsor	King & Queen arr.W. 6.20pm
30.04.1918	9.30am	Windsor–Chatham	King & Queen arr.W. 2.30pm
	1.00pm	Chatham–Windsor	
30.08.1918	9.00am	Windsor–West St.Leonards	King arr.Windsor 3.45pm
	1.30pm	West St.Leonards–Windsor	
16.09.1918	9.00am	Windsor–Porton	The King
16.09.1918	4.45pm	Salisbury–Windsor	King arr.Windsor 6.30pm
28.04.1924		Swindon–Windsor	The King & Queen visit to Swindon Works

SPECIAL OR EXCURSION PASSENGER TRAIN JOURNAL

(For full instructions in making out this Journal, see Circular No. 4829 dated January, 1935)

B.R. 29752/7

UP

1X01 { Description of Train 19.00 m. from Matlock — Windsor & S. Br. C

GROVE.

Fri day, May 10 19 68

Stations and Dividing Points Between each District	Actual Time of				Late away from Station Mins.	Minutes Lost							Minutes Gained		Vehicles				Tare Weight in Tons or where load is altered	Remarks as to cause of Detention at Stations, Signals, etc., also information shewing the various places where Train is crossed from M.L. to R.L., or vice versa
	Arrival		Departure			At Stations				By Signals	By Eng. Checks	By Exceptional Causes	At Station	By Engine	Attached		Detached			
						Att'ch'g or De- taching	Other Station Delays	Waiting Conn- ections	By Engine						Loaded	Empty	Loaded	Empty		
	H.	M.	H.	M.																
Heyford			21 45		6										8					
Wolverton Jct			21 58		6			4												
Oxford			22 02		6															
Didcot E. Jct			22 15		7				1											
Reading			22 32		5								2							
Slough East			22 51										3							
Windsor	23 00																8			
TOTALS						5							7 8		8					

Minutes Late Leaving District or at Destination

Total of all Minutes in District
Lost 5 Gained

Scale of Weather during Journey, if Wet, Frost, Fog or Snow and between what Points — wet

General Remarks, e.g. Occurrences to Train, Causes of Delay, whether Coaches fully and correctly labelled, properly heated and suggestions for improvement of Working, etc.

Show "Yes" or "No" if Train is formed in accordance with programme, etc

---

FORMATION OF TRAIN AT COMMENCEMENT OF JOURNEY

Vehicles to be shewn IN ORDER FROM ENGINE

	VEHICLE				
Region	Number	Tare Weight Tons	Description	Lav. or Corr.	FROM	TO
	5133	BK 1		Matlock	Windsor
	799		Kng E Saloon		
	499		Dining Saloon		
	6901		Saloon		
	2023		Sleeping Car		
	806		Saloon		
	325		Dining Saloon		
	31209		Power Bk		

B.R. 29752/7

WORKING OF GUARDS, TICKET COLLECTORS, ETC.

Head Guard to be shewn as H.G.
Senior Guards to be shewn as S.G.
Train Ticket Collector to be shewn as T.C.
Travelling Porter to be shewn as T.P.

Name	Grade	From	To	Stop at
G. Buckingley	G.	Banbury	Windsor	

TRAIN ENGINE WORKING

No. of Engine	From	To	Name of Enginemen	Stationed at
3226	Banbury	Windsor	Yates	Banbury
3223				

ASSISTANT ENGINES

No. of Engine	From	To	Whether Second Engine assisted or worked home

SPECIAL OR EXCURSION PASSENGER TRAIN JOURNAL

Mr. F. D. Patterson

BRITISH RAILWAYS (W.R.)

Reading STATION, W.R.

19.00 Train Matlock to Windsor & Slou

1X01 Date May 10 68

The guard's journal for the last Royal train to operate on the Windsor branch, 1900 hrs Matlock to Windsor, 10th May, 1968.

Date	Train	Remarks
05.06.1925	Windsor–Stoke and return	The King
21.04.1927	Windsor–Cardiff & return	The King
24.04.1928	11.45am Windsor–Wool & return	The King
28.01.1936	FUNERAL OF KING GEORGE V	See Chapter Eight
18.03.1941	7.00pm Windsor–Portskewett	The King
21.03.1941	6.55am Frome–Windsor	The King arr.Windsor 8.55am
01.04.1941	Windsor–Weston-s-Mare	The King
11.12.1941	Bridgend–Windsor	The King
02.05.1942	Windsor–Bath & rtn	The King
08.05.1942	Exeter–Windsor	The King
12.02.1944	Swanage–Windsor	The King
30.03.1944	Swansea–Windsor	The King
20.04.1950	6.00pm Stratford-o-A–Windsor	The King visit to theatre
04.04.1951	10.00pm Windsor–Coventry	The King
05.04.1951	5.45pm Leamington–Windsor	The King
15.02.1952	FUNERAL OF KING GEORGE VI	See Chapter Eight
15.04.1953	10.00pm Windsor–Dumbarton	The Queen
16.04.1953	Clydebank–Windsor	The Queen arr.W. 9.45am
10.07.1953	5.15pm Llangollen–Windsor	The Queen arr.W. 10.15pm
26.03.1955	Town Green–Windsor	The Queen from Grand National
12.04.1955	10.00pm Windsor–Morecambe	The Queen
14.04.1955	Colne–Windsor	The Queen arr.W. 9.45am
05.04.1956	10.45pm Windsor–Hull	Duke of Edinburgh
16.04.1956	11.15pm Windsor–Bristol	The Queen
22.04.1957	Windsor–Hagley	The Queen
08.11.1957	10.15pm Leicester–Windsor	Duke of Edinburgh
27.01.1958	10.30pm Wolferton–Windsor	The Queen
21.03.1958	10.30pm Liverpool–Windsor	Duke of Edinburgh
05.12.1958	4.20pm Bristol–Windsor	The Queen arr.W. 7.06pm
08.04.1959	9.30am Windsor–Banbury	The Queen
08.04.1959	5.15pm Henley–Windsor	The Queen
24.03.1961	11.10pm Edinburgh–Windsor	Duke of Edinburgh
12.05.1961	Marylebone–Windsor	Duke of Edinburgh
18.06.1961	Windsor–Corby	The Queen
27.07.1962	Totnes–Windsor	The Queen
21.10.1962	11.10pm Windsor–Reading	Duke of Edinburgh (fwd by ordinary service to Salop)
26.10.1962	Llanwern–Windsor	The Queen
29.04.1963	Windsor–Kemble & bk	The Queen
10.05.1963	Pontypool Rd–Windsor	The Queen
30.04.1964	10.55pm Windsor–Cardiff	Duke of Edinburgh
24.05.1964	Birmingham(SH)–Windsor	The Queen
15.06.1964	Barnwell–Windsor	The Queen
08.08.1965	Windsor–Holyhead	The Queen
03.04.1966	Windsor–Buckingham	The Queen
04.04.1966	Bletchley–Windsor	The Queen
23.04.1966	12.40pm Stonehouse–Windsor	The Queen
03.06.1966	Castle Cary–Windsor	The Queen
17.03.1967	Cosford–Windsor	The Queen
29.05.1967	11.05pm Windsor–Nidd Bridge	Duke of Edinburgh
07.08.1967	Windsor–Soton Docks	The Queen
15.03.1968	3.15pm Moreton-in-Msh–Windsor	Duke of Edinburgh a.W.4.45pm
30.04.1968	10.45pm Windsor–Birmingham(NS)	Duke of Edinburgh
10.05.1968	7.00pm Matlock–Windsor	The Queen arr.W. 11pm

THE LAST ROYAL TRAIN OVER THE WINDSOR BRANCH

NOTES

Sources of information: The Public Record Office; The Royal Archives; BR Records; *Railway Reminiscences* by G.P. Neele (for some Balmoral journeys).

Only those journeys of the Monarch (&/or consort) and the equivalent foreign Kings/Queens or Head of State are listed here. There were, of course, special train journeys by other relatives (but far fewer), and very occasionally the Monarch used ordinary trains; these are not listed either. There are gaps in the records available, principally 1849–1864, 1889–1899 (for the Paddington trains), 1919–1924, so this list cannot claim to contain every Royal Train used by the Monarch on the Windsor branch. But it is sufficiently comprehensive for the reader to understand the importance of the Castle to the line.

Between 1854–1861 the Balmoral journeys ran from the SWR station.

(a) last use of Broad Gauge RT on branch? (10.07.1874)

(b) via Basingstoke

(c) Queen Victoria was allowed 35 mins

BG=Broad Gauge; NG=Narrow Gauge; QV=Queen Victoria; RAO=Return as ordered; ?=Royal Train, but occupant not identified.

†First use of new Royal Train.

Appendix Four

Windsor Station Masters

1854	William B. Page
1861	John Matthews
1867–1876	Hubert Simmons (Resigned)
1882	John George Smythe
1888	Frederick H. Frazer
1891	F.H. Frazer
1891–1903	Sidney Frederick Johnson (to SM Paddington)
1903–1925	Samuel Thomas Maun (Retired)
1925	O.T. Fenner
1930	O.T. Fenner
1932	O.T. Fenner
1947	O.T. Fenner
1950	E.H. Lucking
1956	E.H. Lucking
1962	E.H. Lucking (last SM at Windsor)

Sources:

Billing's Directory & Gazetteer 1854

Kelly's Directory 1861, 1891, 1895, 1899, 1930, 1932, 1947, 1950, 1956

GWR Magazine

Ernest Struggles, or the Life of a Station Master (H. Simmons)

There is a reference in a letter in the Eton College Records dated 7th December, 1849 ('. . . if you will ask Perkins to ask Mr Howell at Windsor for his wages – he will get them – and pray let him in future always do so').

Mr Howell was station superintendent at Slough, and possibly also covered Windsor, after opening, at first?

Appendix Five

'The Railways and the Windsor Review'

Although the interest of the general public in the recent volunteer review at Windsor may have somewhat waned, a few details concerning the part which the railways played in conveying such an immense number of men safely and efficiently will, we are sure, command the attention of most of our readers. We have, at present only received statistics from one of the companies engaged in the conveyance of troops to Windsor – viz, the Great Western, but the general outline of arrangements on that system may be taken as applying to the regulations, in force on the South Western. The total number of men conveyed to and from Windsor is estimated at from 55,000 to 56,000 and of these the Great Western carried 26,000, the metropolitan volunteers being despatched to and from Windsor and the provincial regiments to and from Slough. The South Western Company divided the forces committed to them between their stations at Ascot, Datchet, Egham, and Virginia Water. To prevent confusion, a statement was printed and circulated amongst the railway authorities and volunteer forces showing the particular army corps to which each regiment belonged, its division and brigade, the number of conveyances required for the officers and men of each corps, the station, either provincial or metropolitan, from which it started, and the time of arrival at, and departure from, the particular station to which it was allotted, and the order of return. In addition to this the Great Western – and, we presume, the South Western – company published a statement of over forty pages for the use of their servants, giving every detail of the day's arrangements and instructions for their proper execution. This compilation gives a very fair idea of the enormous amount of labour and forethought endured by and required from the general manager and his staff on such occasions, and forms in itself a marvel of administrative ability and organisation. The block telegraph was suspended for the day as far as Slough, and platelayers were stationed every quarter of a mile, or nearer, if necessary, to signal the trains. Their posts were, as may be imagined, no sinecure, and amongst their orders was the following:

'If the preceding train has passed the next man in advance, the platelayer will show a caution signal, a green flag by day and a green light by night; but if he does not feel quite certain that the preceding train has passed the next man in advance, he must put down detonators and show his danger signals to stop the train; he must then tell the driver to draw up with great care to the tail of the train in advance. Over this part of the line between Langley and Slough and Slough and Hay Mill signal box, the engine drivers must run with great caution; and they must be prepared to stop at each platelayer they come to. The guards of the train must also keep a sharp look-out and be prepared to apply their brakes instantly if required.'

This most elaborate and carefully compiled programme was indexed, and a few of the heads may serve to give some idea of the many things that had to be thought of: forming return country trains; supply examination, labelling, lighting, and cleansing of coaches; fares and rates for volunteers, horses, troopers; instructions to guards; conveyance of public; position of London trains on down Windsor line; pilotmen; storing, disposal, composition, and arrival of special trains; extra staffs; signal boxes; spare engines; tickets for volunteers and the public; and a summary of trains, ordinary volunteers, and special. In order to facilitate the grouping of the different corps in their special trains, different coloured tickets were issued for the officers and other grades according to whether their point of departure was Paddington, Metropolitan stations, West London stations, or on other lines via London. They also bore the number and name of each corps in the centre, which number corresponded with a similar figure on the train in which the holders' corps was to travel.

The number of carriages employed in the conveyance of volunteers was 800, and these were made up into forty-seven trains, of which twenty-one were set apart for the metropolitan corps and twenty-six were devoted to bringing up forces from all points on the company's system. The storage of such an immense number of carriages after their freight had been disembarked was a matter of no small difficulty, and to place them in any one spot would have required sidings miles in extent. Room was, however, found for them at Acton, West London Junction, Uxbridge, and other convenient points to which they had of course all been allotted long before the eventful day. It may perhaps surprise some of our readers not acquainted with the inner working of railways to learn that although the company's trains started from Bristol, Birkenhead, Manchester, and numerous other intermediate stations, the last train had arrived and had discharged its passengers, who were off the company's premises, *within five minutes of the time fixed for its arrival!*

The chief difficulty in the manipulation of this vast traffic lay, however, in the return journey. As the volunteers had to leave their great coats and other impedimenta in the carriages in which they travelled, it was, of course, necessary that they should return in the same train that carried them to their destination. Each train had, therefore, to be so placed as to be in its proper order in drawing up to the platform, whether they were stored one or a dozen miles from Slough or Windsor. The arrangements had, however, been so carefully made by Mr Grierson, Mr Beasley, and their assistants that no hitch of any kind occurred, and each train drew up at the platform at its appointed time to embark the particular corps which it had conveyed to the scene of action.

The arrangements made for the conveyance of the public were planned and carried out with the same care and forethought, and the Great Western Company could have carried a very much greater number of lookers-on than those who ventured to Windsor by rail. The announcement of the number of volunteers who were to take part in the review seemed so enormous that very many people came to the conclusion that the railway companies would have all they could do to carry the corps, and that a comfortable journey to, or, at any rate, from Windsor, was out of the question so far as the general public were concerned. Such, however, was not the case; for, in spite of the fact that the Great Western station at Windsor is a *cul de sac*, and every train had, therefore, to be backed out before another could enter, that company had made arrangements to carry double the number which they did.

The massing of so many men from all parts of the country at one point in so short a time was a feat which has certainly never been accomplished before, and one which, we have no hesitation in saying, could not be managed in any country where the railways are under State control. Neither expense nor trouble was spared to make the operation successful, and the results reflect the highest credit on the railway system of the country, and more especially on the ability and forethought of the officials of the two companies more immediately concerned.

(From The Railway News, 30th July, 1881)

Appendix Six

A Note on the proposed
Windsor & Ascot Railway (GWR)

The proposal with which we are concerned here is the Windsor & Ascot Railway of 1898, which had GWR support, indeed one of its promoters was Charles Rivers Bulkeley, son of Captain Bulkeley, former Director of the GWR, who had been so much involved in bringing the broad gauge branch to the town. But, before 1898, there had been no less than nine separate schemes for a direct railway between the two towns, the first in 1871, and the ninth in 1883. Further details may be found in *The London & South Western Railway* (Vol. 2) by R.A. Williams (pub. David & Charles).

Initially planned with its own terminus at Ascot, but also to join the LSWR Aldershot branch at Ascot with a triangular junction, running powers to Aldershot were sought but were dropped when the LSWR abandoned its opposition on these terms. The Windsor & Ascot Railway Act obtained Royal Assent on 12th August, 1898 and contained a Working Agreement with the GWR which was to operate the line on the smaller company's behalf. The railway was to be built and ready for opening by 30th September, 1901.

No progress had occurred by then, however, and in its Act of 1901 the GWR transferred the powers of the Windsor & Ascot Railway to itself. A further five years was allowed for completion of the line. Yet further extensions of time were given by Acts passed in 1904 and 1909.

Meanwhile the GWR had opened a motorbus service between Windsor and Ascot on 5th April, 1905. Thereafter the chances of a railway being built must have been fairly unlikely and, eventually, the GWR obtained powers by its 1912 Act to abandon the line. The bus service was one of the longest-lived of those operated by the GWR, not being given up by the company until 31st May, 1931 when the service was taken over by the Thames Valley Traction Co.

During the years after World War I until the GWR gave up running motorbuses, the holding of race meetings at Ascot entailed the withdrawal of buses from many other depots to boost the service from Windsor. This was particularly the case during Ascot week each June and no less than 26 GWR vehicles were photographed lined up on the racecourse in 1920 (see *Railway Motor Buses and Bus Services* Vol. 2 by John Cummings pub. OPC, page 141).

The theme of the seal of the Windsor & Ascot Railway (1898) was, as might have been expected, the Sport of Kings.   *British Rail*

Appendix Seven

Passenger Counts Windsor Branch
Monday to Saturday 10th–15th February, 1969

(Note: Totals for the six days shown)

Train Down, Slough to Windsor	1st class	2nd class	Number included in previous columns from main line	Train Up, Windsor to Slough	1st class	2nd class	Number included in previous columns for beyond Slough
0608		15	10	0621 (SO)		3	2
0647		23	13	0626 (SX)	3	27	22
0708 (SO)		1	–	0656 (SO)		7	2
0715 (SX)		30	22	0700 (SX)	5	139	78
0733 (SX)	1	88	70	0721 (SO)		4	3
0747 (SO)		15	10	0726 (SX)	27	227	231
0750 (SX)		103	86	0742 (SX)	9	162	150
0809		119	93	0756 (SO)		22	19
0832 (SX)	5	307	247	0802 (SX)*	139	1102	1193
0847 (SO)		11	9	0819	61	559	443
0856 (SX)	2	135	111	0843 (SX)	23	333	236
0908 (SO)		4	1	0856 (SO)	1	17	13
0917 (SX)	1	79	67	0905 (SX)	8	184	144
0947	3	106	62	0921 (SO)		13	9
1008		51	33	0934 (SX)	6	24	24
1047	4	101	56	0956	5	75	60
1108		46	19	1021	1	68	41
1147	10	96	63	1056	2	102	63
1208	10	86	27	1121	3	77	30
1247	5	119	75	1156	3	65	38
1308	1	114	69	1221		88	34
1347	7	162	105	1256	1	127	87
1408		57	23	1321	6	74	42
1447	1	124	66	1356	2	132	45
1508	1	55	20	1421		82	42
1547	2	141	78	1456		91	40
1608 (SO)		17	9	1521		79	38
1616 (SX)		82	32	1556		124	54
1635 (SX)	3	138	68	1621 (SO)		27	6
1647 (SO)	2	41	13	1626 (SX)		87	47
1703 (SX)	3	268	192	1650 (SX)		163	117
1708 (SO)		11	2	1656 (SO)		34	14
1735 (SX)	11	327	245	1715 (SX)		99	64
1747 (SO)		20	11	1721 (SO)		14	9
1754 (SX)	23	326	309	1745 (SX)		86	46
1808 (SO)		5	–	1756 (SO)		16	8
1817 (SX)	15	371	359	1803 (SX)		73	44
1835 (SX)		285	274	1821 (SO)		29	20
1847 (SO)		14	10	1826 (SX)		24	6
1853 (SX)		54	53	1844 (SX)		40	14
1908 (SO)		8	4	1856 (SO)		20	12

The extent of the enlarged Royal waiting room behind platform 4 at Windsor can be judged from this further scene at Madame Tussaud's in 1990. Although Queen Victoria is approaching her coach in this tableaux, she, of course, never knew the Royal rooms when they were this size. Behind the Queen comes Princess Henry of Prussia and her two children, then the Prince of Wales and Prince Henry. *Author*

13th June, 1992 was the 150th anniversary of the first Royal Train from Slough to Paddington, and to mark the event the owners of the Royalty & Empire exhibition at Windsor and BR jointly arranged 'a special weekend of fun, including a steam engine in (Windsor) platform'. 'Hall' class 4−6−0 No. 6998 *Burton Agnes Hall*, in steam but static, headed former GWR Royal saloon No. 9004 on the buffer stops at Windsor. It had been intended to place 'King' class 4−6−0 No. 6024 *King Edward I* there, as more appropriate to the Royal connection, but at the last moment it was decided that the locomotive was too heavy for the River Thames bridge, and No. 6998 was substituted. *Author*

Train Down,Slough to Windsor	1st class	2nd class	Number included in previous columns from main line	Train Up,Windsor to Slough	1st class	2nd class	Number included in previous columns for beyond Slough
1917 (SX)	6	157	146	1902 (SX)		26	14
1947	1	88	62	1921 (SO)		9	9
2012		13	7	1934 (SX)		22	9
2047	1	93	88	1956		37	23
2112		24	13	2021		14	9
2147	1	87	68	2056		6	3
2212		8	3	2121		33	20
2247		41	32	2156		21	8
2312 (SO)		–		2221		18	5
2347 (SO)		16	16	2256		24	11
				2321 (SO)		2	1
	119	4682	3451		305	4915	3702

Notes
*Through to Paddington
Only four trains, the 0715 and 0750 down and the 0726 and 0802 up were booked to convey first class accommodation. This may explain the discrepancy in numbers of first class passengers, 305 'up' but only 119 'down'. Some staff may have counted such tickets as 'first', despite no first class accommodation available, others may not have done so.
Over the course of the week some 400 more passengers, or approximately 70 a day, left Windsor by train than arrived by train.
SX=Saturdays Excepted; SO=Saturdays Only.

Appendix Eight

Madame Tussaud's Exhibition at Windsor

In 1979, British Rail, faced with the maintenance of a much larger station at Windsor than it needed, but, the building being listed, able to do little about it, approached Madame Tussaud's to see if the famous waxworks would wish to open an exhibition there. The firm welcomed the idea and the long process of restoring the disused part of the station, including the Royal waiting room and the large roof built to shelter the parading troops, began. Every effort was made to achieve authenticity, right down to the colour of the decorations and furnishings. The 130 wax models were based on photographs of the actual characters present when the Royal Train pulled into Windsor Station for the celebration of Queen Victoria's Diamond Jubilee in June 1897.

'Royalty and Railways' opened on Good Friday 1983, the major exhibit being a life size reproduction of part of the Royal Train. Hauled by reproduction 4−2−2 locomotive The Queen, built by Steamtown, Carnforth, one of the two carriages in tow was actually an original 1897 saloon, rescued from use as a seaside bungalow, as mentioned in Chapter Four.

Combined rail and admission tickets were made available by BR from 1st May, 1983 at just £4 (£2 child) from Paddington or Waterloo and either route could be used for outward and return journeys. The leaflet boasted that the 'Exhibition is not a station museum, but a fascinating glimpse of Victorian England'. Later the Exhibition was renamed 'Royalty and Empire', no doubt to widen its appeal.

In January 1990 new owners L & R Leisure Group plc took over the Exhibition from Madame Tussaud's, and, although somewhat modified by the new owners, the railway element is still large and the Royal Train is still there. A visit is well worthwhile, and it also gives an opportunity to visit parts of Windsor Station otherwise unavailable to rail passengers, particularly the Royal waiting room.

The most interesting feature in this 1990 scene from the Madame Tussaud's exhibition is coach No. 9002 in the background, the *original* 1897 vehicle which formed part of the GWR Royal train until 1927. Sent to Aberporth in 1935 to become a seaside bungalow, it was rescued 50 years later and restored at Windsor station.

Author

Replica 4–2–2 locomotive No. 3041 *The Queen* under the original platform 4 canopy at Windsor, part of the Madame Tussaud's exhibition, pictured in 1990.   *Author*

Appendix Nine

The Slough and Windsor Railway Society
by Jim Gander

The society was formed in 1983 by a group of local enthusiasts when, at the time, there was concern for the future of the old GWR branch line from Slough to Windsor. It was the original intention either to purchase or lease the branch and run it, not only as a tourist attraction but as a commercial railway.

So far those aims remain frustrated but remain long term ambitions. Plans have, however, been formulated for the creation of a living steam museum and nature conservancy area in the land that formed the Slough triangle.

The society has purchased Slough Estates No. 3, a Hudswell, Clarke & Co. 0–6–0 saddle tank of 1924 vintage. It is one of only two survivals of the local system and is being restored locally for future use at the museum. The society also own a GWR 'Toad' brake van and an LNER wooden van.

The society organises excursions to places of interest to the transport enthusiast and holds weekly meetings in 'The Manor'. This is an ancient wooden GWR building of uncertain origin at Slough station. Under the care of the society it houses a small museum, library and refreshment area.

The society meets every Friday throughout the year with guest speakers on a variety of mainly transport and railway related topics. Meetings are advertised in the railway press. Visitors are welcome to just turn up. For further information please contact:

J.A. Gander
73, Seacourt Rd
Langley, Berks
SL3 8EP

John Bourne's drawing of the up station at Slough, with the Refreshment Rooms and Royal Hotel in the background, c.1845. The Royal Hotel (not owned by the GWR) fell upon hard times after the opening of the Windsor branch and it closed in 1852.
British Rail

Bibliography

RAILWAYS

GWR Records at Public Record Office, Kew (RAIL Series)

Board of Trade/Ministry of Transport Records at Public Record Office, Kew (MT series)

GWR, BR and Bradshaw's timetables

Crown, College and Railways by Raymond South (Barracuda Books) (An excellent in-depth look at the 15-year-struggle to bring railways to Windsor.)

The Locomotives of the GWR (RCTS)

History of the Great Western Railway by E.T. MacDermot (Revised Clinker) (Ian Allan)

An Historical Survey of Selected GW Stations (Vol. 4) by C.R. Potts (OPC)

The Royal Trains by C. Hamilton Ellis (Routledge & Kegan Paul)

Railway Reminiscences by G.P. Neele (re-published by EP Publishing Ltd, 1974)

Ernest Struggles, or the Life of a Station Master (Vol. 2) by Hubert Simmons (pub.1880, out of print)

Steaming Spires by Richard Tolley (David & Charles)

News Bulletin of the Middle Thames Archeological & Historical Society (in Slough Library)

The GWR Magazine, The Railway Gazette, The Railway Magazine, The Railway Times, The Railway News

Windsor & Eton Express

WINDSOR AND SLOUGH

The Story of Windsor by Maurice Bond (Local Heritage Books)

Windsor in Victorian Times by Angus Macnaghten (pub. by author)

Windsor Town and Castle by Henry Farrar (Phillimore)

Windsor and Eton by B.J.W. Hill (Batsford)

Windsor Castle by Sir Owen Morshead (Phaidon Press)

The History of Slough by Maxwell Frazer (Slough Corporation)

A Town in the Making by the Slough & Eton branch of the W.E.A. (Berkshire County Council)

The Story of Slough by Judith Hunter (Local Heritage Books)

Royal River Highway by Frank L. Dix (David & Charles)

ETON, TOWN AND COLLEGE

A Town called Eton by Selina Ballance (Eton Press Ltd)

Eton Medley by B.J.W. Hill (Winchester Publications)

Eton College Records

ROYALTY

V.R.I. Her Life and Empire by the Duke of Argyll (Eyre & Spottiswoode)

Victorian R.I. by Elizabeth Longford (World Books edition)

Life with Queen Victoria by Victor Mallet (John Murray)

The Court at Windsor by Christopher Hibbert (Longmans)

Recollections of Three Reigns by Sir Frederick Ponsonby (Eyre & Spottiswoode)

Master of the Horse Day Books at the Royal Archives, Windsor (RA MOH DB5–9)

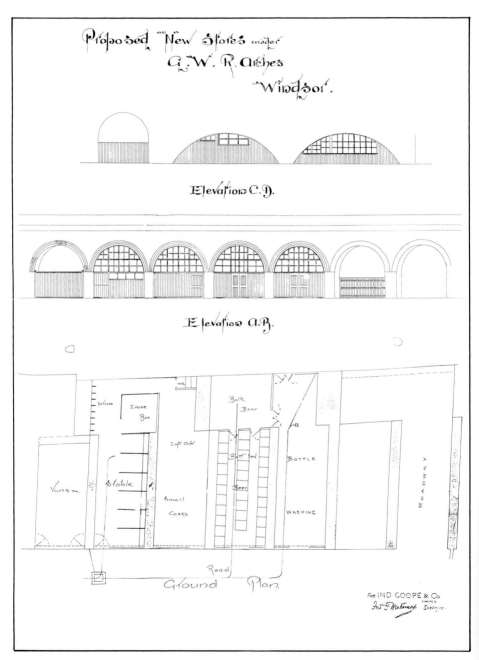

Plan for Bottling Stores and Stables in five arches near the Goods Yard, leased to Ind Coope & Co. in 1902.

Index

A through train service is restored to Windsor after more than 17 years! On 14th June, 1993 (the first day of operation), Driver Cliff Day and Trainee Driver Jim Byron stand beside their class '166' Network Express forming the 10.18am Paddington to Windsor.

C.C. Young